A *New*
and Native
Beauty

A New and Native Beauty

The Art and Craft of Greene & Greene

Edited by

Edward R. Bosley *and*

Anne E. Mallek

THE GAMBLE HOUSE

USC *School of Architecture*

MERRELL

LONDON · NEW YORK

First published 2008 by Merrell Publishers Limited

81 Southwark Street
London SE1 0HX

merrellpublishers.com

in association with

The Gamble House/USC
4 Westmoreland Place
Pasadena, CA 91103

gamblehouse.org

Published on the occasion of the exhibition A "New and Native"
Beauty: The Art and Craft of Greene & Greene

The Huntington Library, Art Collections, and Botanical Gardens,
San Marino, California
October 18, 2008–January 26, 2009

Renwick Gallery, Smithsonian American Art Museum,
Washington, D.C.
March 13–June 7, 2009

Museum of Fine Arts, Boston
July 14–October 18, 2009

A catalog record for this book is available from the Library
of Congress.

British Library Cataloguing-in-Publication Data:
A new and native beauty : the art and craft of Greene & Greene
1. Greene, Charles Sumner, 1868–1957 – Exhibitions
2. Greene, Henry Mather, 1870–1954 – Exhibitions
3. Arts and crafts movement – California – Exhibitions
I. Bosley, Edward R. II. Mallek, Anne E. III. Gamble House
(Pasadena, Calif.)
747'.0922

ISBN-13: 978-1-8589-4452-4 (hardcover)
ISBN-10: 1-8589-4452-X (hardcover)
ISBN-13: 978-1-8589-4453-1 (softcover)
ISBN-10: 1-8589-4453-8 (softcover)

Produced by Merrell Publishers Limited
Designed by Phil Cleaver & Emily Berry of etal-design
Copy-edited by Katherine Reilly
Proof-read by Barbara Roby
Indexed by Hilary Bird

Printed and bound in Singapore

KEY TO ABBREVIATIONS USED IN NOTES

Avery: Greene & Greene Architectural Records and
Papers Collection, Drawings and Archives, Avery
Architectural and Fine Arts Library, Columbia
University, New York

CSG: Charles Sumner Greene

EDA: Charles Sumner Greene Collection (1959-1),
Environmental Design Archives, University of
California, Berkeley

GGA: Greene and Greene Collection, Greene and
Greene Archives, The Gamble House, University
of Southern California at The Huntington Library,
Art Collections, and Botanical Gardens, San Marino

HMG: Henry Mather Greene

Contents

ANNO DOMINI MCMLII

ARCHITECTS MUCH HONORED IN YOUR HOMELAND
FOR GREAT CONTRIBUTIONS TO DESIGN, SENSITIVE
AND KNOWING BUILDERS WHO REFLECTED WITH
GRACE AND CRAFTSMANSHIP EMERGING VALUES
IN MODERN LIVING IN THE WESTERN STATES, FORMU·
LATORS OF A NEW AND NATIVE ARCHITECTURE

THE AMERICAN INSTITUTE OF ARCHITECTS

NOW HAILS AND HONORS YOU

HENRY MATHER GREENE

AND

CHARLES SUMNER GREENE

FOR YOUR CONTRIBUTIONS TO THE DESIGN OF THE AMERICAN
HOME. YOUR GIFTS HAVE NOW MULTIPLIED AND SPREAD TO ALL
PARTS OF THE NATION, AND ARE RECOGNIZED THROUGHOUT THE
WORLD, INFLUENCING AND IMPROVING THE DESIGN OF SMALL AS WELL
AS GREAT HOUSES. YOU ENRICH THE LIVES OF THE PEOPLE. YOU
HAVE MADE THE NAME OF CALIFORNIA SYNONYMOUS WITH SIMP·
LER, FREER AND MORE ABUNDANT LIVING. YOU HAVE HELPED SHAPE
OUR DISTINCTIVELY NATIONAL ARCHITECTURE, AND IN GIVING TAN·
GIBLE FORM TO THE IDEALS OF OUR PEOPLE, YOUR NAMES WILL BE
FOREVER REMEMBERED AMONG THE GREAT CREATIVE AMERICANS.

SECRETARY

PRESIDENT

Foreword

When I was a student of architecture at the University of Southern California in the 1950s, the instructor I respected most, Calvin Straub, was also the one who taught us about Greene and Greene. Straub brought his students—a postwar generation of hopeful Modernists—to the idea that design and building in the West could be radically different. And since we were feeling full of ourselves, he reminded us that Greene and Greene had grasped this concept fifty years before the rest of us. We learned that "modern architecture" did not have to be all glass, concrete, and steel, but that materials and progressive design could also come from more regional media—wood, stone, brick—without sacrificing beauty, function, or dynamism. We can thank the Greenes, and such instructors as Straub, and Harwell Hamilton Harris before him, that twentieth-century California architecture evolved into an era of holistic design and craft that has shaped a larger debate, nationally and internationally. Where it goes from here is up to today's architecture students, but I believe that we must continue to teach them about important legacies, such as that of Greene and Greene.

Frank O. Gehry, FAIA

Preface

A "New and Native" Beauty: The Art and Craft
of Greene & Greene *accompanies a traveling
exhibition of the same name. The impetus for the
book and the exhibition has been the centennial of
the Gamble house, designed by Greene and Greene in
1907–09. In 1966, the heirs of Cecil and Louise Gamble
made a gift of the house and its architect-designed
furnishings to the city of Pasadena in a joint
agreement with the University of Southern California
School of Architecture, which operates the house as a
historic site open to the public for regular tours. In
1990, in cooperation with The Gamble House/USC,
the Huntington Art Collections opened a permanent
exhibit of Greene and Greene decorative arts in the
Virginia Steele Scott Gallery of American Art to
enhance public awareness and understanding of these
California architects of international reputation.
Since then, public understanding and enjoyment of
Greene and Greene have grown enormously, and
the brothers' work is now represented in museums
internationally that deal with design in the early years
of the Modern movement. On this basis, it seemed
clear that a traveling exhibition and accompanying
book incorporating the fruits of recent research
would provide additional context for the Greenes'
work both locally and to the international audience.
The Huntington and The Gamble House/USC are
proud to collaborate in this important work, and we
extend heartfelt thanks to the many friends, colleagues,
lenders, and financial supporters who have assisted in
so many ways to make this possible.*

John Murdoch
*Hannah and Russel Kully Director, The Huntington
Art Collections, San Marino, California*

Edward R. Bosley
*James N. Gamble Director,
The Gamble House, University of Southern California
School of Architecture*

EDWARD R. BOSLEY

Introduction

Architects much honored in your homeland for great contributions to design, sensitive and knowing builders who reflected with grace and craftsmanship emerging values in modern living in the western states, formulators of a new and native architecture ...

With these words, Charles and Henry Greene were celebrated by the American Institute of Architects in 1952. To say that they were "much honored" had only recently been true. After the firm of Greene and Greene was dissolved in 1922, the brothers were for many years virtually ignored by the architectural profession and the press. Reading between the lines of the AIA citation, one senses a slightly guilty feeling of catching up, as if the profession had suddenly become aware of having kept the Greenes waiting too long to receive peer recognition. Henry Greene died just two years after the AIA award, and Charles was too frail of body and mind to attend the convention at which the award was announced. The AIA further ventured that the Greenes' names would be "forever remembered among the great creative Americans." While such a prediction now seems reasonably prescient, it could as easily have been regarded at the time as a wistful hope.

Relatively few authors have published scholarly texts focused exclusively on the Greenes and their work. The essential historical facts have been covered, and informed opinions offered on the important characteristics of their architecture and decorative arts, but much remains unstudied. It seems fitting to mark the centennial of their greatest achievements with additional scholarly perspectives on the men and their work; on their collaborators, clients, and influences; and on the specific areas of craft into which the Greenes ventured.

In this group of independent essays, fresh observations on the Greenes begin, in Anne E. Mallek's text, with a moment of enlightenment, when the Greenes' design aesthetic—with the encouragement of an astute and passionate client, James Culbertson—moved boldly into the Arts and Crafts idiom. In the following essay, Virginia Greene Hales and Bruce Smith offer biographical sketches of Charles and Henry Greene. Their study benefits in part from the direct kinship of one of the authors, a Greene family historian. Smith's second contribution—"Sunlight and Elsewhere"—examines why the most exotic influence on the Greenes' work may have been within the borders of Southern California itself, a region that has always attracted diverse cultures that are manifested in ways both real and metaphorical. As Smith argues, the Greenes appropriately mined these cultures for design inspiration.

The focus narrows in the next chapter, where Margaretta M. Lovell trains her perceptive eye on the Greenes' drawings and building specifications in order to interpret how they accommodated the characteristics of the materials they used, including metal, glass, textiles, masonry, and many varieties of wood. Despite the assumed antimodernism that attaches to most figures within the Arts and Crafts movement, Lovell submits that the Greenes operated with convincing fluency in a modern economy of global scope. She also explores their designs and use of materials in the context of household caste, whereby something as subtle as a shift from pine to oak flooring might signal transition from the world of the serving to that of the served.

Next, the Greenes' furniture designs are viewed in the context of the history of furniture making, demonstrating that such work can reveal much about cultural values. Edward S. Cooke, Jr., examines particular pieces for their structural design, suitability of use, and uniqueness of ornament. In explaining what the Greenes knew about significant trends—such as the "structural style" of Gustav Stickley and the influence of Europe—Cooke brings into sharper view the context within which the brothers worked. He also provides new perspective on the legacy of the Greenes among contemporary woodworkers. The exquisite craftsmanship of the Swedish brothers John and Peter Hall is celebrated, too, in recognition of the fact that without the Halls and their associates, the Greenes' reputation would lack a measure of its luster.

Nina Gray's essay on the Greenes' metalwork brings new information to light on the designs and fabrication of this frequently bypassed component of their decorative arts. From door hardware to fireplace furnishings and metal lighting fixtures, the Greenes achieved subtle effects through collaborations with skilled craftsmen and an understanding of the possibilities of the medium. Particularly surprising is the breadth of manufacturing methods the Greenes employed. Cast, wrought, spun, chased, incised, and overlaid, metal seems to have been of no less significance to the Greenes than wood.

Bedroom wardrobe, mahogany and ebony, with copper, silver, abalone, and wood inlay, 1909, Robert R. Blacker house, Pasadena, 1907–09
Private collection. Photograph © Ognen Borissov/Interfoto

A study of the Greenes' stained glass follows, in which Julie L. Sloan challenges earlier scholarship to establish that Emil Lange was not the sole glass artist to execute their finest designs. Beginning with the Greenes' initial attempts to follow the international trend toward domestic stained and leaded glass, Sloan reveals how the brothers' early, unsophisticated work in glass quickly attained proficiency and distinction. Copper-foil wrapping and other techniques are credited with making possible the beautiful effects the Greenes ultimately achieved.

The women clients of Greene and Greene were an impressive cadre of individuals who were both independent and determined. Some were wealthy, but others worked hard to afford an architect. Surviving letters in the Greene and Greene Archives suggest that Charles Greene particularly held the attention of the firm's women clients. Henry, too, was interested in a woman's perspective on design and building. According to his daughter, the late Isabelle McElwain, he would consult his wife, Emeline, on design details that would help a household operate more conveniently and efficiently. Ann Scheid presents the diverse backgrounds of several of the Greenes' women clients and establishes that many of the houses function as well as they do—and are as beautiful as they are—in part because these determined women commanded the attention and respect of their architects.

Charles Greene traveled to England twice, and was married to an Englishwoman. The first international publication of the Greenes' work was in Britain's *Academy Architecture*, and the brothers were aware of William Morris and English Arts and Crafts. But to what degree were they influenced by this knowledge? In his essay, Alan Crawford peers at England through the eyes of Charles Greene; in the telling, he persuasively counters the prevailing notions of influence. Charles's personal papers—scrapbooks, travel diaries, collected postcards, and photographs he took while abroad—lead to new conclusions on what it was about England that was most important to him and how it may have affected his work. Crawford also describes apparent "Englishness" in Greene and Greene from an English perspective and so brings a fresh and relevant view to American readers.

Among the less-studied aspects of the Greenes' work has been garden and landscape design, partly owing to the scant documentation of their intentions. In the penultimate chapter of this book, David C. Streatfield uses archival photographs of the Greenes' gardens, supplemented by original drawings and more recent images, as sources for considering not only the details of their garden designs, but also how the outdoors complemented the architecture of their houses. The author traces the divergent traditions of naturalistic and formal gardens as they evolved in the Greenes' work to demonstrate how they realized their version of a "California Garden."

The final essay examines the Greenes' influence on Modernism, illustrated primarily through the visionary photography of Maynard Parker, whose archive of negatives at the Huntington Library served as an important resource. Resonances between the Arts and Crafts aesthetic of Greene and Greene and Modernism may seem counterintuitive, but by the late 1940s and early 1950s, the Greenes were recognized by the AIA precisely for their prescience in designing such features as skylights and long walls of windows to lighten interiors. Such "modern conveniences" as comfortable counter heights and easy-to-access, built-in storage were pioneered by the Greenes but soon forgotten, until interest was revived by a few architects, critics, and journalists after World War II.

In their winter years, the Greenes—and Henry in particular—felt it important to capture for the future the essence of their work before it was forever altered. Henry asked the elderly Mrs. Blacker if she might consider leaving some of her more important pieces of furniture to a museum, but she demurred. The Blacker house furnishings—among the best the Greenes produced—were soon sold at a yard sale, and though some of the objects have made their way into institutions and into the hands of civic-minded owners, other significant examples may never come to the light of public appreciation, either because their owners do not fully understand their value or, ironically, because they do. Either way, some of the most important artistic patrimony of our time is no longer fully accessible to the growing community of scholars and the public who care deeply about it. Pundits have proclaimed villains in the saga of Greene and Greene objects. In recent years, the scarcity, quality, and sheer beauty of these pieces have caused auction prices to soar to unprecedented levels. Dealers, collectors, curators, institutions, and auction houses—each going about their legal and legitimate pursuits—have been criticized for trading in fixtures and furnishings removed from extant Greene and Greene houses. This criticism seems facile and perhaps misses the greater point of collective cultural responsibility. The day has long since passed—some fifty or sixty or more years ago—when we could hope to protect in their entirety such complex and comprehensive works of art as Greene and Greene houses, fixtures, furnishings, and gardens. It is fortunate that the Gamble family, the city of Pasadena, and the University of Southern California recognized the opportunity to act in the public interest to save a significant remnant—the Gamble House—in 1966. While this comprehensive kind of historic preservation may be routinely enjoyed in some other countries, in America it seems surely to remain the exception rather than the rule. For the present, greater appreciation of Greene and Greene is made possible by individuals willing to share their own discernment and good fortune by offering access to their houses and private collections.

A "New and Native" Beauty: The Art and Craft of Greene & Greene seeks to foster access to and appreciation for the genius of two brothers whose work was so elusive, self-effacing, and sufficiently out of the ordinary that it was overlooked for decades in favor of more familiar or explainable styles. The architecture and decorative arts of Greene and Greene may, as a result, be better known and studied, and we are tremendously grateful to the lenders who have made this book and its accompanying traveling exhibition possible. The editors, contributors, and participating institutions trust that this will not be the last word on Greene and Greene, but rather the next in a continuing discussion leading to a fuller recognition of their legacy.

ANNE E. MALLEK

The Beauty of a House:
Charles Greene, the Morris Movement,
and James Culbertson

During a visit to Southern California in January 1909, Charles Robert Ashbee, the celebrated self-appointed "successor to William Morris in England," took time in his personal diary to comment on Charles Greene and his "beautiful houses."[1] Ashbee's near-poetic response to Greene's architecture was both personal and emotional as he described, almost enviously, its "tenderness," "subtlety," and "repose." His reaction was similarly poetic following his visit to the workshops of Peter and John Hall (contractor and cabinetmaker, respectively), who were carrying out the Greenes' furniture designs for the David B. Gamble house in Pasadena, among others.[2] Ashbee remarked that it was

without exception the best and most characteristic furniture I have seen in this country. ... quite up to our best English craftsmanship, Spooner, Barnsly [sic], Lutyens, Lethaby. ... Here things were really alive—and the Arts and Crafts, what all the others are screaming and hustling about, are here actually being produced by a young architect, this quiet, dreamy, nervous, tenacious little man, fighting single-handed until quite recently against tremendous odds.[3]

The description appears self-consciously constructed, even romantic, as if Ashbee were telling the story of the Arts and Crafts movement. His visit to California came just two years before the *Architectural Review* would declare the English Arts and Crafts Exhibition Society (from which the movement had derived its name) to be "dead."[4] Ashbee (1863–1942) had mourned the death of his own business enterprise in 1907, when the Guild of Handicraft had gone into liquidation. And yet here in Pasadena were the Greenes, whom Ashbee compares to some of the great architects, designers, and craftsmen of the English movement.[5] It is not only sympathy that Ashbee expresses; his is almost the voice of a parent, as if he viewed the movement then beginning to fade in England revived and continued in the work of the Greenes, particularly Charles Greene. Charles, in turn,

had shown an interest in the English Arts and Crafts style seven years earlier, with the design and decoration in Pasadena of the James Culbertson house, the only work that he would ever identify as being influenced by the "Wm Morris movement."[6] In the house for Culbertson, one finds the earliest manifestation in the Greenes' work of that magical trinity—an inspiring site, a sympathetic client, and an architect, as Ashbee characterized him, willing to dream.

THE "MORRIS MOVEMENT" AND AN ENGLISH HOUSE
It was William Morris's power to dream and his innate curiosity that were so alluring to all who met him or read his words. Morris (1834–1896) was captivated by nature, by the picturesque, by the romance of older buildings. The movement that he inspired was also essentially romantic, and American followers paid tribute to him by sometimes dubbing it "the Morris movement."[7] Self-styled successors included not only Ashbee in England, but also the craftsman–editor–marketing guru Gustav Stickley in America. The editor of *The Studio* magazine, Charles Holme, went so far as to purchase Morris's Red House in Bexleyheath, Kent, designed for him by Philip Webb in 1859 and decorated with the help of his artist friends in 1860–62. At the turn of the century, the *Ladies Home Journal* remarked, "a 'William Morris wave' or 'craze' has been developing, and it is a fad that we cannot push with too much vigour."[8] Morris & Company had exhibited in 1883 at the Boston Foreign Fair, where its booth was accompanied by a detailed brochure that freely and specifically suggested the possible uses for the beautiful embroideries, stained glass, printed and woven textiles, tapestries, and other items on display. Morris's firm also had representatives in New York and Philadelphia as early as 1878.[9] Many had made the pilgrimage across the Atlantic to meet Morris in person (as he never visited America), not least the Harvard professor and scholar Charles Eliot Norton, the famed Boston architect H.H. Richardson, and the founder of the utopian

[15]

FIGURE 2
*Design for carved
paneling in dining
room, 1902, James A.
Culbertson house*
Courtesy of Charles Sumner
Greene Collection (1959-1),
Environmental Design
Archives, University of
California, Berkeley

Roycrofters community, Elbert Hubbard.[10] Morris personalized the Arts and Crafts movement while standing for its broader goals; he was representative not only of an aesthetic ideal, but also of a country and a way of life. It is part of the essential romanticism of the movement that he was and still is so often referred to as its "father."

For Morris, architecture had been primary and all-encompassing. In his lecture "The Beauty of Life," he promised, "Architecture would lead us to all the arts, as it did with earlier men: but if we despise it and take no note of how we are housed, the other arts will have a hard time of it indeed."[11] The Culbertson house as built in 1902 began as an exercise in nostalgia, but, over the following thirteen years, it evolved internally and externally, reflecting the Greenes' changing structural and decorative vocabulary. Morris's Red House also began as a tribute to his love for the medieval in its style and its use of local materials. Its furnishings, however, presaged his career in the decorative arts, as he took great care in every detail, from windows to cabinetry to fireplaces. Both of these early works express the ideals of their owners, quite literally in the mottoes inscribed over fireplaces, set in windows, and carved into walls.[12] In the Culbertson house, these appeared over the front door, on the living-room mantel, in the entry hall, and on the dining-room walls: "The Blessing of the House is Contentment," "The Crown of the House is Godliness," "The Glory of the House is Hospitality," and "The Beauty of the House is Order" (fig. 2). Nor were these houses alone in this whimsical form of self-expression: Frank Lloyd Wright used nearly the same mottoes in his house of 1905 for William Heath in Buffalo, New York.[13] In Sweden, the artist Carl Larsson painted them over the doorways in his family home in Sundborn, and, more locally, Charles Lummis had employed mottoes above the fireplaces at his Los Angeles home, El Alisal. M.H. Baillie Scott wrote in his treatise *Houses and Gardens* (1906), "when decoration becomes articulate in the writing on the wall it affords a more definite revelation of the character and tastes of its owner."[14] Such expressiveness was characteristic of the Greenes' work at this time. Charles Greene's own home on Arroyo Terrace, the Colonial house for George H. Barker in Pasadena, and the James Culbertson house were all in disparate styles dictated largely by clients and owners. These projects kept the Greenes' minds running on a variety of aesthetic themes, encouraging them to look both locally and abroad for inspiration.

The James Culbertson house was only the second house designed by the Greenes situated along Pasadena's dry riverbed, the Arroyo Seco. It followed Charles Greene's own house, the construction of which had begun in March 1902, just four months before the Culbertson contract was issued. It was also the Greenes' second essay within four years in the half-timbered vernacular, commonly known and promoted as "Old English." These houses, which recalled a romantic past with their seemingly "honest" construction, appealed to American architects in search of an architectural identity, just as the Gothic Revival and medieval guild structure had been impetus for Morris's firm and its projects. Charles Eastlake, in his *History of the Gothic Revival* (1872), had praised the integrity of the original model, "untrammeled by the consideration of dates or mouldings, or any of the fussiness of archaeology."[15] English-born Boston architect H. Langford Warren wrote in praise of the English style in 1904: "it is not too much to say that no other nation has succeeded in developing a domestic architecture having the subtle and intimate charm which in the English country house makes so strong an appeal to the love of home as well as the love of beauty. … our own best work, like that of England, will be done by founding it on the sound traditions of England's past."[16] Wilson Eyre, a successful Philadelphia architect who had traveled to Britain on a sketching trip early in his career, enjoined American architects to "look to England rather than France for models and inspiration for the country house."[17] In England, the "Old English" style was practiced by C.F.A. Voysey as early as the 1880s,[18] and by Richard Norman Shaw, who was largely responsible for the proliferation of this and the "Queen Anne" styles, following a sketching trip to Kent and Sussex in the early 1860s.[19] From the early 1890s, *American Architect and Building News* was peppered with photographs and drawings of buildings—both domestic and public—in the "Old English" style. It seemed that every architect had to try his hand at it, as if in a kind of tribute to what they saw as their architectural patrimony.[20] Indeed, this common stylistic vogue in both England and America was made boldly manifest in 1893 at the World's Columbian Exposition in Chicago. "Victoria House," the British government building at the fair, was designed to resemble an English country house of the sixteenth century, with a half-timbered second floor and brick-clad first floor (fig. 3). A brochure even described one of its ceilings as having been modeled after one in the medieval Haddon Hall in Derbyshire.[21]

Charles Greene descended into this "Old English" melee in 1888, the very year of the founding of the Arts and Crafts Exhibition Society in London. Greene not

THE BEAUTY OF THE HOUSE IS ORDER

only studied architecture in Boston with his brother, Henry—just behind Copley Square and H.H. Richardson's Trinity Church, with its Morris & Company window— but also later apprenticed with H. Langford Warren. There is a sense, then, that he was thoroughly immersed in an Anglophilic environment during the last ten years of the century, leading to his marriage to an English woman and subsequent first voyage to the British Isles. Morris's presence was nearly a decade old by the time the Greenes began their studies at the Massachusetts Institute of Technology, but such journals as *American Architect and Building News*, which reported on the activities of the Arts and Crafts Exhibition Society in London, still promoted his works and the movement he inspired.[22] Like the "Old English" style itself, Morris may have been somewhat watered down by time and over exposure, but Greene's awareness of both—and his nearly ten years in architectural apprenticeship and practice—could have heightened his sensitivity to the meaning and the romance of much of what he encoun- tered during his four-month tour of England and Europe in 1901. The England he visited was passing into its fifth year of mourning for Morris, and the Arts and Crafts

movement was at its height. Whether Greene recognized or cared about this at the time is debatable. What is per- haps more important is that, eight years after this visit and at the peak of his own career, he should be viewed by Ashbee—by the English movement—as its American heir apparent. First, however, Greene required a client who not only sympathized with his objectives, but also had the wealth to realize them.

AN ENLIGHTENED CLIENT

At the same time that Charles Greene was immersed in the highly Anglicized atmosphere in Boston, a business- man was moving his family from Wilson Eyre's native state of Pennsylvania to another major outpost of the American Arts and Crafts movement—Chicago, Illinois. This man also had a romantic turn of nature, and, rather than live in the city, he saw the promise of a newly devel- oped suburb named for one of Sir Walter Scott's Waverley novels. Called "Chicago's ideal home suburb," Kenilworth was situated just 17 miles (27 km) north of Chicago on a bluff overlooking Lake Michigan, "from which a charming view is afforded of the restless waters, passing sails, and the ever changing panorama of this

FIGURE 4

*Franklin Burnham,
James A. Culbertson
house, Kenilworth,
Illinois, 1893*

Courtesy of Greene
and Greene Archives,
The Gamble House,
University of Southern
California, gift of Mary
and Howard Durham

great inland sea."[23] James Culbertson, described on his death in 1915 as being "forever bent on doing things in the best way, in the enduring way," and as a man whose "moral fiber" was "superfine,"[24] had been born in Girard, Pennsylvania, the third of seven children and the eldest son. At age sixteen, he had begun to assume responsibility for his father's business, the Girard Lumber Company, and by 1882 he was its secretary and treasurer, becoming president in 1910. His move to Chicago may have stemmed in part from a desire to be closer to the company's headquarters in Michigan,[25] as well as his intention "to devote himself to cultural pursuits."[26]

The Kenilworth community had been the brainchild of Joseph Sears, a devout Swedenborgian and recent retiree of N.K. Fairbank & Company, known for its refined lard, cooking oil, and washing powder. Sears had read Scott's novel of 1821 and had visited the ruin of Kenilworth near Warwick on a trip to England with his family in 1883. The 223-acre (90-ha) Chicago suburb that he founded in 1889 began with the idea of a country home and place of retirement, "a community with the atmosphere of the country and the convenience of the city."[27] In 1893, Culbertson was one of its earlier resi-

dents. He built in the nostalgic "Old English" style that was sympathetic with its surroundings, siting his house for the trees that lined a neighboring ravine (fig. 4).[28] The interior of the seven-bedroom house, with its carved stairway and bedroom suites in a variety of precious woods, "bespoke his love of lumber."[29] Culbertson proved himself an engaged member of the community, becoming first president of the Kenilworth Club (1894–95) and first village president (1896–97), establishing the Kenilworth Improvement Association (1897), and providing funds for the assembly hall of 1907 designed by George Washington Maher.[30]

The Culbertson residence, at 220 Melrose Avenue, was designed by the Kenilworth Company architect, Franklin Burnham.[31] Burnham was responsible for fourteen other homes in Kenilworth, including his own Shingle-style house, and for the railway station, with its rusticated stone arches and Romanesque flourishes. Like Culbertson, he had begun his career at a young age, becoming an architectural apprentice when he was only fourteen. Born in Illinois in 1853, Burnham moved to Chicago in 1860 with his parents; he later entered into partnership there with Willoughby James Edbrooke.[32]

Burnham eventually settled in Southern California; in a letter to Joseph Sears in December 1899, he spoke of hoping to stay in the area: "Los Angeles is growing steadily—no boom—and will in time be the Great Suburb of the U.S."[33] Though he wrote that the new houses were "Uniformly Handsome," he called the Mission style the "finest." In the announcement of his death in *Western Architect*, he is said to have moved to Los Angeles in 1903,[34] when he became involved in the development of the Mount Rubidoux district in Riverside, an elite suburb not unlike Kenilworth, which was situated to take advantage of views of the San Bernardino Mountains and the Santa Ana River. His commissions (primarily for civic buildings) in Riverside, San Diego, and Pasadena, however, show him working in a much more Neo-classical, "White City" vein; the exception is the Carnegie library he designed for Riverside in 1903 in the Mission Revival style.[35] By the time of his death in 1909, the *Los Angeles Times* lauded him as "one of the best-known Southern California architects."[36]

Given that Culbertson was familiar with Burnham's work from the Kenilworth project and that the architect was working in Los Angeles within a year of Culbertson's own arrival in California, one wonders why Culbertson looked to the relatively inexperienced Greenes to build his Pasadena home. The "Old English" design of Culbertson's Kenilworth house was likely due to his own inclination toward the style; not many of Burnham's other buildings for the community bear such an overt reference to this romantic mode. The death in 1896 of the Culbertsons' only child, Lloyd (then only eight), may have precipitated the building of a winter residence in Pasadena. James and his wife, Nora, like many of the Greenes' future Midwestern clients, had been visiting the area for several years, taking advantage of the healthful climate and such beautiful resort hotels as the Hotel Green. A desire to dissociate themselves further from their personal tragedy may have led them to look for new people and new partners in building. It is tempting to imagine how an initial and serendipitous meeting between Culbertson and Charles Greene may have come about. Culbertson, who recognized the importance of siting for his Kenilworth home, naturally would have been drawn to the arroyo, where Charles Greene had begun building his own home in March 1902. In surveying the neighborhood, Culbertson would not have failed to notice the new construction and may well have inquired after the name of the architect. A conversation may then have taken place between architect and potential client that would signal the beginning of a sympathetic partnership (fig. 5).

This sympathy and shared purpose are evident in the letter written by Charles Greene to his new client in October 1902, just three months after signing the contract, in which he remarks that Culbertson's suggestion for the living room "pleased me very much, as I am in through [sic] sympathy with the Wm Morris movement, in fact the whole inside of the house is influenced by it in design."[37] Greene goes on to answer several questions regarding a rug, the wall colors, and the size of a window seat, revealing Culbertson's keen involvement in the project, as well as demonstrating Greene's Anglophilic tendencies and awareness of current trends in art and architecture. Having at that point spent more than nine years in the Chicago area, Culbertson could not have been immune to the activity of the "Morris movement": designer and socialist Walter Crane had lectured and exhibited at the Art Institute of Chicago in 1891; Ashbee's Guild of Handicraft had exhibited at the Chicago Art Club in 1898; and Ashbee had delivered ten lectures around the city in 1900.[38] Apart from this, Culbertson's involvement in the development of Kenilworth likely brought him into close contact with several influential Chicago architects involved in its evolution, including Maher, J.L. Silsbee, and Daniel Burnham (overseeing architect of the World's Columbian Exposition).

Culbertson was soon as involved in his new community in Pasadena as he had been at Kenilworth, becoming an active supporter of fellow Chicagoan Amos Throop's Polytechnic school, which had been inspired by the teachings of Morris and John Ruskin, and offered training in various manual skills and crafts.[39] In 1912, he would become a board member of the newly established Pasadena Music and Art Association. Its founder, George Ellery Hale, had also come to Pasadena by way of Chicago within a year of Culbertson. There could be no doubt that Culbertson would have felt himself to be a member of a cultured, Midwestern, and English-appreciative community.[40] In examining details of his house in Pasadena, it is evident that this sympathy was investigated in greater depth, with architect and client each encouraging the other to explore and expand mutual strengths and interests.

From the completion of the Culbertson house in 1902 (fig. 6) until James Culbertson's death in 1915, the Greenes were either attending to its various additions and alterations or working on other houses in a similar style. Throughout these years, it is as if the Culbertson house became a bellwether of their developing architectural and decorative vocabulary. Early photographs of

the Culbertsons' living room show Gustav Stickley furniture (like the mottoes, these objects were expressive, though structurally rather than verbally) mixed with Tiffany lamps and a variety of Asian and other art objects (figs. 7 and 8).[41] These were set in an eloquent framework with details reminiscent of Japanese temple construction (specifically the brackets above the window seat and over the mantel). This idea of "staging" one's collection was not uncommon at the time, the novelist Edith Wharton having gone so far as to call it a *"mise en scène."*[42] In an article of 1906 for *Good Housekeeping,* Una Nixson Hopkins remarked on the resonance of this framework, mentioning the "Japanese gray" of the living room and noting, "At least a part of the detail of this house suggests Japanese influence ..."[43] The unique character of this room is further enhanced by the treatment of the windows; the leaded glass shows a branching geometrical form, in contrast with the more conventional English diamond pane used elsewhere.

This mixture of Japanese and English elements, which lends the house a "picturesque" or eclectic quality, raises an interesting point about the compatibility of the styles.

It is commonly believed that the Greenes visited the Japanese exhibits and Ho-o-den pavilion at Chicago's Columbian Exposition, and that they may have seen examples of other Japanese structures at subsequent expositions in San Francisco (1894) and St. Louis (1904). However, the first exhibition of Japanese work in the West took place long before, at the International Exhibition of 1862 in London. This was also where the fledgling firm Morris, Marshall, Faulkner & Co. made its first public appearance. Medieval met Japanese and discovered that they were sympathetic, truth to materials being paramount in both the design of buildings and the creation of beautiful objects. Hermann Muthesius would write in his treatise *Das englische Haus* (1904–05), "we must see in this mixture of Japanese and Gothic one of the influences that has helped to shape the new art of the interior in England."[44]

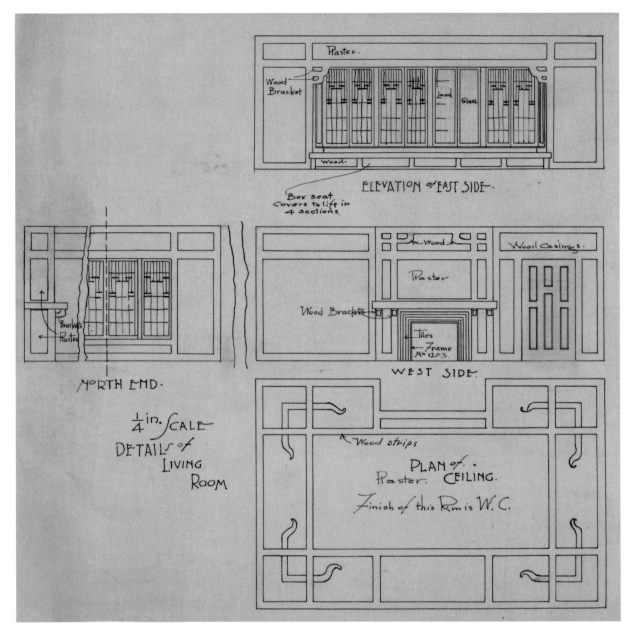

FIGURE 8

*Elevation drawings of
living room, showing
Japanese architectural
details in recessed
window seat, above
mantel, and in
ceiling, James A.
Culbertson house*

Courtesy of Avery
Architectural and
Fine Arts Library,
Columbia University

Though there was a strong awareness of Japan in America, both during the Greenes' time in Boston and later in California, perhaps this earlier-established sympathy facilitated the Greenes' incorporation of Japanese elements in their design for what was ostensibly an English house. The next commission the Greenes undertook in the English style, the brick and half-timbered house for Adelaide Tichenor in Long Beach (1904–05), goes some way toward supporting this hypothesis. Here the Japanese elements are more overt in the treatment of garden, roof, and furniture. Chairs for the Tichenor house also evidence the same Japanese bracket form seen in the Culbertson living room; this motif would reappear in 1909 and 1910 in later furniture for the Robert R. Blacker and Laurabelle A. Robinson houses, both in Pasadena (figs. 9 and 10).

The Greenes had returned to the Culbertson commission in 1903 to develop the terrace and foundation wall, which included clinker bricks. Such brickwork was

FIGURE 9
*Plant stand,
mahogany, ebony, and
marble, 1909, Robert
R. Blacker house,
Pasadena, 1907–09*

Courtesy of American
Decorative Art 1900
Foundation. Photograph:
Gavin Ashworth,
© American Decorative
Art 1900 Foundation

FIGURE 10
*Desk chair, ash,
Adelaide A. Tichenor
house, Long Beach,
1904–05*

Courtesy of Guardian
Stewardship. Photograph
courtesy of Sotheby's
New York

employed again in the foundation for the house designed for Charles Greene's sisters-in-law in 1903 and in the Tichenor house the following year. Its use has become one of the hallmarks of the Greenes' structural work, and is itself a reference to medieval building.[45] The Laurabelle A. Robinson house, built in 1905–06, returned once more to the half-timber aesthetic, but with a greater emphasis on the horizontal. C.F.A. Voysey had felt strongly about accentuating this attribute in his own houses: "When the sun sets horizontalism prevails, when we are weary we recline … What, then, is obviously necessary for the effect of repose in our houses, [is] to avoid angularity and complexity in colour, form or texture and make our dominating lines horizontal rather than vertical."[46] The Robinson house, facing east–west, is in perfect accord with Voysey's dictum.

In 1906, the Greenes executed six drawings for Louis K. Hyde of Plainfield, New Jersey, evidence that, by means of such publicity as the *Good Housekeeping* article and the exhibition of their work in St. Louis, they (as West Coast architects) were becoming identified with the popular East Coast English style.[47] The Hyde drawings are essentially identical to the Culbertson design as built in 1902. At the same time, the Greenes also began modifying the house of Culbertson's friend and neighbor Theodore Irwin, with additions including a brick-and-tile terrace, wide balconies, and exposed-timber construction. The last element was in evidence in 1907 in the Mary E. Cole house on Westmoreland Place; its monumental arroyo-boulder chimney, with its stones "floating" in pebbledash, shows the reappearance of Charles Greene's whimsical nature. The brothers

FIGURE II

Garage, 1906, James A. Culbertson house

Courtesy of Greene and Greene Archives, The Gamble House, University of Southern California, gift of Mary and Howard Durham

worked on two projects for the Culbertson house in 1906, including a few minor alterations and the addition of a garage (fig. 11). This building was peculiarly situated in front of the house, but the trelliswork along its sides and roof not only helped it to blend in with its garden surroundings, but also disguised its stylistic departure from the main house. Here there was no gable or half-timbering, though the trelliswork may have been an intentional allusion to this.

The year 1907 saw an extensive addition to the Culbertson house and the beginning of two commissions now ranked among the Greenes' greatest achievements—the Robert R. Blacker and David B. Gamble houses.[48] The addition of a kitchen and service area to the southeast of the main Culbertson residence resulted in an L shape much like that of Morris's Red House; it also effectively separated the service wing from the rest of the house, thereby creating a den and moving the dining room to the front, facing northeast. The new den and dining room, with their decorative frieze work and carved details, reveal a return to a more Japanese aesthetic. The Greenes were gradually making each room more distinctive, demonstrating a new adherence to the German principle of *Gesamtkunstwerk*, or the environ-

ment as a complete work of art.[49] In the Blacker house, this idea of distinctive thematic treatments of rooms—including both decoration and furniture—was more fully and elaborately explored. But we know it to be a fresh preoccupation with the Greenes in the Culbertson house, perhaps indicative of a greater influence of architect-designer over client. This new development further emphasized the picturesque nature of the house, previously hinted at only in the glass in the front door, which presented a scene of a rustic house in a rolling landscape. Nature was framed and imported into the house. In the den, which overlooked the Arroyo Seco, was a painted frieze of trees and, above the mantel, a relief carving of mountains (figs. 12 and 13). The dining room reflected an overt Japanese influence in the gilded frieze work of stylized cloud forms; inverted brackets (almost like a *torii* gate); and, over the fireplace, a relief carving of Mount Fuji with cloud-like repoussé work in the copper hood below (fig. 1). Gone are the "dull blue" ceiling and frieze, blue rug, and cream-colored curtains that Hopkins had described in 1906. They have been replaced by a more fully realized aesthetic—one that was refined, ornate, and unified. While the dining-room details were reminiscent of the lotus-themed living room of the Blacker house,

with its gilded plaster frieze, the painted frieze in the den recalled the dining room of the William T. Bolton house in Pasadena (see Cooke essay, fig. 9) and foreshadowed the delicate painted friezes in the dining and living rooms of the William R. Thorsen house in Berkeley (see Gray essay, fig. 20).

These thematic treatments were further pursued in 1909 in the alteration of the entry hall (fig. 14), which carried the rural theme of the front-door decoration to the frieze level, where carved panels of fruit trees interspersed with birds and flowers spelled out "The Glory of the House is Hospitality." Such carved and painted decoration referenced not only the new German aesthetic but also the English country houses designed by Philip Webb and Voysey, and even the buildings that occupied Morris's dream world in *News from Nowhere* (1890).[50] They also recalled the words of Edward Morse, in his *Japanese Homes and Their Surroundings* (1886): "Within these plain and unpretentious houses there are often to be seen marvels of exquisite carving, and the perfection of cabinet work …"[51] Once again, we find English and Japanese motifs and aesthetics sharing the same space and proving complementary rather than contradictory.

In the later alteration of the entry hall and the installation of new light fixtures for the hall, den, and living room, one senses Culbertson's reemerging presence. In 1909, he was also instructing Maher on details regarding the new gymnasium and addition to the Kenilworth Union Church.[52] He was equally attentive to his Midwest and West Coast commissions, as was his wife, Nora.[53] Lighting became a strong focus of the Greenes in these later years; following Morris's instruction, they were beginning to address the "popular arts" as well as architecture. As the basket-shaped art-glass lanterns in the Blacker living room echoed the lotus motif and threw light upward on to the gilded frieze, so the light fixtures in the Culbertson house were designed to reflect distinctive room personalities. The entry-hall lantern, situated in the center of the room, was hexagonal, making it an object of interest and beauty from all angles. The geometric leading in the living-room lanterns reflected the style of leading in the windows, while the clear glass and abstract leading design in the new staircase windows allowed for light and views, at the same time reminding the viewer of the wisteria vines growing along the west-terrace pergola directly below.

The extension of the north side of the house in 1910 reflected the mature Greene and Greene vocabulary in the complex timber support structure at the northwest corner. The conventional and derivative English half-timbering here was permitted to rest side by side with the exposed-wood construction that had come to define so much of the Greenes' work, as if in that juxtaposition alone one might chart their progress (fig. 16). While one can see evidence of the triumph of a Japanese aesthetic and new German design theory in their work for the Culbertson, Blacker, and Gamble houses in 1909–10, Greene and Greene returned to their English "roots" in the following two years, in four commissions that demonstrate an even greater maturity and refinement. This is no coincidence, since England and the Morris movement had re-entered their lives in 1909 in the form of C.R. Ashbee and Charles Greene's second trip to England.

In March 1911, the Greenes received a commission from A.M. Drake in Pasadena, which resulted in a design with a half-timbered upper level and slightly steeper gables over the front door. In April came a commission from Woodside for Mortimer Fleishhacker, who requested an English-style house with a thatched roof. The Greenes' unexecuted design for S.C. Graham in Los Angeles is even more reminiscent of earlier work in its use of half-timbering over stucco (recalling the Robinson house), art glass, carved frieze work, and an L-shaped plan. The Mary M. Kew house of 1912–13 in San Diego quotes from the Culbertson house in its staircase window, linenfold paneling, and pergola, and from the Fleishhacker house in its rolled-eave roof. While in the midst of such work in an English vein, Charles Greene also designed some of his greatest and most refined case pieces—for the Charles M. Pratt house in Ojai and the Cordelia Culbertson house in Pasadena—and exceptionally beautiful metalwork in the fireplace furniture for the Thorsen and Blacker houses.

The Greenes would return to the Culbertson house in 1914 to add particularly English details to the front elevation, in the form of two bay windows (fig. 15).[54] By this time, the Greenes had designed eight houses in a direct or implied English style, entire interior schemes (including furniture) for at least seven houses, and nearly as many gardens and landscapes. The picturesque vision of the romantic building in a landscape had resolved itself into a building that emerged from a landscape and was of the landscape. So when the Greenes focused once again on the James Culbertson house—which they had worked on consistently for the previous twelve years—they brought it into a closer relationship with the land. They lined the property along Grand Avenue with an extensive pergola and brick wall, and added to the garden in a way that invested the house with a look of permanence and organic growth.

FIGURE 14

*Entry hall, showing
alterations and
addition of fixtures
of 1909, James A.
Culbertson house.
Photograph by Leroy
Hulbert, c. 1915*

Courtesy of Avery
Architectural and
Fine Arts Library,
Columbia University

Very little evidence exists to prove that Charles Greene was drawn to examine British Arts and Crafts architecture in person on his visits to Britain in 1901 and 1909. Nor do his writings, scrapbooks or holdings in his library suggest a strong interest. However, it is clear that Greene, like Morris, was drawn to the monuments, countryside, and literature that helped to inspire this romantic movement. For it must be remembered that when Morris made his various pilgrimages to these medieval buildings, the Arts and Crafts movement had not yet formally begun. Red House was built nearly forty years before the first society of Arts and Crafts was founded in America.[55] Perhaps the reason Charles Greene described himself as being in thorough sympathy with the Morris movement was due in part to an innate sympathy with its ideas, as well as with the man credited as its founder.

DREAMERS OF DREAMS

This personalized aspect of the movement is interesting not only for the study of such an original and dynamic figure as William Morris, but also for the examination of the work of the Greene brothers, and more specifically the ideas and person of Charles Greene. As assiduously as some might have followed Morris and parroted fragments of his lectures, there were other artist-dreamers like Charles Greene who shared Morris's ideals, seeking "the greatest possible amount of Truth with the greatest amount of Pleasure."[56] The term "Wm Morris movement," which Greene employed in his letter to Culbertson, comes to have a broader and deeper resonance when one examines not only the common purpose of Morris and Greene, but also their common nature.

Both Morris and Greene were dreamers who loved romantic fiction as much as the details of a medieval

building. Morris's own fiction and poetry often deal with the landscapes of romance and of dreams, from the early *Earthly Paradise* (1868–70) to the later and more politicized *News from Nowhere* (1890). These dreams are interwoven with architecture, real and imagined, foreign and ancient.[57] The protagonist in Charles Greene's unpublished novel, a young architect kidnapped and forced to build a house for a sickly but beautiful opera singer (with whom he subsequently and rather predictably falls in love), describes himself as "a dreamer," who finds the "guiding motive" for the design of the house in the "spirit" of a bronze urn.[58] Morris and Greene shared an admiration for the romantic novels of Sir Walter Scott,[59] rife with "allusions to the Architecture, either military or ecclesiastical of a bygone age … [that invest] with a substantial reality the romances which he weaves."[60] Directed by Scott, Morris looked to the countryside and the Gothic for examples, and though he could appreciate the medieval beauty of Haddon Hall, and was awestruck by the anonymous engineering of cathedrals in Chartres and Rouen, it was ultimately to the domestic level that he looked for inspiration: "if you do not feel the beauty of the little grey cottage, which has stood so many storms and evil days, and is still sound and trim; or of the little village church, brimful of the history of six centuries, you cannot feel that of the stately cathedral …"[61] The photographs, postcards, drawings, and notes from Charles Greene's trips to England reveal that he was also drawn to such medieval precedents as Haddon Hall and the Old Post Office in Tintagel, Cornwall, the center of Arthurian romance.[62] We must not forget that Morris, as a young man, had read Thomas Malory's *Morte d'Arthur*, which his friend and artist Dante Gabriel Rossetti had proclaimed to be on a par with the Bible.[63] Greene's library was also stocked with the works of such romantic poets as Thomas Gray and such classics as John Bunyan's *Pilgrim's Progress*.[64] Morris and Greene were creating a host of memories with the same romantic architectural vocabulary.

Both men had also dreamed of becoming artists but were forced early in their careers to conclude that their livelihoods lay elsewhere—for Morris, in decorative arts and ultimately in advocating for a social revolution, and for Greene, in architecture. Perhaps these foiled artistic attempts made them that much more sensitive to the romantic, to the building in the landscape, where Nature and Art meet in harmony. This intersection is very important in the work of both Morris and Greene: each built his own house in a country setting, Morris's Red House overlooking the valley of the Cray River (fig. 17),

and Greene's house poised on the edge of the Arroyo Seco in Pasadena. Both houses are idiosyncratic, playful, personal—from Charles's "ingenious"[65] octagonal studio tower to Morris's turreted well-house—to the point that Red House was described as "more a poem than a house."[66] They are whimsical, and yet their disparate elements harmonize with one another as much as they do with their surroundings. In an article of 1905 titled "California Home Making," Charles Greene instructed the readers, or "art loving people," of the *Pasadena Daily News* to "love nature first, then the rest will follow."[67] Morris and Greene were not alone in this desire to be closer to nature. The country-house retreat was becoming a common phenomenon in America, and Arts and Crafts architecture in Britain was also being constructed primarily in the countryside. Architect and author Claude Bragdon urged that the architect searching for "a more characteristic and sincere architecture … should study, not books alone, but first of all, Nature, for in Nature the simple yet subtle laws in accordance with which all things have their being, by which they wax and wane, are written large in time and space."[68] It was the countryside in Britain that both inspired and nurtured the movement, and it is thus perhaps not surprising that the Greenes should in turn have discovered their own unique architectural identity in the "country peacefulness" of Pasadena.[69] As Morris's textile patterns and dyes were inspired by his garden in Oxfordshire and the rivers that wind through the south of England, so the greatest concentration of Greene and Greene houses can be found in the Park Place tract along the Arroyo Seco.

On February 21, 1894, William Morris offered the following words of advice about house-building to the students of the Birmingham Municipal School of Art:

… if you build them solidly and unpretentiously, using good materials natural to their own countryside, and if you do not stint the tenant of due elbow room and garden, it is little likely that you will have done any offence to the beauty of the countryside or the older houses in it. Indeed, I have a hope that it will be from such necessary, unpretentious buildings that the new and genuine architecture *will spring, rather than from our experiments in conscious style more or less ambitious, or those for which the immortal Dickens has given us the never-to-be-forgotten adjective "Architectooralooral."*[70]

Morris's self-declared pursuit of "a life of art,"[71] though it ultimately led to the establishment of a firm that specialized in the decorative arts, was rooted in "the glorious art of good building."[72] For him, architecture

was not only a beginning; it was the origin and "foundation of all the arts."[73] His idealistic injunctions inspired a generation of artists and architects, who followed him loyally in the pursuit of an individual identity and, in turn, a national identity, that the arts and buildings of a nation might be reflective of both its soil and its people. More than fifty years after Morris delivered his lecture to the Birmingham students, the American Institute of Architects honored two of its own—born in the Midwest, trained on the East Coast, and practicing on the West Coast—with a Special Citation, declaring them to be "sensitive and knowing builders" and "formulators of a new and native architecture."[74] Charles and Henry Greene, it would seem, had fulfilled Morris's intention almost to the letter—as recognized by Ashbee in 1909. It can be argued that their success began with the development of a rather romantic individual (not at all unlike Morris)—his mind, his dreams, his ambition—who, seasoned by the experience and experiment offered in particular by a thirteen-year relationship with a house and its enlightened owner, James Culbertson, ultimately attained a mature architectural style and philosophy.

1. Quoted in Edward R. Bosley, *Greene & Greene* (London: Phaidon, 2000), p. 140. Taken from Ashbee Papers, Modern Archive Centre, King's College Library, Cambridge University, doc. no. 108a, p. 6.

2. Bosley, *Greene & Greene*, p. 141.

3. Quoted in *ibid.*, p. 140. Taken from Ashbee Papers, doc. nos. 72–74.

4. Quoted in Alan Crawford, "United Kingdom: Origins and First Flowering," in Wendy Kaplan, *The Arts and Crafts Movement in Europe and America: Design for the Modern World* (New York: Thames & Hudson, 2004), p. 64. Taken from the *Architectural Review*, 30 (1911), p. 285.

5. It is worth noting that in the same journal passage, Ashbee acknowledges the Japanese influence on both the work of the Greenes and that of Frank Lloyd Wright. However, it is for the Greenes that he reserves comparison with the English Arts and Crafts movement.

6. Letter from CSG to James Culbertson, October 7, 1902, GGA.

7. "Stages in the Development of Household Art," *The Craftsman*, 1, no. 3 (December 1901), p. vi.

8. Edward Bok, "Is It Worthwhile?" *Ladies Home Journal*, 17 (November 1900), p. 18. This essay reprinted in David Shi, *In Search of the Simple Life: American Voices, Past and Present* (Layton, Ut.: Gibbs M. Smith, 1986), pp. 207–11.

9. Linda Parry, *William Morris Textiles* (London: Weidenfeld & Nicolson, 1983), p. 137. Parry notes that Morris & Company was represented in New York by the firm of Cowtan & Tout, Inc., on Madison Avenue. In Philadelphia, its products were sold at Woodville & Company on Walnut Street.

10. Norton and Richardson each met Morris in 1882, and Hubbard claimed to have met him in 1894. Norton also corresponded with Morris, and had been the firm's primary contact in Boston in preparing for the fair of 1883.

11. William Morris, "The Beauty of Life," in *The Collected Works of William Morris*, ed. May Morris (London: Longmans, Green & Company, 1915), XXII, pp. 51–80. The lecture was originally delivered by Morris to the Birmingham Society of Arts and School of Design on February 19, 1880. This is an early, if not his earliest, use of one of his most oft-quoted dictums: "Have nothing in your houses that you do not know to be useful or believe to be beautiful."

12. Over one of the fireplaces at Red House was the motto, "Ars longa, vita brevis."

13. The motto on the mantel at the Heath house read, "The reality of the house is order. The blessing of the house is contentment. The glory of the house is hospitality. The crown of the house is coolness." I am grateful to Bruce Smith for bringing this to my attention.

14. M.H. Baillic Scott, *Houses and Gardens: Arts and Crafts Interiors* (Woodbridge, Suffolk: Antique Collectors' Club, 1995), p. 85. Originally published 1906.

15. Charles Eastlake, *A History of the Gothic Revival*, ed. J. Mordaunt Crook (New York: Humanities Press, 1970), p. 2. First published in 1872 by Longmans, Green & Company, London.

16. H. Langford Warren, "Recent Domestic Architecture in England," *Architectural Review*, 11 (1904), pp. 5, 12.

17. Wilson Eyre, "My Ideal for the Country Home," *Country Life in America*, 24 (May 1913), pp. 35–36.

18. Voysey executed a drawing in 1884 for a building with half-timbering on the second floor, leaded windows, and a door under a Tudor arch. According to Peter Davey, his last use of the style appeared in 1890 for Walnut Tree Farm in Castlemorton, Hereford and Worcester, as laws passed at that time restricted half-timbering to boarding over rendered brickwork, which Voysey felt to be a "sham." See Peter Davey, *Arts and Crafts Architecture: The Search for Earthly Paradise* (London: Architectural Press, 1980), p. 87.

19. *Ibid.*, p. 38. Shaw, like Morris and Webb, had been an apprentice in the office of Gothic Revival architect George Edmund Street in the late 1850s.

20. Frank Lloyd Wright made his own attempt in this style in the house he designed in 1895 for Nathan Moore in Oak Park, Illinois.

21. *The Graphic History of the Fair* (Chicago: Graphic Company, 1894).

22. The journal praised the work of George Jack (who worked for Morris & Company) as well as Morris and Edward Burne-Jones's medieval *Holy Grail* tapestries. *American Architect and Building News*, 42 (December 1893), pp. 122, 135.

23. *Kenilworth: The Model Suburban Home* (Kenilworth Company, n.d.), pp. 4, 7. Copy in the archives of the Kenilworth Historical Society.

24. Obituary written for the *American Lumberman* by Dr. Charles Horswell, pastor of Kenilworth Union Church and longtime friend of Culbertson, n.d. Copy in the archives of the Kenilworth Historical Society.

25. In the 1860s, Culbertson's father had purchased over 62,000 acres (25,000 ha) in Michigan and Wisconsin; he also had a mill and a sash, door, and blind factory in Covington, Kentucky, where Culbertson would meet his future wife, Nora Lloyd. See entry for "William C. Culbertson" in Benjamin Whitman, *Nelson's Biographical Dictionary and Historical Reference Book of Erie County, Pennsylvania* (Erie, Pa.: S.B. Nelson, 1896), pp. 788–89.

26. See Culbertson obituary, *American Lumberman*. Culbertson might also have been drawn to this English-themed suburb by genealogy; his family could be traced back to fifteenth-century Scotland, thence to Ireland in the seventeenth century, and Philadelphia in the early eighteenth century.

27. Colleen Browne Kilner, *Joseph Sears and His Kenilworth: The Dreamer and the Dream* (Kenilworth, Ill.: Kenilworth Historical Society, 1990), p. 19.

28. Kenilworth street names also referred to a romanticized English and Scottish past, and included "Roslyn," "Warwick," and "Essex." Given the timing of Culbertson's move to the Chicago area, it is also likely that he visited the Columbian Exposition, where he might very well have encountered the half-timbered British government building. It is known that he visited other expositions; he remarks in a letter to Charles Horswell of August 18, 1909, that he and Nora were returning home via Seattle to visit the Alaska–Yukon Exposition. Copy in the archives of the Kenilworth Historical Society.

29. Colleen Kilner, "James A. Culbertson" (typed document for Kenilworth Historical Society, 1969).

30. Maher, like Frank Lloyd Wright, had worked for Louis Sullivan and J. Lyman Silsbee; he designed his own house in Kenilworth in 1893.

31. Burnham had been hired by Sears in 1889.

32. Together Burnham and Edbrooke designed a number of public buildings across the country, including many of the campus buildings of the University of Notre Dame in Indiana, opera houses, the Georgia state capitol, and, in 1909, Pasadena's First Church of Christ, Scientist.

33. Letter from Franklin Burnham, 2727 Ellendale Place, Los Angeles, to Joseph Sears, December 11, 1899. Copy in the archives of the Kenilworth Historical Society.

34. *Western Architect*, 15 (February 1910), p. 24. The announcement also notes that Burnham's "work was creditable, his personality genial."

35. In all, Burnham was responsible for nine Carnegie libraries in Southern California between 1903 and 1909. I would like to thank Ann Scheid for helping me track down this information.

36. *Los Angeles Times*, December 17, 1909, p. 117. The article makes special mention of Burnham's designs for the Riverside County Courthouse (1903) and the Masonic Temple in San Diego (1909).

37. Letter from CSG to James Culbertson, October 7, 1902, GGA.

38. Ashbee had been sent by the National Trust (established 1895) to encourage support and raise funds for the organization. In the process, he met Frank Lloyd Wright, who agreed to be the local secretary for the Trust. See Davey, *Arts and Crafts Architecture*, p. 188.

39. Amos Throop came to Pasadena in 1886 after serving as a politician and civic leader in Chicago. He established Throop University in 1891, which became Throop Polytechnic in 1892. By 1910, it had changed its emphasis from the manual arts to engineering and was renamed the California Institute of Technology. Culbertson was a trustee from 1908 until his death in 1915.

40. It is worth noting that the Pasadena Music and Art Association was housed in the Stickney Memorial School of Fine Arts, former home to the local Shakespeare Club. Both it and the Art Department building at Throop Polytechnic were designed in the English half-timbered style.

41. Receipt in GGA dated May 1, 1906, showing purchase of a "Shigoioki jardinière" from John C. Bentz, Importer, Japanese and Chinese Fine Art Works and Curios. Bentz had a shop in Pasadena that was also frequented by the Greenes.

42. Edith Wharton, *The House of Mirth* (New York: Charles Scribner's Sons, 1905), p. 212. In 1902, Wharton had published *The Decoration of*

Houses with Boston architect and interior decorator Ogden Codman, Jr.

43. Una Nixson Hopkins, "A Study for Home-Builders," *Good Housekeeping,* March 1906, pp. 262, 260.

44. Hermann Muthesius, *The English House* (London: Crosby Lockwood Staples, 1979), p. 157. Translation of *Das englische Haus* (Berlin: Wasmuth, 1904–05).

45. Thomas C. Sorby, "Domestic Architecture in England during the Middle Ages," *American Architect and Building News,* 76 (May 1902), pp. 59–60. The author notes the use of "fire-stained bricks" in medieval buildings, an example of "the tactfulness and originality of the architects of the time … converting apparently blemished materials into an effective means of decoration." He cites examples at Hampton Court Palace, among others.

46. C.F.A. Voysey, *Individuality* (London: Chapman & Hall, 1915), p. 111.

47. Wilson Eyre specifically identifies this style with the East Coast. He claims, "California has … its distinctive style to suit its climate and natural scenery; the Middle West is still experimental; and we here in the East are continuing to concentrate on a few styles, such as the English manor house and the smaller French chateaux, but especially the English." Wilson Eyre, "The Development of American Dwelling Architecture during the Last Thirty Years," *Architectural Review,* 5 (1917), p. 243.

48. The Greenes were working on the Culbertson project as early as June 1907, when an announcement was made in the *Pasadena Star.* On May 4, 1907, the *Pasadena News* announced that the plans for the Blacker house had been completed. Construction of the Gamble house would not begin until early 1908. For the Culbertson house, an invoice from Ernest Grassby, "Architectural Sculptor," dated December 1, 1907, shows a commission for three carvings for an upright piano. Charles Greene had saved an article titled "The Designing of Piano Cases" from the *Architectural Review* (1905), which illustrated a semi-grand and an upright case designed by C.R. Ashbee, the semi-grand with elaborate painted decoration and the upright with beautiful inlay. Greene's copy of the article is in the EDA.

49. Charles Greene would have seen the German exhibits at St. Louis, which were reviewed in *The Craftsman* as "remarkable for charm of color and completeness of design … Each room was in fact a complete work of art as a room." Charles Shean, "The New Art: A Personal and Creative Art," *The Craftsman,* 8, no. 5 (August 1905), pp. 606–607.

50. In *News from Nowhere,* Morris writes of a guesthouse in Hammersmith, west London: "I found it difficult to keep my eyes off the wall-pictures … . I saw at a glance that their subjects were taken from queer old-world myths and imaginations which in yesterday's world only about half a dozen people in the country knew anything about …" William Morris, *News from Nowhere* (London: Routledge & Kegan Paul, 1970), p. 85. Originally published in installments in *The Commonwealth* in 1890.

51. Edward S. Morse, *Japanese Homes and Their Surroundings* (New York: Dover, 1961), p. 9. Originally published by Ticknor & Company in 1886.

52. The original Gothic-style building had been designed by Franklin Burnham in 1892.

53. Letter from James Culbertson to CSG, July 22, 1910: "Mrs. Culbertson thinks that pink is not the best color for the blossoms in the hall lanterns and that yellow would be better … The drawings promise a very satisfactory result." Copy of letter in GGA.

54. This addition also included delicate carvings of birds and rather Japanese-style clouds (similar to those illustrated in Morse) set in relief inside the dining-room bay. The leaded glass in this bay showed heraldic roundels in painted glass. This again strikes a particularly English note; M.H. Baillie Scott praises the use of such heraldry: "in its symbolic birds and beasts … one finds the elements of a kind of decorative language." Baillie Scott, *Houses and Gardens,* p. 82.

55. Boston Society of Arts and Crafts, founded 1897. Red House was built in 1859.

56. CSG, as quoted in Bosley, *Greene & Greene,* p. 33.

57. "From his first sight of Canterbury a cathedral became Morris's dream building. Quite literally so: his own dreams were filled with buildings, and cathedrals are the setting for several of Morris's dream narratives." Fiona MacCarthy, *William Morris: A Life for Our Time* (London: Faber & Faber, 1994), p. 19.

58. CSG, "Thais Thayer," unpublished typescript, GGA, pp. 69, 94.

59. Morris mentions this in "The Lesser Arts of Life" (1882); the list of books in Charles Greene's library in his Carmel studio includes Scott's *Tales of a Grandfather* (1828–30).

60. Eastlake, *A History of the Gothic Revival,* pp. 112–15.

61. William Morris, "An address delivered at the distribution of prizes to students of the Birmingham Municipal School of Art on February 21, 1894," in Morris, *The Collected Works of William Morris,* XXII, p. 429.

62. For more on this subject, see the essay in this volume by Alan Crawford, pp. 197–211.

63. MacCarthy, *William Morris: A Life,* p. 97.

64. The following books from Charles Greene's library were each inscribed with his name, "London," and the date "1909": William Carleton's *Fawn of Springvale & Other Tales* (Dublin, 1841); Thomas Gray's *Poems* (London, 1821); James McPherson's *Poems of Ossian* (Edinburgh, 1830); Thomas Moore's *Epistles, Odes and Other Poems* (London, 1817); John Oxenford's *Tales from the German* (London, 1844); A.A. Proctor's *Legends and Lyrics* (London, 1860); Friedrich Schiller's *Ghost Seer!* (London, 1831), which contained a receipt for the Clovelly hotel; and Sir Walter Scott's *Tales of a Grandfather* (Paris, 1828–30).

65. Bosley, *Greene & Greene,* p. 43.

66. Dante Gabriel Rossetti, as quoted in MacCarthy, *William Morris: A Life,* p. 156.

67. CSG, "California Home Making," *Pasadena Daily News,* January 2, 1905, pp. 26–27.

68. Claude Bragdon, "The Sleeping Beauty," *The Craftsman,* 4, no. 5 (August 1903), p. 347.

69. Ann Scheid, *Pasadena: Crown of the Valley* (Northridge, Calif.: Windsor Publications, 1986), p. 93.

70. "An address delivered at the distribution of prizes to students of the Birmingham Municipal School of Art on February 21, 1894," in Morris, *The Collected Works of William Morris,* XXII, pp. 429–30. Emphasis in original.

71. See MacCarthy, *William Morris: A Life,* p. 95. Quote from Georgiana Burne-Jones, *Memorials of Edward Burne-Jones,* 2 vols. (London: Macmillan & Co., 1904).

72. William Morris, "The Arts and Crafts Today," delivered in Edinburgh, 1889, in Morris, *The Collected Works of William Morris,* XXII, p. 360.

73. *Ibid.,* p. 365.

74. "A Special Citation to Henry Mather Greene and Charles Sumner Greene," *Journal of the American Institute of Architects,* 18 (July 1952), pp. 4–5.

VIRGINIA GREENE HALES AND BRUCE SMITH

Charles and Henry Greene

Late in life, after they no longer shared an architectural practice, Charles and Henry Greene each produced an architectural magnum opus, a work as distinguished and distinct as its author. In 1918, Charles began his last major commission, two years after leaving behind both Pasadena and his brother: "I left my acquaintances, friends, my vocation, my brother with whom I was associated, and business connections, and went to Carmel in the pine woods—'right at the highest point of your career' claimed my more intimate friends." He was abandoning his work, he wrote, "so to ponder life and art." But then, "I broke my vow just once, for one house to grow out of rock cliff over hanging the Pacific Ocean impelled by myself and a gathered group of men without a contractor." This house was for D.L. James (fig. 1), an "unruly client," Charles Greene later called him. James was an aspiring playwright; a wealthy merchant of fine imported china, glass, and silver; and, fortunately for Charles, a patron who lived in faraway Kansas City. James came to Carmel only in the summertime, giving Charles the freedom to work on his own, designing the house and then supervising it as stone was laid upon stone. James finally called a halt to Greene's labors in 1922 so that he and his family might at last occupy the house. "I am everything," Charles wrote, "without office boys, draftsmen, and secretary." This was his masterpiece, and his alone.[1]

It leaves one wondering whether it was really the practice of architecture that Charles was vowing to forsake when he left Pasadena, or—as was more likely—whether it was the constraints of working with contractors, draftsmen, and secretaries, all tethers to his creativity and to his role as an artist. During his years in Northern California, the architecture he produced was meager in quantity when compared to that created by his younger brother. Henry, changing the name of the firm in 1922 to simply Henry M. Greene, Architect, continued the architectural practice he had begun with his older brother in 1894. By the late 1920s, because of a slow economy and changing stylistic demand, the practice was falling off. Henry's last major commission, in 1929, was for a ranch house in California's Central Valley (fig. 2). The client, Walter Richardson, a native Californian who had been raised in Pasadena, came to Henry with the idea of a simple house built around a courtyard, something very much in tune with the early work of the brothers. Richardson wanted to act as his own contractor, and to construct the house economically from adobe bricks made on site. Henry agreed to these conditions.[2]

There followed a series of letters from architect to client giving an extraordinary portrait of Henry Greene, both as an architect and a person. The twinkle in his eye, so often described by friends and family, comes out in his writing when he tells the discouraged Richardson, "Cheer up, the worst is yet to come!"[3] He guided Richardson through each step of the building; when a builder failed to provide cost estimates for the house, Henry undertook the task himself.[4] He was careful, exacting, and uncomplaining, providing in words and drawings in letter after letter details on everything from the finish of the redwood ceiling to the spacing and nailing of the shingles.[5]

Charles Greene's house for D.L. James represents one man's artistic vision expressed upon the landscape, a stone house melding into rock cliffs rising from the raging sea; Henry created—with his client—a home gently settled on the hillside, both skillfully integrated with the landscape, and made from it. The adobe bricks of the walls were made from clay taken from the property; rocks from the hillside were used for the foundation and chimney; the terrace is sandstone quarried from the site. It is about the land and the process, and it is about the fulfillment of the client's wishes, carried beyond the client's expectations. It too is a masterpiece of architecture, largely for its embodiment of all things Californian, which had been the thrust of the Greenes' work throughout their careers.

As these houses illustrate, Charles and Henry Greene were extraordinarily different men, each accomplished and dedicated to his art in his own way. They were born and bred, though, of the same stock, growing up together, learning architecture together, sharing an architectural practice for twenty-two years, and, throughout their lives, staying close and caring for each other. It was their innate differences, however, that enabled the body of work they produced to come into being, balancing each other, working in tandem toward the beauty they created together.

The brothers arrived just fifteen months apart, Charles on October 12, 1868, and Henry on January 23, 1870 (figs. 3 and 4). Born in Cincinnati, a bustling city of 216,000, they

FIGURE 1
"Seaward,"
D.L. James house,
Carmel Highlands,
1918–22

Courtesy of Greene and Greene Archives, The Gamble House, University of Southern California

were the only children of Thomas Sumner Greene and Lelia Ariana Mather. Their father, also born in Cincinnati, after graduating from high school, spent five years fighting in the Civil War. Just prior to his discharge in Louisiana, he met Lelia Mather, who was there visiting relatives, having traveled from her family's farm near Barboursville, West Virginia.[6] Married in 1867, they chose to live in Cincinnati, near Thomas's parents.[7]

There was already a history of architects and craftsmen in the family. On the paternal side, the Greene family had owned and operated an anchor forge, grist mill, sawmill, and cotton mill in Warwick, Rhode Island, from 1684 until well into the 1880s. There the brothers' great-grandfather Christopher and his brother, Nathanael Greene, of Revolutionary War fame, had lived.[8] On Thomas's mother's side were James Sumner and his son, Thomas Waldron Sumner, noted shipwrights, housewrights, and architects in Boston and Brookline, Massachusetts.[9] These ancestors had no formal training in their crafts; as was often the case in those times, they had largely learned their skills by apprenticeship and on the job.

But the Greene boys had been born into a world that was rapidly transforming. Individual craftsmanship was

being replaced by standardized production, and the fields of medicine, law, and architecture were becoming professionalized. Their father, Thomas, always a powerful force in their lives, set his sights on two goals for the boys: giving them the best education for entering the profession of architecture, and guiding them toward working together in their own firm.

Cincinnati, which had been the leading cultural and industrial center in the Midwest, had by now passed its zenith, replaced by Chicago and St. Louis. Thomas moved the family to St. Louis in 1874, working first as a clerk, then as a bookkeeper. Following the death of both his father and an older brother, he returned to Cincinnati, where he enrolled in the Joseph A. Pulte Homeopathic College.[10]

During Thomas's time of study, Lelia took Charles and Henry to her parents' farm in West Virginia.[11] It is not known whether they attended the local elementary school or were tutored at home. At their grandparents', the boys—who had always lived in the city—were introduced to nature and to all that went into running a self-sufficient farm. They learned to ride on horseback through the fields; they saw how wool was turned into thread and cloth, how butter was churned, and how

carpentry and blacksmithing were done.[12] It may have been during this time, when the brothers were between ten and thirteen years old, that the foundations of their later working relationship were laid. As the oldest sibling and prone to dreaming and using his imagination, Charles may have originated the idea of building together, say, a fort; it may then have been up to Henry, who was of a more practical bent, to come up with the way of doing it.[13]

Charles and Henry were influenced during early childhood by the interest of their parents in the arts. Their mother, Lelia, was very artistic, making quilts and painting porcelain china.[14] Both she and Thomas played the piano and attended concerts and the opera. Charles learned to play the violin, and Henry played the flute and sang; both played the piano.[15] The boys also painted in watercolors from the time they were young.

After Thomas Sumner Greene finished his medical course, he moved the family back to St. Louis.[16] There he established his own practice, which emphasized the curing of "catarrh" and other respiratory illnesses. He decided that, to further the boys' education, he would place them both in the Manual Training School, a three-year high school started by Calvin M. Woodward in 1879 and connected with Washington University in St. Louis. Charles entered the school in 1884, and Henry followed in 1885. This education served as an excellent foundation for their later careers. The purposes of the school were to foster the discovery of "inborn capacities and aptitudes" in the students and to give them a broad foundation in liberal arts, with hands-on training in working with "tools, materials, drafting and methods of construction." The students studied mathematics, English, and drawing, as well as the practical arts of "carpentry, wood-turning, pattern-making, iron chipping and filing, forge-work, brazing and soldering, and the use of Machine shop tools."[17]

No doubt it was Thomas who decided that the next step would be for his sons to apply to the Massachusetts Institute of Technology, better known then as "Boston Tech." So that the boys could go east together to college, Thomas arranged for Charles to be "settled in a real architect's office" in St. Louis during Henry's final year at the Manual Training School. Charles was distressed; years later he wrote, "my father suggested I enter an architect's office. I had a feeling of keen disappointment. I wanted to be an artist."[18]

In the fall of 1888, the Greene brothers traveled together to Boston. In looks, they differed somewhat. Both were slightly built, Henry a few inches taller

than Charles, with a sharper nose and more prominent ears; Charles had a dreamlike quality to his eyes. Starting "Tech," they shared rooms at Miss Rachael's Boarding House just a few doors off Copley Square in the Back Bay.[19] Boston was the cultural center of the country, and an exciting place to be for two young men studying architecture. The Back Bay project of filling in the old Mill Pond, begun in the 1860s, was still underway, and hundreds of new, elegant townhouses were being built along Beacon Street and Commonwealth Avenue. H.H. Richardson's Romanesque Revival architecture had reached its apex with his design for Trinity Church, completed in 1877 in Copley Square, adjacent to the Museum of Fine Arts and down the street from the Rogers Building of Boston Tech, where Charles and Henry attended classes. The new Boston Public Library by McKim, Mead & White was also being built opposite Trinity Church.

Even so, in later years, Charles remembered "a sinking feeling when walking up the dull, red sandstone steps of the Rogers Building ... It was a day without the rising of the sun ... work had to be done, classes didn't wait."[20] It was not a happy time for the sensitive twenty-year-old. He wanted to be studying art. Several of the other students took a dislike to Charles, and one of them blackballed both boys from the architectural club because Charles had been critical of the Rogers Building. It pained Charles deeply that Henry was also blackballed: "My brother was very quiet and industrious and uniformly gracious to everyone."[21]

There were other difficulties. Henry's health suffered. He had stomach problems for which his father prescribed medication by letter, and, during the Christmas vacation of 1889, when he and Charles were in New Bedford with their grandmother and great-aunt Emily, he contracted bronchitis. They nursed him back to health, but he worried in letters to Charles that he would not be able to catch up on his schoolwork.[22]

Charles fared better physically; he seemed to have more energy and a stronger constitution. But he tended to become reclusive, staying indoors, writing poetry and plays, and dreaming in his own inner world. Their parents encouraged both Charles and Henry to join a gym for exercise, and Thomas urged them to be more sociable and to "meet the right people," especially those recommended by their relatives. They went to social, musical, and theatrical events; Charles studied watercolor painting and piano, and became involved in photography.[23]

Henry also took piano lessons and enjoyed choral singing. He had a brief romance with a young woman named Annie Calendar, whose family lived on Nantucket during the summers. Both Henry and Charles visited them there, and Henry painted watercolor scenes of the seashore (fig. 5). Their father sent money for them to purchase bicycles, for ease in getting around. Sometimes they would cycle down to East Braintree, where their cousins the Ogdens and Averys lived when they were not at home in Boston.[24]

Henry's grades were somewhat better than Charles's, and he was apparently content with their circumstances at Boston Tech. Charles wrote years later, "My brother, Hal, seemed very comfortable and happy and had better marks than I received, which made me very unhappy and discouraged."[25] Charles was more restless and did not like the strictness of the schedules and routines. All of this, combined with his desire to become an artist, not an architect, made him resistant to completing his certificate. But Thomas warned him, "I differ with you Charlie about the value of the Tech certificates. I think you will find that without them you will not be able to enter any of the Architectural Societies and in order to take proper work among first class architects you will have to join the associations. I therefore wish you to get up that back work and get your certificates."[26] During these years, the influence of the brothers' grandmother and great-aunts was also important in informing their architectural tastes. It is very likely that their grandmother, Matilda Ray Sumner Greene, would have told Charles and Henry about the architecture of her grandfather James Sumner, known for his fine carpentry work on Thomas Dawes's Brattle Square Church (1772) in Boston and for his great engineering feat in the building and erection of the steeple for the First Baptist Meeting House in Providence, Rhode Island (1774–75).[27] Matilda's father, Thomas Waldron Sumner, designed Harvard's Divinity Hall (1825) and the East India Marine Hall in Salem (1824).[28] The Marine Hall was one of the earliest museums in America, and held many items that East India Company ships brought back from the Far East in the late 1700s. Although the Brattle Square Church had been demolished by 1872, Matilda may well have taken Charles and Henry to see the East India Marine Hall.[29] She may have taken them out to Brookline, too, to see where she had grown up on Warren Street, and to see the first Town Hall (1824), just around the corner on Walnut Street, which her father had designed.[30]

Within two years, Charles and Henry had finished their course work and passed all of their exams except "Heating and Ventilation." Lelia wrote in November 1890, encouraging them to keep going:

I am glad you are studying up on heating. I hope you will both get your certificates. I do not want to say anything to hurt your feelings or destroy your ambition, but there are two sides to look at always in everything in life. Practical first. Your bread and butter are necessary first. Ideal and Art are very fascinating. I can appreciate all that, but it is very necessary for some one to work for the means and substance to keep the pot boiling and get the wherewithal to indulge such Luxuries ...[31]

Both parents must have been pleased when their sons completed their last exams and received their certificates in a ceremony at Trinity Church on March 28, 1891.[32]

In the spring of 1890, nearly a year before receiving their certificates, the brothers began to work in various architectural firms as apprentice drafters.[33] Charles was initially employed by Andrews, Jacques & Rantoul, which had designed the William Cox residence called Roughwood in Brookline.[34] He also worked briefly for R. Clipston Sturgis, but his restlessness kept him searching for another job. In March 1891, he was invited to work for H. Langford Warren, where he happily stayed for eight months. He then shifted to the office of Winslow & Wetherell; the firm's design can be seen in the S.S. Pierce building still standing at Coolidge Corner, Brookline. In these offices, Charles would have become familiar with the Shingle style, the Queen Anne style, and the use of clinker brick.[35]

Henry went to work in the spring of 1890 for Chamberlain & Austin, staying through the summer. He then changed to Stickney & Austin, commuting to the firm's office in Lowell. Part-time work for Edward R. Benton soon followed, but perhaps his best job, however brief, was with Shepley, Rutan & Coolidge, the successor firm to H.H. Richardson.[36]

By early 1892, Thomas and Lelia Greene were facing difficulties in St. Louis. Thomas's homeopathic business was declining, and Lelia suffered from asthma. They began to consider a major move, to join Thomas's sister Alice Sumner Longley and her family in Southern California; in the spring of 1892, they traveled west by train to Pasadena.[37] In January 1893, the boys considered moving to California to join their parents, but decided their prospects were far brighter in Boston. Their parents reluctantly agreed: "... there is nothing for you to do here and you would lose by giving up your prospects there," Lelia wrote. Then, in May 1893, the New York Stock Exchange crashed, and the United States entered the worst depression to that point in its history. Charles lost his position, and Henry's office would soon begin laying off draftsmen. They decided to go west.[38]

Aug 17/92
Nantucket, Mass.

13

Henry and Charles arrived in late August 1893 in Pasadena, a city of perhaps 10,000 people with dusty, unpaved roads—not like Boston in the least. But Pasadena was growing; it had nearly doubled in size over the previous three years.[39] By 1894, the brothers had hung their sign on Colorado Street in Pasadena as the architectural firm of "Greene and Greene." Years later, Henry wrote to Charles reminding him of their first job: "designing concrete boxes for old Mr. Hutchenson, the candy man."[40] Over the next eight years, they obtained commissions for approximately thirty houses, along with sundry other jobs that included Sunday school rooms for a local church, stables, offices for the local ice company, and an office block on a prominent downtown corner, to which they moved their offices in 1896.[41]

By the spring of 1899, Henry, who by now wore glasses and sported a full beard and mustache, was courting a young woman named Emeline Augusta Dart (fig. 6). He became very ill with "inflammatory rheumatism," which kept him bedridden for three months. In July, to recuperate and to prepare for their wedding, he traveled to Emeline's hometown of Rock Island, Illinois. They were married in August, honeymooning in Kansas City.[42] On their return to Pasadena, they moved next door to the house occupied by Thomas, Lelia, and Charles, at the corner of Lake and Colorado streets. Both homes were owned by Thomas, creating a nice family enclave, especially with the birth of Henry and Emeline's first child, in September 1900.[43]

In February 1901, Charles, now with a trim mustache and glasses, also stepped into marriage; his wife, Alice

Gordon White, was an English heiress, one of four sisters who lived just east of the Greenes on Colorado Street (fig. 7). Her father—listed as a "Capitalist" in the local city directory—had passed away a few years before, leaving his daughters well off. The newlyweds' honeymoon included a tour of England, Scotland, and the Continent; visits to museums, art galleries, churches and cathedrals; and purchasing postcards of architecture; Charles took time out along the way to paint watercolors. It was a Grand Tour, perfect for an architect with a lively interest in the arts.[44]

While Charles and Alice were overseas, the financial panic of 1901 occurred. Thomas's investments had not done well, and he was forced to sell both of the Colorado Street homes. He and Lelia decided to move to Kansas City and set up his medical practice there.[45] Thomas wrote to Charles in Europe, "We will miss your return, and of course it is very uncertain when we will see you again ... I am afraid you will never do much in California."[46]

Henry seized this opportunity to move with his family and his mother-in-law, Charlotte A. Whitridge, to Los Angeles, where they settled in two adjacent houses in the fashionable West Adams district. He opened a "branch" office for the firm in downtown Los Angeles in an attempt to expand the practice. He had written to his brother in England, "There seems to be a good deal of work in the City [Los Angeles], but not much here [Pasadena]. I am anxious to get a start there. We'll never make our salt in this blooming place."[47]

When Charles and Alice returned in the late summer of 1901, they lived in a rental home in Pasadena; for the first time, the two brothers did not share their daily lives. By the end of 1901, Charles had arranged to build a house in Pasadena on a property overlooking the Arroyo Seco. In 1903, with the house completed, the Pasadena office of Greene and Greene was closed. Charles now saw clients and worked from the studio in his new home.[48]

Henry continued working in Los Angeles until 1904, when he and his family moved back to Pasadena. They found a pleasant lot on Bellefontaine Street, which his mother-in-law purchased; she then commissioned Henry to design a large duplex home for them all (fig. 9).[49] She was unusually protective of her only daughter, Emeline, who was partially deaf and had a weak heart as a result of contracting scarlet fever at age four. Unable to attend school, Emeline was taught to read and write by her mother. She was a quiet and rather elusive young woman, quite lovely in her elegant gowns and hats.

For the next several years, Henry commuted daily to downtown Los Angeles on the "Red Car" as Charles continued to work from his home studio. Most of the

FIGURE 5
Coastline and lighthouse, Nantucket Island, Massachusetts. Watercolor by Henry Greene, 1892

Courtesy of Greene and Greene Archives, The Gamble House, University of Southern California

FIGURE 6
Studio portrait of Henry and his wife, Emeline, c. 1900

Courtesy of Henry M. Greene Family Collection

commissions they received at this time, however, were based in Pasadena. In 1907, they closed the Los Angeles office and opened a new office in Pasadena, reflecting the financial and social reality that the majority of their clients were wealthy tourists who came to Pasadena either to stay or merely to spend the winter.

It was during this period—from 1902 to 1906—that the designs of the Greenes began assuming the individuality and sophistication that led to their expansive, costly, extraordinary works of 1907 to 1911. It was a step-by-step progression that involved developing a unique vocabulary, experimenting with materials and forms, finding competent craftsmen who could accurately interpret and execute the work, and building a clientele who not only had the wealth to commission an "artistic" house, but also the good judgment to do so. The clients that the Greenes were able to attract were not the only proof of their success; their style was widely imitated by fellow architects, by contractor-builders, and in bungalow plan books. It is also interesting to note that it was during the brothers' most architecturally productive period, from 1902 to 1911, that all but one of their children were born; Charles and Alice had five, and Henry and Emeline had four.[50]

The different natures of the two brothers were manifested in the way they worked together.[51] Henry's son remembered, "Uncle Charles was by nature an artist and designer, and my father excelled in the construction and the 'getting things done' categories."[52] There is little question that Charles was the lead designer of the firm, that much of the unique aesthetic came from him. However, during the Greenes' most prolific period (1902–11), it is equally clear that there were too many projects for one man alone to design. In 1906, for example, according to their job book, they had twenty-two commissions, six of them for houses in the range of $18,000. Processing these jobs involved not only producing designs and working drawings, but also bookkeeping and correspondence. For the latter work, Henry and Charles asked their father, who had returned from Kansas City, to join the office and use the bookkeeping skills he had learned when young.

The Greene and Greene style was well recognized in both professional journals and popular magazines during this time. The first article devoted to the brothers, just as their work was reaching full maturation, was in 1906 in the *Architectural Record*;[53] the last major article was just six years later, in *The Craftsman*.[54] Surprisingly, the writers of both pieces described the same features as the key elements in the Greenes' style: the low, wide spreading roof lines and projecting beams that "cast heavy shadows," the "utter absence of ornamentation and display" on the exterior, and the "shingled or clapboarded walls." Both writers perceived the work of the Greenes as uniquely Californian, though noted the influence of Japan and the related "frank use of structural beams." The only distinguishing difference between the two articles was that in 1906, the author was emphasizing that good architecture, as exemplified by the work of the Greenes, need not incur great expense; whereas the

writer of 1912 stressed that "the quality of materials and workmanship that goes into the house built by Messrs. Greene & Greene renders them of necessity expensive."[55]

In spite of the Greenes' success in developing a new architecture and in obtaining clients who could afford the design of interiors, furnishings, lighting, and landscaping, Charles still felt the drive to pursue his own artistic directions (fig. 8). He often referred to himself as an artist, at one point describing a job for a client as a "transaction between artist and patron."[56] In 1909, he left Pasadena and his brother to spend seven months in England with his family, visiting museums, attending parties, and painting watercolors. On his return, he took

time to write stories, poetry, and an imaginative novel about a young, "timid, retiring" architectural student at the Massachusetts Institute of Technology who is kidnapped from Boston and taken to an island where he is told to build a house for a beautiful woman.[57] He tried to have the novel published, unsuccessfully, and wrote several articles on architecture for professional journals; the last ones express frustration, almost anger, about the current state of the architectural profession in California, about the mass manufacture of homes, and about the bungalow books, which "offer a selection degrading to the art … because they are ready-made."[58] Describing his final departure from Pasadena in 1916, when he

FIGURE 9

Henry and Emeline, their children and spouses, in front of the Greenes' home on Bellefontaine Street, Pasadena, 1931. From left to right: Elbert Mather Greene and Alyce Adair Greene, Alan R. McElwain and Isabelle Horton Greene McElwain, Henry Dart Greene and Ruth Elizabeth Haight Greene (Charlotte A. Whitridge in front of Ruth), Henry Mather Greene and Emeline Dart Greene, and cousins, Will and Phoebe Barth

Courtesy of Greene and Greene Archives, The Gamble House, University of Southern California

moved his family to Northern California, Charles wrote: "I wondered, what is art? Is there more in life than art? Is there anything in architecture without art?"[59]

In the years following his move to Carmel, Charles painted, puttered, appeared in plays with his family, composed poems, and wrote on spiritual matters. He built a home for his family, and a studio for himself within which he could work, think, meditate, and, at times, gather around him those who were of like mind.[60] He dressed for the role of an artist, letting his hair grow long and wearing smocks sewn for him by Alice (fig. 10). Despite his vow, Charles did continue with some architectural work: two houses for clients and homes for family members, the studio for himself, magnificent gardens for a former client, a war memorial for the city of Carmel, a stable for horses, and additions and alterations, mostly for past clients. And then there was his last major work—the home for D.L. James—built "to grow out of rock cliff over hanging the Pacific Ocean …"

During these years, Henry, still in Pasadena, completed almost eight times as many jobs as Charles, designing houses and gardens, alterations and additions, and essentially maintaining a full architectural practice; but major commissions were few. By 1928, he wrote Charles, "work is pretty scarce down here now and all [are] struggling to get what there is going on."[61] The following year, just before the Depression set in, he received his final great commission, from Walter Richardson, for the simple courtyard house on a hillside in Porterville, a project that he turned into something extraordinary, and very Californian.

In the decade following completion of these last commissions, the work of the two brothers was largely forgotten.[62] During the 1930s and through the war years, in the writings of such architectural historians as Lewis Mumford, Henry Russell Hitchcock, Sigfried Giedion, Talbot Hamlin, and James Marston Fitch, only scant mention was made of the Greenes. It is not inconceivable that their work could have been bulldozed into oblivion; of approximately 140 houses designed by the two brothers, sixty-six have been demolished and another fourteen substantially altered, leaving about sixty homes to represent their body of work.

These were difficult years for Henry. His beloved wife, Emeline, died June 27, 1935, one day shy of her fifty-ninth birthday. Henry lived on at the Bellefontaine house, taking care of his mother-in-law until she entered a rest home in 1939. It was then no longer practical for him to remain in the house; after making it available for rent, he moved to Altadena to live with his son's family (fig. 12).[63]

In 1945, Henry was visited by a lively, intelligent, and outspoken woman, Jean Murray Bangs, the wife of architect Harwell Hamilton Harris. She had decided to write about the work of the brothers. Although she had grown up just a block from the enclave of Greene and Greene homes along the Arroyo Seco in Pasadena, she had not learned the names of these architects until one of her husband's assistants had said to her: "They got Greene and Greene and they'll get your husband, too." He was referring to the fact that when architects develop a style that is worthy of being imitated, as did the Greenes, it is copied widely and the power of its uniqueness is diluted. The original works—and their creators—subsequently risk being lost to history.[64] The phrase haunted Bangs until finally, returning with her husband to California in 1944, she searched out the Greenes and found Henry living with his son in Altadena. Speaking with him about his work, she inquired about the firm's drawings, only to be told that they had been left in the garage of his former home; she soon rescued the drawings from the "backless and rat-infested cabinet" in which they had been stored.[65]

One of the first mentions of the Greenes in print in a decade and a half was probably thanks to Jean Murray Bangs. In 1946, her friend Carey McWilliams, in his seminal cultural study *Southern California Country*, mentioned that between 1900 and 1915, the brothers "began to adapt the bungalow form in an interesting way."[66] Bangs never wrote the book she planned on the Greenes, but she did publish her research in articles in architectural journals and popular magazines, especially in *House Beautiful*, edited by her friend Elizabeth Gordon.[67] The work of the brothers was recognized in 1948 by the Southern California chapter of the American Institute of Architects, which awarded them a special Certificate of Merit, specifically citing "merit in the design and execution of work in Architecture and the Fine Arts …"[68] Charles was seventy-nine years old (fig. 11) and unable to attend the banquet at the Biltmore Hotel in Los Angeles, but Henry, seventy-eight, and many of his family were there. In 1952, the Greenes received a Special Citation from the national AIA for being, among other things, the "formulators of a new and native architecture." Not long after this, Henry Mather Greene passed away after a short illness on October 2, 1954, at the age of eighty-four. Three years later, on June 11, 1957, Charles Sumner Greene passed away at his home in Carmel at the age of eighty-eight.[69]

It matters that this commendation finally came to these two brothers, these two very different men, and that it came not just in time for them to be acknowledged while they were still alive, but also in time for

FIGURE 10

Charles with his mother, Lelia Ariana Mather Greene; his wife, Alice; and his daughter, Anne (the concert pianist, Ariana Cressy Giles Greene), standing in front of his studio in Carmel, 1931. Photograph by Henry Dart Greene

Courtesy of Greene and Greene Archives, The Gamble House, University of Southern California

FIGURE 11

Charles in his studio,
Carmel, 1947

Courtesy of Greene
and Greene Archives,
The Gamble House,
University of Southern
California

FIGURE 12

Henry at the home of
his son Henry Dart
Greene, Altadena,
March 6, 1949

Courtesy of
Henry M. Greene
Family Collection

[*page 55*]
FIGURE 13

Panel detail, living-
room light fixture,
Robert R. Blacker
house, Pasadena,
1907–09

Courtesy of American
Decorative Art 1900
Foundation. Photograph:
Gavin Ashworth,
© American Decorative
Art 1900 Foundation

[*page 56*]
FIGURE 14

"The Bathers."
Henry, Emeline, and
Henry Dart Greene
(aged five years),
vacationing in
La Jolla Cove, 1905

Courtesy of
Henry M. Greene
Family Collection

much of their best work to be better appreciated and preserved. Fortunately, acclaim for their work today has grown far beyond any they received during their lifetimes. It is recognized not only for the heights of craftsmanship and artistry they attained and for their achievement in developing a manifestly Californian style of architecture; but also, most importantly, today their work is valued for its original, individual, artistic style, the result of the combined vision and efforts of two brothers, Charles and Henry Greene.

1. The quotations by Charles Greene are from his scribbled notes in Misc. Papers, EDA. Inner quotation marks have been added for clarity of text. Regarding the D.L. James house, the best overview is Edward R. Bosley, *Greene & Greene* (London: Phaidon, 2000), pp. 193–200. See also Charles Miller, "The James House: Charles Greene's Masterpiece in Stone," in *Fine Homebuilding Great Houses: Craftsman-Style Houses* (Newtown, Conn.: Taunton Press, 1991), pp. 52–58. The initial design of the James house was entirely Charles's work, but in 1940, when James requested the addition of a library, Charles turned to Henry for help in the engineering. See letters from CSG to HMG, June 17, 1940, and from HMG to CSG, September 13, 1940, EDA.
2. For Henry's commission for Walter Richardson, see Bosley, *Greene & Greene*, pp. 187–89.
3. Letter from HMG to Walter Richardson, September 23, 1929, GGA.
4. Letter from HMG to Richardson, June 21, 1929, GGA.
5. Henry wrote, "I also like to leave a space of ¼" between each shingle and its neighbor and have the alignment irregular. It makes a more interesting texture." Letter from HMG to Richardson, July 26, 1929, GGA.
6. Lelia was descended from Rev. Richard Mather and his son, Timothy, a farmer in Dorchester, Massachusetts. Timothy was an uncle of Cotton Mather, famous for his role in the Salem witch trials. Horace E. Mather, *Lineage of Rev. Richard Mather* (Hartford, Conn.: Press of the Case, Lockwood & Brainard Co., 1890), p. 362.
7. Thomas's parents were Elihue Greene and Matilda Ray Sumner. Elihue was a clerk and bookkeeper most of his business life. *Cincinnati City Directories*, 1834–78.
8. Louise Brownell Clarke, from the manuscript of George Sears Greene, *The Greenes of Rhode Island, with Historical Records of English Ancestry, 1534–1902* (New York: Knickerbocker Press, 1903), pp. 200–12.
9. William Sumner Appleton, *Record of the Descendants of William Sumner of Dorchester, Mass. 1636* (Boston: David Clapp & Sons, 1879), pp. 21, 42; and HMG, "Ancestors of Matilda Ray Sumner Chart," handwritten draft, GGA.
10. It is possible that an inheritance from his father enabled this change

in Thomas's life. It is probable that he stayed with his widowed mother in Cincinnati during this period, helping to take care of her. About Thomas's older brother, William Ward Greene, there is a marker stone but no burial record in the family plot, Spring Grove Cemetery, in Cincinnati. It states that he died January 7, 1879, in Bodie, California, and it is assumed he was buried there also.
11. 1880 U.S. Census, Barboursville, Cabell County, West Virginia, June 1, 1880 enumerated.
12. As told by Henry Dart Greene, in *The Memoirs of Henry Dart Greene and Ruth Elizabeth Haight Greene*, ed. Virginia Dart Greene Hales (La Jolla, Calif.: Virginia Dart Greene Hales, 1996), I, p. 7.
13. This was the predominant pattern throughout the brothers' lives, up to when Charles called upon Henry from long distance to help solve a structural problem for the library at the D.L. James house. See letters between CSG and HMG, September 13 and November 11, 1940, EDA.
14. A quilt made by Lelia is in the possession of Charles Greene's granddaughter Jane Roberts McElroy; painted plates signed "L.A.G.," with dates ranging from 1888 to 1892, are owned by Henry's granddaughter Virginia Dart Greene Hales.
15. Letters between CSG and HMG and their parents, 1888–93, GGA.
16. The different locations the Greenes lived in St. Louis are listed in *Gould's St. Louis Directories*, 1875–93.
17. *Prospectus of the Manual Training School of Washington University* (St. Louis: Globe-Democrat Job Printing Company, 1879), p. 5.
18. CSG Misc. Papers, EDA. Charles spent the year working with the St. Louis architect Alfred F. Rosenheim.
19. Bosley, *Greene & Greene*, p. 13.
20. CSG Misc. Papers, EDA.
21. *Ibid.*
22. Letter from HMG to CSG, January 2, 1890, GGA.
23. Letters between CSG and HMG and their parents, 1889–93, GGA.
24. *Ibid.*
25. CSG Misc. Papers, EDA.
26. Thomas Greene, St. Louis, to CSG and HMG, Boston, July 1, 1890, GGA.
27. James Sumner also designed the fortifications on Prospect Hill in Providence during the Revolutionary War. See Frederic C. Detwiller,

"Thomas Dawes's Church in Brattle Square," *Old-Time New England*, LXIX, nos. 3–4 (Winter–Spring 1979). About the building of the First Baptist Meeting House in Providence, in 1774–75, see also Norman Morrison Isham, *The Meeting House of the First Baptist Church in Providence: A History of the Fabric* (Providence: Akerman-Standard Co., 1925).
28. Christopher P. Monkhouse, "Biographical Sketch of Thomas Waldron Sumner, Architect of East India Marine Hall, (1824)," in Philip Chadwick Foster Smith, *East India Marine Hall: 1824–1974* (Salem, Mass.: Peabody Museum of Salem, 1974).
29. Charles and Henry might well have met Edward S. Morse, the director of the museum, whose book *Japanese Homes and Their Surroundings* had been published in 1886. About the influence of this book on the work of the Greenes, see Bosley, *Greene & Greene*, pp. 51–52, 59; and the essay in this volume by Bruce Smith, pp. 59–83.
30. We thank Roger Reed of the Brookline Preservation Commission for showing us the first Town Hall of Brookline and the location of Thomas Waldron Sumner's property.
31. Lelia Mather Greene, St. Louis, to CSG, Boston, November 2, 1890, GGA.
32. Bosley, *Greene & Greene*, p. 18.
33. We thank Robert Judson Clark for supplying us with a copy of the Greenes' MIT transcript records. See also Bosley, *Greene & Greene*, pp. 16–17.
34. Roughwood is now the administration building for Pine Manor College.
35. For a good overview of the Greenes apprenticeships in Boston, see Bosley, *Greene & Greene*, pp. 17–21. See also Barbara Ann Francis, "The Boston Roots of Greene and Greene" (master's thesis, Tufts University, 1987), copy on file at the GGA.
36. Richardson had died in 1886. Henry worked for Shepley, Rutan & Coolidge in the summer of 1893; the firm had just completed that April the new First Parish Unitarian-Universalist Church at 382 Walnut Street in Brookline, next to the first Town Hall that Charles and Henry's great-grandfather had designed. It is unknown whether Henry worked on the drawings for this building. The church looks like a small-scale afterthought of the buildings at Stanford University, which the same firm designed in 1888. The church

stands today, its back joined to the old Town Hall. See Greer Hardwicke and Roger Reed, *Brookline's Historic Places: A Compilation of Brookline Properties Including Those Listed in National and State Registers of Historic Places and in Local Districts* (Brookline, Mass.: Brookline Preservation Commission, 1995), p. 18.
37. This is well documented in letters to Charles and Henry from their parents prior to their move in 1892 to Pasadena, GGA.
38. Surprisingly, over the years, much importance has been given to an undocumented visit by Charles and Henry to the World's Columbian Exposition in Chicago during their move from Boston to Pasadena. It has been written that "they were both impressed by the design and the simple but dramatic construction of the Ho-o-den, the official exhibit of the Japanese government," which so impressed them that "the following year they made a special effort to attend the Midwinter Exposition in San Francisco in order to visit the Japanese hill and water gardens." Randell L. Makinson, *Greene & Greene: The Passion and the Legacy* (Salt Lake City: Gibbs Smith, 1998), p. 5. Others have taken this a step further: "The Greene brothers … owed the start of their successful careers as architects to seeing the Japanese displays at the Columbian Exposition, Chicago in 1893 and in 1894 at the Midwinter Exposition, San Francisco." Lionel Lambourne, *Japonisme: Cultural Crossings between Japan and the West* (London and New York: Phaidon, 2005), p. 185.

The only primary-source recollection in print for this assertion is an interview published by Clay Lancaster in 1957, the month following Charles Greene's death. (Henry had died three years previous.) Lancaster had visited with both Charles and Henry; Henry was his primary source, given Charles's advanced senility. Henry recollected for Lancaster that "they admired the Japanese buildings at both" the Chicago fair of 1893 and the San Francisco fair of 1894. It is Lancaster, not Henry, who mentions the Ho-o-den in Chicago. Clay Lancaster, "My Interviews with Greene and Greene," *Journal of the American Institute of Architects*, 28 (July 1957), p. 205.

There is nothing in the seminal writings of the two earlier historians who interviewed both Charles and

Henry about the influence of the exhibits of 1893 and 1894. In 1948, Jean Murray Bangs wrote, "Greene and Greene ran head on into this influence [the influence of oriental art] on the Pacific Coast," clarifying that "one had only to walk down the street to feel it. There were beautiful Japanese tea gardens in Pasadena and in San Francisco oriental shops, run by discriminating connoisseurs, were full of objects [that] would be museum pieces now … The brothers fell under the spell of this art." Jean Murray Bangs, "Greene and Greene," *Architectural Forum*, 89, no. 4 (October 1948), pp. 83, 85. According to L. Morgan Yost, Charles stated that the source of Japanese influence came from the book purchased from an "itinerant bookseller" with "pictures of Japanese homes and gardens." L. Morgan Yost, "Greene & Greene of Pasadena," *Journal of the Society of Architectural Historians*, 9, nos. 1–2 (March–May 1950), p. 13.

In 1949, Henry said that "he first experienced an awakening to the possibilities of 'foreign developed architecture' in school and gained a further appreciation of it when he discovered its applicableness to the restful climate of the Southland." Frank Purcell, "Two Brothers Pioneered the Future: City's Almost Forgotten Geniuses, Greene and Greene Acclaimed at Last," *Pasadena Independent*, March 6, 1949.

Sources for the Japanese influence on the Greenes' work are complex, and include not just written materials, but also the Japanese tea garden in Pasadena, Japanese import stores in both the Southland and San Francisco, and the fascination with Japan during the brothers' time in Boston. However, it is important to remember that the Japanese influence in their work did not begin to blossom until after Charles Greene's visit to the world's fair in St. Louis in 1904.

39. The 1890 census had Pasadena at 4882, but according to a promotional publication published in 1893, the population had already grown to "nearly ten thousand." Harry Ellington Brook, *The Land of Sunshine: Southern California—An Authentic Description of Its Natural Features, Resources, and Prospects* (Los Angeles: World's Fair Association and Bureau of Information Print, 1893), p. 64.

40. HMG, Pasadena, to CSG and Alice Greene, Carmel, October 6, 1938, EDA.

41. The best reconstruction of the Greene and Greene office job list is in Bosley, *Greene & Greene*, pp. 227–36.

42. See letters from HMG to CSG, July 28, 1899, and from Bess Hulbert to CSG, August 24, 1899, GGA.

43. Hales, *Memoirs*, I, p. 13.

44. Charles and Alice crossed the Atlantic to Southampton, then traveled around Italy and to Paris. Alice was English-born, so they returned in May to Great Britain for a lengthy visit, including London, Devon, Cornwall, Somerset, and Manchester in their travels. They visited Alice's childhood homes in Lancaster and the Lake District, as well as Scotland, where the Glasgow International Exhibition was in progress. On their way overland to California, they stopped in Buffalo to see the Pan-American International Exposition, where Charles had his first exposure to the new line of "Craftsman Furniture" being produced by Gustav Stickley. See Edward R. Bosley, "The British Connection," *The Tabby: A Chronicle of the Arts & Crafts Movement*, 1 (July–August 1997) pp. 6–21. Charles's copy of the catalogue from the Glasgow International Exhibition, dated and signed in his handwriting, is at the EDA.

45. Lelia's brother, Valcolon Mather, had a practice as a homeopathic doctor in Kansas City from 1887 to 1920; this was possibly the reason Thomas and Lelia moved there.

46. Letter from Thomas Greene, Pasadena, to CSG, abroad, April 12, 1901, GGA.

47. Letter from HMG to CSG and Alice Greene, April 5, 1901, GGA.

48. The property belonged to Alice Greene and her sisters, as indicated in the tax assessor's field book, 1902–03, vol. 2, May, p. 34, Pasadena City Archives. A notice on March 21, 1902, in the *Pasadena Star* states that construction had begun on the house for Mr. Charles Greene. See Margaret Meriwether, "Charles Sumner Greene and Henry Mather Greene, Architects, an Annotated Bibliography," typescript (1993), GGA. Presumably Charles and Alice would have been moving in by year's end, and by the beginning of 1903, Charles would have started working from his new home. Pasted into the office scrapbook in the GGA is an announcement: "Mssrs Greene and Greene, architects, announce that

on and after February 1, 1903, their office will be in the Grant Bldg NW Corner Fourth and Broadway, Los Angeles, Rooms 722 and 723. The Pasadena office will be discontinued. Mr. Charles Sumner Greene will be found at his studio on Arroyo View Drive, Pasadena, Monday, Wednesday, and Friday afternoons."
49. Hales, *Memoirs*, I, p. 14.
50. After Henry Dart Greene, 1900, Emeline and Henry had William Sumner Greene, 1906; Isabelle Horton Greene, 1907; and Elbert Mather Greene, 1910, as listed in the family copy of *Kate Greenaway's Birthday Book*, in possession of Virginia Dart Greene Hales. Charles and Alice had Nathaniel Patrickson Greene, 1902; Bettie Storey Greene, 1903; Alice Sumner Greene, 1905; Thomas Gordon Greene, 1907; and Ariana Cressy Giles Greene, 1910, as noted in the "Charles Sumner Greene Family List," compiled by Thomas Gordon Greene, April 13, 1990, GGA.
51. About the different nature of the brothers, see also Bosley, *Greene & Greene*, p. 4; and Makinson, *Passion*, pp. 12–13.
52. Henry Dart Greene, in Hales, *Memoirs*, I, p. 18.
53. Written by the editor of the *Architectural Record*, Herbert Croly, under the pseudonym Arthur David, "An Architect of Bungalows in California," *Architectural Record*, 20 (October 1906), pp. 305–15. Croly was probably led to the Greenes' work through his connections with Elmer Grey and Myron Hunt, both of whom had written for the journal. The issue in which the article on the Greenes appeared had as its lead article a piece on the work of Hunt and Grey, written by Croly under his own name. Grey would serve with Charles Greene the following year on a judging committee for the exhibits for the Los Angeles Architectural Club and the Arts and Crafts Society of Los Angeles. See *Pasadena Daily News*, April 13, 1907; and Meriwether, "Bibliography." Hunt and Charles Greene were neighbors; their children played together around the reservoir. Hunt's son remembered that his father "admired [Greene's] work tremendously. ... I always thought of Greene as Dad did, that he was a great artist." Jan Muntz, *Pasadena Oral History Project Interview with Hubbard Hunt* (Pasadena, Calif.: Pasadena Historical Society, Friends of the Public Library, 1984), p. 8.

54. "Domestic Architecture in the West: California's Contribution to a National Architecture: Its Significance in the Work of Greene and Greene, Architects," *The Craftsman*, 22, no. 5 (August 1912), pp. 532–47.
55. "Cast heavy shadows"; "shingled or clapboarded walls," Croly, "An Architect of Bungalows," pp. 310, 311. "Utter absence of ..."; "frank use of ..."; "the quality of ...," "Domestic Architecture," pp. 545, 533, 547.
56. CSG to Charles M. Pratt, Ojai, n.d. [probably 1912 or 1913], GGA.
57. Copies of Charles's typescript, "Thais Thayer," are at the GGA and EDA; the typescript is undated, but his son Patrickson remembered his father writing the book about 1914 while still in Pasadena. Nathaniel Patrickson Greene, interview with Robert Judson Clark, April 1959, in Bosley, *Greene & Greene*, p. 223 n. 59. It is also worth noting that the description of the house designed by the protagonist strongly resembles the house designed by the Greenes in 1911 for Cordelia Culbertson and her sisters.
58. CSG, "Impressions of Some Bungalows and Gardens," *The Architect*, 10 (December 1915), p. 278.
59. CSG Misc. Papers, EDA. The question mark at the end of the phrase was added by the authors.
60. Charles scribbled in his notes, "I have a studio where I work, but it is hardly a studio. We have all kinds of story telling, songs and recitals, lectures from faraway places, from Russia, from England and other lands—some from Salinas lettuce fields." CSG Misc. Papers, EDA.
61. Letter from HMG to CSG, October 12, 1928, EDA.
62. In 1927, Greene and Greene were included in a listing of architects of the period that included Reginald Johnson, Myron Hunt, Louis Mullgardt, Francis Underhill, and George Washington Smith. They were described as "the Greenes who invented the California bungalow." Thomas E. Tallmadge, *The Story of Architecture in America* (New York: Norton, 1927), p. 270. A history of 1930 ignores them in the text, relegating them to a footnote on the California style and "the distinctive bungalow type associated with the names Greene and Greene." Sheldon Cheney, *The New World Architecture* (New York and London: Longmans, Green & Co., 1930), p. 288. The

Greenes' work was thereafter nearly ignored until the late 1940s.
63. Hales, *Memoirs*, I, p. 197.
64. Lisa Germany, *Harwell Hamilton Harris* (Austin: University of Texas Press, 1991), p. 94.
65. *Ibid.*, p. 109.
66. Carey McWilliams, *Southern California Country: An Island on the Land* (New York: Duell, Sloan & Pearce, 1946), pp. 357–58.
67. One wishes that the work of the Greenes had been rediscovered simply based on its own merits, but the reasons for their work being brought back into the limelight were far more complex; see the essay in this volume by Edward R. Bosley, pp. 231–57. Their reemergence had to do with the social, cultural, and political battles being waged during the Cold War years of the 1940s and 1950s; the Greenes were promoted as part of an alternative lineage, an American democratic alternative to the European influence of the imported International Style. As Elizabeth Gordon writes, "Two ways of life stretch before us. One leads to the richness of variety, to comfort and beauty. The other, the one we want fully to expose to you, retreats to poverty and unlivability. Worst of all, it contains a threat of cultural dictatorship." Elizabeth Gordon, "The Threat to the Next America," *House Beautiful*, April 1953, p. 127. Gordon places on the side of poverty, unlivability, and cultural dictatorship the likes of Walter Gropius; on the other side, she finds the roots of good modern design in the work of Frank Lloyd Wright, Bernard Maybeck, and Greene and Greene.
68. The certificate that was presented to Henry is reproduced in Hales, *Memoirs*, II, p. 148.
69. Henry Greene's death was noted by his son Henry Dart Greene in the family copy of *Kate Greenaway's Birthday Book*, p. 13, along with his place and time of burial; Charles Greene's death is noted in the "Charles Sumner Greene Family List."

BRUCE SMITH

Sunlight and Elsewhere: Finding California in the Work of Greene and Greene

Over the nearly three decades of their practice, more than 96 percent of the houses designed by Charles and Henry Greene were built in Southern California.[1] That the Greenes grew to love California, as was shown in both their writings and their work, was as evident as the truth that California, for a while, grew to love the Greenes. And then for several decades, from the mid-1920s into the late 1940s, they were forgotten. But by that time, many of their ideas—central courtyards, porches and pergolas, verandas and piazzas rejoicing in the fresh air and the pleasures of life out-of-doors; an aesthetic that celebrated the exoticness of the western edge of the nation; and broad, gently sloping rooflines offering protection from the sun—had become part of the common vocabulary of the architecture of the Southland. In their efforts to represent California in their work, to design, as Charles wrote, as "a man dependent upon his own power of expression rather than that of rigid custom,"[2] they had created not only an architecture that imagined what California meant to those who had come there, but also an aesthetic that had become one of the layers of meaning by which California understood itself.

This essay examines a number of examples of the early work of the Greenes in an attempt to trace the development of their aesthetic. Most of these designs were built; two were only drawings indicative of the dreams of the brothers. The first of these designs is from the beginning of their careers, about 1895; the last dates to 1904, several years before their masterworks came into being. These are not the *tours de force* that the Greenes produced from 1907 to 1911, for which interiors, furniture, carpets, lighting, and gardens were designed for clients who were not only able to afford meticulous craftsmanship, but were also sufficiently cosmopolitan to appreciate the brothers' artistry. Yet, these early works were extraordinary in their own right, involving leaps of inspiration and imagination. They held within their designs visions of what California might mean, seen through artistic eyes, and they set the course toward the distinctive and individualistic aesthetic of the Greenes.

The most exotic, the most "foreign" land that Charles and Henry Greene would ever travel to in their lifetimes was that of Southern California. Departing the third week of August 1893 from Boston's Fitchburg Depot, the Greene brothers journeyed the width of America, traveling through Chicago and across the Great Plains, passing the "buffalo capital" of Dodge City, where the last great cattle drive had taken place just seven years before.[3] Coming over the Rockies, they descended into what was truly the far West, frontier territory where horse-driven stagecoaches still raced the steam engine, just a half-dozen years after the last battles between the U.S. Cavalry and Geronimo. Through the windows of their Pullman Sleeper, they could see scattered Mexican villages and ancient Indian pueblos still inhabited, as well as the vestiges of the old Santa Fe Trail, described by the railroad guidebook of 1893 as having been, not many years before, "almost continuously sodden with human blood and marked by hundreds of rude graves dug for the mutilated victims of murderous Apaches and other tribes."[4] Charles and Henry had left behind the gentility of brick buildings, cobbled streets, and five years of architectural study and apprenticeship in Boston—the "Athens of America"—to make a long journey, measured in more than just miles.

Arriving in Pasadena, stepping down on to the station platform, the brothers were faced with a dirt street and the immensity of the new Hotel Green, a grand tourist hotel built five stories high in the Moorish style, something that did not seem out of place with the swaying palm trees and bright sunshine of the California Southland. They had arrived in a city incorporated less than a decade before, populated with 10,000 people, up from the 390 residents of the 1880 census. It had all been created over the past two decades. It was all new. It was all invented.

The Greenes had arrived in an "elsewhere," an area as much held in the imagination as it was geographical.[5] It was a landscape just decades before ruled by Spain, then Mexico. The 8000-year-old culture of the California Indians had essentially disappeared, replaced by the idealized, imagined world of the Indians in Helen Hunt Jackson's *Ramona* (1884). There were remnants of rancheros and haciendas, old adobes and the ruins of the missions. And the brothers were near a coastline very conscious of "Facing West from California's Shores,"[6] soon to abound with Japanese and Chinese curio stores, its landscape dotted with Japanesque gardens and teahouses.

Yet there was a familiarity to it all. The Greenes entered an enclave of Midwestern civility, of respectable American homes appropriate to the middle-American cities where they had passed their childhoods. It was a region defined by metaphors, often of European origin, recognizable to any urbane visitor. An advertisement for the recently completed Mt. Lowe funicular railway that ran from Pasadena to the mountain peak above it trumpeted it as connecting "Switzerland and Italy … From Roses and Orange Groves to Snow in Two Hours Time."[7] A travel narrative published the same year the Greenes arrived described Pasadena as having "Spanish Breezes, Italian Sky and sunsets, Alpine mountains, tropical luxuriance of vegetation,"[8] all part of the push to market Pasadena and its environs as a winter resort, a domestic alternative to Europe for the wealthy tourist. Those who journeyed across the continent required reassurances that they were venturing to a civilized, cultured locale, like Switzerland or Italy. The Spanish heritage, the picturesque ruins of the missions, provided sightseers with visions of a past civilization. The fact that the oldest one had been constructed only a century and a quarter before and the most recent just seventy years before was politely ignored, as was the reality that the missions, far from being remnants of a thriving past culture, were the most distant, rusticated outposts of a defunct colonial empire. They were a valued tourist destination, a substitute for Roman ruins and medieval abbeys, a part of the creation of the romantic "elsewhere."

Charles and Henry Greene were relatively young men when they came to Southern California in the late summer of 1893; on opening their architectural office in Pasadena just over four months after their arrival, Charles was twenty-five, Henry just a few weeks shy of twenty-four.[9] They were the principals in their new practice, and probably initially the only employees; their early years of architectural work were thus no doubt ones of learning. Despite their years of education and apprenticeship,

neither of the two young men would have had any experience in the actual running of an office or much, if any, experience in dealing directly with clients.[10]

The Greenes spent the first eight years of their partnership—from 1894 through 1901—gaining this experience. Their clients were local residents without grand budgets: the owner of the local meat market, who was also a neighbor of their parents; the president of a Pasadena bank; and his son, the bookkeeper. Two houses were designed for a local investment company, and several for doctors, surely introduced to Charles and Henry by their father, a physician with his own office in Pasadena. Their largest commission was for an office building on a prominent downtown corner into which, at the end of 1896, they moved their offices.

What is striking about these first houses designed by the brothers is how inappropriate they were to the California Southland: rectangular boxes with steep pitched roofs, colonnaded porches, and applied plaster ornament. They are houses that might have been perfectly suitable for the eastern seaboard or for the Midwestern towns of their youth. Novice architects, even if they have the inspiration and desire, often do not have control of the design. Clients have dreams, expectations, dictates, and especially budgets. Not until midway through their fourth year of practice did the Greenes have a client who would spend more than $4000 on a home, and it was another year before they had a commission over $10,000.

One early project is indicative of the direction in which the Greenes' dreams and aspirations were heading. In the archives of their work, there is a set of plans labeled simply as "Job No. 11" (figs. 2–4). No client's name is attached; it was probably a house they designed on speculation.[11] Its early number indicates a date of late 1895 or early 1896, just as the brothers were entering their third year of practice. Unlike their other work of the time, this design is expansive: a string of rooms around an enclosed central courtyard, with the heart of the house not a fireplace, but a fountain in the middle of the inner court. All the main rooms both open into the courtyard and face out-of-doors.

"Job No. 11" is recognizably Californian. Incorporated into the curved staircase that rises from the courtyard is a scalloped parapet wall that could have been taken from an *espadaña*, the curved parapet that defines the front of many California missions. It also has the first roof by the Greenes designed for sunshine, not snow; its gradual slope allows the eaves to stretch outward from the walls, providing shelter from the bright California sun. The eaves do not extend as far as they do in later designs, yet

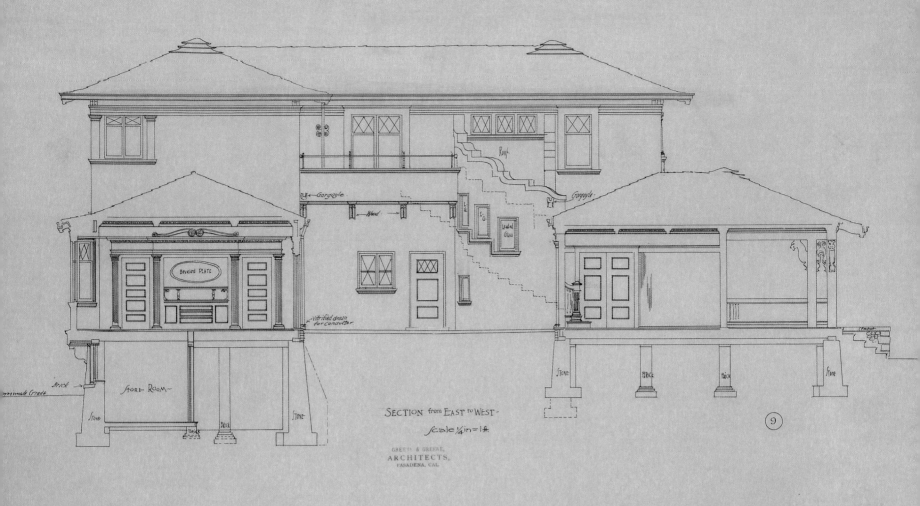

SECTION from EAST to WEST

Scale ¼ in = 1 ft.

GREENE & GREENE,
ARCHITECTS,
PASADENA, CAL.

⑨

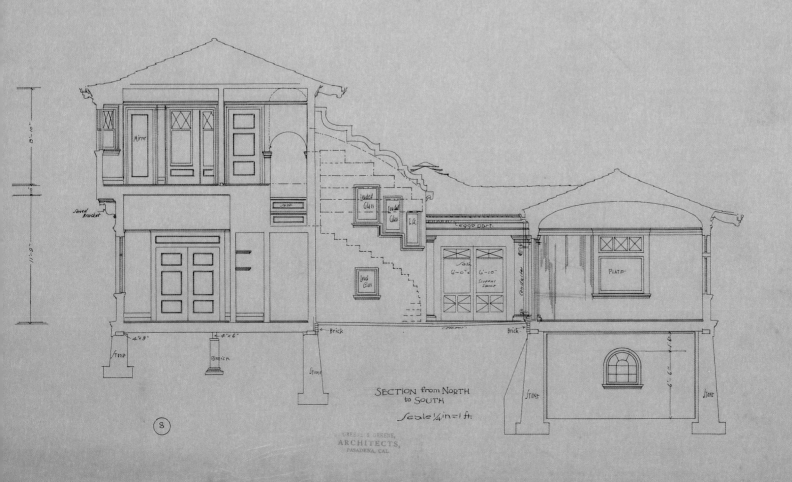

SECTION from NORTH
to SOUTH

Scale ¼ in = 1 ft.

⑧

GREENE & GREENE,
ARCHITECTS,
PASADENA, CAL.

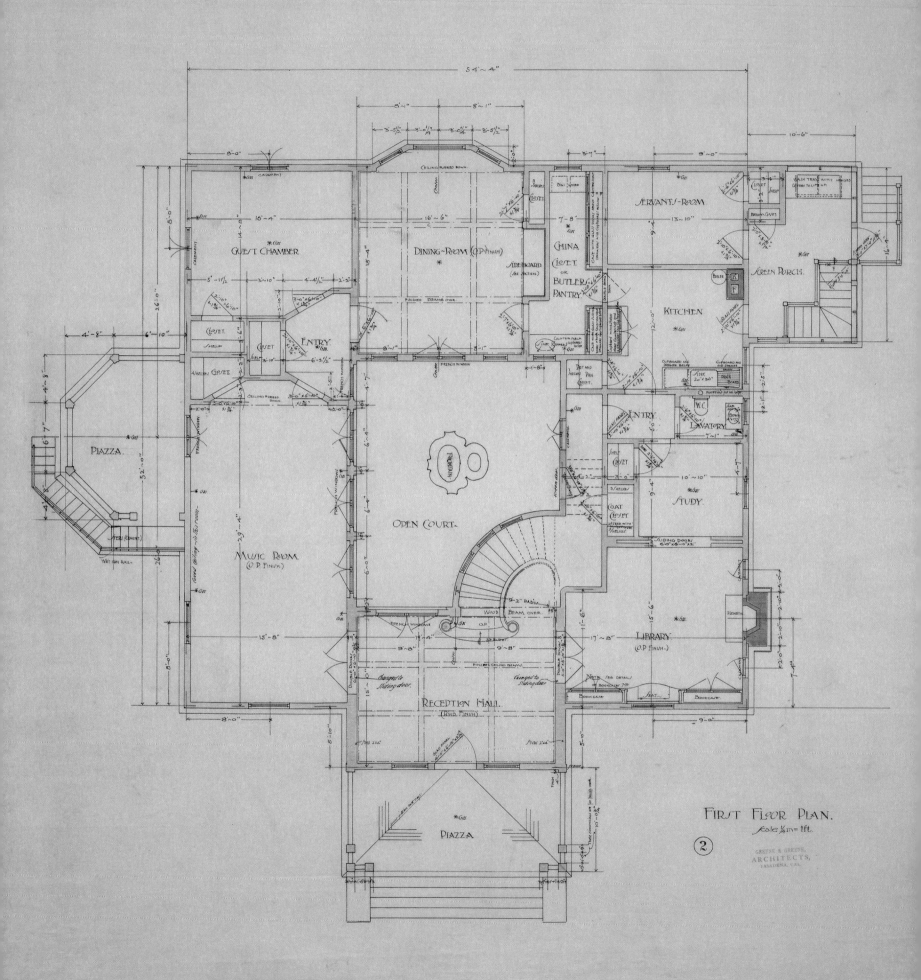

FIRST FLOOR PLAN.
Scale ¼ in = 1 ft.

②

GREENE & GREENE,
ARCHITECTS,
PASADENA, CAL.

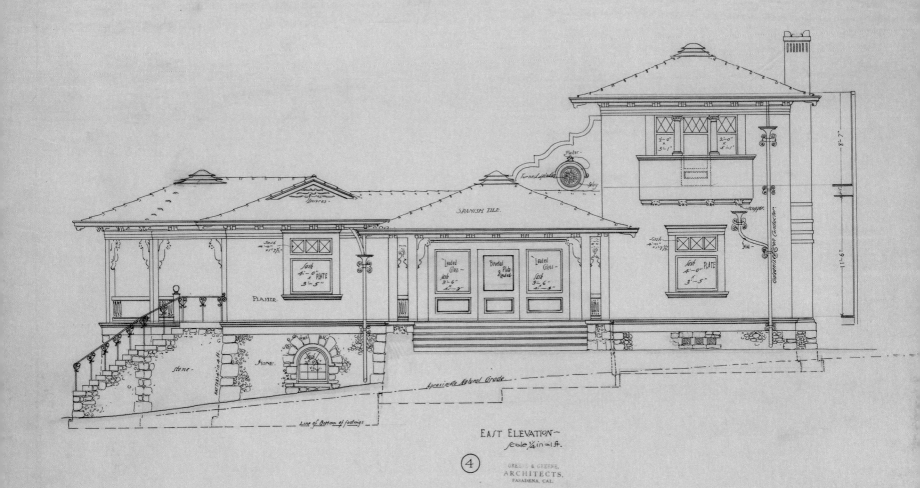

EAST ELEVATION
Scale ¼ in = 1 ft.

④

GREENE & GREENE,
ARCHITECTS,
PASADENA, CAL.

SOUTH ELEVATION
Scale ¼ in = 1 ft.

GREENE & GREENE,
ARCHITECTS,
PASADENA, CAL.

⑤

here, for the first time, there is a sense of California in the work of the two brothers.

The Greenes were discouraged by their first eight years of practice; their work had up to that point been confined entirely to the Pasadena area. They had made the journey west to be near their parents, but in 1901, their parents decided to move to Kansas City, and sold the houses where the brothers were living.[12] Henry took this opportunity to open a "branch office" in Los Angeles, moving his family out of Pasadena to the fashionable Los Angeles district of West Adams. Charles had just returned from his European honeymoon. He chose to remain in Pasadena, and for the next five years the two brothers labored apart. Charles at first worked by himself out of the Pasadena "main office," but by early 1903, he had closed the Pasadena office and begun to work from a studio in his newly completed home on the edge of the Arroyo Seco. It was there that he met with clients, sketched out his ideas, did preliminary drawings, and designed the firm's first lighting fixtures and furniture.[13]

From 1902 until the start of 1907, the brothers expanded their business beyond Pasadena, building houses in Hollywood, Los Angeles, and Long Beach, and even one in Vancouver, British Columbia; still, four-fifths of their commissions were for residents of Pasadena.

The Greenes were finally attracting a different clientele: members of the traveling leisure class who came to Pasadena for their health or the winter sunshine, and sometimes stayed, if only for the winter. They came for the orange groves and rose blossoms; for the spectacle of chariots racing on New Year's Day after a parade of flower-covered floats; for the picturesque romance of life on the western edge of the continent with cowboys and rancheros; for the stores selling Oriental imports and Indian basketry; for carriage rides to visit the local mission or to see the fields of poppies in bloom; for the pageants, fashion shows, and polo matches; and for horseback rides up into the wilderness of what was called the Devil's Gate at the head of the arroyo. But most of all, they came for the California sunshine.

Importantly, it was during this period that the elements that came to define the architecture of the Greenes—the shingled walls with expressed timbered joinery, massive pilings of stones, clinker bricks interwoven with cobblestones, low-pitched roofs with broad overhangs and extended rafters, verandas and pergolas, open courtyards, and a spread-out plan often clinging to the earth—were all explored, mostly in Pasadena, often in the houses designed and built around Charles Greene's own home overlooking the arroyo.[14]

Early attempts to define the burgeoning aesthetics of the Greenes coupled this body of work with the existing identification of Pasadena with Switzerland.[15] At the beginning of 1907, a lengthy article in the *Pasadena News* about the gathering of houses around Charles Greene's home referred to the neighborhood as "Little Switzerland." The writer freely admitted that none of the houses there was "purely Swiss"; but she cited the "long, plain roof lines, the wide gables and heavy timberwork" that were "suggestive of the motif," and she stated, "all their wealth of picturesque stonework and terracing is decidedly Swiss." She did concede "there is also in many of them the feeling of the Japanese …"

The centerpiece of this assemblage of homes, "the largest and most elaborate of these dwellings," was the house recently remodeled by the Greenes for its new owner, Theodore Irwin (fig. 6). The author of the article wrote how "an extension of the rafters about the top accentuates the Swiss effect." Next door to the Irwin house was, she wrote, "one of the architects of Little Switzerland," living "in the midst of the beauty his pencil has called into being." His home, according to the writer, was "a charming little Swiss Chalet."[16]

Years later, Charles Greene wrote, "People of Pasadena called my first group of successful houses little Switzerland. From my own understanding there was nothing Swiss about it—it all started from my interest in Japanese early temple design."[17] This was perhaps a bit disingenuous of him; one even wonders at his complicity in the Swiss attribution. Even though there was nothing identifiably Swiss about his own home (fig. 5), there were distinct Swiss stylistic elements in the house next door that he designed in 1903 for the three maiden sisters of his wife, Martha, Violet, and Jane White (fig. 7).[18] The upper story was sided with split redwood shakes overhanging the first-story basement of cobblestone walls. It had a broad, low-pitched, sloping roof—in Switzerland designed with an overhang and strong supports to allow snow to gather and act as a blanket for the winter—here serving to protect the occupants from the strong California sunshine.[19]

The house for the White sisters was only the first of the Greenes' chalet-like homes. It was followed almost immediately by the broad-gabled design for Mary Reeve Darling in Claremont. Again sided with split shakes, the house has an open loggia over the front door in place of the traditional Swiss balcony.[20] A year and a half later, when Charles wrote an article called "California Home Making" for a local newspaper, he chose to illustrate it with a drawing of this Swiss chalet–styled design for Darling (fig. 8). Its caption read: "A California House."[21]

FIGURE 6
*View looking
northeast, Theodore
Irwin, Jr., house*
Photograph © Alexander
Vertikoff

FIGURE 7
*View looking
southwest, Martha,
Violet, and Jane
White house,
Pasadena, 1903*

Courtesy of Charles Sumner
Greene Collection (1959-1),
Environmental Design
Archives, University of
California, Berkeley

FIGURE 8
*Mary Reeve Darling
house, Claremont,
1903. Illustration of
ink-and-wash
drawing by Charles
Greene as it appeared
in* Academy
Architecture *(1903)*
Courtesy of Bruce Smith

Charles's musings on "California Home Making," published January 2, 1905, in the special New Year's Day Tournament of Roses edition of the newspaper, came at a propitious time.[22] The Greenes had since had the opportunity to design a house costing more than $20,000; they had gained other commissions allowing them greater artistic freedom; and they had found clients for whom they could design furniture and lighting. When Charles wrote his article, there was no mention of Switzerland or the Swiss chalet; however, he did discourse on the Spanish missions. Through the years, he grew to love the missions of California, supporting their restoration, painting pictures of them, and eventually visiting them as he traveled up the coast, camping with his family. In this article of 1905, he described their architecture as "the old art of California." "Study it," he preached, "and you will find a deeper meaning than books tell of sun-dried bricks and plaster show." The missions were built by "those old monks [who] came from a climate not unlike this"; they were constructed "after their own fashion, and their knowledge of climate and habits of life were bred in the bone ... simple as it is, and rude, it has something that money cannot buy or skill

conciliate. It runs in every line, turns in every arch and hangs like an incense in dim cathedral light."

What Charles had no patience for were "the styles and what a host of them there are." "[H]ow glibly we all chatter about them," he wrote. He singled out an imaginary "Mrs. Knowit," who had just completed a house, "Old Colonial": "Of course there is the portico with its white classic columns and pediment, its paneled door and fan light and all the rest."[23] What is interesting is that the largest commission the two brothers had received to date, their first one over $20,000, and one that they had chosen to represent their work at the Louisiana Purchase Exposition of 1904 in St. Louis, was for just such a Colonial-styled house. Complete with white columns and fanlights, the George H. Barker house was designed by the firm only two years before Charles wrote this article.[24]

Charles's compelling point is that "the styles" were not about California:

When one follows a style, says Mrs. Knowit, one always has something one may give an excuse for. ... We admit that many things do need [an] excuse, but surely the thing that serves a

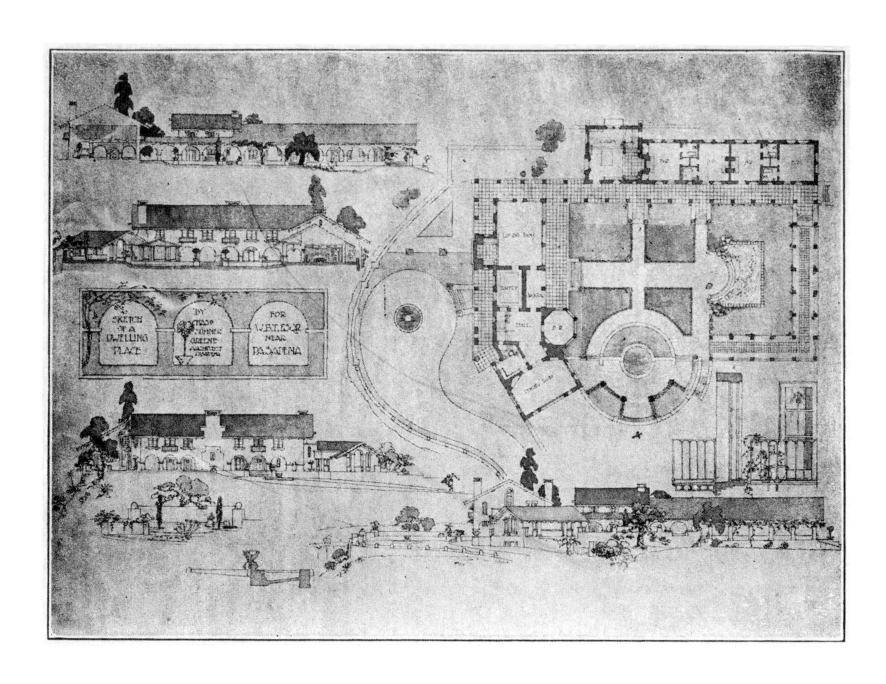

SKETCH OF A DWELLING PLACE BY CHARLES SUMNER GREENE ARCHITECT PASADENA FOR W.B.T.... NEAR PASADENA

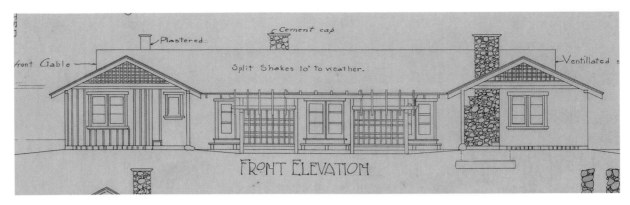

FRONT ELEVATION

FIGURE 9
*Charles Greene,
"Sketch of a
Dwelling Place …
for W.B.T. Esqr. Near
Pasadena," 1903*
Courtesy of Greene
and Greene Archives,
The Gamble House,
University of Southern
California

FIGURE 10
*Detail of front
elevation, Arturo
Bandini house,
Pasadena, 1903*
Courtesy of Avery
Architectural and
Fine Arts Library,
Columbia University

purpose and that one finds continued pleasure in using must carry its own motive. Then let us try and suit ourselves. This is the principle of California's best thought and there are many people who have found solace in the theory that one may do anything one likes if one only knows how.[25]

Charles was the one who wanted to do anything he liked, if only he could convince the client to allow him sufficient freedom. It is enlightening from this perspective to look at which work the brothers chose to represent them at the St. Louis exposition.[26] Submitted from the Los Angeles office of Greene and Greene were photographs of two houses: one of them the aforementioned Neo-classical house with white columns and fanlights, the other in the English Tudor style.[27] The Neo-classical was the Greenes' largest commission to date; the English Tudor their first opportunity to design a winter house for one of the wealthy Midwesterners coming to California for the sunshine, James Culbertson of Illinois.

Significantly, Charles also separately submitted a large presentation drawing, a "Sketch of a Dwelling Place … for W.B.T." (fig. 9).[28] In the official catalogue, it was listed just beneath the entries from the office of Greene and Greene, designated as being by Charles Sumner Greene, Pasadena.[29] In stark contrast to the office submissions, Charles's entry was for a very Californian, fully landscaped, rambling estate, spread out like an old hacienda. There were two separate buildings, both living spaces, set at right angles to each other and connected by arched colonnades. As with Job No. 11, all the major rooms opened on both sides to the outside. There was a formal garden within the space created between the buildings, further defined by the covered colonnaded walkways, seeming to draw inspiration from the California mission courtyards. Unlike the other entries, it was a house and garden designed for a specific location, and a specific climate, that of Southern California.[30]

Charles's very Californian project was never built; there were no plans, elevations, or specifications, only the one presentation piece. But it was evidently submitted to the exposition just as Charles was designing what was to be the firm's first authentic Californian house, a commission from a true Southern Californian, Arturo Bandini.[31] Quite a romantic figure, Bandini was described as being "slender, very good looking," and having a dashing presence.[32] With a cigarette hanging from his lips, he could as easily ride horses as discourse eloquently on grizzly bears and Indians. He called himself not of Mexican background but "Castellano"; his ancestors were from Andalusia, his grandfather and father playing a part in California's history from the time of Spanish rule up to statehood. He was born in San Diego in the simple, single-story, U-shaped courtyard adobe built by his father, Juan, at the beginning of the Mexican era.[33] And it was such a house—a patio house with a series of connecting rooms around a courtyard—that Bandini requested in 1903 from the Greenes. He called it a "California house" (figs. 10 and 11).[34]

It was a style of house that evoked a way of life where "the orange grove [was] always green, never without snowy bloom or golden fruit; the garden never without flowers, summer or winter," as Helen Hunt Jackson described the vista from the home of her heroine in her novel of 1884, *Ramona: A Story*.[35] Ramona's house was built—as was Arturo Bandini's birth home—"of adobe, low, with a wide veranda on the three sides of the inner court, and a still broader one across the entire front." These verandas were "supplementary rooms to the house. The greater part of the family life went on in them. Nobody stayed inside the walls, except when it was necessary."[36] Jackson's story of Ramona, the beautiful half-Indian girl raised on one of the old rancheros in California who falls in love with and marries the doomed Indian Allesandro, became an important element of

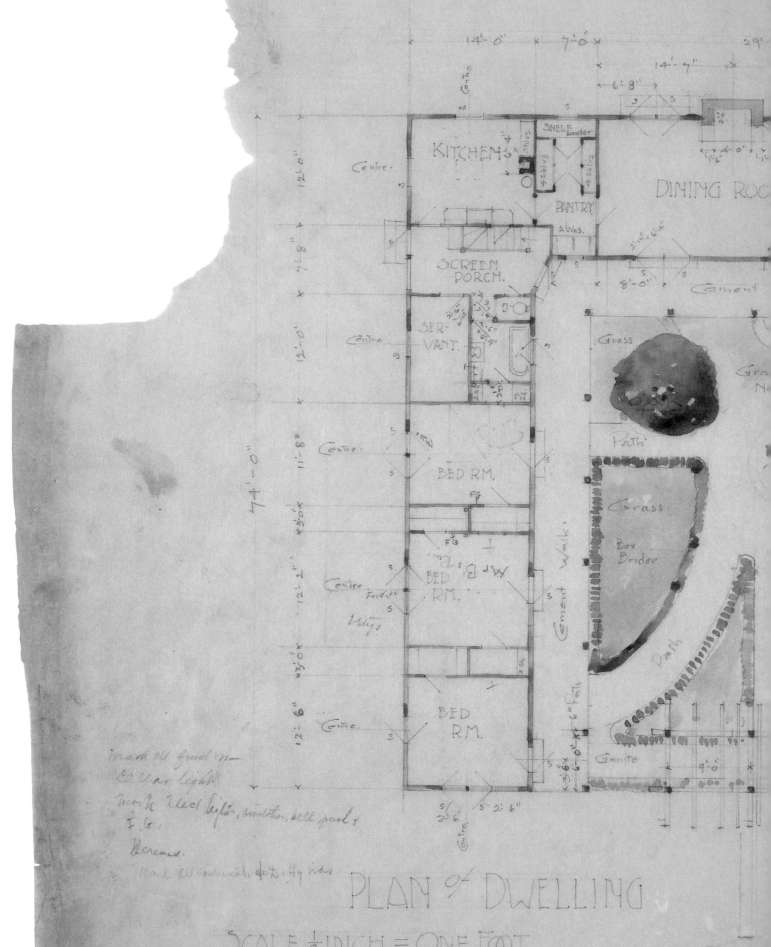

14'-0"   x   7'-0"   x   29'
14'-4"
6'-8"

Centre

KITCHEN

SHELF   Under

DINING ROO

PANTRY

SCREEN
PORCH.

Centre

SER-
VANT.

Centre

Grass

Path

BED RM.

Grass

Grass

Box
Border

Centre

BED
RM.

Cement Walk

Path

Utils.

BED
RM.

Centre

Granite

9'-0"

Mark all front m—
Cellar light.
Mark Elect light, insulation, bell push &
F.G.
Mercans.
Mark all casements hot & cold water sides.

PLAN of DWELLING

SCALE ⅛ INCH = ONE FOOT.

PASADENA

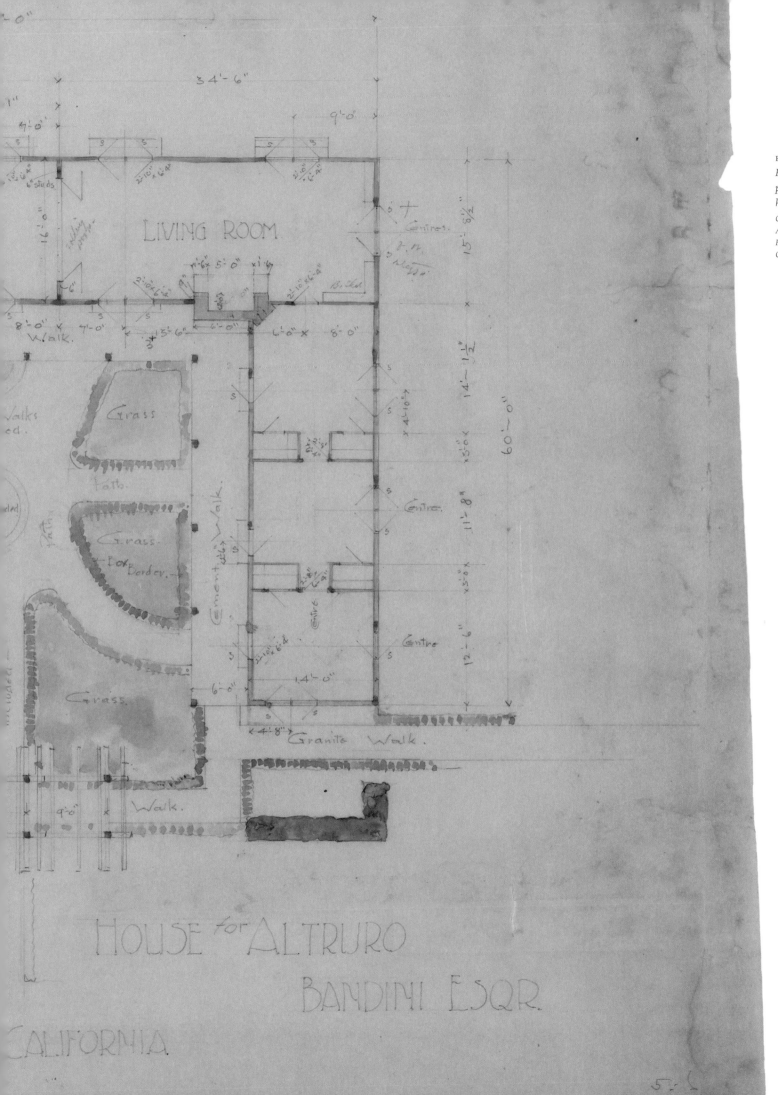

FIGURE 11
Pencil-and-watercolor plan, Arturo Bandini house

Courtesy of Avery
Architectural and
Fine Arts Library,
Columbia University

LIVING ROOM

Grass

Grass

Border.

Grass.

Walk.

HOUSE FOR ALTRURO

BANDINI ESQR.

CALIFORNIA

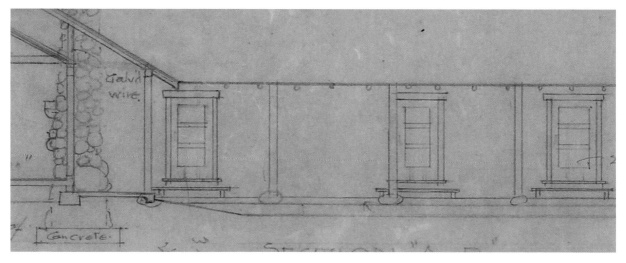

California's invented folklore, a vital part of the defining of the romantic "elsewhere." Ramona landmarks were fashioned all over the Southland. Casa de Estudillo in San Diego, a U-shaped adobe house around a courtyard built by Juan Bandini's father-in-law, became known as Ramona's marriage place.[37] There was the "Home of Ramona" at Rancho Camulos in Ventura County, and the "birth place of Ramona" at the San Gabriel Mission just south of Pasadena. These were tourist sites to be visited, as Charles and Henry's parents did, writing to their sons in 1893 about driving "over to the old mission the other day, where 'Ramona' [was] born."[38] Later that same month, their mother wrote to "My Dearest Boys," requesting that they purchase and send her a copy of *Ramona* so that she could read it for herself.[39]

Ramona's home had become a familiar, recognizably Californian image, portrayed on postcards and orange-crate labels, and described in travel narratives. When the Greenes designed Arturo Bandini's "California house," it was as a variation of this style, built not of adobe, but of unpainted, upright board-and-batten siding with a massive cobblestone fireplace in the living room.[40] Charles Greene explained it was "a house on the old Mission plan, that is to have a court about 60 ft. square." But he clarified, "It is all of wood and very simple—not in the so called mission style at all."[41] It was, in other words, Californian without the pastiche of one of "the styles," the Mission Revival style in this case.[42]

The Greenes did design in the Mission Revival style, as they did in the Colonial or English Tudor styles when clients requested it. In 1897, they had produced a Mission Revival design that was not built. A few months later, they attempted to have an *espadaña*-style dormer placed on a house commissioned by the brother-in-law of one of their aunts; the element was rejected. The one Mission Revival project that was constructed—an apartment building of 1903 that has since been demolished—employed a complete Mission Revival idiom, with *espadaña*-shaped parapets on the front and red-tiled roofs over the doorways.[43]

It was obvious that the requests of clients needed to be satisfied, but Charles had a vision of the design process that meant not turning to "the styles," but rather drawing upon "anything one likes if one only knows how." He wrote in his article of 1905 about the "possibility [that] lies in the plasticity of such a mind," stating, "No wonder we have experiments sometimes startling, but often they lead to new and better thoughts. That is the reason why [Californian] houses are interesting." It was not meant to be a smooth road to follow; mistakes were made, wrong

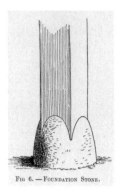

FIG 6. — FOUNDATION STONE.

directions taken. And the poor clients would have to "pay for them and have to live with them while the aesthetic architect paints his picture for the next." Design for Charles was a step-by-step process of developing an aesthetic, justified in his mind since "the public is in the end the benefactor. So we need not fear experiments."[44]

With the growing confidence of the Greenes during these years of 1902 to 1906, there was more freedom to experiment, to incorporate diverse elements into their evolving vocabulary as their way of defining their own aesthetic. In the Bandini house, Charles added a design element at the last moment that was not Californian at all, but one that was so suited to the "California house" that it was possible the client was not even aware of its addition. Just twelve days after the Bandini contract was signed, Charles obtained a copy of what was at the time the preeminent book on Japanese domestic architecture, Edward S. Morse's *Japanese Homes and Their Surroundings* (1886).[45] He must have pored over it intently, for, before construction progressed very far along, he penciled in on the tracing paper a change for the footing stones for the porch roof posts (fig. 13). The alteration is distinctive; it was a Japanese style illustrated in the Morse book (fig. 14).[46] In the context of the Bandini house, though, the footing stones do not look Japanese at all, merely rustic, weathered, and appropriate to the carefree Arcadian lifestyle intended for the courtyard.

It was not the first time that the Greenes had borrowed from Japan. The year before, they had incorporated a "Japanese temple" bracketed-beam-and-column motif in the design for the living-room walls of the English Tudor–style house for James Culbertson. A *Good Housekeeping* article of 1906 on the Culbertson house, after mentioning a number of Japanese elements, declared that "Japanese influence … is fast creeping into the architecture of California" and that the design incorporated "ideas which are the newest and most artistic to be found."[47]

Japanese elements in a house design did proclaim the home as artistic, as did the careful placement of a *kakemono* (scroll painting) on a wall or the display of "several Japanese pieces of old Imari blue" on a "shelf over the fireplace," as in the home of Charles Greene's sisters-in-law.[48] Such objects signified that the household was cultured, cosmopolitan, and had a refined taste. And odd as it might seem, as the *Good Housekeeping* article noted, this love of things Japanese was becoming very Californian.

The idea of Japan, and things Japanese, had become yet another layer in the inventing of California, a part of the romantic "elsewhere." Southern Californians were

FIGURE 15
*Adelaide A. Tichenor
house, Long Beach,
1904–05. Watercolor
by Charles Greene,
c. 1905*
Courtesy of Greene
and Greene Archives,
The Gamble House,
University of Southern
California

aware they faced toward Asia, not Europe. On Venice Pier, looking out over the Pacific, there was an exhibition of Japanese objects, "rare Oriental goods and curiosities," previously displayed at the St. Louis and Portland expositions.[49] "You have come to the front door of America," proclaimed one Pasadena writer on New Year's Day 1903. "Look out upon the Orient."[50] From 1903, on a prominent downtown corner in Pasadena, there was a Japanese teahouse and garden—one of a series built in the state—where one could sip tea after strolling through the garden, or purchase Japanese *objets d'art*.[51] Even the local ostrich farm in South Pasadena had a Japanese tea garden to visit after having an ostrich ride. And starting in 1903, an annual dinner celebrating the cherry blossom was hosted in Pasadena by the Japanese artist Toshio Aoki, who taught painting to the children of the wealthy.[52] By 1906, there were eight stores in Pasadena selling "Japanese Art Goods," many of them congregated around the grand tourist hotels, near their market of wealthy easterners who traveled west, looking for something different, something exotic and artistic, something Californian.

Only rarely can the source for a given design element be fairly conclusively pinpointed, as with the Bandini house and the Morse book. More often, we look back and locate the first use of a motif—one of Charles's "experiments"—and then see it adapted and played with in subsequent works. We are able only to speculate on its source, possibly missing the truth that sources, as with ideas, often do not arise from a single fount, but rather build one upon the other, gathering momentum over time.

The Greenes had a number of Japanese reference points around them in Pasadena, but these would have built upon a long exposure to things Japanese. During their five years in Boston, the brothers were in the city that was at the center of the "Japan Craze."[53] Then—according to Henry's late-in-life recollections—the brothers visited both the World's Columbian Exposition in Chicago in 1893 and the Midwinter Exposition the following year in San Francisco, where they "admired the Japanese buildings at both fairs for the way they tied in with the landscape."[54] It is worth noting that the Greenes' letters and diary entries from this period make no mention of anything Japanese. They had other concerns: their schooling, their work, their music studies. And when they began their architectural practice in 1894 in Pasadena, they showed no interest in Japanese design elements for nearly a decade.

The "Japanese temple" motif of the bracketed beam and column in the Culbertson house in 1902 was the Greenes' first allusion to Japan. Charles's self-confessed

interest in "Japanese early temple design"—written in reaction to the Swiss appellation placed on their work—may have built upon what he had seen at the expositions or been spurred by the construction of the Japanese teahouse in Pasadena. According to his own later account, in about 1903, an itinerant bookseller showed him a set of books on travel: "Idly he leafed through the pages until his attention was arrested by pictures of Japanese homes and gardens. This was what he had been seeking. Here was that expression of post and beam construction, of articulated structure. Here, too, were the house and garden as one, an informal yet carefully conceived whole."[55]

In July 1904, at the behest of a client, Adelaide Tichenor, Charles visited the St. Louis exposition.[56] While exploring the fairgrounds, he would have been able to walk through and around a number of examples of Japanese architecture, set in the invented "elsewhere" of the fair. There was a full-scale copy of the large gate at Nikko as the entrance to "Fair Japan," an area devoted to teahouses, a Japanese theater, restaurants, bazaars, a typical "street of Tokio," and "forty pretty Geisha girls." In the Japanese Imperial Gardens, there were replicas of the Kinkaku-ji, the Golden Pavilion; and the Shishinden, the reception hall of the Imperial Palace in Kyoto. And in the Fine Arts Building, where Charles's own work was exhibited, elevations and plans by Japanese architects showed a gateway in the "temple style" and an ornate residence in Tokyo with an *irimoya* (hipped-gable) roof, the same style of roof used on the Shishinden.[57]

A few months after his return home, Charles clipped pictures of the Japanese exhibits from a magazine and pasted them in his scrapbook. More significantly, he took what he had seen at the fair and incorporated it into the design for Tichenor's Long Beach house (fig. 15). Much of the design was imitative: the roof was in the *irimoya* style; porch railings were in a Japanese post-and-panel style; and there was a curved Japanese bridge in the garden (see Hales–Smith essay, fig. 8).

But there was an additional element of experimentation here that was more interpretative than imitative, that was about "that expression of post and beam construction, of articulated structure" Charles would speak of so many years later. The timber structuralism of the building at first seems to relate to English Tudor half-timbered houses—especially with the infill of clinker bricks—but the absence of diagonal bracing points to a Japanese influence. In British and European buildings, diagonal bracing was needed for stability. In Japan, however, diagonal bracing was eschewed; flexibility within the frame was needed to withstand earthquakes.

FIGURE 16
*Detail of front
elevation, Adelaide A.
Tichenor house*
Courtesy of Avery
Architectural and
Fine Arts Library,
Columbia University

FIGURE 17
*View of south (front)
façade, Adelaide A.
Tichenor house*
Courtesy of Charles Sumner
Greene Collection (1959-1),
Environmental Design
Archives, University of
California, Berkeley

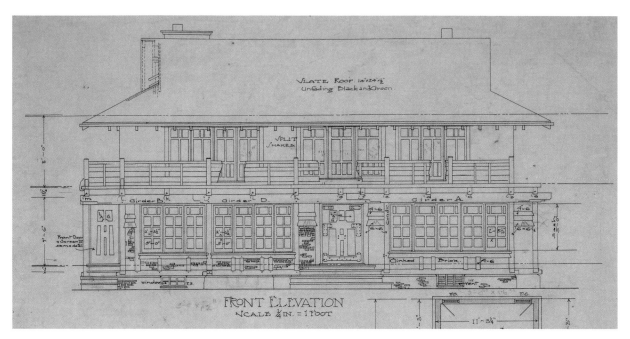

FIGURE 16
*Detail of front
elevation, Adelaide A.
Tichenor house*
Courtesy of Avery
Architectural and
Fine Arts Library,
Columbia University

FIGURE 17
*View of south (front)
façade, Adelaide A.
Tichenor house*
Courtesy of Charles Sumner
Greene Collection (1959-1),
Environmental Design
Archives, University of
California, Berkeley

Thus, in Japanese building, the structure becomes not about the bracing, but about the joinery. A high level of joinery had been refined through the centuries to maintain stability yet allow elasticity in the structure, which would be lost without the use of diagonal members. Also, in Japanese construction, the structural carcass is what defines the architecture. Walls are secondary to frame, especially since spaces between structural columns are frequently "filled in" not with fixed walls, but with sliding *fusuma* doors or *shoji* screens.[58]

In the Tichenor house, no diagonals were used in the half-timbered walls. What is evident is a design aesthetic based on the timbered structure: the column-and-post walls with infill of clinker bricks; the bands of casement windows reminiscent of sliding *shoji* screens; corner posts holding up crossbeams supporting purlins, rafters, and the roof (figs. 16 and 17).[59] It was a structuralism that, even when decorative, expresses the construction. It is this that conveys Japan, as much as the direct imitation of the roof form and the Japanese bridge. It is also—as the Greenes incorporated it into their aesthetic over the next half-decade—something that became decidedly Californian.

The Greenes added one more architectural "experiment" to their design for Tichenor that has been considered Japanese, although it actually was not. At the rear of the garden was what Charles called a "Tea House,"[60] an outdoor, open-sided roofed structure, not at all a teahouse in the Japanese sense (fig. 18). Stylistically, it was closer to the pergola the Greenes built just two years before for Culbertson's English Tudor house; the primary difference was that the "Tea House" was roofed, whereas the pergola was not. The innovative "experiment" in this case was the extension of the rafters beyond the edge of the tiled roof; called "rafter tails," these became a standard part of the Greenes' mature vocabulary.

Rafter tails were perhaps the one element of the Greenes' style most imitated by others. Within a few years, other architects were extending rafters beyond rooflines; the design element was readily adopted by builder-contractors and used in magazines to illustrate emblematic California bungalows. In the article of 1907 on "Little Switzerland," rafter tails were said to accentuate "the Swiss effect"; just a few months later, in an article in *The Craftsman*, they were considered "strongly suggestive of Japanese influence"; by 1918, the architect Peter Wight was counting them as one of the defining elements of "true and rational bungalows."[61] Charles

himself, when questioned by a client "why the beams project from the gables," answered, "because they cast such beautiful shadows on the sides of the house in this bright atmosphere."[62] In actuality, they were not about Switzerland—or Japan—but all about Southern California and its sunshine.[63]

These were the years, up to 1904, of the Greenes' "experiments sometimes startling," each one being constructed "while the aesthetic architect paints his picture for the next." These projects, especially "Job No. 11," the "Sketch of a Dwelling Place," and the houses for Arturo Bandini and Adelaide Tichenor, allowed the brothers the opportunity to try new concepts, to put on to paper, and sometimes build, forms and images leading toward their own individual style. By 1905 and 1906, the firm's lexicon had become more cohesive, as evidenced in designs for Henry and Laurabelle Robinson, Robert Pitcairn, and the extraordinary additions and alterations for Theodore Irwin. The Greenes' work was also becoming recognized as part of the climate and geography of California, built with gardens graced by pergolas, with sleeping porches and verandas that blurred the division between outside and in, with massive cobblestone chimneys and meandering walls of clinker brick embedded with boulders from the creek bed, reminding one of the nearness of wilderness.

Then, in 1907, the Greenes closed their Los Angeles office, and for an all-too-brief period—until about 1911—the brothers began to work together again in Pasadena. In designing houses for Robert Blacker, David Gamble, Freeman Ford, William Thorsen, and Charles Pratt, their aesthetic found its full artistic bloom. These were costly houses, some used only in winter, and all were furnished and variously appointed with art glass, carpets, hanging lanterns and chandeliers, even picture frames designed by the architects. Though called Japanesque, or Swiss—the Gamble house, for instance, was described as "A Chalet in the Japanese Style"—it was an architecture about California and all that it represented: the sunshine, the outdoors, the western edge of a young nation facing the Far East, a place of recovery and renewal and throwing off constraints of East Coast conservatism, and, as Charles wrote in 1908, a place that represented "the wondrous climate of California and the freedom of life one may lead here."[64] Perhaps most importantly, the aesthetic of the Greenes not only imagined what California meant to those who went there, but also itself formed a part of the romantic "elsewhere" by which California would forever be understood.

FIGURE 18
*Garden "Tea House,"
Adelaide A. Tichenor
house*
*Courtesy of Charles Sumner
Greene Collection (1959-1),
Environmental Design
Archives, University of
California, Berkeley*

[*pages 82–83*]
FIGURE 19
*Theodore Irwin, Jr.,
house. Photograph by
Harold A. Parker,
c. 1907*
*Courtesy of
The Huntington Library,
San Marino, California*

1. Of approximately 121 houses constructed from designs by the firm of Greene and Greene between 1894 and 1922, 117 were documented as built in Southern California, that is, from Santa Barbara to the Mexican border. Of these, 101 were built in the Pasadena area. These figures are incomplete, however, as there are projects missing from the Greene and Greene office job list. The best reconstruction of the job list is in Edward R. Bosley, *Greene & Greene* (London: Phaidon, 2000), pp. 227–36, which has been my primary source for the numbering sequence of jobs and building costs.

2. CSG, "Bungalows," *Western Architect*, 12, no. 1 (July 1908), p. 3.

3. I am deeply in debt to Marta Pardee-King, Curator of Social Sciences at the Boston Public Library, for her detailed answer to my query on Boston train stations and schedules. She cited Richard C. Barrett, *Boston's Depots and Terminals: A History of Boston's Downtown and Back Bay Railroad Stations from 1834 to Today* (Rochester, NY: Railroad Research Publications, 1996), pp. 1–5, 13.

4. C.A. Higgins, *To California and Back* (Chicago: Passenger Department, Santa Fe Route, 1893), p. 17.

5. In having physical reality, California was an idealized "elsewhere," as compared to Thomas More's invented island of Utopia, an idealized "nowhere."

6. Walt Whitman wrote his "Facing West from California's Shores" in 1860 for the first Japanese embassy visiting America, only one year after Japan had opened its ports to trade.

7. This was in a promotional booklet put together for the World's Columbian Exposition in Chicago: Harry Ellington Brook, *The Land of Sunshine: Southern California—An Authentic Description of Its Natural Features, Resources, and Prospects* (Los Angeles: World's Fair Association and Bureau of Information Print, 1893), p. 98.

8. Kate Sanborn, *A Truthful Woman in Southern California* (New York: D. Appleton & Co., 1893), p. 68.

9. "Dr. T. S. Greene's two sons, Messrs. Henry M. and Charles M. [*sic*] Greene, who arrived from Boston a short time ago, have opened an architect's office in the Eldredge block. They are late graduates of the Boston School of Technology and come fully prepared to prove their qualifications as architects." *Pasadena Star*, January 13, 1894, p. 5.

10. On architectural office practice at the end of the nineteenth century, see Mary N. Woods, *From Craft to Profession: The Practice of Architecture in Nineteenth-Century America* (Berkeley: University of California Press, 1999), esp. pp. 139–40. On the Greenes' education and apprenticeships, see Bosley, *Greene & Greene*, pp. 13–21; and Barbara Ann Francis, "The Boston Roots of Greene and Greene" (master's thesis, Tufts University, 1987), pp. 15–59.

11. Bosley, *Greene & Greene*, pp. 27–28.

12. Charles had been living with his parents. Henry was living with his wife, Emeline, and their firstborn son next door, in a house owned by their father.

13. For extrapolation of this sequence of events, see Bruce Smith, *Greene & Greene and the Duncan-Irwin House: Developing a California Style* (Salt Lake City: Gibbs Smith, forthcoming).

14. From 1902 through 1907, Greene and Greene designed eleven houses very near Charles's home.

15. An article of 1907 promoted the San Gabriel Mountains above Pasadena as "America's Alps," touting "mountain peaks that … would tax the skill and endurance of the hardiest Alpine Climber." *Pasadena Daily News*, March 23, 1907, p. II-1. The Swiss chalet as a style had been popular since its introduction to America by Andrew Jackson Downing, who called it "the most picturesque of all dwellings built of wood." Andrew Jackson Downing, *The Architecture of Country Houses: Including Designs for Cottages, and Farm-Houses and Villas, with Remarks on Interiors, Furniture, and the Best Modes of Warming and Ventilating* (New York: D. Appleton & Co., 1850), reprinted as *The Architecture of Country Houses* (New York: Dover, 1969), p. 123.

16. Grace Hortense Tower, "'Little Switzerland': Pasadena's Boast for Homes," *Pasadena News*, March 16, 1907, p. II-1.

17. CSG Misc. Papers, EDA.

18. It is worth noting that a two-volume set on Switzerland with a beautiful chalet on the title page eventually ended up in Charles Greene's library. It is inscribed "Martha White, Nov. 1, 1902"; this was just about the time that Charles was designing the house for the White sisters. The book was William Beattie, M.D., *Switzerland Illustrated in a Series of Views Taken on the Spot and Expressly for this Work by W. H. Bartlett, Esq.* (London: G. Virtue, 1835). The full series of inscriptions is "T. White 1836, Martha White, Nov. 1, 1902, Chas. Sumner Greene, Sept. 9th 1905." See Bruce Smith, "Library of Charles Sumner Greene," typescript, GGA.

19. For the White sisters' house, see Bosley, *Greene & Greene*, pp. 52–54.

20. For the Darling house, see *ibid.*, pp. 54–56.

21. Greene had already used this same drawing of the Darling house in 1903 in a British journal, where it was published as "House at Pasadena [*sic*], California, Chas. Summer [*sic*] Greene, Architect," under the section "American Domestic Architecture," *Academy Architecture*, 24 (1903), p. 54.

22. CSG, "California Home Making," *Pasadena Daily News*, January 2, 1905, pp. 26–27. An edited version of this essay, titled "Home Making in California," was reprinted two years later in *A Book of the Crown City and Its Tournament of Roses* (Pasadena, Calif.: Pasadena Daily News, 1907).

23. CSG, "California Home Making," p. 26.

24. See Bosley, *Greene & Greene*, pp. 47–48.

25. CSG, "California Home Making," p. 26.

26. Frederick Skiff *et al.*, *Official Catalogue of Exhibitors, Universal Exposition, St. Louis, 1904* (St. Louis: Official Catalogue Company, 1904), p. 65.

27. This was the James A. Culbertson house (1902); see Bosley, *Greene & Greene*, pp. 48–52.

28. "Sketch of a Dwelling Place by Chas. Sumner Greene, Architect, Pasadena, for W.B.T. Esqr. Near Pasadena" (36 × 46 in.; 91.5 × 116.8 cm); the current location of the presentation drawing is not known. It was exhibited again in 1911 at the second annual exhibition of the Architectural Club of Los Angeles. See *Architectural Club of Los Angeles, Year Book, 1911, of the Second Annual Exhibition under the Auspices of the Architectural League of the Pacific Coast, Los Angeles, Ca., January 17–21, 1911*. Most likely W.B.T. are the initials of an earlier client, William B. Tompkins.

29. Skiff *et al.*, *Official Catalogue*, p. 65. It is interesting to note that in Charles Greene's correspondence with the exposition organizers, even though he has written on Greene and Greene office letterhead, he signs his name as "Chas. Sumner Greene" and provides the return address of his home in Pasadena. Correspondence on file, Archives, St. Louis Art Museum.

30. For the "Dwelling Place … for W.B.T.," see Bosley, *Greene & Greene*, pp. 63–64.

31. Although the Bandini job number was 109, seven job numbers before that of W.B.T. (job number 116), the contract for Bandini was reported in the *Pasadena News* on November 19, 1903, so Charles would have been working on the design for Bandini over the late summer or fall of that year. Charles wrote a letter on September 23, 1903, to Halsey Ives, Chief of the Department of Art for the St. Louis World's Fair, stating his desire "to exhibit some of my work" in the architectural section of the arts exhibition at the fair; the work he exhibited was the W.B.T. project. Correspondence on file, Archives, St. Louis Art Museum.

32. "Autobiography of Walter L. Richardson of Porterville, California, September 1954," manuscript, GGA, p. 17.

33. For Bandini, see *ibid.*, pp. 17–18; C. Fred Shoop, "Bandini Home Recalls Past," *Pasadena Star News*, July 26, 1961, p. A-8; and "Ralph Bandini Remembers: Mountain Lions and Other Game," *Pasadena Community Book* (Pasadena: A.H. Cawston, 1955), pp. 40–41. For Juan Bandini and the home where Arturo was born, see San Diego Historical Society, "San Diego Biographies: Juan Bandini (1800–1859)," http://www.sandiegohistory.org/bio/bandini/bandini.htm (accessed August 29, 2007); Patricia Baker, "The Bandini Family," *Journal of San Diego History*, 15, no. 1 (Winter 1969), http://www.sandiegohistory.org/journal/69winter/part2.htm (accessed August 29, 2007); and Sally B. Woodbridge, *California Architecture: Historic American Buildings Survey* (San Francisco: Chronicle Books, 1988), p. 201.

34. According to Jean Murray Bangs, "Greene and Greene," *Architectural Forum*, 89 no. 4 (October 1948), p. 85.

35. Helen Hunt Jackson, *Ramona* (New York: Grosset & Dunlap, 1912), p. 19. Originally published in 1884.

36. *Ibid.*, p. 17. See also Dydia DeLyser, *Ramona Memories: Tourism and the Shaping of Southern California* (Minneapolis: University of

Minnesota Press, 2005); Carey McWilliams, *Southern California Country: An Island on the Land* (New York: Duell, Sloan & Pearce, 1946), pp. 70–83; Kevin Starr, *Inventing the Dream: California through the Progressive Era* (New York: Oxford University Press, 1985), pp. 55–63; and George Wharton James, *Through Ramona's Country* (Boston: Little, Brown, 1909).

37. San Diego Historical Society, "Old Town State Historic Park," http://www.sandiegohistory.org/links/oldtown.htm (accessed August 29, 2007).

38. Letter from Lelia Mather Greene to CSG and HMG, January 1, 1893, GGA.

39. Letter from Lelia Mather Greene to CSG and HMG, January 29, 1893, GGA.

40. Interestingly, the first house built in Pasadena by one of the founders of the city—called a "California House" by the builders—was a simple, three-room, board-and-batten structure, left unpainted to stand "in naked ostentation until clambering vines hid its bareness." J.W. Wood, *Pasadena Historical and Personal* (Pasadena, Calif.: published by the author, 1917), p. 61.

41. Letter from CSG to Lucretia Garfield, [October 1903], GGA. Though the letter is undated, Charles mentions that his wife has just come home from the hospital after giving birth to their second child, Bettie Storey Greene, who was born on October 21, 1903.

42. By "mission style," Charles meant the Mission Revival style. When used to describe architecture, this term referred to the styles derived from California missions. For example, in Gustav Stickley's magazine, *The Craftsman*, "Mission Style" in architecture specifically referred to buildings influenced by the Franciscan missions; see "A Craftsman House Founded on the California Mission Style," in *Craftsman Homes* (New York: Craftsman Publishing Co., 1909), p. 9. The meaning of "Mission Style" when referring to furniture was more ambiguous, alluding either to the California missions or, more probably at the turn of the last century, to the style of Arts and Crafts furniture begun by Joseph McHugh and popularized by Stickley. For "Mission Style" in reference to furniture, see Anna Tobin D'Ambrosio, "'The Distinction of Being Different,'" in *The Distinction of Being Different: Joseph P. McHugh and the American Arts and Crafts Movement*, exhib. cat., Utica, NY, Museum of Art, Munson-Williams-Proctor Institute, 1993, esp. p. 18. See also "How 'Mission' Furniture Was Named," *The Craftsman*, 16, no. 2 (May 1909), p. 225. Eugene Neuhaus, "The Genealogy of the Architecture," in *The San Diego Garden Fair: Personal Impressions of the Architecture, Sculpture, Horticulture, Color Scheme, & Other Aesthetic Aspects of the Panama California International Exposition* (San Francisco: Paul Elder, 1916), p. 14, discourses on the origins of the architecture of the Franciscan missions, distinguishing this meaning of "Mission Style" from two other meanings, the first considered as "an original product of California, absolutely detached from any style of the past," and the second as "recent production of the Stickley Brothers furniture plant."

43. There was also of course the Greenes' "Job No. 11," with its courtyard plan and *espadaña*-styled parapet. The Mission Revival house was for Edward B. Hosmer. The brother-in-law of one of their aunts was Howard Longley; often misidentified as an uncle, he was the brother to Albert Longley, who married Alice Sumner Greene, sister to Henry and Charles's father; see Virginia Hales, "Greene Connections with the Longleys," typescript, June 9, 2003, GGA. I am grateful to Virginia Hales for sharing this with me. The apartment building was designed for F.J. Martin. Plans and elevations for all four jobs are at Avery.

44. CSG, "California Home Making," p. 26.

45. There were few other books available specifically devoted to Japanese architecture. Notably, there was Christopher Dresser's well-known *Japan: Its Architecture, Art, and Art Manufactures* (1882); but Dresser focuses on the more ornate forms of temple architecture. Moreover, this book was not included in the list of what is known to have been in Charles Greene's library. Charles did have several books on Japan published earlier than his designs for the Culbertson house; but, with the exception of a book of 1902 on European and Japanese Gardens, these works were on Japanese culture and literature. See Smith, "Library of Charles Sumner Greene."

46. It is inked in more carefully on the final elevation drawing, probably done in the Los Angeles office under Henry's supervision. The plans are at Avery. Clay Lancaster first noted this Japanese-inspired use of stone for porch posts in the Bandini house. Clay Lancaster, "The American Bungalow," *Art Bulletin*, 40, no. 3 (September 1958), p. 246.

47. Una Nixson Hopkins, "A Study for Home-Builders," *Good Housekeeping*, March 1906, p. 264. The article cites walls that are stained a "Japanese brown," p. 262, or a "Japanese gray," p. 262, and "a lattice frame for a rose … shows the careful consideration of the Japanese in the making of small things," p. 263. Oddly, the writer does not mention the "Japanese temple" motif in the living room.

48. CSG, "Bungalows," p. 4. Interestingly, for Christmas of 1911, one of the sisters, Jane White, gave Henry Greene's mother-in-law a small calendar depicting Japanese *ukiyo-e* prints, probably from a store selling Japanese art goods in Pasadena. The calendar belongs to Virginia Hales, Henry Greene's granddaughter.

49. *Official Monthly Handbook: Balloon Route Excursion Souvenir* (Los Angeles: Balloon Route Publishing Co., December 1908), pp. 7, 9–11. A photograph in Specialized Libraries and Archival Collections, Information Services Division, University of Southern California Doheny Memorial Library, Los Angeles, shows downtown Los Angeles looking north on Broadway from Sixth Street; a large banner strung up across the street advertises the "opening, grand winter carnival and oriental exposition Venice Jan. 14 1906." Record ID chs-m1113 USC-1-1-1-117 5200. At that time, the office of Greene and Greene was in the Pacific Electric Building at Sixth and Main streets, three blocks away.

50. Rev. Stephen G. Emerson, "At America's Front Door," in *Pasadena, New Years Day, Tournament of Roses, Pasadena Beautiful; Crown of the San Gabriel Valley, The Ideal City of Homes* (Pasadena, Calif.: Pasadena Daily News, [1903]), p. [43].

51. See *Pasadena Oral History Project, Talking about Pasadena: Selections from Oral Histories* (Pasadena, Calif.: Junior League of Pasadena, 1986), pp. 26–27. This incorrectly credits the teahouse and garden to Victor Marsh; city directories and postcards from the period correctly identify them as belonging to George Turner Marsh, the leading merchant of Japanese

goods in San Francisco from 1876. See Clay Lancaster, *The Japanese Influence in America* (New York: Walton H. Rawls, 1963). The teahouse remained on the corner of Fair Oaks and California in Pasadena until 1912, when it was purchased by Henry Huntington and moved to his estate in nearby San Marino. See William Hertrich, *The Huntington Botanical Gardens, 1905–1949: Personal Recollections of William Hertrich* (San Marino, Calif.: Huntington Library, 1949), pp. 78–79.

52. For Aoki and his annual cherry blossom dinners, see "Artist Aoki's Artistic Dinner," *Pasadena Evening Star*, March 7, 1903, p. 1; "Cherry Blossom Dinner Tonight," *Pasadena Daily News*, March 7, 1908; and Grace Hortense Tower, "A Cherry Blossom Dinner," *Good Housekeeping*, March 1904, pp. 283–84. Tower also wrote the local newspaper article on "Little Switzerland" connecting the work of the Greenes to the Swiss style.

53. Edward S. Morse dubbed it the "Japan Craze." See *The Japan Idea: Art and Life in Victorian America*, exhib. cat. by William Hosley, Hartford, Conn., Wadsworth Atheneum, 1990, p. 31. Morse lectured on Japan and things Japanese during these years; in 1890, his protégé Ernest Fenollosa, acknowledged as the leading expert on Japanese art in America, became the first curator of Japanese art at the recently expanded Museum of Fine Arts, Boston. In 1893, Fenollosa held his first exhibition, *Hokusai and His School*, accompanied by an extensive annotated catalogue. See Kojiro Tomita, *A History of the Asiatic Department: A Series of Illustrated Lectures Given in 1957 by Kojiro Tomita (1890–1976)* (Boston: Museum of Fine Arts, 1990), p. 29; see also *Museum of Fine Arts, Department of Japanese Art, Special Exhibitions of the Pictorial Art of Japan and China No. 1: Hokusai, and*

His School. Catalogue, Boston, Museum of Fine Arts, 1893. The museum was just down the street from where the Greenes were living at the time; their freehand drawing class at the Massachusetts Institute of Technology took place in the museum galleries. At least peripherally, they would have been aware of the local fascination with things Japanese. Also, Charles's favorite professor at MIT, the artist Ross Turner, was a close friend to both Morse and Morse's Japanese charge, Bunkio Matsuki. Matsuki later became Boston's leading seller of Japanese imports. See Frederic A. Scharf (ed.), *"A Pleasing Novelty": Bunkio Matsuki and the Japan Craze in Victorian Salem* (Salem, Mass.: Essex Institute, 1993), p. 18. A Japanese house was designed for Matsuki in 1893, for the vacant lot next to Morse's home in Salem. The design was based on sketches of houses that Matsuki had seen in Japan and on Morse's book *Japanese Homes and Their Surroundings*. The architectural firm that undertook the Matsuki commission was Andrews, Jacques & Rantoul, where Charles had apprenticed from 1890 to 1891. See Dean Lahikainen, "Bunkio Matsuki's Japanese House in Salem, Massachusetts," in Scharf, *"A Pleasing Novelty,"* pp. 60–87. The "Japan Craze," however, was not about architecture; it was about things that showed how modern one was. *The Japan Idea*, exhib. cat., pp. 45–46.

54. Clay Lancaster, "My Interviews with Greene and Greene," *Journal of the American Institute of Architects*, 28 (July 1957), p. 205.

55. This was narrated when Charles was in his late seventies, some four decades after that moment of epiphany, and it feels a bit romanticized in the retelling. The architect who was told the story

reported that Charles then went over to the bookshelf in his Carmel studio, pulled down the same book, and "turned almost automatically to the page and remarked sadly that he had never gotten to Japan." L. Morgan Yost, "Greene & Greene of Pasadena," *Journal of the Society of Architectural Historians*, 9, nos. 1–2 (March–May 1950), p. 13. It is impossible to know if the book to which Charles referred was Morse.

56. Tichenor had written from St. Louis, on June 10, on stationery with the letterhead of the California Building at the fair, practically ordering Charles to get on a train to St. Louis. The timing of Charles's trip is inferred by a letter he wrote to his wife from Kansas City; presumably he stopped there on the way home from the fair to see his parents and "enjoy Mother's cooking." CSG to Alice Greene, July 18, 1904, GGA. By August, Charles was receiving correspondence from Grueby Faience Company indicating that he had already visited the fair.

57. Kwanjiuro Yamashita, *The Illustrated Catalogue of Japanese Fine Art Exhibits in the Art Palace at the Louisiana Purchase Exposition, St. Louis, Mo. USA* (Kobe, Japan: Kwansai Shashin Seihan Insatsu Goshi Kaisha, 1904), pp. 106–107.

58. *Fusuma* doors are traditionally made of paper and wood and serve as solid opaque removable barriers between rooms or for closets. They slide on wooden grooves, as do *shoji* screens, which are made of rice paper and wood and are translucent, allowing light into a room. See Klaus Zwerger, *Wood and Wood Joints: Building Traditions of Europe and Japan* (Basel, Berlin, Boston: Birkhauser, 2000), esp. p. 155, on diagonal bracing; see also Hideo Sato and Yasua Nakahara, *The Complete Japanese*

Joinery (Vancouver, BC: Hartley & Marks, 1995); and S. Azby Brown, *The Genius of Japanese Carpentry: The Secrets of a Craft* (Tokyo, New York, London: Kodansha, 1995).

59. Even an article of 1912 published in Japan about the Greenes noted the size of the windows was comparable to *shoji*, compared to the narrower windows usually seen in the West: "If we open up all these windows, the effect must be very much like *shoji* windows." Noboru Yoshida, "Japanesque," *Kenchiku kougei soushi* [Architecture and Craft Journal] (August 1912), 8, no. 1, pp. 33–34. Translation by Yoshiko Yamamoto.

60. CSG, "Impressions of Some Bungalows and Gardens," *The Architect*, 10 (December 1915), plate 1.

61. Tower, "'Little Switzerland,'" p. II-1; Henrietta P. Keith, "The Trail of Japanese Influence in Our Modern Domestic Architecture," *The Craftsman*, 12, no. 4 (July 1907), p. 451; and Peter Wight, "California Bungalows," *Western Architect*, 27, no. 10 (October 1918), p. 98.

62. Letter from CSG to Lucretia Garfield, June 5, 1903, GGA.

63. In Charles's article "California Home Making," one of his illustrations was "A Cobblestone Gateway" showing the firm's first built structure with rafter tails. As can be deduced from Bosley's "Complete Job List," it was probably designed after the Tichenor teahouse, but was constructed first because of delays in the Tichenor project. Later in 1905, rafter tails would be used for the first time on a house. Designed for Dr. Arthur A. Libby, it was a modified form of the Greenes' Swiss chalet style.

64. CSG, "Bungalows," p. 3.

F.S. DETAIL of INLAY for TABORETTE
RESIDENCE FOR
FREEMAN A FORD, ESQ AT PASADENA CAL.
SHEET No (75)   SEP. 16, 1908.

√ Silver

{ Project 1/64 in.
{ beyond face

Ebony

Ebony
Silver } 1/64" Projection above face

MARGARETTA M. LOVELL

The Forest, the Copper Mine, and the Sea: The Alchemical and Social Materiality of Greene and Greene

"There are things in it Japanese; things that are Scandinavian; things that hint at Sikkhim, Bhutan, and the fastnesses of Thibet [sic]," remarked Ralph Adams Cram in 1913, "and yet it all hangs together, it is beautiful, it is contemporary, and for some reason or other it seems to fit California. Structurally it [displays] … honesty. … It is a wooden style built woodenly."[1] Cram was evoking for his New England readers the novel style of Greene and Greene's great bungalows, their realization of William Morris's and John Ruskin's dream of honest building and sincere living, but his comment also pointedly describes the physical materiality of these most wooden of wooden structures. "Bermese [Burmese] teak," for instance, is frequently listed on the firm's specifications as a material with unique geographic coordinates, sensuous properties, and cultural associations, as well as functional strengths and visual characteristics. Harvested by elephants and transported efficiently in the global economy of the *pax Britannia*, teak provided a touchable metonym of both the old worlds of Asian "fastnesses" and the new modernity of a materials palette unbounded by localness.[2] "[I]t all hangs together," said with a degree of wonderment, signals Cram's reassurance to himself that the multiplicity of materials gathered—ebony and mahogany, "Oregon pine" and redwood, copper and silver, wrought iron and steel, Grueby tiles and leaded art glass, cobblestones and clinker bricks, ivory and abalone—settles into wholeness and results in beauty.[3]

This "hanging together" is not just a matter of the Greene brothers' mastery of visual assemblage—what we usually term "style"—it is also the result of a supra-spatial understanding of architecture. More than most other designers, the Greenes were attentive to all the qualities of the materials they specified. Although visual and functional characteristics predominated, olfactory and aural experiences were also attended to: teak and Port Orford cedar are aromatic, and heavy felt placed under copper and oak deadened the sound of rain and

footsteps.[4] Tactile qualities were even more important. The Greenes frequently selected close-grained woods, such as mahogany and teak, for interior surfaces and furniture, their finish meticulously specified to yield a silky smoothness not found in the work of any other designers:

All exposed surfaces of wood work shall be sanded perfectly smooth with 00 sandpaper and given a coat of Wheelers Paste Filler wiping across the grain to remove surplus filler. Forty-eight hours or more after filler has been applied the work shall be sanded a second time over the whole surface with 0000 sandpaper and given a coat of raw linseed oil with proper amount of dryer. Oil shall be applied over a small amount of surface and immediately wiped off with clean cheese cloth. After this last process and work has been allowed to stand a sufficient time it shall be repeated. To the oil of this final coat shall be added a small amount of Pratt and Lambert's '61' Quick Drying Varnish. After this polish the whole with clean Cheese cloth.[5]

Such careful specifications not only underline Charles Greene's literacy in materials and fabrication methods, and the need he felt to parse such matters, in this case to unfamiliar and remote craftsmen; they also press urgently toward a tactile effect, specifically, "leaving wood all smooth and perfect."[6] Perfection here is a function of smoothness to the hand as well as structural integrity and visual effect. Touch is invited and rewarded in Greene and Greene interiors; banisters, doors, wainscoting, and windows beg for contact. Even more so, furnishings, the use of which requires touch, gratify the hand. Not only their structural parts but also their decorative motifs seem to call for fingering: the design for a taborette for the Freeman A. Ford house in Pasadena specifies that here—as in so many other of the firm's designs—the ebony elements are to project 1/64 of an inch beyond the surface (fig. 1). Touching this faint relief, one would also note the coldness of the silver inlay that laces through the imaginative ebony trellis. The micro-universe created

FIGURE I

Full-scale detail of silver-and-ebony inlay for a taborette (small table), September 16, 1908, Freeman A. Ford house, Pasadena, 1906–08

Courtesy of Charles Sumner Greene Collection (1959-1), Environmental Design Archives, University of California, Berkeley

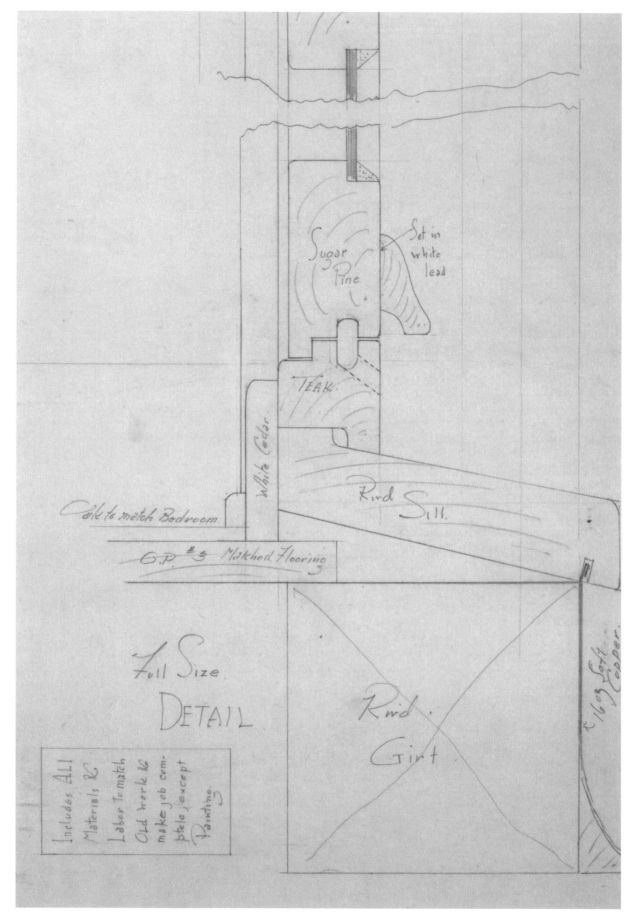

by the Greenes in their houses is a rich, sensuous land-scape, appealing strongly to four of the five senses, a symphony of effects that have for a century "hung together" and enriched human experience.

MATERIALS

Broadly speaking, we can say that the Greenes selected their materials and used them in combination with each other with an eye to sensory effect (as noted above), to function, and to aesthetic effect. They were also attentive to the price, and to the cultural resonance of their materials. Frequently they used materials to express social distinctions. This essay will touch on each of these considerations. The functional dimension of the Greenes' selection of materials was, for the most part, unexceptional in West Coast building. Like others in their day, they specified eastern white oak for flooring and thresholds because it resists wear; redwood and Douglas fir (*Pseudotsuga menziesii*, known to Greene and Greene as "Oregon Pine" and abbreviated "O.P.") for large structural members because the first-growth cuts of these Pacific coast trees produced exceptionally large, straight-grained dimensioned lumber; and sheet lead for flashing and copper for downspouts because they have the flexibility, impermeability, and longevity required to keep water out or in. What is exceptional in the Greenes' functional selections of material is the specificity to which they tailored their selections and the sheer number of different materials called for. A quick survey of specifications for some of their buildings yields more than a dozen different woods used structurally (and a dozen more employed decoratively). For instance, fragrant, strong, and densely grained Port Orford cedar (*Cupressus lawsoniana*, known to Greene and Greene as "White Cedar" and abbreviated "W.C.") was used in door frames, stair risers, wainscoting, window frames, towel bars, and other interior fittings.[7] Douglas fir and redwood are the most common woods specified, employed for all structural timbers as well as for internal and external sheathings; redwood, being resistant to damp and insects, was often used in exposed sites.[8] Redwood was one of the few western lumber trees to which the Greenes would have been introduced in their training at the Massachusetts Institute of Technology; however, in such East Coast publications of the period as a textbook of masonry, carpentry, and joinery, it is commended only as an interior finish.[9] Water-resilient sugar pine was specified for screen-door frames, window sashes, and kitchen drain boards and counters.[10] Exceptionally weather-durable teak was employed for some external applications, although its use in the Greenes' commis-sions was most often aesthetic. For instance, of sixty-six doors ordered for the William R. Thorsen house in Berkeley in 1910, two are teak: the door opening from the front hall to the den, which was wainscoted in teak, and the exterior door opening from the front hall to the back terrace.[11] The first, therefore, was primarily an aesthetic choice, the second a functional one.

Other woods specified for more specialized purposes in the major commissions include ash, birch, mahogany, maple, and red oak. Hickory appears once; reputed to be "the heaviest, hardest, toughest, and strongest of all American woods … [one especially noted for its] flexibility," this is the wood the firm specified for a chin-up bar in one of the Thorsen bedrooms.[12] A drawing from Charles Greene's studio of a window detail for an addition to the Thorsen house provides a good example of his extensive knowledge of the characteristics of different woods (fig. 2). A redwood girt, protected by copper skirting, supports a redwood sill at floor level where "Oregon Pine" (Douglas fir) subflooring supports the finished oak floor. Water- and weather-resistant "White Cedar" (Port Orford cedar) and teak members support a glazed sugar-pine French door. Six woods, gathered from the forests of southwest Oregon, northwest California, the Sierra Nevada mountains, the river valleys of southern New England, and the distant kingdom of Burma, come together in this drawing to create an exceptionally functional symphony of materials designed to remain stable and watertight for a century.

Time is the fourth factor that the Greenes took into consideration. They not only expected their houses to endure, they also designed them so that changes over time would strengthen rather than weaken structure. They note, for instance, in their directions to the company preparing the mahogany trim for the Thorsen house dining room: "Screws and [ebony] Plugs fix slots so that top can shrink towards front."[13] The functional responses of various species of woods—to water, shrinkage, abrasion, load, and flexing—may well have been a prominent feature of their high school education at the Manual Training School of Washington University, which incorporated a vigorous curriculum in woodworking, metalworking, and toolmaking.[14] It is likely that at MIT the Greenes had further training in the nature of specialized materials, but one suspects that the breadth and depth of their appetite for the unique capacities of a geographically heterogeneous array of woods was fed primarily at the world's fairs—Chicago in 1893, San Francisco in 1894 and 1915, and St. Louis in 1904—and at the dazzling lumberyards of Los Angeles and San Francisco.[15]

While the Greenes were primarily interested in the functional capacities of various woods—and of copper, which they so idiosyncratically used to sheathe and protect external wood, especially end-grain posts of Douglas fir[16]—they were also sensitive to other important qualities. Cost was one of these. In 1914, Douglas fir was the least expensive wood they used; Port Orford cedar cost twice as much; oak cost three times as much; and teak cost five times as much.[17] Even in the most lavish of the "ultimate bungalows," the board feet of Douglas fir is considerable although largely invisible on the interior.

If the first reason for the Greenes' use of a wide variety of woods and other materials is function and the second is price, the third is aesthetic choice. By juxtaposing different kinds of wood, or different kinds of art tiles, the Greenes achieved specific aesthetic effects, both on the scale of the house as a whole and on the smaller scale of individual motifs. Furniture ordered for the David B. Gamble house in Pasadena, for instance, included room-specific suites in black walnut (David and Mary Gambles' bedroom), ash (Mary Gamble's sister's bedroom), maple (guest bedroom), and mahogany (dining and living rooms).[18] Moving from room to room, one feels a uniformity of vocabulary within the specific and slightly differing "dialects" of the various woods. The effect is one of rich variety, similar to that of variations on a musical theme, where one listens simultaneously for familiar reiteration and for radical difference.

Like music, the architecture of Greene and Greene is designed to envelop the viewer; one experiences it both visually and somatically as surface and as structure. A section of the Freeman A. Ford house, for instance, gives one a sense of the musculature of the building, resisting gravity with a complex assemblage of beams overhead, and of the enveloping surface woods, each with its own color, figure, scent, and perhaps also acoustic properties (fig. 3). The drawing also suggests the rather different forests from which the two principal woods were extracted, with the narrow board and batten of the "W.C." (Port Orford cedar) recalling the growth pattern of those Oregon-sourced trees and the wider slabs of redwood evoking those Northern California giants. Further variety is provided by the specification of "Curly Redwood," lumber made from logs cut from the base of the most massive trees, where the grain of the wood has actually been compressed by the weight of the behemoth it supports. Other materials brought into the composition include diamond-paned casements and leaded art-glass panels providing points of transparency, translucency,

color, iridescence, and non-rectilinear form to the wall. Combined in harmonic patterned cadences, these elements add up to spaces that, in Cram's terms, "hang together" richly, and evoke the forests from which their principal materials were extracted.

The exuberant yet subtle contrast of materials that we see in the selection of woods for furniture suites and for interior wall surfaces is also evident in the inlaid pictorial motifs with which the Greenes enlivened their most elaborate furniture. A watercolor sketch of two sprigs of a flowering plant, perhaps a clematis, provides an example of Charles Greene's "painting" with wood (fig. 4). Annotations indicate that the stems are to be lignum vitae; the leaves are to be maple with white oak veins, and white oak with maple veins; a hole in a chewed leaf is to be mahogany. The flower petals are to be maple, with ebony, vermillion, and "Knurled" white oak adding points of contrast and color. In each building as a whole and in each pictorial inlay, the Greenes anticipated that the viewer would see fine distinctions between materials. While probably unable to identify correctly all the materials—Cram, after all, was in error about where that Burmese teak grew—the inhabitants and their visitors would have understood that allusions were being made (to the "fastnesses" of inner Asia, for instance), that distinctions were being made for structural and for aesthetic effect, and that they were being asked to respond to these buildings with their ears, noses, and fingers as well as with their eyes. Few architects in the Greenes' era, or ever, marshaled such a plethora of materials to create habitation. Cram speaks of Greene and Greene houses as "contemporary," and certainly the amplitude of choice and selection evidenced in these designs is one of the key elements of the firm's modernity. But to what degree do the materials themselves (and the handling of those materials) evidence the Greenes' modernity, and to what degree do they exhibit the antimodernism to which most of the literature so insistently points?

REVOLUTIONARY

"One must see the real and revolutionary thing in its native haunts of Berkley [sic] and Pasadena to appreciate it in all its varied charm and striking beauty," Ralph Adams Cram reported enthusiastically in 1913, associating "revolutionary" with those two progressive university towns and with the Greene brothers.[19] California, a scarce fifty years after the Wild West days of the gold rush and urban vigilantism, was new to American middle-class culture, and such commentators as Cram understood the architecture of the Greenes to be "native" to this, the state's new identity. It was "native," but only in the radical sense that this indigenousness was a matter of migrant architects working for migrant clients with materials and motifs gathered largely from elsewhere. One of the key attributes of California and of the architecture that suited "the kind of climate and soil, the habits of the people, and their ways of looking at civilization and nature"[20] was this assumption that everyone and everything was from elsewhere and thus could manufacture identity and form from scratch, fictionalize it, and play "what if …" with high stakes. California, the Greenes, and their clients were revolutionary in their easy shrugging off of ancestral and local traditions. But when the American Institute of Architects belatedly honored the firm in 1952 for having "made the name of California synonymous with simpler, freer and more abundant living,"[21] it was mostly wrong, or at least overstating the case, as we shall see. What the Greene brothers and their clients were doing was neither "simpler" nor "freer," although it was, in very important ways, "abundant" and new.

What was truly "revolutionary" about the Greenes' practice was a modernism of trade and finance that broke down natural and national spatial barriers; their use of abstract design motifs; their unexpected juxtapositions of incongruous materials; and their authoritarian role in the building process. This is not to make a case for that proto-Modernist identity that Reyner Banham so effectively rebutted, but rather to underline those aspects of their practice that were already "modern" in the first decade of the twentieth century.[22] Most conspicuously, the revolution that the firm embraced was a previously unknown, "freer" internationalism of money and materials. Ebony from the forests of Africa, abalone from the seabed off the cliffs of Northern California, and copper from Nevada, Michigan, or Rhodesia, came by steam power, in regularly scheduled shipments to vendors in Los Angeles and San Francisco. The infrastructure that made the "ultimate bungalows" possible included the Suez Canal.

The Greenes' thinking in these expansive, global terms, I hypothesize, began with the world's fairs, where objects of technological ingenuity and formerly scarce or unknown raw materials were presented to designers, artisans, businessmen, and potential clients eager to imagine, make, distribute, and buy new finished goods. The Greenes at the World's Columbian Exposition of 1893, in other words, saw much more than the Japanese Ho-o-den. They took advantage of this buoyant internationalism largely in terms of the influx of raw materials,

but they also, on occasion, used these links for fabrication: the carpet designed for the Gamble living room, for instance, was ordered from a London firm and woven in Bohemia (fig. 7). Moreover, the Greenes participated actively in the international movement of capital that fueled these far-flung trade relationships. Beginning in the first decade of the twentieth century, Charles Greene began investing in local companies, such as the Pasadena Ice Company, which he knew well as a customer and as designer of their modest offices. He was investing on a national scale (in Union Oil, for instance) by 1915; by 1920, he was receiving dividends from power companies in New York and Alabama, and bond payments from the cities of Montreal and Winnipeg. In 1920, his income from these sources exceeded $420 a month, and he expanded further, investing in the kingdoms of Italy and Hungary, and the republics of Peru and Chile.[23]

It could be argued that Charles's practice shrank after his move to Carmel in 1916 because he did not actively have to seek commissions. He kept his license current, built himself a studio (albeit used three hours a day for his daughter's piano practice), and subscribed to *Architectural Record* and *Architectural Forum* (as well as *National Geographic*), but he and his family lived comfortably on these investments until the crash of 1929, when his cashbook lists a rash of defaults.[24] Charles was, in the sense of all shareholders, a capitalist, and he invested in the "revolutionary" technologies of his day, such as electric power and oil. He bought a Cadillac in 1908, had a telephone by 1910, and purchased a motorcycle for his son Patrickson in 1917.[25] Congruent with these early adoption practices, he patented his furniture designs.[26] Credited with being the dreamy-artist half of the Greene and Greene partnership, Charles actually exhibited shrewd business acumen in a thoroughly contemporary mode.

As important to the Greenes' modernity as the movement of materials and money was the movement of information. Professional journals, imported books, correspondence, and personal travel kept the brothers in contact with their peers elsewhere.[27] The New Englander Ralph Adams Cram and the Englishman C.R. Ashbee made the pilgrimage to California to see the Greenes' work, and Charles spent both his honeymoon of 1901 and his "sabbatical" of 1909 in England. The Greenes were also in touch with their Midwestern counterpart, Frank Lloyd Wright. An important dimension of their modernity was their non-isolation.

One of the characteristics that made Greene and Greene homes decisively modern and "freer" (although not "simpler") was their up-to-date domestic technology.

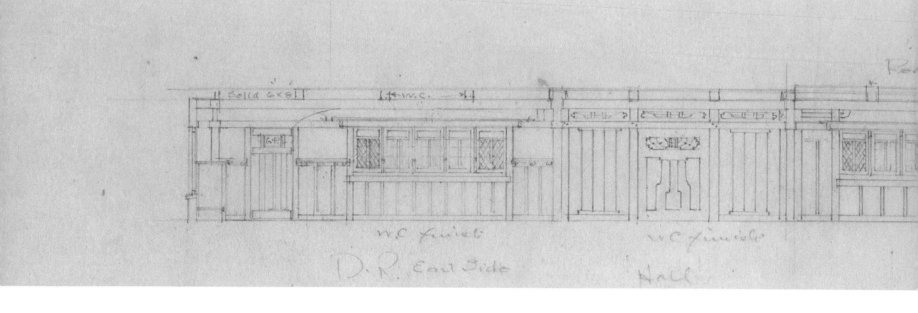

Solid 6×5 | t.w.c. |

W.C. finish   W.C. finish

D. R. East Side   Hall

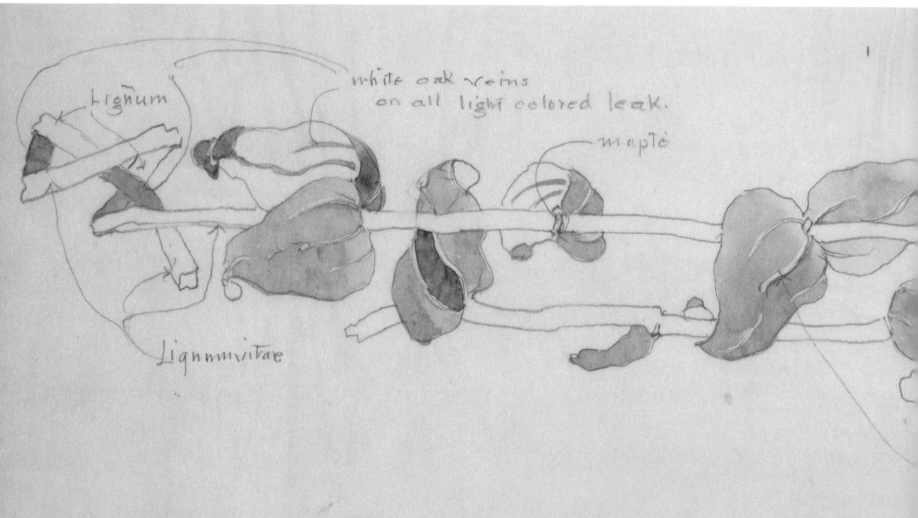

Lignum

white oak veins
on all light colored leak.

maple

Lignumvitae

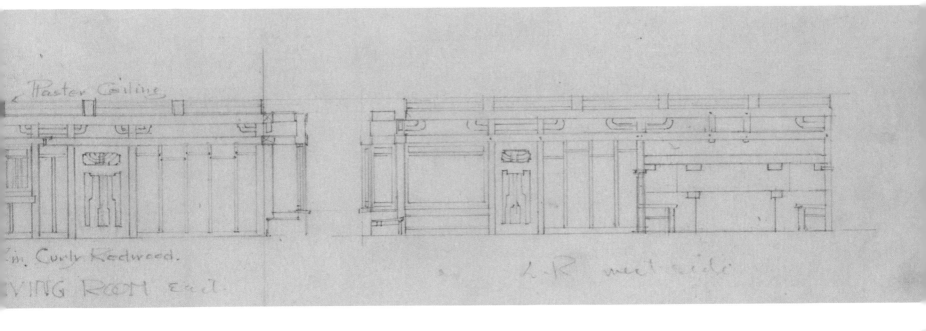

Plaster Ceiling

in Curly Redwood.

VING ROOM End.

L.R. west side

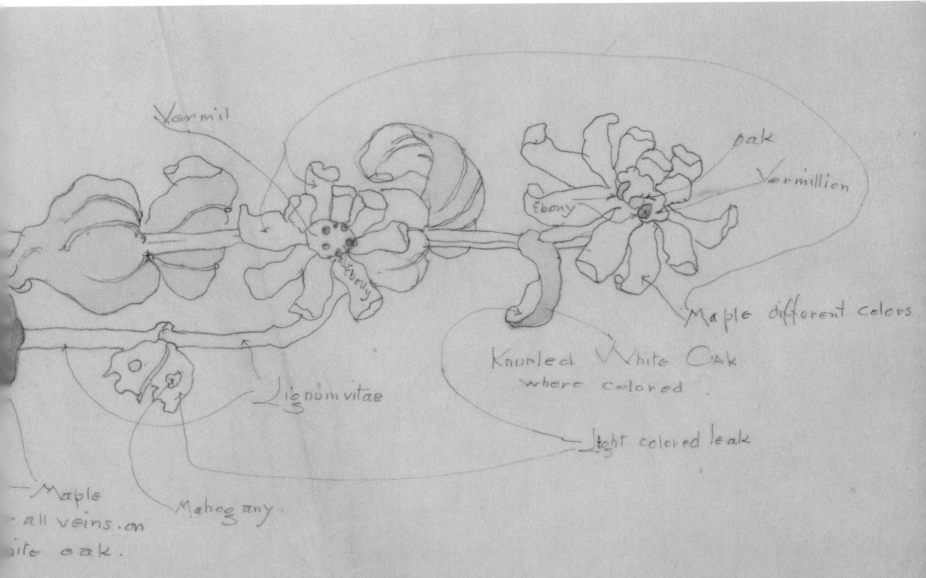

Vermil

oak

Vermillion

Ebony

Ebony

Maple different colors

Lignumvitae

Knurled White Oak
where colored

light colored leak

Maple

all veins on

hite oak.

Mahogany.

FIGURE 5
*1¼-inch scale details
of living-room table,
1912, Charles M. Pratt
house, Ojai, 1908–11*
Courtesy of Charles Sumner
Greene Collection (1959-1),
Environmental Design
Archives, University of
California, Berkeley

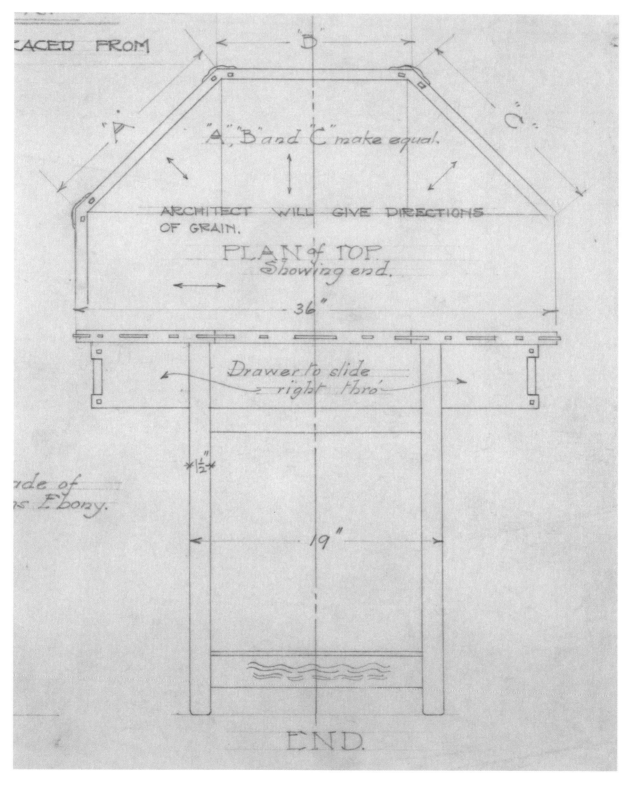

Central heating, central vacuum-cleaning systems, garages, electricity, telephone, indirect lighting, recessed lighting, sliding glass windows, plate-glass windows, window and door screens, specialized cabinetry of all kinds, and an amplitude of three-unit bathrooms made Greene and Greene houses designed before 1912 truly "revolutionary."[28] Their exteriors often displayed new patented materials; most were roofed with fire-retardant "malthoid," many were surfaced with "gunite," and at least one, the Cordelia Culbertson house in Pasadena, was set on an extremely sophisticated reinforced-concrete foundation.[29]

The designs with which Greene and Greene surfaces were embellished were sometimes illusionistic (as fig. 4), sometimes stylized, and often abstract (as figs. 1 and 7). Before painters understood the piquancy of treating a flat surface as a two-dimensional abstract design field, those creating decorative arts objects—whether quilters or cabinetmakers—were experimenting with abstraction. Charles Greene's watercolor designs for the living-room carpet in the Gamble house, his composition of such inlays as that for the Ford taborette, and his choice of wood grain as a design medium make clear that, while he may not have been theorizing abstraction, he was doing it. Certainly many of his designs are pictorial, usually stylized, but these other ventures into pure line, color, and shape show him to be masterful in this mode. Equally "revolutionary," the designs of Greene and Greene frequently included the unusual and unexpected insertion of one material into another, such as metal into wood (as fig. 1), arroyo boulders into brick walls, and semiprecious stones into an ebony footstool.[30]

The yoking together of disparate materials and the embracing of cutting-edge technology and abstraction are aspects of aesthetic creativity that gave a "contemporary" (to use Cram's term) edge to the work of Greene and Greene. However, a drawing by Charles Greene (fig. 5) gives an indication of a new, equally modern role being assumed by architects. As in many other specifications and drawings, the clarity of the description or design—here the "direction of [wood] grain" is plainly indicated by arrows—is reinforced by "Architect will give directions of grain." The architect looms as arbiter of all decisions, small as well as large, and is clearly somewhat nervous about the delegation of judgment in aesthetic matters, in spite of Ruskin's hope for the redemptive ingenuity of the artisan at the base of Arts and Crafts theory. Even building in the unfamiliar material of quarried stone with a master stonemason, Charles Greene acted as contractor and was on the site of the D.L. James

house in Carmel daily, adjusting the stonework.[31] In a drawing for a built-in bathroom case for the Thorsen house, the architect minutely directed exactly which boards were to be screwed into the frames and what kinds of washers and screws were to be used.[32] With patrons, the Greenes were prudently more deferential. There is, for instance, a series of handwritten notes on small scratch-pad sheets that apparently records a conversation between Charles Greene and Mrs. Gamble in which she expressed and he transcribed some of her ideas for the house on Westmoreland Place:

Front hall 1st floor ~~teak~~ mahogany. ... Outside lanterns on west not too straight and stiff or heavy; Lanterns something like Mr. R.R.B.'s. ... hanging clock with swans and water of abalone shells ... Chair high backs dignified. ... 1st floor Hall— Couch or davenport—teak, not to have hat rack: [then] small hat rack. ... door knobs 3' 2" above floor / Mrs. Gamble. ... Mrs. Gamble's suggestion for Hall Chairs [with sketch]. Not like Mrs. Bush's.[33]

The record of this exchange displays active thinking and accommodation that become invisible in the decisive final directives to workmen in the plans and specifications. In the controlling confidence of the formal specification documents, one senses the Greenes' professional modernity as much as in their ready adoption of technological innovation and the global reach of their materials mart. Ralph Adams Cram, Gustav Stickley, and the American Institute of Architects, however, were almost certainly using the terms "contemporary," "revolutionary," and "freer" to signal not these dimensions of modernity but the bungalowness, the seeming social informality, of these structures.

What made the work of Greene and Greene startlingly modern to their contemporaries was the absence in these expensive homes of aristocratic imagery, of grandeur, so familiar a characteristic of the well-publicized New York City and Newport homes of the wealthy at the turn of the century. No François I turrets or symmetrical Louis XIV galleries evoked the historic resources of European potentates in the Greenes' Pasadena bungalows; their universe of allusion was to nature. This eschewal of monarchical theatricality—and of the social formality presumed to inhabit such spaces— was noted in those comments about the "honesty" of these structures, about their "simpler, freer," and "revolutionary" character. It also, paradoxically, aligned Greene and Greene houses with the antimodernism inherent in the Arts and Crafts movement.

ANTIMODERNIST

In the heyday of the American system of manufactures, the advantages of heavily capitalized large-scale production and distribution, standardization, reduced unit price, and greater efficiency created fortunes and, thus, increased architectural patronage. In designing homes for the owners of these new industrially based fortunes, Greene and Greene (and some other design firms) adopted the seemingly inverted ethic of the Arts and Crafts movement. Key features of the Greenes' antimodernism include handcraftsmanship, historic construction techniques, "honest" use of materials, and archaic imagery.

Eschewing the qualities of mass production, machined precision, and replication that marked their era, the Greene brothers insisted on handwork and on construction techniques that predated the development of the balloon frame in the 1830s. When they specified for the outside walls of the F.W. Hawks house in Pasadena, "all timbers are of rough sawed redwood. … All mortised, tenoned and held by oak pins," and when they indicated on the plans for light fixtures for the Thorsen house, "all joints morticed [sic] and pinned [with] Ebony Plugs / Mahogany wood," they were directing the craftsmen to make individual joints and to secure them with a system of all-wood joinery that had been universally used in seventeenth-century Euro-American construction and just as universally abandoned by the mid-nineteenth century, except in the construction of barns.[34] While much of Greene and Greene construction is fixed by more modern countersunk brass screws capped by slightly protruding ebony plugs, the joints are still individually crafted. The designs underline the principle of "conspicuous construction" (to use Banham's term) that hearkens back to an earlier era, although not to the role of the craftsman-as-thinker envisioned by Ruskin and Morris.[35]

Greene and Greene left little to chance, and even less to artisan initiative, carefully detailing all aspects of their designs; these were delivered with extraordinary polish, especially the commissions executed by the Hall brothers. However, handcraftsmanship was one of the Greenes' key desiderata. The word "hand" appears repeatedly in the directives concerning the fabrication and finishing of materials of all kinds: bricks are to be "sand moulded, hand made, [and] hard burned"; tiles are to be "hand pressed with rounded corners, not mechanically straight, nor yet misshapen"; posts and beams are to be "redwood roughed off with the axe"; "all woodwork as it comes from the mill shall be finished by hand. … All corners are to be rounded and surfaces scraped according to the personal direction of the Architect";

brass plates are to be "hand chased and gilt"; a mirror frame was to have its "Surface Scraped by hand, slightly [sic] wavy. All hand Work."[36] Consistent with Arts and Crafts principles, Greene and Greene endorsed both the look and the reality of unique components touched by human individuality, manual know-how, and care.

As important as handwork was the "honest" expression of materials. Charles Greene was quoted as opining, "We have got to have bricks and stone and wood and plaster; common, homely cheap materials, every one of them. Leave them as they are—stone for stone, brick for brick, wood for wood, plaster for plaster. Why disguise them? Thought and care are all that we need, for skill we have. The noblest work of art is to make these common things beautiful for man."[37] Here he endorses the alchemy of craftsmanship—the elevation of the common to the status of art through the efforts of designer and fabricator.

Last, the Greenes' antimodernism is marked by the inclusion of archaic elements. While they excluded Greco-Roman forms, coded "dishonest" in their "false" expression of material and their historic association with imperial power, they embraced other historical forms, especially those coded "colonial" (and therefore "native"). The inglenook, the settle, the beamed ceiling, and the wood-burning fireplace are key features of many Greene and Greene designs, most notably the extraordinary construction at the heart of the Gamble house living room. Charles Greene's sentiments about this cluster of forms are clear in his description of the fireplace as a "simple but generous shelter for the great back log and glowing embers."[38] Evoking historic open-fire cooking technology and cozy inglenook sociability, these visual quotations confirmed colonialesque romantic antimodernism as much as beamed ceilings, elaborated trusses, and diamond-paned casement windows;[39] such elements in the Greenes' repertory signaled "retro" even more loudly than other elements signaled, to Cram and others, "revolutionary." Colonial houses were frequently documented and featured in the architectural press from the 1870s on; the Greenes also knew these forms personally, having summered as youngsters on Nantucket, where intact seventeenth- and eighteenth-century buildings were omnipresent.[40] In keeping with this Arts and Crafts affection for pre-industrial technology and human relations, for objects marked by tradition and by the individual maker, Charles Greene bought an antique Shoshone basket from a Fred Harvey shop so that he—like so many other Arts and Crafts practitioners—could display Native American handwork within the hand-finished "colonialness" of his own home.[41] The argument for the Greenes' antimodernism is, overall, as strong as it is for their modernism.

MATERIALS OF DISTINCTION

Finish floors: 1st story living room, den, hall, dining room and butlers pantry shall be quarter-sawn white oak ... ; balance of house finish floors shall be ... face matched rock maple. ... Stairs: ... [shall be] quartered white oak treads, ... back stairs maple treads. Cellar stairs ... O. P. [Douglas fir].[42]

The most marked area in which Greene and Greene were not revolutionary was in their expression of social distinctions as material distinctions. They followed precedent meticulously in the organization, surface finish, and somatic effect of their interiors, so that one could identify instantly which of the two spatial moieties— servant or served—one stood in. Oak underfoot meant something very different from maple or fir underfoot. When the AIA praised Greene and Greene for having "made the name of California synonymous with simpler, freer and more abundant living," it was probably thinking about the translation to the West of the wide apertures between major rooms and the many terraces for easy outdoor living that the brothers had seen in eastern Shingle-style homes (such as the Pierre Lorillard house of 1878 in Newport by Peabody & Sterns). The terms seem to imply a renovation of human relations, but in this respect, the Greenes' houses were no "simpler" or "freer" than those of their predecessors or contemporaries. The lives of those who spent their days on maple and Douglas fir flooring were not simpler, freer, or more abundant than those of their counterparts elsewhere.

To speak generally of Greene and Greene houses, the served spaces contained more archaic forms—fireplaces, beamed ceilings, wainscoting, built-in settles, inglenooks, bay windows. These vehicles of cultural memory and variant room shapes are not to be found in the business-like, strictly rectilinear spaces of the servant areas. Finished in different materials, the back hallways, stair treads, and doors were narrower, the ceilings often lower, and winder staircases—never found in the front of the house—economized on space, reminding those in the "back" areas of the variant behaviors expected in these two different zones.[43] These two parts of the house were in every respect somatically distinct. The dimensions were not tighter in the back areas because there was an expectation that servants were physically smaller. Nor was the absence in the servant spaces of some materials

(such as leaded art glass, mahogany, and teak) simply a matter of economy, for the code was extended to such small matters as the finish on the doorbell buttons (mother-of-pearl in the front and plain in the back) so that inhabitants, visitors, and tradesmen, all initiated into the language of materials, would understand spatially specific expected behaviors and social interactions.[44] No expense was spared on ingenious cabinetry for the servant spaces; the issue in the usage of distinctive materials was not economic, it was social.

Designs for light fixtures for the Freeman A. Ford house exhibit these characteristic differences (fig. 6). Sconces for the front bedrooms are on large brackets with 8-inch (20-cm) arms. They incorporate chains and hooks (suggesting adjustability and historic methods of fastening and hanging), and their supports are to be made out of "WHITE CEDAR" (Port Orford cedar). Support blocks for ceiling fixtures have dimpled corners and are of cedar as well. Light fixtures for the kitchen wing, on the other hand, are fixed, smaller, plainer, and on 4-inch (10-cm) arms; most are to be made of "O.P." (Douglas fir). Design and materials are spatially and socially specific, not just functionally specific in these houses.

Looking at the plans of the four floors of the Thorsen house, one can also begin to understand other distinctions between the served and servant halves of Greene and Greene houses (figs. 8, 9, 10, 11). There is considerable specialized plumbing in the kitchen, pantry, and laundry areas, for instance, and the family baths are consistently three-fixture units; however, in two areas, only a toilet or a toilet and a sink are provided for the staff, suggesting an expectation of sink-bathing or bowl-and-pitcher washing (as was common in Europe as well as in working-class urban and rural America at the time). The "man" in the "man's room," using the basement-level facility, and the chauffeur in the garage are provided with only rudimentary plumbing. The women on the attic floor share a three-unit bath; however, as in other Greene and Greene homes, this is marked as a service bath in its linear arrangement and 4 ½-feet (1.3-m) tub; tubs in the family bathrooms are 5 or 5 ½ feet (1.5 or 1.7 m) long. The Thorsen house plans also exhibit the characteristic array of specialized cupboards and shelving in the butler's pantry, kitchen, and other service rooms that made these areas highly efficient and orderly, as well as expensive to construct. These were work areas, and the expectation was that people in these spaces would be, generally, on the move, with the oven almost constantly in operation and generating heat. Perhaps for these reasons, at least

FIGURE 6
*Details of electric
fixtures, c. 1906,
Freeman A. Ford
house*

Courtesy of Charles Sumner
Greene Collection (1959-1),
Environmental Design
Archives, University of
California, Berkeley

one Greene and Greene commission, the Robert Pitcairn house of 1906, in Pasadena, is designed with no heating ducts in the kitchen area.[45]

The Thorsen house in Berkeley (see Bosley essay, fig. 4) differs from the Greene and Greene designs for Pasadena in that it has a servants' dining room. Usually the Greenes' plans provide only a "Screened Porch" as a sitting room for servants. In the Pasadena bungalows, is open-air area was also the site of household deliveries, a cool place to work, sometimes the location of laundry tubs, often the location of the icebox, and the point of access to the toilet for outside help. The interior placement and more specialized character of this room in Berkeley may be a function of the rawer winter weather in the north, but the location of the service side of the house directly on the property line also suggests that the "screening" function of a screen porch would have been insufficient so close to the street. We are reminded that the screens on the "Screened Porch" were not primarily about insects (as the family porches were not equipped with screens); rather, they were about vision.

That there were outsiders within the secure envelope of the "ultimate bungalows" is evident from the presence of locks on the doors, on the furniture, and, in at least one house, on the medicine cabinets.[46] We have the sense from one client that the Greene brothers were pressing her toward a more open plan, one that dispensed with the formalities of a reception room (where visitors were traditionally "parked" while the servant sought out the pertinent family member), a concept she resisted: "The sun room is to be a reception room and as such must be shut off. I have told you that all sorts of persons who are strangers to me, come and ask for me by name. The maid must not allow them to enter my living rooms. I have told you I had had things stolen in that way."[47] It is clear from such an exchange that the relative openness of the principal rooms of the Greene houses was a move toward both greater informality among peers and a culture of greater trust; yet the fact of disparate populations of visitors and different social classes in the "family" space is also clear.

The Greenes' clients were not exceptional in having live-in servants. In 1910, one in twelve American families had live-in help, in all, there were about 1.5 million domestic servants in the country.[48] Helen and Robert Lynd, in their classic study of Muncie, Indiana, published in 1929, calculated that for a family of five to live in "health and decency," it needed rent, food, fuel, clothing, insurance, union dues, and wages for a maid; they estimated that 30 percent of "Middletown's" families comfortably

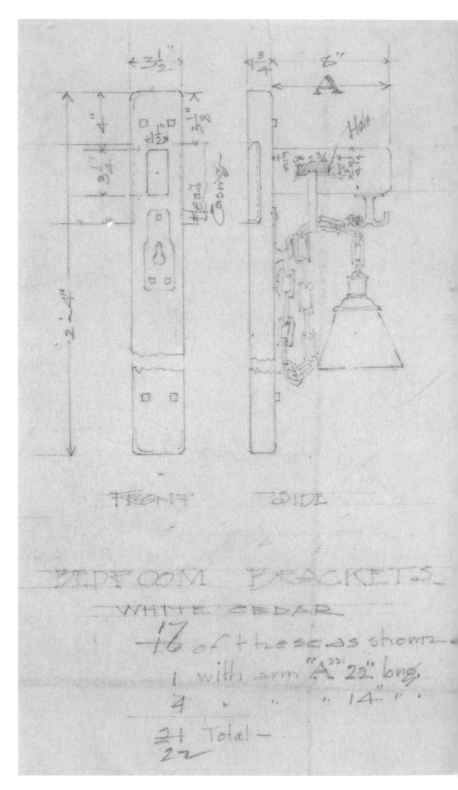

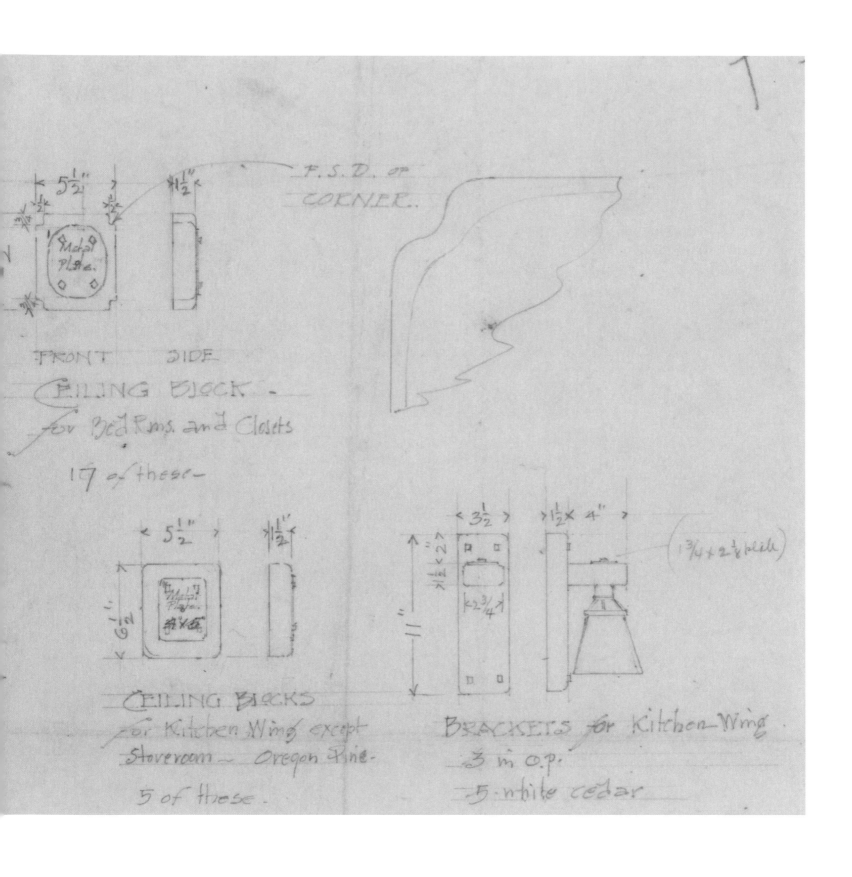

F.S.D. of
CORNER.

5½"   1½"

Metal
Plate.

FRONT   SIDE

CEILING BLOCK.

for Bed Rms. and Closets

17 of these.

5½"   1½"

6½"

Metal
Plate.
4" X 6"

CEILING BLOCKS

for Kitchen Wing except

Stoveroom – Oregon Pine.

5 of these.

3½"   1½" X 4"

11"   2"

2¾"

(1¾ + 2⅛ high)

BRACKETS for Kitchen Wing

3 in O.P.

5 white cedar

met this middle-class minimum.[49] In 1910, Charles Greene paid his maid $25 a month; Peter Hall billed $.25 an hour (or about $50 a month) for the labor of his (male) unskilled workmen and $.43¾ an hour (or $88 a month) for his skilled craftsmen.[50] Domestic servants were, in other words, relatively inexpensive, and as standard to the single-family middle-class home as administrative staff are in small businesses today. This system prevailed until the 1920s, when immigration restrictions and labor shortages associated with World War I raised the cost of such "help," and entry-level labor (culturally speaking) shifted from private homes to hotels, restaurants, and industrial farming, where it remains today.[51]

One singular design by Greene and Greene, the A.C. Brandt house of 1905 in Pasadena, does not show the consistent pattern of distinct served and servant spaces, coded in distinctive materials, room shapes, and finishes.[52] Rather, it is a working-class plan, treated as housing one rather than two social classes. The only staircase is a winder stair; the only bath is off the screened porch. The house's three equally sized bedrooms open directly from the living room, the dining room, and the kitchen, respectively, without any buffering hallways; and no pantry separates the dining room from the chatter, odors, and population of the kitchen. The plan of the Brandt house resembles those of prefabricated homes sold nationally by the Aladdin Company to large firms establishing company towns for their workers. Its inclusion of a bathroom puts it toward the upper end of the offerings of Aladdin, a company with a motto—"a housed labor supply is a controlled labor supply"—that clarifies both the motivation of presumed purchasers and the population expected to inhabit such structures.[53] Occupied by a contractor, the Brandt house is unique in the work of Greene and Greene and underlines the social distinctions so clearly built into their other, better-known houses, even their most modest middle-class homes. The praise lavished on the Greenes for evolving houses "freed from the tight formality of traditional plan forms" might better suit this uni-class home, adapted from plans contractor-builders had established for working-class families decades earlier than the "ultimate bungalows."[54]

Greene and Greene designed some very inexpensive houses; indeed, the firm was identified early on as creating homes of great beauty at low cost.[55] Many were not significantly more costly than other moderate buildings (Charles's Carmel studio, for instance, cost $2500 in 1923), but others were expensive (the Henry A. Ware house in Pasadena cost $15,000 in 1913), and some were extremely expensive (the Gamble house cost more than $80,000 in 1908, while the Cordelia Culbertson house in Pasadena cost more than $150,000 in 1911).[56] A key aspect of the Greenes' success was their versatility; a key aspect of their enduring reputation was their consistency.

Most commentary on the work of Greene and Greene focuses on their accomplishment of extraordinary design feats. Underlying this just praise is the appreciation all visitors feel, as they walk through the principal rooms of any of these houses, for the well-proportioned and interestingly shaped spaces, the rich character of the materials used, and the hand finish of those materials with finest-grained sandpaper. They sense, with Cram, that these are houses that "hang together." As they move from the front rooms, with their teak and mahogany overhead beams and intimate inglenooks, into the rectilinear maple and fir service areas lined with well-fitted cupboards and cabinets, they still feel surrounded by masterly design. But we are ill-equipped today to read the subtle material cues that would have signaled to the original inhabitants and visitors of these houses, as clearly and loudly as uniforms, the spheres of two tightly interlocked but disparate social groups. It is important to note that this design was simultaneously an expression of "revolutionary" ideas and comfortable status quo relationships.

Overall, the materials specified in Greene and Greene designs, and the firm's use of these materials, signal both the "contemporary" and the pre-modern; the brothers' work is a product both of California and of the global movement of design ideas, materials, and money. Like a touchstone, the œuvre of Greene and Greene reveals the concerns of its observers, and thus it is simultaneously "contemporary" and historicist, "revolutionary" and implacably wooden; it allows us to imagine a world of "simpler, freer and more abundant living" while partitioning that world explicitly into "haves" and "have-less-es." The Greenes exhort us to use our rich sensory resources to imagine a better, more abundant world than that we find in any other corner of the built environment, or, if truth be told, of the natural environment.

No.1 SIZE 13'6"×13'0" LIVINGROOM RUG FOR THE D.B. GAMBLE RESIDENCE. Chas. Sumner Greene
at Pasadena, Cal. U.S.A. Greene & Greene, Architects, Pasadena. del. 1908.

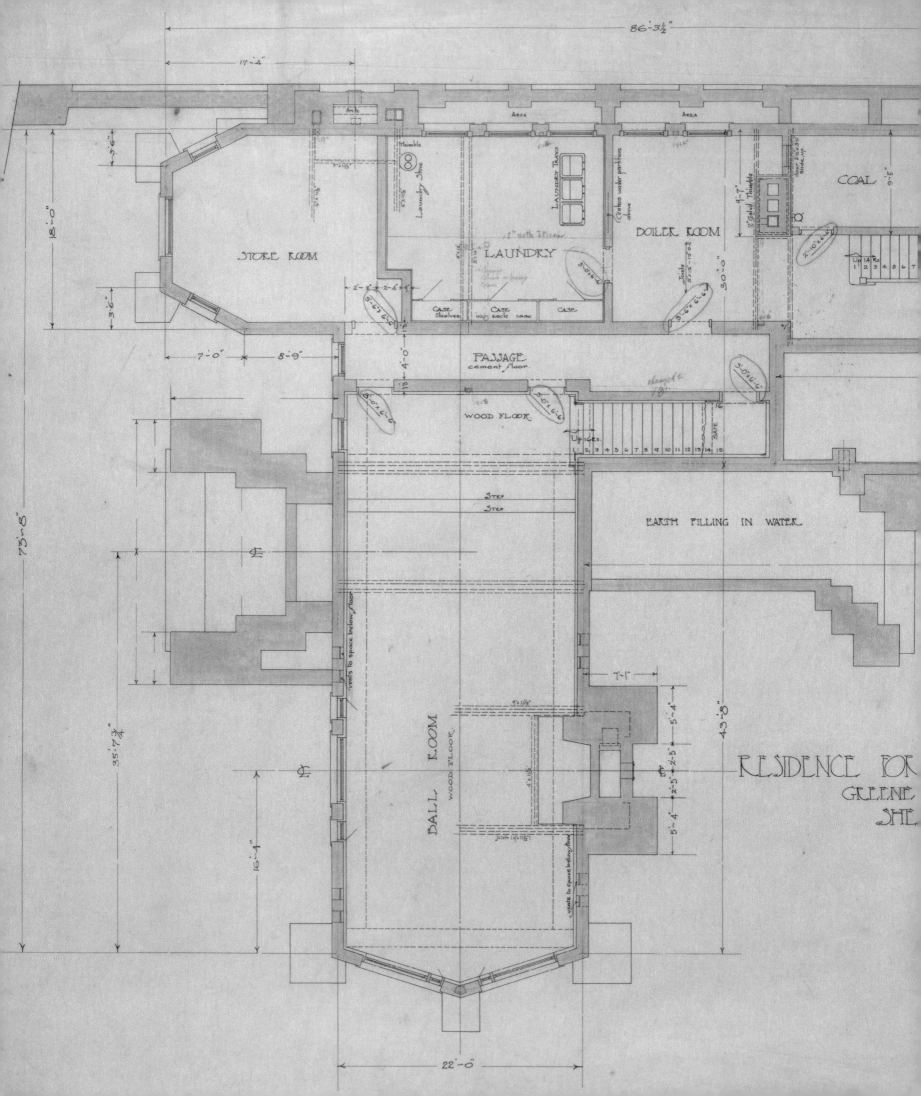

STORE ROOM

LAUNDRY

BOILER ROOM

COAL

PASSAGE
cement floor.

WOOD FLOOR.

EARTH FILLING IN WATER

BALL ROOM
wood floor.

RESIDENCE FOR

GREENE

SHE

86'-3½"

17'-4"

18'-0"

3'-6"

3'-6"

7'-0"

8'-9"

4'-0"

75'-8"

35'-7¾"

16'-4"

43'-8"

22'-0"

7'-1"

30'-0"

9'-7"

2'-6"

9'-0"

AREA

AREA

AREA

Thimble

Laundry Stove

LAUNDRY TRAYS

CASE
Shelves

CASE
iron each case

CASE

STEP

STEP

Up 16 Rs.
1 2 3 4 5 6 7 8 9 10 11 12 13 14 15

SAFE

Up 14 Rs
1 2 3 4 5 6 7

5'-4"

5'-4"

2'-5"

2'-5"

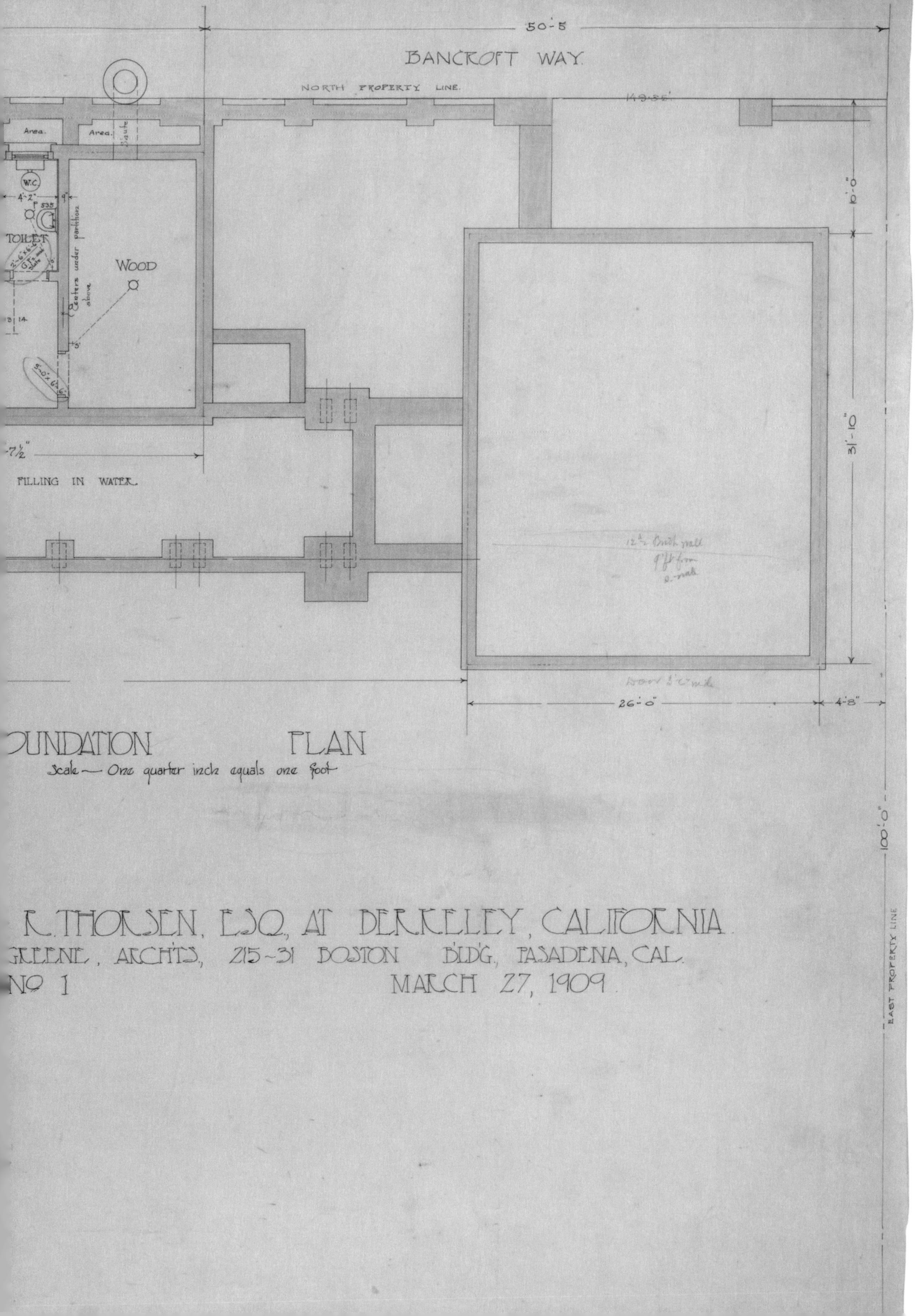

50'-5"

BANCROFT WAY

NORTH PROPERTY LINE.

149.35"

Area. Area.

W.C.

TOILET

WOOD

Gutters under partition above.

FILLING IN WATER.

12½" thick wall 9 ft from e-wall

6'-0"

31'-10"

26'-0"   4'-8"

100'-0"

FOUNDATION   PLAN

Scale— One quarter inch equals one foot

R. THORSEN, ESQ., AT BERKELEY, CALIFORNIA.
GREENE, ARCHTS, 215~31 BOSTON   BLD'G, PASADENA, CAL.
Nº 1   MARCH 27, 1909.

EAST PROPERTY LINE

FIGURE 8
*Foundation plan,
March 27, 1909,
William R. Thorsen
house*

Courtesy of Charles Sumner
Greene Collection (1959-1),
Environmental Design
Archives, University of
California, Berkeley

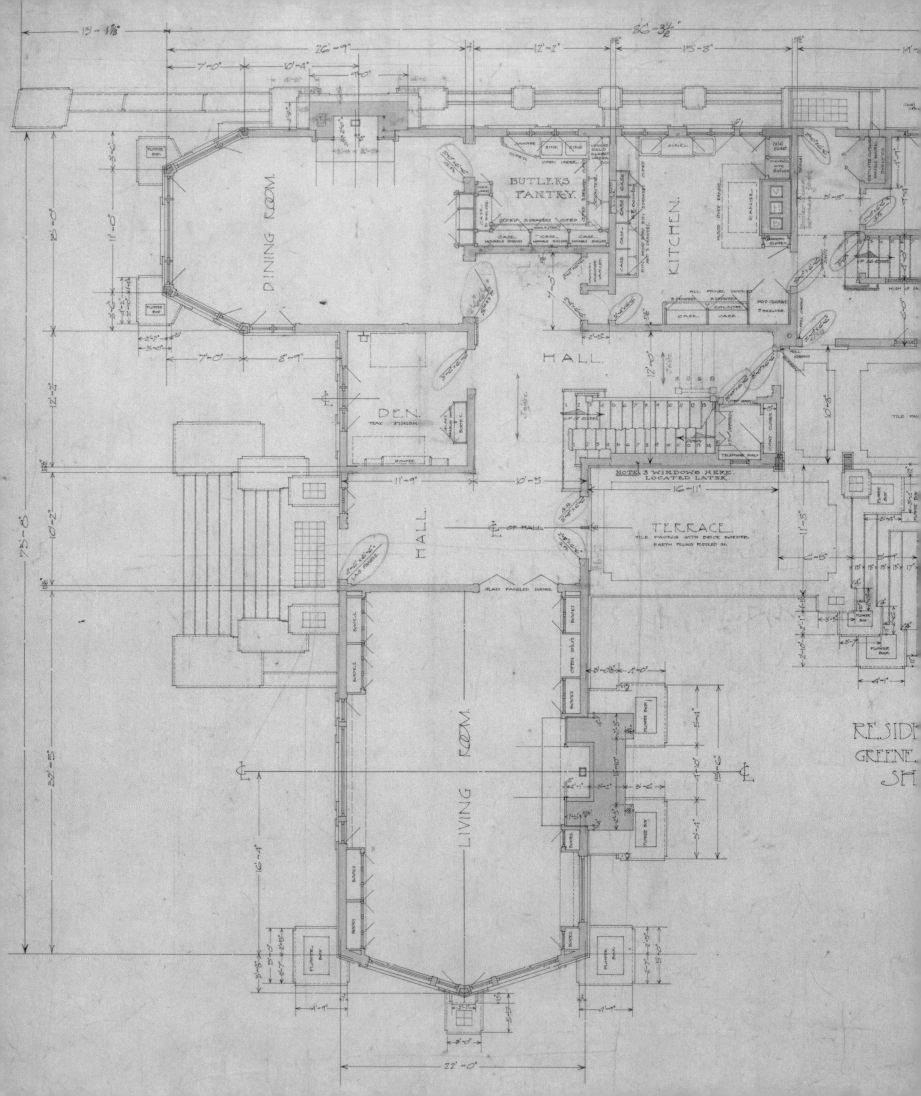

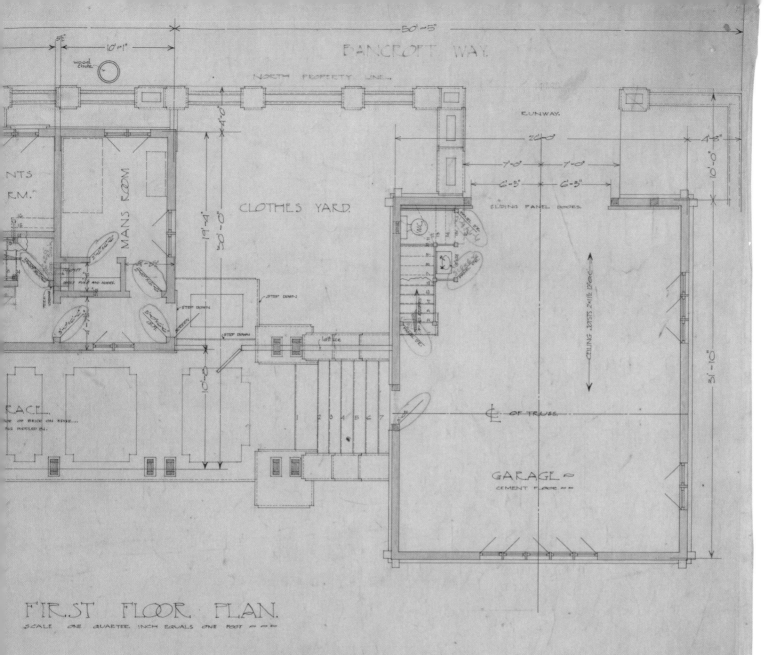

BANCROFT WAY

NORTH PROPERTY LINE

RUNWAY.

CLOTHES YARD.

MANS ROOM

SLIDING PANEL DOORS.

CEILING JOISTS 24×12 16"oc

CL OF TRUSS.

GARAGE
CEMENT FLOOR

FIRST FLOOR PLAN.
SCALE ONE QUARTER INCH EQUALS ONE FOOT

NOTE. ALL SASH TO OPEN OUT,
UNLESS MARKED "OPEN IN."

FOR WM. R. THORSEN ESQ. AT BERKELEY CALIF.
GREENE ARCH'TS, 215-31 BOSTON BLD'G, PASADENA CALIF
No. 2   MARCH 27th '09

FIGURE 9
*First-floor plan,
March 27, 1909,
William R. Thorsen
house*

Courtesy of Charles Sumner
Greene Collection (1959-1),
Environmental Design
Archives, University of
California, Berkeley

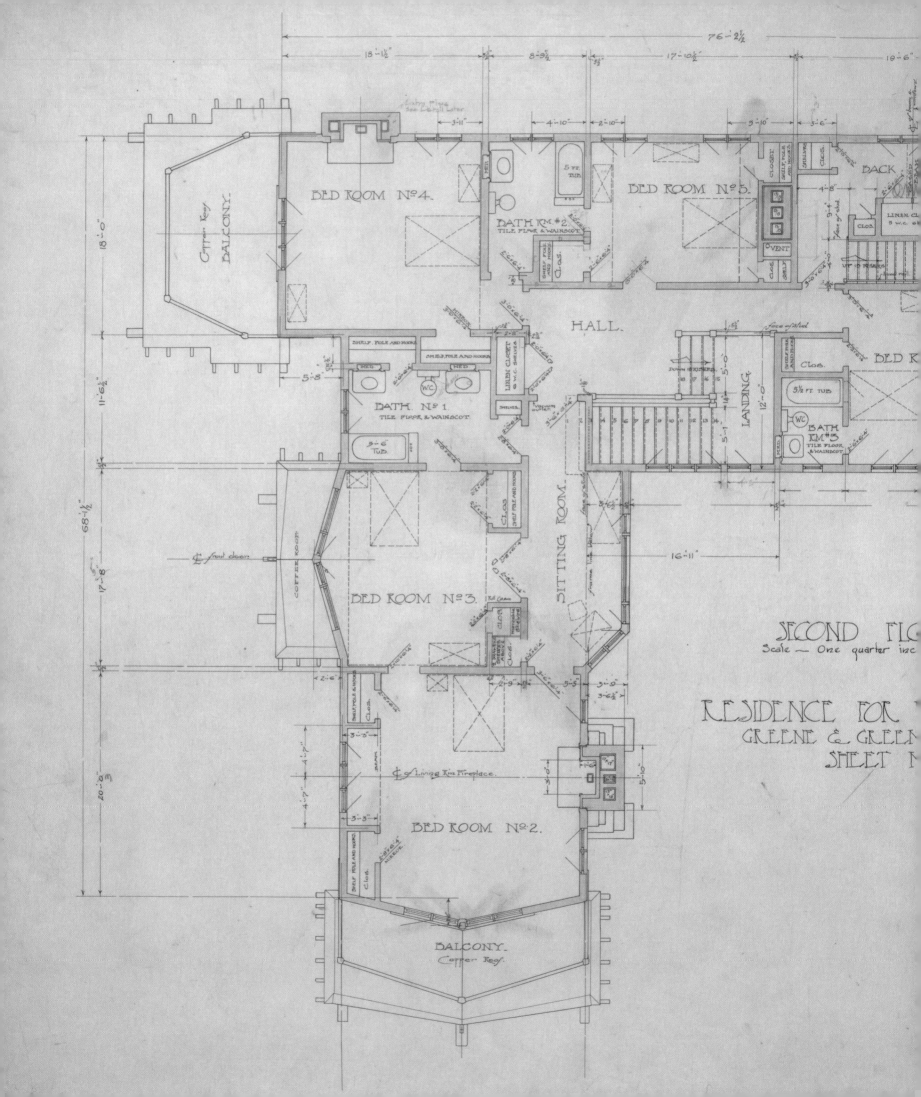

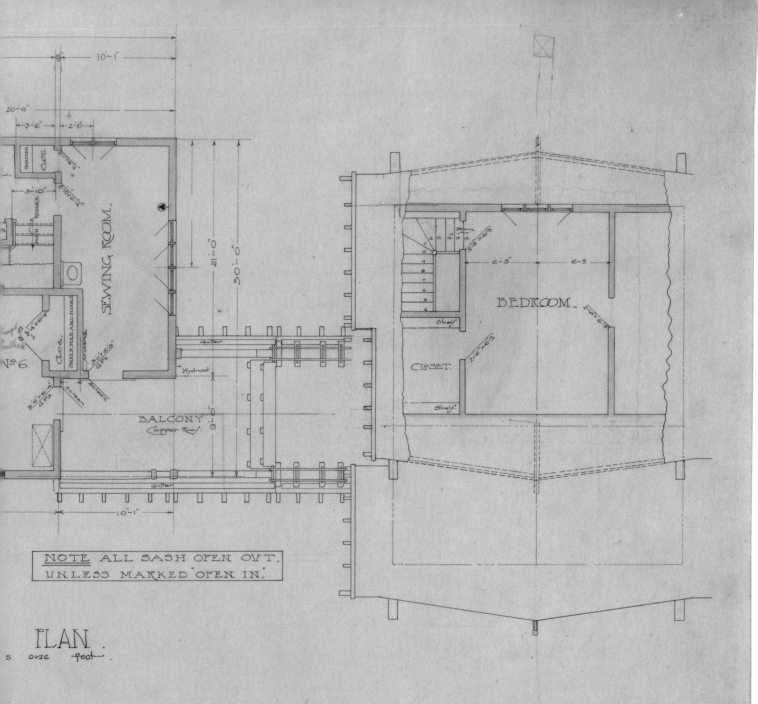

SEWING ROOM.

CLOS.

No. 6

BALCONY.
Copper Roof.

gutter

Hydrant

gutter

NOTE ALL SASH OPEN OUT,
UNLESS MARKED 'OPEN IN.'

BEDROOM.

CLOSET.

Shelf

Shelf

PLAN.
s one foot.

THORSEN, ESQ, AT BERKELEY, CALIFORNIA
RCHTS. 215-31 BOSTON BLD'G, PASADENA, CAL.
MARCH 27, 1909.

FIGURE 10
*Second-floor plan,
March 27, 1909,
William R. Thorsen
house*

Courtesy of Charles Sumner
Greene Collection (1959-1),
Environmental Design
Archives, University of
California, Berkeley

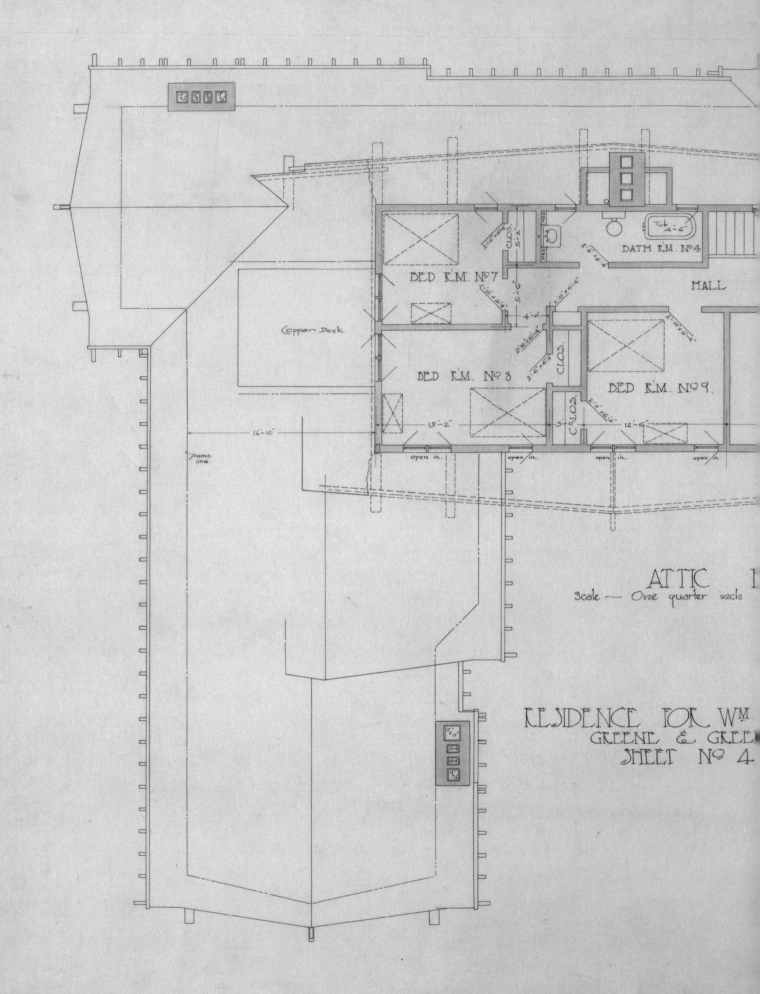

Copper Deck.

BED R.M. No 7

BED R.M. No 8

BED R.M. No 9.

CLOS.

CLOS.

CLOS.

CLOS.

BATH R.M. No 4

HALL

16'-10"

15'-2"

12'-6

frame line.

open in.   open in.   open in.   open in.

Tub 4'-6"

ATTIC

Scale — One quarter inch

RESIDENCE FOR Wm

GREENE & GREE

SHEET No 4

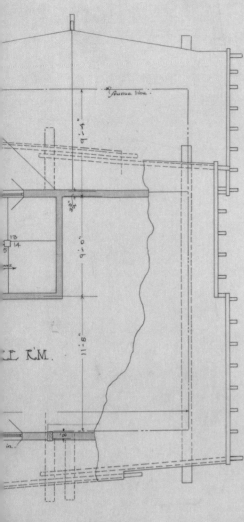

E. RM.

NOTE. ALL SASH OPEN OUT,
UNLESS MARKED 'OPEN IN.'

one foot

HORSEN, ESQ., AT BERKELEY, CALIFORNIA.
RCHTS, 215-31 BOSTON BLDG., PASADENA, CAL.
MARCH 27, 1909.

FIGURE II

Attic plan, March 27, 1909, William R. Thorsen house

Courtesy of Charles Sumner Greene Collection (1959-1), Environmental Design Archives, University of California, Berkeley

[page 109]

FIGURE 12

Living-room table, mahogany, ebony, and silver, 1912, Charles M. Pratt house

Private collection. Photograph courtesy of owner

The author wishes to thank Waverly Lowell and Miranda Hambro of the EDA, and also Paul Groth, Kathleen Moran, Richard Hutson, Ian Carmichael, Joe McBride, Edwin Harvey, and Linda Phipps for their assistance on aspects of this essay.

1. Ralph Adams Cram, *American Country Houses of Today* (New York: Architectural Book Publishing Co., 1913), pp. iv–v.
2. C.H. White, "Teakwood for Interior Decoration," *Architect and Engineer*, 24, no. 2 (March 1911), pp. 94–97.
3. A partial list of the materials Greene and Greene include in their specifications or indicate on their drawings includes the following:
Woods: ash, birch, black walnut, cedar (also white cedar and Port Harford [Orford] cedar), ebony, hickory, koa, lignum vitae, mahogany (also mahogany veneer on chestnut core), maple (also rock maple and white maple), oak (also quarter-sawn white oak, knurled white oak, and red oak), Oregon pine [Douglas fir], redwood (also curly redwood), southern red gum, sugar pine, teak (also Bermese [Burmese] teak), vermillion (both heartwood and sapwood).
Metals: brass, copper (also 16-oz. soft copper, copper bronze wire, copper wire, copper pins, and tinned 18-oz. copper), galvanized iron wire (also galvanized black wire), gold leaf, lead (also 4-lb. sheet lead), silver (also silver wire inlay and silver rivets), steel 2¼-in. bars (also steel 1½-in. bars, and locks), wrought-iron bars (also galvanized wrought iron, wrought-iron plates, cast iron, and porcelain enameled iron).
Glass: leaded art glass, leaded glass, cut-glass panels, plate glass, French plate mirror, plate mirror.
Ceramics: Grueby tiles, Rookwood tiles, white hexagonal floor tiles.
Masonry: Caen stone, Ishian stone, cobblestone, pink stone, clinker brick (also blue brick and old brick), marble (also Numidian marble, Benou Jaune marble, and Tavernelle marble), travertine.
Other: abalone, ivory, mother-of-pearl, turquoise.
4. "Felt under copper," plans for William R. Thorsen house, Berkeley, 1908–10, EDA; "heavy deadening felt under all oak," specifications for Jesse H. Payne house, Carmel, 1925, EDA.
5. Specifications for Mortimer Fleishhacker addition, 2418 Pacific Ave., San Francisco, after 1916, EDA.

6. Payne specifications, EDA.
7. Specifications for Mortimer Fleishhacker addition, Woodside, n.d., EDA, include "White or Port Harford [Orford] Cedar" for door panels. A White Brothers Lumber circular advertises "white cedar" as a "Pacific coast wood," Catalogues and Samples 1908–30, EDA. Of the three tree species known by this familiar name, only Port Orford cedar is a West Coast wood, and supplies of Atlantic white cedar were exhausted by 1900. See also specifications for Robert Pitcairn, Jr., house, Pasadena, 1906, EDA; drawings for Freeman A. Ford house, Pasadena, 1906–08, EDA; and specifications for Mary E. Cole house, Pasadena, 1906, EDA.
8. See, for instance, Cole specifications, EDA; Pitcairn specifications, EDA; and Thorsen plans, EDA.
9. *Masonry, Carpentry and Joinery* (Scranton, Pa.: International Library of Technology, International Textbook Co., 1899; repr. Chicago: Chicago Review Press, 1980), pp. 23–24.
10. Pitcairn specifications, EDA; drawings for Robert R. Blacker house, Pasadena, 1907, EDA; and Payne specifications, EDA.
11. Thorsen plans, EDA. According to White, "Teakwood," p. 94, "teak … is the only known wood that can be wet on one side and dry on the other without warp or decay." The teak front door, including leaded art glass, was evidently ordered separately.
12. *Masonry, Carpentry and Joinery*, p. 25; "F. S. D. [full-scale design] of Exercising Bar in Bedroom No. 2," Thorsen plans, EDA.
13. "Mah[ogany] Trim for Dining Room" drawn by E.L.B. for Matthew Bros Mfg Co., Milwaukee, Wis. 3/16/10, Thorsen plans, EDA. Elsewhere the architects direct the specifics of construction of built-in chests of drawers for the same house: "Screw from outside into dust panel from frames. Fix so that sides will shrink towards front of case," Thorsen plans, EDA.
14. Randell L. Makinson, *Greene & Greene: Architecture as a Fine Art* (Salt Lake City: Peregrine Smith, 1977), pp. 26–27.
15. *Ibid.*, p. 32; Correspondence with Vendors, 1904, EDA; and EDA folder 43: design for an Exhibition Building for the Southern Pine Association, New Orleans, LA, 1916. Two of the Greenes' most important clients were in the lumber business, William

R. Thorsen and Robert R. Blacker (Makinson, *Architecture as a Fine Art*, p. 209); newsletters and sales lists from White Brothers Hardwood Headquarters, San Francisco, are among Charles Greene's papers, EDA.
16. See fig. 2; "copper caps" on balcony uprights, North Elevation, Henry K. Bradley house, 1910, EDA; and "14 inch copper caps" on the upright posts of the balcony rail at the Thorsen house, West Elevation, EDA.
17. Invoice from Hall Manufacturing Co. to CSG, November 30, 1914, Receipts 1908–44, EDA.
18. "Itemized Report of Gamble Furniture Billed," November 30, 1908–January 1, 1910, EDA.
19. Cram, *American Country Houses*, p. iv.
20. Gustav Stickley, *The Craftsman*, 22, no. 5 (August 1912), as quoted in Makinson, *Architecture as a Fine Art*, p. 212.
21. AIA Special Citation (1952), GGA.
22. Reyner Banham, "Introduction," in Makinson, *Architecture as a Fine Art*, pp. 12–23.
23. Cashbook 1909–41, EDA.
24. *Ibid.*; letter from CSG to Pasadena rug merchant Haigag H. Khazoyan, February 27, 1926, about the use of his studio, EDA. Makinson describes 1916–27 as Charles Greene's "lean period" (*Architecture as a Fine Art*, p. 241), but his cashflow was excellent.
25. Cashbook 1909–41, EDA; and Virginia Dart Greene Hales (ed.), *The Memoirs of Henry Dart Greene and Ruth Elizabeth Haight Greene* (La Jolla, Calif.: Virginia Dart Greene Hales, 1996), I, p. 19.
26. Trademark/Copyright 1913, EDA.
27. On the importation of books, see Cashbook 1909–41, EDA.
28. For central vacuum system, see Thorsen plans, EDA; and Bradley plans, EDA. For an instance of indirect lighting, see the Mary M. Kew house, San Diego, 1912–13 (Makinson, *Architecture as a Fine Art*, p. 210). In 1907, only 8 percent of American residences were wired for electricity. Thomas Schlereth, "Conduits and Conduct: Home Utilities in Victorian America, 1876–1915," in *American Home Life, 1880–1930: A Social History of Spaces and Services*, ed. Jessica H. Foy and Thomas J. Schlereth (Knoxville: University of Tennessee Press, 1992), p. 233.
29. Blueprints for the Cordelia A. Culbertson house, Pasadena, 1911–13, EDA.

30. Ebony footstool designed for Mary J. Moore, 1930, University of Southern California, on loan to the Huntington Library. Harvey Ellis was the other designer of this era who used metal inlays, a practice rarely found in American furniture, although used by some urban shops of the Empire period.
31. Makinson, *Architecture as a Fine Art*, p. 222. In a detail drawing of the Thorsen house chimney, EDA, every course of brick is noted.
32. Thorsen plans, EDA.
33. CSG, handwritten notes on conversation with Mrs. David Gamble, n.d., EDA.
34. Specifications of the F.W. Hawks house, Pasadena, 1906, EDA; "F. S. Details of Ceiling Lights …," Thorsen plans, EDA; and "F. S. Central Lantern," Thorsen plans, EDA.
35. Banham, "Introduction," in Makinson, *Architecture as a Fine Art*, p. 18.
36. Fleishhacker addition specifications, 2418 Pacific, EDA; Payne specifications, EDA; and furniture for Mrs. Dudley P. Allen, 1917, EDA.
37. Quoted in J.M. Guinn, *A History of California and an Extended History of Its Southern Counties* (Los Angeles.: Historic Record Co., 1907), II, pp. 540–41, as quoted in Makinson, *Architecture as a Fine Art*, p. 160.
38. CSG, "California Home Making," *Pasadena Daily News*, January 2, 1905, p. 27, quoted in Makinson, *Architecture as a Fine Art*, p. 148.
39. For pronounced living-room inglenooks, see also the Philip L. Auten house of 1903, Pasadena; the Samuel P. Sanborn house of 1903, Pasadena; the Martha, Violet, and Jane White house of 1903, Pasadena; the Jennie A. Reeve houses of 1903–04, Long Beach; the Cora C. Hollister house of 1904–05, Hollywood; the Adelaide A. Tichenor house of 1904–05, Long Beach; the Josephine Van Rossem house of 1905–06, Pasadena; the Mary E. Cole house of 1906–07, Pasadena; and the Freeman A. Ford house of 1906–08, Pasadena. For diamond-paned casements, see fig. 3; and Fleishhacker house, Woodside, North Elevation, EDA. For settles, see the Kate A. White house of 1904, Pasadena; and the Louise T. Halsted house of 1905, Pasadena.
40. CSG, "California Home Making," p. 28.
41. Letter from Fred Harvey office, Albuquerque, to CSG, July 1 [1904],

EDA. Harvey (1835–1901) built hotels, restaurants, and souvenir shops along the railroads in the Southwest.

42. Pitcairn specifications, EDA; see also Payne specifications, EDA.

43. For door dimensions, see listing of doors ordered for Thorsen house, EDA.

44. "Pushes shall be Midget with [mother of] pearl buttons, except rear door, which shall be Standard," electric wiring specifications for Charles S. Witbeck house, Santa Monica, 1917, EDA.

45. Pitcairn house, blueprint for foundation floor, EDA.

46. "Lock[ing] Med[icine] Case" noted in two baths, Fleishhacker house, Woodside, EDA; "Locks for all doors and drawers" noted on

drawing of a secretary for the Cordelia Culbertson house, EDA. For a discussion of locks, see Faye E. Dudden, *Serving Women: Household Service in Nineteenth-Century America* (Middletown, Conn.: Wesleyan University Press, 1983), pp. 177–78.

47. Letter from Adelaide Tichenor to CSG, September 27, 1905, quoted in Makinson, *Architecture as a Fine Art*, p. 99.

48. Daniel E. Sutherland, "Modernizing Domestic Service," in Foy and Schlereth, *American Home Life*, p. 245; and Ruth Schwartz Cowan, "Coal Stoves and Clean Sinks: Housework between 1890 and 1930," in *ibid.*, p. 215.

49. Robert S. Lynd and Helen Merrell Lynd, *Middletown: A Study in American*

Culture (New York: Harcourt Brace, 1929), pp. 84, 169–70, as cited in Cowan, "Coal Stoves," p. 213.

50. Cashbook 1909–41, EDA; invoice from Peter Hall to CSG, June 21, 1911, Receipts 1908–44, EDA.

51. Cowan, "Coal Stoves," p. 215.

52. For the Brandt house plan, see Makinson, *Architecture as a Fine Art*, p. 111. For a discussion of workers' housing, see Paul Groth, "Workers' Houses in West Oakland," in *Sights and Sounds: Essays in Celebration of West Oakland*, ed. Suzanne Stewart and Mary Praetzell (Rohnert Park, Calif.: Anthropological Studies Center of Sonoma State University, 1997), pp. 53–57.

53. Scott Erbes, "Manufacturing and Marketing the American Bungalow:

The Aladdin Co., 1906–20," in *The American Home: Material Culture, Domestic Space, and Family Life*, ed. Eleanor McD. Thompson (Winterthur, Del.: Henry Francis du Pont Winterthur Museum, 1998), pp. 46, 49, 54.

54. Makinson singles out the hall-less Arturo Bandini house of 1903 in Pasadena as the breakthrough design, *Architecture as a Fine Art*, p. 70.

55. Una Nixson Hopkins, "A Study for Home-Builders," *Good Housekeeping*, March 1906, quoted in Makinson, *Architecture as a Fine Art*, p. 68.

56. By comparison, prefabricated Aladdin bungalows cost $313 to $1578 (plus the costs of foundation and erection on site) in 1916 (Erbes, "Manufacturing," p. 49).

EDWARD S. COOKE, JR.

An International Studio:
The Furniture Collaborations of the
Greenes and the Halls

The furniture designed by Charles and Henry Greene has long fascinated those who have seen it firsthand. On his visit to Pasadena in January 1909, the British designer C.R. Ashbee went to the workshops of John and Peter Hall, where much of the Greenes' furniture was made, and saw some of the pieces being produced for the David B. Gamble house. Ashbee praised it as "the best and most characteristic furniture I have seen in this country," noting in particular the "supreme feeling for the material" and "exquisite dowelling and pegging" that decorated it.[1] However, at that time, few people actually got to experience the Greenes' furniture. As custom-made work for specific homes, their furniture remained relatively unknown, appreciated largely by a small circle of original clients and their families.

Only with the renewed interest in the Arts and Crafts movement during the 1970s did a broader public in California and throughout America have the opportunity to see Greene and Greene furniture in person. Early in the decade, several exhibitions featured the Greenes' work, and in 1979, Randell Makinson published his seminal *Greene & Greene: Furniture and Related Designs*.[2] At the same time, the direct forms, sensuous materials, and visible craftsmanship resonated with studio furniture makers who valued technical virtuosity and the refined use of wood. Such California studio furniture makers as Alan Marks, Philip O'Leno, and Morris Sheppard saw the Greenes' designs firsthand and drew inspiration from them to develop their own style of "fine furniture."[3] Public awareness and the emergence of makers able to work in a Greene and Greene idiom, either crafting reproductions or adapting their approach to new forms, such as entertainment centers or bathroom vanities, spawned a Greene and Greene revival. The attraction of the Greenes' furniture remains strong to this day; clients ranging from the readers of *Style 1900* to the Walt Disney Company eagerly call for Greene and Greene–style furniture, and makers from David Hellman in the Northeast to Thomas Stangeland in the Northwest and James

Ipekjian in California meet the demand. The furniture of early twentieth-century Pasadena retains its value as the ultimate balance of craftsmanship and design and has emerged as an Arts and Crafts brand.[4]

The marketplace and scholarship have canonized the Greenes in the last forty years and developed a narrative that charts the seemingly inevitable evolution of their particular genius. The allure of their furniture prompts us to explore how Greene and Greene actually developed their specific philosophy and vocabulary, why the designs were so successful at the time of their creation, and why they continue to resonate today. As we know more about the design arts of this period, it is possible to place the brothers within a larger international context, to recognize their dependence on skilled artisanal collaborators, and to chart how they responded to certain trends or opportunities. It is a complex but telling chapter in furniture history that demonstrates how furniture can embody and reveal communication systems and cultural values, both at the time of its creation and throughout its existence.

Many scholars have attributed the Greenes' affinity to furniture making and craftsmanship to their education at Calvin M. Woodward's Manual Training School in their hometown of St. Louis. During the 1880s, when the Greenes attended the school, manual training did not teach specific trades or a complete set of skills but rather acquainted students with industrial processes, developed some proficiency with tools, and provided a base of technical literacy. Instructors used a series of small discrete exercises to expand the students' broad technical knowledge and eye for pleasing details and proportions. Thus the Greenes would have gained a general introduction to a variety of subjects, such as carpentry, woodturning, forge work, and machine tools, but they did not master the art of cabinetmaking and thus did not possess the requisite abilities to make anything but extremely simple furniture. The basic level of their expertise can be seen in the table that Charles made as a wedding present for his wife in about 1901 (fig. 2). It is comprised of stock

FIGURE 1
Detail of living room, Laurabelle A. Robinson house, Pasadena, 1905–06

Courtesy of Charles Sumner Greene Collection (1959-1), Environmental Design Archives, University of California, Berkeley

FIGURE 2
*Table, Douglas fir,
cedar, oak, mahogany,
and birch, designed
and constructed by
Charles Greene
during his
engagement to Alice
Gordon White, c. 1900*
Courtesy of Guardian
Stewardship. Photograph
courtesy of Sotheby's
New York

molding and readily available boards and veneers and is assembled with glue and nails. More than actual cabinet-making skills, manual training provided the Greenes with a basis for the appreciation of and curiosity about craftsmanship.[5]

In 1901 and 1902, probably as the result of Charles's honeymoon, his August visit to the Pan-American International Exposition in Buffalo on the return trip home, and the brothers' awareness of new design ideas through such shelter magazines as *The Craftsman*, the Greenes began to develop an interest in the tenets of the Arts and Crafts movement: the integration of interior furnishings with architecture, the use of natural materials honestly wrought and expressed, and an emphasis on craftsmanship. Previously the brothers designed Queen Anne–style houses that were furnished by the clients in a cluttered Victorian fashion, but in 1902, for the James Culbertson house, they undertook the decoration themselves, turning to such commercially available furnishings as Gustav Stickley furniture, Rookwood and Tiffany ceramics, and Navajo rugs (see Mallek essay, fig. 7). At this time, the Greenes acted more as decorators than designers.[6]

In early 1903, the Greenes tried their hand at designing furniture for their interior spaces. For the living room of a house for Charles's three sisters-in-law,

the White sisters, the brothers designed an oak settee and an oak-and-cedar tea table (fig. 3). Both pieces reveal their indebtedness to the structural style of Gustav Stickley (1858–1942). For the table, the reliance on the figure of ring-porous oak for rough, authentic surface decoration, the thick-dimensioned stock of the straight legs and the top's frame, and the proud pegs of the mortise-and-tenon joinery are all derived from the Stickley vocabulary. The Greenes' interest in the Stickley style is also evident in their illustrations of a domestic interior published in 1903 in the British journal *Academy Architecture*. During this period, it seems that Stickley and his journal *The Craftsman* held the greatest influence on the Greenes.[7]

Two commissions of 1903 and 1904 for houses in Long Beach, the Jennie A. Reeve house and the Adelaide A. Tichenor house, reveal that the Greenes built upon the Stickley furniture vocabulary and began to design full interiors, including suites of furniture, built-in sideboards, stained-glass windows, and electrical lighting, all designed to fit in with the paneling and woodwork. A desk for the Tichenor house is particularly close to Stickley work (fig. 4); the two slab sides with a fall-front writing surface over heavily battened doors borrow from one of Stickley's earliest designs. The butterfly splines on the sides of the desk, the protruding tenons and pegs of the Reeve bureau and Tichenor easy chair, the

FIGURE 3
Tea table, oak and cedar, Martha, Violet, and Jane White house, Pasadena, 1903
Courtesy of Guardian Stewardship. Photograph courtesy of Sotheby's New York

over-engineered rectilinearity of the Reeve sideboard, and the solidity of the Tichenor living-room chairs with upholstered leather seats and a series of thin vertical splats all underscore the influence of Craftsman prototypes. However, some of the joinery on the work of this period falls short of the Craftsman ideal. On the Tichenor chairs, the side and rear seat rails are simply let into a dado, and the side and front rails are mitered around rabbeted front legs (see Mallek essay, fig. 10). Even with the additional reinforcement of stretchers, these joints do not withstand the pressures of seating. The Greenes' furniture of this time was probably made by an as-yet-unknown Pasadena millwork shop more accustomed to interior finish work.[8]

The Tichenor work reflected the Stickley aesthetic, but it also revealed new ideas, particularly the influence of Asia. The Greenes' designs incorporated many features from Japanese architecture, derived from Charles's copy of Edward S. Morse's *Japanese Homes and Their Surroundings* (1886) and from his visit, at the urging of Mrs. Tichenor, to the Japanese pavilions at the Louisiana Purchase Exposition in St. Louis in July 1904. The cloud-lift motif seen on the drawer pulls of the case furniture and the stepped edges of boards and rails suggest that Charles had been exposed to Chinese designs as well. The cloud lift is an abstraction of the humpback stretchers found on chairs and small tables of the Ming and Qing periods, and the stepping of board edges was a familiar technique for lightening the aprons of Chinese tables. Stickley used similar cloud-lift details on his "Tokio" plant stands (fig. 5; see also Mallek essay, fig. 9), which were illustrated in his catalogue of 1900 and exhibited at the world's fair in Buffalo in 1901.[9]

While the Greenes may have been initially inspired by the Stickley interpretation of Chinese furniture, physical evidence suggests that they also had access to real Chinese examples; they began to use housed mortise-and-tenon joints, explore the visual effects of mitered joints, and adapt elements of simple Ming-style furniture. At a time when most Westerners eagerly sought and collected carved and lacquered Chinese furniture and when displays at world's fairs emphasized such elaborate work, the Greenes seem to have had the opportunity to examine less common plainer examples firsthand. Some local Pasadena dealers in Asian art, such as Grace Nicholson, sold porcelains and textiles, but they did not seem to show any furniture. It is unclear whether the dealer John Bentz, who hired the Greenes to design a commercial block in 1901 and a home in 1905, carried any furniture, but Fong See's shop, F. Suie One, began to

sell Chinese furniture in downtown Los Angeles and Pasadena in 1902. It may have been Fong See who opened the Greenes' eyes to Chinese furniture. From 1904 on, their designs reveal a sophisticated knowledge of Chinese examples; at the same time, the brothers occasionally placed authentic Chinese furniture in their clients' houses. Charles even used some Chinese pieces in his Carmel studio.[10]

Stickley continued to be the dominant influence in the furniture the Greenes designed from 1904 through early 1906. The sideboard of Douglas fir for the Bentz house in Pasadena (1905) showcases the resinous tangential figure of the native conifer and features a thick top through-tenoned into the substantial sides and wedged; battens are screwed on to the door fronts as in the Tichenor desk. A similar use of pine can be found in the kitchen cabinets and living-room settee designed for Caroline de Forest in the spring of 1906 and in the dining-room sideboard and hall case for Josephine Van Rossem of the same period. For the Edgar Camp bungalow in late 1904, the Greenes designed a desk that featured a new type of carcass construction. While the fall-front writing surface and desk compartments closely follow

FIGURE 6
*Living room,
Laurabelle A.
Robinson house*

Courtesy of Charles Sumner
Greene Collection (1959-1),
Environmental Design
Archives, University of
California, Berkeley

FIGURE 7
*Living-room
secretary, mahogany,
1906, Laurabelle A.
Robinson house*

Courtesy of The Gamble
House, University of
Southern California.
Photograph © Ognen
Borissov/Interfoto

Stickley prototypes, and the faceted door pulls resemble those on the Reeve furniture, the sides were attached to the top and bottom with finger joints, a millshop's version of a dovetailed carcass.[11]

In the latter half of 1906, the Greenes' furniture assumed a very different character. In October, they began to design pieces for the Laurabelle A. Robinson house (fig. 6). While the entry hall featured railings and a shoe bench very much in the mode of the Tichenor designs and the den contained a red oak settee and writing table as well as a library table with a flat-wedged through-tenoned stretcher, the living room and dining room were distinguished by differences in form, materials, and cabinetmaking. Unlike the ahistorical modern work of Stickley, the Robinson designs were based on historical examples, such as Chinese Ming-style chairs, Anglo-American Neo-classical sideboards, and Empire-style leafed pedestal tables. The grace of this historicism was emphasized by thin-dimensioned verticals and softened, modeled edges. The primary show wood was mahogany, a material preferred by cabinetmakers for its good weight-to-strength ratio, few imperfections, consistent grain structure, suitability for shaping, and capacity to take an even finish. Whereas oak and ash were rough and authentic, mahogany was smooth and refined. Finally, the Robinson furniture displays a more technically sophisticated approach to workmanship: the dining-room armchairs feature splined miter joints at the juncture of the arms and front posts; the living-room desk consists of a mitered carcass with well-fit doors and drawers and with well-modeled pulls in a Chinese style (fig. 7); the sideboards incorporate inlaid decoration; and all the pieces have rounded edges and smooth oiled finishes with no visible tool marks. The technical foundation of the

furniture for these two rooms was accomplished cabinetmaking rather than self-conscious craftsmanship."[12]

From late 1906 onward, Greene and Greene furniture remained at this high level of refinement. The William T. Bolton house, for which the Greenes designed furniture in March 1907, included such early American forms as a gateleg table and dining chairs with pierced slats in their backs. The Stickley-influenced rectilinear dining table, with thin secondary stiles echoing the legs, and the tall-back hall chairs relate closely to the contemporary designs of Charles Rennie Mackintosh and Frank Lloyd Wright (figs. 8 and 9). The Bolton commission also marks the Greenes' earliest use of square ebony plugs to cover pinned joints and to provide a contrasting color. The Greenes' conception of suites, whether the Anglo arrangement of the dining room or the Chinese use of a tall hall table flanked by a pair of chairs, also suggests a wide-ranging awareness of historical design.[13]

Many scholars have focused on the innate design genius of the Greenes and attributed this change in their approach to the development and natural maturation of their own vision. Evolving aesthetics, however, cannot fully account for what happened after 1906. The Robinson living-room and dining-room furniture embodied a whole new structural logic. It was fundamentally different from the inside out, from the forms, to the technical means to carry out the intended design, to the final appearance. Such a dramatic change did not take place in the minds of the architects or on their drawing boards, but rather on the shop floor. For the Robinson house furniture, the Greenes worked exclusively with the brothers Peter Hall (1867–1939) and John Hall (1864–1940), both of whom had been previously employed by a millwork firm known as the Pasadena Manufacturing Company.

Although Peter had started up his own contracting business in 1902 and worked for the Greenes on the architectural renovation of the Tod Ford, Sr., house in 1905, John remained as a foreman for the Pasadena Manufacturing Company until late 1906, when he joined his brother in business in a recently expanded 5000-square-foot (465-sq.-m) shop with a gas-powered line shaft on South Raymond Avenue in Pasadena. The furniture for the Robinson and Bolton houses embodies a distinctive craftsmanship characterized by millwork preparation and joinery, and highly skilled handwork fitting, decorating, and finishing.[14]

With trusted, skilled collaborators in place, the Greenes and Halls were able to respond to a series of extraordinary clients from 1907 through 1913, producing more than four hundred pieces of furniture. During this period, they designed and furnished complete houses in which each room had a distinct aesthetic identity and a specific group of furniture forms with unifying ornament. The roots of this approach to total design can be found in Charles Greene's annotations in the periodical *International Studio*, which suggest a great interest in German design philosophy in the early twentieth century. In an issue from 1901, an extensive discussion of the artists' colony at Darmstadt highlighted the work of German painter-turned-designer Peter Behrens (1868–1940). For Behrens, the practical pleasurable object was neither totally functional nor simply decorative but blended elements of both utility and beauty into a form of aestheticized structure. Behrens was the most publicized early practitioner of *Gesamtkunstwerk*, the

integration of architecture and interior furnishing to create a harmonious whole. He was interested not only in providing a coherent look to the furniture, textiles, metalwork, and tableware in a single room, but also in developing a series of distinctive coherent spaces. To create intimate domesticity for his house at Darmstadt, Behrens developed a different feel for each room: the music room had gray-stained maple furniture decorated with intarsia and inlay, walls faced with gray and pink marble, and a gilded ceiling; the dining room featured japanned work;[15] the drawing-room paneling and furniture were executed in yellowish birchwood; plain elm decorated the library; and polished lemonwood fitted out the lady's bedroom. A later review of an Arts and Crafts exhibition of 1904 in Dresden provided additional insight into the tenets of the German approach: the artist/designer supervises the construction of his designs, the entire piece of furniture is constructed in one shop, and nothing is done speculatively. The interest in developing a different coherent aesthetic in each room, the close involvement of the architect, and the focus on the art of building characterized the Greenes' work after 1906.[16]

While the German approach provided the philosophical basis for the Greenes, little of their work resembles the designs of Behrens or his Viennese contemporary Josef Hoffmann. For most of the specifics of their furniture vocabulary, the Greenes continued to draw inspiration from Stickley, Japanese architecture, and Chinese furniture (seen most clearly in the horse-hoof feet of the Blacker entry-hall furniture; fig. 10), as well as from three other European sources. Charles

FIGURE 8

Hall table and chair, mahogany, 1907, Dr. W.T. Bolton house, Pasadena, 1906

Courtesy of Guardian Stewardship. Photograph © Ognen Borissov/Interfoto

FIGURE 9

Dining room, Dr. W.T. Bolton house

Courtesy of Charles Sumner Greene Collection (1959-1), Environmental Design Archives, University of California, Berkeley

highlighted an article of 1901 on furniture produced at the Royal School of Art Craftsmanship in Prague. The writer praised a stained oak chest and several other forms "for the simplicity of their general lines and angles and the effectiveness of their decoration, consisting generally of inlaid wood of various colors." Another article marked by Charles was a feature of 1902 on the designs of the Scots James Salmon and J. Gaff Gillespie, who carefully blended together "originality of treatment and new combinations of orthodox features with a wholesome obedience to precedent and to the restraining influences of the classical idea ... and the reticent use of decorative detail always subservient to the whole effect." The accompanying illustrations showcase many elements found in the Greenes' interiors: entrance doors with multiple stained-glass lights, fireplaces with tiles around a small firebox, plasterwork ceilings, extensive wood paneling, and integral settees with dovetail keys keeping backboards together. This sort of plain British vernacular work, more than the more flamboyant designs of Mackintosh or M.H. Baillie Scott, caught the Greenes' attention. Although Charles did not mark the volume of *International Studio* with an article on the German Pavilion at the St. Louis fair of 1904, there is strong material evidence that Richard Riemerschmid also inspired the Greenes. The Director's Room that Riemerschmid designed for the German Pavilion was somewhat restrained, but his reception room of 1903 for Carl Thieme's urban villa in Munich bears a striking connection to the work of the Greenes from late 1906 onward. The richly integrated elements and simple furniture forms share a similar spirit with the Pasadena work, but the most compelling feature of the Thieme suite was the somewhat random application of inlaid squares to conceal screwed joinery and provide surface ornament. It is Riemerschmid's lyrical free patterning, more than Hoffmann's rigid geometry, that seems to have inspired the Greenes' use of square ebony plugs to cover screw holes and to provide rhythmic decoration.[17]

The Greenes' furniture for Robert R. Blacker (1909), David B. Gamble (1908–09), Freeman Ford (1908–09), William R. Thorsen (1909–10), Charles M. Pratt (1910–12), and Cordelia Culbertson (1912–13) manifests a Behrens-like notion of unified aesthetics as well as the mature woodworking systems of the Hall shop. The most notable change is in the sophistication of the chairs, which are no longer shoddily constructed, as in the Tichenor furniture. The chairs for these houses often include compound curves in the shaping of the crest rails, elaborate wood and metal inlays, low-relief

carving, sinuous arms, and leg sections that are rarely rectangular (resulting in complex angles where seat rails and stretchers are joined to the legs). Rather than displaying the Stickley Craftsman idiom of the earlier work, many of these chairs seem descended from historical examples of the mid-eighteenth-century Georgian style. Even the Morris-type chair of the Blacker hall and the more unusual boxed wing chair of the Ford living room are rendered in a refined vernacular manner. The complexity and resolution of these pieces suggest an accomplished, experienced chair maker who was able to accommodate some of the Greenes' motifs.[18]

Case furniture made during the years of the "ultimate bungalows" is also distinctive. In the Pratt living room, a suite of mahogany furniture, including a *tour de force* fall-front desk, features a common decorative approach: fruitwood inlay, inlaid silver wire in a wavy pattern (fig. 11), and smoothed ebony pegs to cover countersunk screws or provide visual rhythm. Typical of the Halls' cabinetmaking was the concern for efficient, practical joinery and the accommodation of the expansion and contraction of wooden boards owing to changes in humidity. In the process of assembling the paneled carcass, they did not fit intersecting parts in the same flush plane, which required careful laying out of joints to ensure a tight level fit and fine adjustments with a plane to remove any slight variations, but rather used slightly offset joints in which the tolerances were not so critical. This joinery also provided subtle surface variety. Characteristic of the tops of case furniture, as well as many tables and benches, is the use of battens or breadboards at the end of a wide board. These battens were secured to the end of the wide boards with a series of screws set within oversized mortises with slotted washers, a fastening system that allows the top to expand and contract without cupping.[19]

The drawer construction on the Halls' furniture is also noteworthy. On the Pratt desk, the drawer fronts are secured to the sides with blind tongue-and-groove joints that were easily and tightly cut on a table saw. The backs were simply butted against the inside surface of the drawer sides and screwed in place. For the bottoms, plywood was floated in machine-cut grooves along the insides of the drawer front and sides. The bottom was screwed to the underside of the drawer back, and an oak center strip was screwed to the underside of the bottom. This oak strip slid within a matching rabbeted strip along the upper surface of the full-depth dust panels and ensured the proper action even if the opening was oversize or the drawer out of square. Like the offset joinery

FIGURE 10

Entry-hall bench, mahogany and ebony, 1909, Robert R. Blacker house, Pasadena, 1907–09

Courtesy of American Decorative Art 1900 Foundation. Photograph: Gavin Ashworth, © American Decorative Art 1900 Foundation

FIGURE 11

Detail of inlay in side panel of living-room fall-front desk, mahogany with oak, silver, and fruitwood inlays, 1912, Charles M. Pratt house, Ojai, 1908–11. Photograph by Leroy Hulbert, c. 1915

Courtesy of Avery Architectural and Fine Arts Library, Columbia University

FIGURE 12

Dining-room sideboard, mahogany with fruitwood, oak, and abalone inlays, 1909, William R. Thorsen house, Berkeley, 1908–10

Courtesy of The Gamble House, University of Southern California. Photograph © Tim Street-Porter

of the panel construction, this detail made it easy to tune the smooth operation of a drawer and obviated time-consuming fitting and planing.

A second drawer construction found on the Halls' work for the Greenes is a proud finger joint for which the craftsman cut finger joints on the front and sides with a table saw with multiple dado cutters. He then rounded the edges, smoothed the end grain, and interlocked the fingers, securing them with countersunk screws concealed with square ebony plugs. These two types of drawers are unparalleled in American furniture of this period and are more typical of Scandinavian modern work. The only example of dovetailed drawer construction is the case furniture for the Thorsen house (fig. 12), all of which was built on site in the house's basement "Jolly Room" without the benefit of the powered

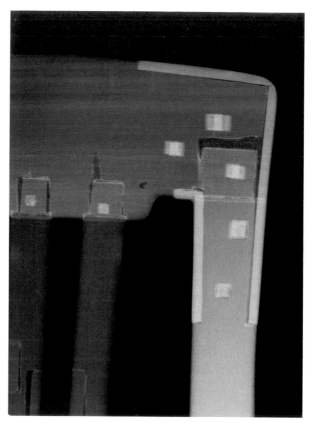

machinery in the Halls' shop that was so integral to their fabrication process. The expedient preparation and joinery of the drawer systems contrast with the time-consuming inlay, carving, detailing, scraping, sanding, and finishing.[20]

Close analysis and X-rays of several objects from the Blacker house also provide valuable information about the Hall shop. On the Blacker living-room armchair (figs. 13 and 14), X-rays of the joints where the splat is attached to the rear seat rail and to the crest rail reveal that mortises were chopped out very roughly before the splat was finished. Once finished, the splat served as a pattern to scribe tight-fitting, housed mortises in the seat and crest rails. The same approach characterizes the joints that secure the crest rail to the rear post and the arm to the front post. In the former, the mortise in the crest rail is overcut but presumably has tight-fitting cheeks, since there is no evidence of a pin or screw securing the joint. The groove for the ebony beading has ensured this tight fit; an X-ray indicates that the maker chopped from the groove into the mortise, the width of the chisel determining both. The rough depth and undercut ends of the

groove also demonstrate how the maker worked expediently yet accomplished a finished look. The beading fits tightly, adds some strength to the joint, and provides a contrasting detail to distract one's eye from the joint line. Along the front-arm joint, a tight-cheeked tenon is glued into a deeply cut mortise with width determined by the groove; applied decorative ebony plugs are set into holes that had been pilot-drilled and squared off with a chisel; and an ebony beading is pieced and bent along a groove extending beyond the joint, all further demonstrations of the same conventions.[21]

Such a concern with machine preparation and joinery, wood expansion, and modeled surfaces is not typical of American work of 1900 to 1915 and is often associated with Scandinavian furniture made from the early twentieth century onward. The Scandinavian basis of this tradition is given additional credence by examination of the woodworkers employed in the Hall shop. In 1907 and 1908, there was a sudden influx of recent immigrants, including the Swedes David Swanson and Bror Krohn, who collaborated on David and Mary Gambles' bedroom suite; the Swedes Erik Peterson and George Nelson, who

FIGURE 15
*Entry-hall furniture,
Cordelia Culbertson
house, Pasadena,*
1911–13
Courtesy of Charles Sumner
Greene Collection (1959-1),
Environmental Design
Archives, University of
California, Berkeley

[*page 126*]
FIGURE 16
*Gateleg table, oak,
c. 1912, Mary Maud
Earl apartment house
(Herkimer Arms),
Pasadena, 1912*
Private collection.
Photograph © Ognen
Borissov/Interfoto

[*page 127*]
FIGURE 17
*Game-room addition,
1923–25, Mortimer
Fleishhacker, Sr.,
estate, Woodside,*
1911–12
Private collection.
Photograph © Estate
of Mark Fiennes

were skilled chair makers; and the German Gottlob Karl Lapple, who might have been the craftsman who worked on the Thorsen house dovetailed furniture.[22]

The last large group of furniture designed by the Greenes and built by the Halls was the commission for Cordelia Culbertson and her two sisters. The dark mahogany suites in the entry hall (fig. 15) and living room featured traditional Georgian-style forms but each with a different sort of inlay decoration (rose and ribbon for the hall, and fasces with conventionalized flowers in the living room). The lighter mahogany in the dining room was decorated with a rope-and-sheaf inlay. After this commission, the Greenes designed only occasional pieces of furniture for some of their clients and seemed to have familiar craftsmen build them. For the Mary Maud Earl apartments in the Herkimer Arms building of 1912, they designed very simple furniture, such as a space-saving gateleg table (fig. 16) and a bookcase that featured a slide-out bed and a slide-out writing surface tucked into the lower section. The stark austerity of the table, its lack of exposed joinery, and even the placement of the shelf simply on the stretchers all suggest that the Greenes

entrusted this work to another local millshop that could produce pieces in sufficient quantity to furnish a number of the apartments in the two-story building. The differences can be attributed more to this new shop and to budgetary constraints than to whether Henry, always portrayed as more of an engineer than an artist, exerted greater control in the design.[23]

After Charles moved to Carmel in 1916, two different types of Greene furniture emerged: Charles's low-relief carved work, usually on forms made by John Hall or some other trained cabinetmaker, and Henry's spare designs, executed by local millshops. In 1923, Mortimer Fleishhacker added a new game room to the house the Greenes had built for him in Woodside in 1911–12; he turned to Charles to design the room and a card table with four chairs (figs. 17 and 18). Charles had John Hall make the furniture, but Charles may have carved the decoration on the suite, since it resembles his documented carving. From this time forward, Charles seemed to take pleasure in adding carved surfaces to his own studio and to furniture he had others build. Remaining in Pasadena, Henry turned away from the

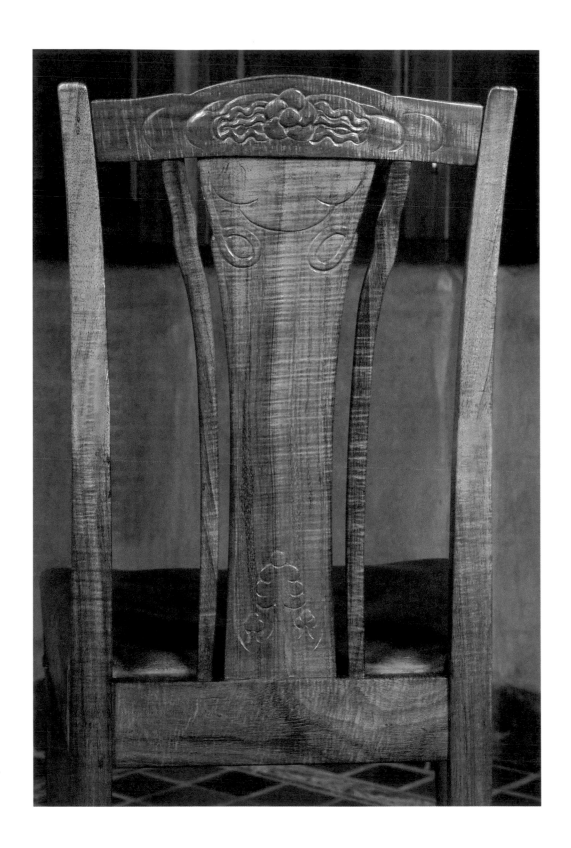

modeled surface. His furniture for V. Ray Townsend in 1927 for the Jennie Reeve house in Long Beach and for the Walter Richardson house of 1929 in the Central Valley was based more on the Stickley-inflected designs for the Bolton house, but it is further distinguished by its simplified joinery. The hard edges, plugs used only for pinning joints, and the simplified breadboard ends all suggest that the use of a shop other than the Halls' contributed significantly to the very different appearance of this work.[24]

What led to this rapid decline in both the quantity and quality of the Greenes' furniture? Several factors seem to have contributed to this softening market, but none of them seems to be the Greenes' inability to cater to or lead popular taste. The primary reason appears to be that custom furniture was time-consuming and expensive, leading to frustrated clients. Charles Pratt complained about the high costs of having Charles Greene personally supervise every single part of the house. With several projects going on simultaneously, bottlenecks occurred in the shop, such as when Peter Hall wrote to Charles Greene in August 1909 that the Gamble furniture was "about completed" and the Blacker furniture "well underway."[25] Popular taste also swung against the lighter forms of Greene and Greene designs. A visitor to the Blacker house in 1909 found the furniture "very excellent for one or two rooms—such as the hall or dining room especially—but in my opinion it is too light in structure and too hard for living rooms. … there is not one deep, soft chair or sofa in the house."[26] It was exactly at this time that the American public began to express a greater interest in combining upholstered modern furniture for the living room and sturdy Colonial Revival styles for other parts of the house. Several of the Greenes' clients hired their own interior decorators to furnish their houses. Charles accompanied Cordelia Culbertson to New York in 1912 and reviewed her orders with F.N. Dowling. Mortimer Fleishhacker turned to Charles for the house and landscaping, but relied on Elsie de Wolfe and Vickery, Atkins & Torrey for the interiors.[27]

Compounding the changing decorating tastes of the Greenes' clients were personnel changes within the Hall brothers' shop. After seven years of frenetic activity, key employees moved on to other firms. David Swanson and Anton Erikson moved to the Binderheim Studios, a Pasadena decorating firm that offered complete mural, upholstery, and fine furniture-making services. Sven Carlson went to a local millwork company named Crown City Manufacturing, where Gottlob Karl Lapple

joined him in 1919. As the furniture business began to decline, the Halls used their machinery for different purposes. By 1918, the craftsmen in the shop were mass-producing distinctive redwood boxes—with finger joints, shaper-produced moldings, and smooth finish—for dried fruits and chocolate. In 1921, a fire destroyed the Halls' shop; among the losses totaling $20,000 were "thousands of boxes in various stages of completion, as well as many thousands of feet of seasoned redwood and valuable machinery." The brothers did not rebuild. Peter simply focused on his work as a contractor, and John worked as an independent finish carpenter and cabinetmaker, taking on occasional discrete jobs for Charles Greene.[28]

Looking back at the whole body of furniture designed by the Greenes, it is obvious that the Halls' shop was critical in realizing the architects' intentions, which were derived from ideas and images drawn from national and international design magazines, close study of Chinese furniture, and an awareness of furniture history. The Halls added their Scandinavian shop traditions and skilled decorative work to create a limited number of objects that seduced wealthy clients and impressed such informed Arts and Crafts leaders as C.R. Ashbee. But the high regard was short-lived. For much of the twentieth century, the furniture collaborations of the Greenes and Halls went unnoticed; many of their finest examples resided in private hands, and the prevailing tenets of Modernism were unsympathetic to their aesthetic. It is striking that the renewed interest in their furniture, made possible by museum exhibitions and a sense of public responsibility for what had been personal possessions, occurred at the very time when a Scandinavian-trained American studio furniture maker named James Krenov wrote passionately about the importance of quiet design comprised of skilled craftsmanship, handwork detailing, and deep respect for the aesthetics of the material. Such values resonate with the collaborative work of the Greenes and the Halls. It is no coincidence that many of the makers currently working in a Greene and Greene style were influenced or trained by Krenov, who waxed so eloquently about the elegance of a "beautifully made drawer with its own whisper and its light movement."[29] The drawers of the Greene and Hall furniture provide a similar sort of experience. The sense of stewardship felt by owners of the Greenes' furniture, the larger number of examples in public museums, and the increasing interest in the Greene and Greene style among contemporary furniture makers have combined to permit more people to enjoy "the best and most characteristic furniture" of the early twentieth century.

[opposite]
FIGURE 18
Back of game-room side chair, walnut, 1923–25, Mortimer Fleishhacker, Sr., estate
Private collection. © Estate of Linda Svendsen

[page 131]
FIGURE 19
Detail, bedroom wardrobe, mahogany and ebony, with copper, silver, abalone, and wood inlay, 1909, Robert R. Blacker house
Private collection. Photograph © Ognen Borissov/Interfoto

I would like to acknowledge the kind assistance of Ted Bosley, Anne Mallek, Ann Scheid, Nancy Berliner, and Freyja Hartzell in developing the ideas in this essay.

1. Quoted in Edward R. Bosley, *Greene & Greene* (London: Phaidon, 2000), p. 140. Taken from Ashbee Papers, Modern Archive Centre, King's College Library, Cambridge University, document nos. 72–74.

2. See especially *The Arts and Crafts Movement in America, 1876–1916*, exhib. cat., ed. Robert Judson Clark, Princeton, NJ, Art Museum, 1972; *California Design 1910*, exhib. cat., ed. Timothy J. Andersen *et al.*, Pasadena, Calif., Pasadena Center, 1974; and Randell L. Makinson, *Greene & Greene: Furniture and Related Designs* (Salt Lake City: Peregrine Smith, 1979).

3. On the rise of studio furniture makers, see *The Maker's Hand: American Studio Furniture, 1940–1990*, exhib. cat. by Edward S. Cooke, Jr., *et al.*, Boston, Museum of Fine Arts, 2003. On the California makers, see Alan Marks, "Greene and Greene: A Study in Functional Design," *Fine Woodworking*, 12 (September 1978), pp. 40–45; *California Woodworking*, exhib. cat., Oakland, Calif., Oakland Museum, 1980.

4. See Darrell Peart, *Greene & Greene: Design Elements for the Workshop* (Fresno, Calif.: Linden Publishing, 2005); and Robert W. Lang, *Shop Drawings for Greene & Greene Furniture* (East Petersburg, Pa.: Fox Chapel Publishing, 2006).

5. On Woodward and manual training, see Calvin Woodward, *The Manual Training School* (Boston: D.C. Heath, 1887); Paul Klein, "Fifty Years of Woodworking in the American Schools," *Industrial-Arts Magazine*, 16, no. 1 (January 1927), pp. 1–5; and Ray Stombaugh, *A Survey of the Movements Culminating in Industrial Arts Education in Secondary Schools* (New York: Teachers College, Columbia University, 1936), esp. p. 30.

6. See Bosley, *Greene & Greene*, pp. 37–50.

7. See *ibid.*, pp. 53–57; Makinson, *Furniture*, pp. 15–21; and Gustav Stickley, "The Structural Style in Cabinet-Making," *House Beautiful*, December 1903, pp. 19–23.

8. Bosley, *Greene & Greene*, pp. 60–69; Edward Cooke, Jr., "Scandinavian Modern Furniture in the Arts and Crafts Period: The Collaboration of the Greenes and the Halls," in *American Furniture 1993*, ed. Luke Beckerdite (Hanover, NH: University Press of New England, 1993), pp. 55–74; and Peart, *Greene & Greene*, p. 17. For an example of a similarly poorly constructed chair, designed by George Grant Elmslie of Chicago in 1910, see *"The Art That is Life": The Arts and Crafts Movement in America, 1875–1920*, exhib. cat., ed. Wendy Kaplan, Boston, Museum of Fine Arts, 1987, p. 204.

9. Ted Bosley and Anne Mallek kindly brought the Stickley use of the cloud-lift shape to my attention. It is interesting to note that Stickley uses the term "Tokio," reflecting a general unfamiliarity with the differences between Japanese and Chinese woodworking traditions. For most Americans of this period, Japan was synonymous with Asian design.

10. Bosley, *Greene & Greene*, pp. 67–68; *Catalogue of the Collection of Chinese Exhibits at the Louisiana Purchase Exposition* (St. Louis: Shallcross Print, 1904); Craig Clunas, "Chinese Furniture and Western Designers," *Journal of the Classical Chinese Furniture Society* (Winter 1992), esp. pp. 66–67; and Edward S. Cooke, Jr., "In and Out of Fashion: Changing American Engagements with Chinese Furniture," in *Inspired by China: Contemporary Furnituremakers Explore Chinese Traditions*, exhib. cat. by Nancy Berliner and Edward S. Cooke, Jr., Salem, Mass., Peabody Essex Museum, 2006, esp. pp. 47–50. With the end of the Boxer Rebellion in early September 1901, more liberal rules for foreign trade and a new Chinese interest in modernization meant that more Chinese were willing to sell their old family furniture. Fong See embarked on a long buying trip in China right at that time.

11. Bosley, *Greene & Greene*, pp. 64–65, 86–88, 91–93; and Makinson, *Furniture*, pp. 43–44.

12. Bosley, *Greene & Greene*, pp. 78–84; and Cooke, "Scandinavian Modern Furniture," pp. 58–59.

13. Bosley, *Greene & Greene*, pp. 86–89; and Makinson, *Furniture*, pp. 46–52.

14. Cooke, "Scandinavian Modern Furniture," pp. 55–74. On the size of the new shop, see Lang, *Shop Drawings*, p. 12.

15. Furniture with a hard, dark lacquer finish.

16. W. Fred, "The Artists' Colony at Darmstadt," *International Studio*, 15 (1901), pp. 22–30; and Hans W. Simger, "Arts and Crafts at Dresden," *International Studio*, 22 (1904), pp. 55–58. Anne Mallek kindly shared with me the fruits of her survey of Charles's notations on his copies of *International Studio*, which are housed in the GGA. Behrens was also extensively featured from 1901 to 1904 in *Deutsche Kunst und Dekoration* and *Dekorative Kunst*. See also Wendy Kaplan, *The Arts and Crafts Movement in Europe and America: Design for the Modern World* (New York: Thames & Hudson, 2004), esp. pp. 77–81.

17. *International Studio*, 14 (1901), pp. 56–58, 63; and W.R. Watson, "Some Recent Scottish Domestic Fittings and Decorations," *International Studio*, 18 (1902), pp. 104–10. On the influence of Riemerschmid and a new assessment of his lyrical qualities, I am indebted to the work of Freyja Hartzell, who is writing a dissertation entitled "Delight in *Sachlichkeit*: The Thingliness of Things in Munich and Berlin, 1890–1930" (Yale University). Charles Greene's scrapbook includes images of the German pavilion at the St. Louis fair of 1904.

18. All dates of the furniture are taken from Bosley, *Greene & Greene*, except Blacker, which appears to be 1909 based on Peter Hall's letter to CSG of August 1909, in the GGA. See note 25. Furniture makers have often identified chairs as a specific sort of subspecialty, since one needs to balance structural demands, cultural notions of comfort, and pleasing aesthetics. An experienced chair maker knows where to provide more substantial mass and where to lighten the structure, how to provide strength in joints subjected to the greatest stress (particularly where the seat rails are set into the legs), what the best dimensions are for seat height and depth, how to account for lumbar support, and what sort of comfort can be provided. On the particularities of the chair, see Galen Cranz, *The Chair: Rethinking Culture, Body, and Design* (New York: Norton, 1998).

19. Studies of the Halls' joinery systems include Marks, "A Study in Functional Design"; Cooke, "Scandinavian Modern Furniture"; Peart, *Greene & Greene*, esp. pp. 74–81; and Lang, *Shop Drawings*, esp. pp. 46–81.

20. Discussions of the Halls' drawer construction can be found in Cooke, "Scandinavian Modern Furniture," esp. pp. 61–63; Peart, *Greene & Greene*, esp. pp. 91–97, 74–81; and Lang, *Shop Drawings*, esp. pp. 35–36. There were at least four different ways that the drawer backs were secured: the drawer back was simply butted within the drawer sides and screwed from the outside surface of the side (Pratt desk and Gamble chiffonier); the back was set within the drawer sides with a tongue-and-groove joint (Robinson dining-room sideboard and living-room desk); the back was set within a groove cut along the inside of the drawer and screwed (Culbertson dining-room sideboard); and the drawer sides were dovetailed to the drawer back (only on Thorsen examples).

21. On the joinery, see Cooke, "Scandinavian Modern Furniture," esp. pp. 63–65; Peart, *Greene & Greene*, pp. 27–28; and Lang, *Shop Drawings*, pp. 23–27.

22. On the personnel in the shop and the connection to Swedish joinery systems, see Cooke, "Scandinavian Modern Furniture," esp. pp. 66–74.

23. Makinson, *Furniture*, pp. 104–11; Bosley, *Greene & Greene*, pp. 156–63; and *Greene and Greene: The Architecture and Related Designs of Charles Sumner Greene and Henry Mather Greene, 1894–1934*, exhib. cat., Los Angeles Municipal Art Gallery, 1977.

24. Makinson, *Furniture*, pp. 122–27; Bosley, *Greene & Greene*, pp. 187–89, 206–209; and *Greene and Greene: The Architecture and Related Designs*.

25. Letter from Peter Hall to Charles Greene, August 9, 1909, as quoted in Bosley, *Greene & Greene*, p. 222 n. 8. On Charles Pratt's frustrations, see *ibid.*, p. 166.

26. Letter from Mrs. J.W. Beswick-Purchas to William and Caroline Thorsen, December 17, 1909, as quoted in *ibid.*, p. 134.

27. *Ibid.*, pp. 158–59, 149. Elsie de Wolfe's involvement in the Fleishhacker commission, while as yet undocumented, is recalled by Fleishhacker family members. On the changing fashions of the time, see Katherine C. Grier, *Culture and Comfort: People, Parlors, and Upholstery, 1850–1930*, exhib. cat., Rochester, NY, Strong Museum, 1988.

28. Cooke, "Scandinavian Modern Furniture," esp. pp. 68–74.

29. James Krenov, *A Cabinetmaker's Notebook* (New York: Van Nostrand Reinhold, 1976), p. 14.

NINA GRAY

"The Spell of Japan": Japonism and the Metalwork of Greene and Greene

In Charles Greene's unpublished and semi-autobiographical novel, "Thais Thayer," the central character, Roy Jones, is a young architect, kidnapped and taken to a tropical island to build a house for an opera diva. Jones becomes enthralled by a Chinese bronze urn, which in turn becomes his muse: "My eye fell upon the bronze urn. Presently I had a revelation ... the spirit of that old bronze was the guiding motive of the design ... my mentor stood before me, bathed in the still morning light where it always met my gaze."[1] It is believed that Greene wrote this novel around 1914, when he was making his most beautiful designs in metal.

Metalwork is typically not what comes to mind when thinking of Greene and Greene, who are primarily known for their masterful use of wood. However, numerous examples of metalwork were incorporated into their architecture and interior decoration—often with spectacular results—from imposing architectural features that included gates, straps, and drainage elements, to lanterns and furniture, to fireplace tools and andirons, to hardware and the decorative inlay of metals. No detail was too small to attract their close attention. The Greenes manipulated metal in many ways, often in combination with other materials. They used iron, copper, brass, bronze, steel, silver, lead, and nickel, which were cast, wrought, hammered, plated, patinated, and inlaid for an astonishing range of surfaces, colors, treatments, and applications.

Greene and Greene began to create metalwork in 1904, at about the time they ventured into their early furniture designs for Jennie Reeve and Adelaide Tichenor. The development of the Greenes' work in metal, like that of their architecture and furniture, was closely linked to the craftsmen who executed their designs.[2] As the Greenes' style matured over the next decade, so did the quality of execution, with hard edges giving way to softer, more rounded forms and more elegant decoration. Their finest designs in metal are found in the four bungalows of their classic period—the Blacker, Gamble, Pratt, and Thorsen houses—for which the Greenes had liberal budgets and enviable artistic freedom. In less opulent commissions, the call for metalwork and other costly decorative arts correspondingly diminished.

Metalwork has long been featured in interior decoration, both out of functional necessity and for aesthetic effect. Fireplace furniture, including andirons and tools, and lighting fixtures employing candles or fuel required the heat-resistant and fireproof properties of metal. Such materials as gilt-bronze or polished brass provided rich, jewelry-like embellishments on walls and furniture. Historically, these elements were integrated with interiors, although they were most often supplied by specialists who worked in iron or bronze. Toward the end of the nineteenth century, the reaction against the eclecticism of the revivalist styles gave rise to a more comprehensive approach to unified interior schemes. The Aesthetic movement called for integrated furniture, accessories, and room treatments that complemented the architecture. The Arts and Crafts movement deepened the commitment to the harmony of architecture with interiors, furniture, and even landscaping, through a comprehensive approach to materials and design.

With few exceptions, until the Arts and Crafts period, metalwork was purchased from suppliers rather than individually designed as part of an interior scheme.[3] Charles Rennie Mackintosh in Scotland and Louis Sullivan and Frank Lloyd Wright in Chicago were among the earliest architects to design most of the constituent parts of architecture and interior decoration, including metalwork, and the Greenes followed their example. Like Wright, the Greenes had a deep respect for materials, and designed with their particular properties in mind. Although Henry was responsible for a handful of wrought-iron andirons and fixtures, it was Charles who fully explored and challenged the limits of the medium.

DESIGN SOURCES

Japonism, or the adoption of Japanese design, was the primary inspiration for the metalwork of Greene and Greene. When C.R. Ashbee visited Charles Greene in 1909, he was impressed with Charles's appreciation of the Japanese aesthetic, writing in his diary: "The spell of Japan is on him, he feels the beauty."[4] Charles became familiar with Japanese architecture, art, and decorative art through world's fairs, books, and collectors. The roots of

FIGURE I
Living-room fire screen, cast and wrought steel, 1914, William R. Thorsen house, Berkeley, 1908–10
Courtesy of The Gamble House, University of Southern California. Photograph © Ognen Borissov/Interfoto

Japonism in the United States can be traced to the mid-nineteenth century, when Commodore Matthew Perry established trade treaties with Japan. Following the Philadelphia Centennial in 1876, Japonism became a minor national obsession.[5] Artists and artisans embraced Japanese motifs and techniques, such as asymmetrical compositions; Japonism was one of the strongest threads running through the Aesthetic movement. Japanese metalwork was especially prized, and its influence can be seen in the highly sophisticated one-of-a-kind pieces made by Tiffany & Company in New York, as well as in mass-produced brass hardware manufactured in Connecticut.

World's fairs provided the greatest exposure to Japanese architecture and design. In America, the expositions held in Chicago in 1893, Buffalo in 1901, and St. Louis in 1904 included examples of Japanese architecture and displays of native goods. While the Greenes were too young to experience directly the Philadelphia Centennial exposition, they did attend the World's Columbian Exposition in Chicago, and they saw the Japanese Tea Garden at the California Midwinter International Exposition in San Francisco in 1894.[6] Subsequent fairs made an even deeper impression on Charles. He and his wife, Alice, visited the Pan-American International Exposition in Buffalo after returning from their wedding trip in Europe and Great Britain. At the urging of his client Adelaide Tichenor, Charles attended the Louisiana Purchase Exposition in St. Louis. Japan had exhibits in the Palace of Manufactures, the Palace of Liberal Arts, and the Palace of Varied Industries, in addition to an official pavilion and a commercial exhibit called "Fair Japan." Charles would have seen entire buildings as well as a vast array of objects and artwork.

Books were another important source of inspiration for Charles Greene. His personal library included such texts as *Mixed Metals* by Arthur Hiorns, published in London in 1901, which describes metal alloys and their properties and would have been useful in determining the best application of particular metals for structural and ornamental use.[7] The Greenes also subscribed to such periodicals as *International Studio*, which widely covered the subject of Japanese art, including metalwork.

In 1903, Charles purchased Edward S. Morse's book *Japanese Homes and Their Surroundings* (1886).[8] Morse, an early scholar of Japan, first traveled there in 1877 to teach zoology at the Imperial University in Tokyo. He soon became interested in all things Japanese, and began to collect pottery and study architecture. Morse was from Boston; with Ernest Fenollosa and William Sturgis Bigelow, he formed an important circle of Japan scholars

in that city. All three men had collections of Japanese fine and decorative arts, much of which entered the Museum of Fine Arts, Boston, before the turn of the century. Charles Greene, who took classes at the museum in the late 1880s and early 1890s, may have known Bigelow's collection of *tsuba*, or Japanese sword guards. *Tsuba* were made of metal, including bronze and iron, and were executed with extraordinary attention to craftsmanship. Their abstracted natural motifs encompassed a variety of techniques. By 1907, the *tsuba* shape figured prominently in Charles Greene's design vocabulary, and he adapted it in creative ways for both furniture and metalwork. He also began to collect *tsuba* himself (fig. 2). Greene's pivotal early education in manual training particularly equipped him to appreciate the possibilities offered by Japanese metalwork.

Many Greene and Greene clients were also keenly interested in Japanese art. In Pasadena, the Greenes designed a retail store in 1901 for John C. Bentz, a collector and dealer in Asian goods and books.[9] Charles is believed to have spent time studying Bentz's objects, prints, and texts. In 1902, the Greenes designed a house for a customer of Bentz, James Culbertson, who collected Japanese screens and other objects. In 1911, they were commissioned by John Bentz's brother, Nathan, also a dealer in Asian art goods, to build a house for him in Santa Barbara.[10]

The scale of Greene and Greene metalwork ranges from massive architectural gates to the most delicate silver inlay for furniture. Charles Greene began to design metalwork and furniture around the same time. As his involvement in interior decoration increased, he exerted ever-widening control over every kind of furnishing. His earliest metalwork, including gates and andirons, was executed in wrought iron. He expanded on both the variety of objects and the range of metals and techniques he employed, culminating in the sophisticated work for the elaborate houses of 1907 to 1911. To cover the extent of the Greenes' metalwork, this essay separately treats architectural elements, including objects that are part of the physical structure of the building, both on the exterior and the interior; objects that are attached but not structural, such as exterior and interior lanterns or lighting devices; furniture and furniture with decorative inlay; and fireplace ensembles, including hoods, fenders, andirons, and surrounds.

ARCHITECTURAL METALWORK
The portal gates for Oaklawn Residential Park in South Pasadena (1904–05) were among the Greenes' earliest

FIGURE 2
A Japanese tsuba,
*or sword guard, from
the collection of
Charles Greene*

Courtesy of Randell
Makinson. Photograph
© Ognen Borissov / Interfoto

works in metal (fig. 3). These monumental gates, the overall silhouette of which is Japanese-inspired, are composed of immense piers of carefully selected granite boulders that frame a wrought-iron grille.

By contrast, the wrought-iron grilles for the Earle C. Anthony Packard showroom in Los Angeles (1911) are an example of Charles Greene's mature style; they were more ambitious in scale and complexity but more delicate and lyrical in composition. The same motifs of abstracted *tsuba* shapes and the Chinese-inspired cloud lift were used in the grilles on each of the door panels, the mezzanine, and the elevator enclosure in the showroom. Tile-covered piers, light fixtures, and ceiling decoration also contributed to a complex geometrical

scheme: octagonal light fixtures harmonize with the octagonal columns, and both vertical and horizontal elements are repeated in the grilles. The decorative potential of wrought iron is accentuated by the repetition of motifs. Whereas the Oaklawn portals emphasize the difference in material between the rough-hewn boulders and the slender wrought iron, here everything plays to the unity of the design.

Similar geometric schemes appear in exterior components of the Greenes' houses for the Blackers, the Gambles, the Pratts, and the Thorsens. Highly sculptural downspouts of sheet copper are a distinctive architectural element of their high-style bungalows (fig. 5). These are artfully shaped into gently rounded forms

[135]

similar to an elongated *tsuba*, and they are "placed and executed with due respect for their contribution to the total design, regardless of location."[11] In contrast to the brownish wood and wrought iron, these downspouts have a greenish patina typical of weathered copper, a subtle coloration that draws attention to them. The downspouts lead into gutters attached to the wooden siding of the house with simple wrought-iron straps that curl over at each end and have visible bolts shaped like the squared ebony plugs of the furniture. There is a playful geometry in the vertical and horizontal directions of the downspouts, gutters, and straps with the wooden siding, beams, and windows. At the Gamble and Cordelia Culbertson houses, the gently rounded shapes of the downspouts are repeated in ceramic planters around the buildings.

Beginning with the Robert Pitcairn, Jr., house in Pasadena (1906), and throughout most of their classic

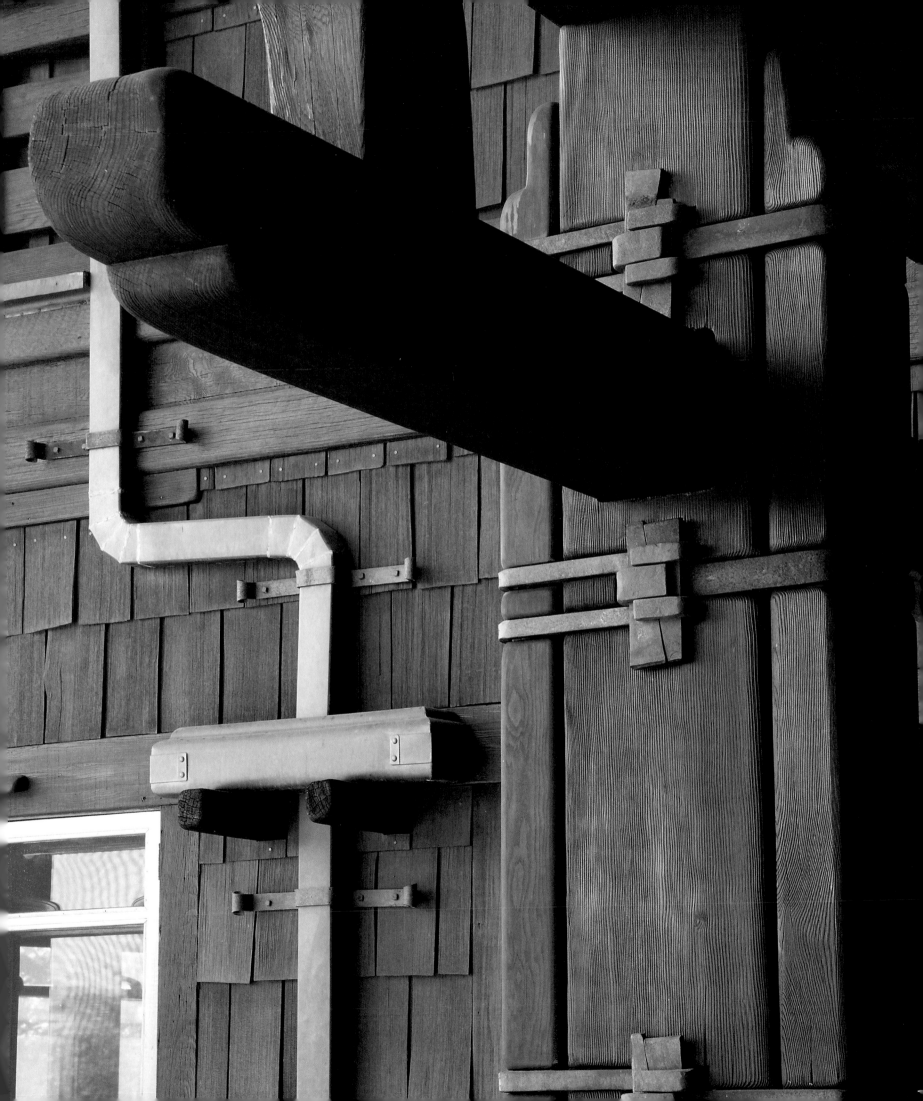

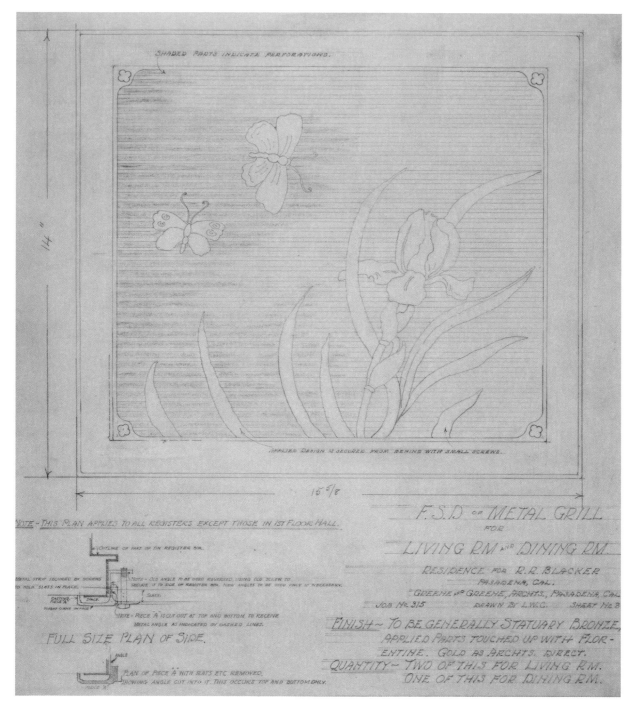

period, the Greenes used large wrought-iron straps strengthened by wedges to bundle massive vertical support posts, creating a bold contrast between materials. The large wooden posts are subtly tapered above and below the straps, giving the impression of the metal actually compressing the wooden beams, perhaps to stress the structural benefit of binding them. The rugged nature of the wrought iron is accentuated, too, by the slightly rusted finish, the total effect being one of strength and structural integrity. When used in the interiors of the classic houses, the straps are more refined. All of the edges are rounded and seem to merge with the woodwork. The finish is soft, with satiny patinas that complement the buttery surfaces and color of the wood. Nowhere is this more evident than in the David B. Gamble house in Pasadena (1907–09), where the metal straps and wedges of the main stairway, and in the dramatic attic trusses, not only serve a structural

FIGURE 7
*Living-room heating
register, bronze,
Robert R. Blacker
house*

Courtesy of Harvey and
Ellen Knell. Photograph
© Estate of Mark Fiennes

function but also break up the regularity of the wood-work (fig. 4). Both metal and wood have a similar luster, a semi-matte finish that contributes to the soothing treatment of an interior space devoid of hard edges.

ARCHITECTURAL INLAY

Inlay was another interior treatment that incorporated metal. Charles Rennie Mackintosh had occasionally used metal inlay to depict patterns of stylized floral motifs. Charles Greene visited Glasgow on his wedding trip in 1901, and would have known Mackintosh's work through articles published in *International Studio*.[12] In America, a similar abstraction of nature appears in the conventionalized rose motif on a folding screen by Gustav Stickley published in *The Craftsman* in early 1905.[13] The Greenes' earliest use of metal inlay is probably the staircase, pilasters, and overmantel for the Arthur A. Libby house in Pasadena (1905). The brass inlay was to have a

"dull satin finish."[14] Greene abandoned this type of applied architectural decoration after the Libby commission in favor of the unadorned beauty of wood or the more subtle straps of the Gamble house.

The small heating registers designed for the living room, breakfast room, and dining room of the Robert R. Blacker house in Pasadena (1907–09) show a different application of metal to interior architecture (figs. 6 and 7). They read as independent framed pictures and are among the most refined, purely Japanesque designs in the Greenes' work. Each of the bronze grilles is a slightly different size, and depicts butterflies and irises in an asymmetrical arrangement. The ornamental details were applied to the grilles and attached from behind with small screws. Several preparatory drawings for the registers survive, with notations suggesting that the ornament be further enhanced with "Florentine Gold."[15] The use of gold, or highly polished and gold-colored

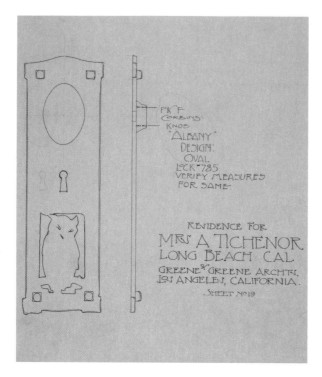

surfaces, is rare in the work of Greene and Greene. The Blacker house has the most lavish embellishment of this kind—in areas such as the gilded frieze in the living room—suggesting that the client favored the effect.

HARDWARE

Owing to its heavy use, door hardware is traditionally made of long-wearing metal. Greene and Greene most often used commercially available hardware, but they occasionally altered such pieces or designed their own. P. & F. Corbin of New Britain, Connecticut, was their major supplier. Founded in 1855, Corbin was one of the four largest American hardware companies. The firm published extensive catalogues in 1895 and 1905 depicting hundreds of models, styles, and finishes for locks, doorknobs, doorplates, and the like. Because of the huge range of hardware available, the Greenes were probably not compelled to venture into custom work in their early years. For the Adelaide A. Tichenor house in Long Beach (1904–05), they adapted Corbin's *Albany* model for a door escutcheon by adding an owl motif (fig. 8).[16] The same motif was used in the backsplash of the bedroom washstand. The Greenes also employed the *Albany* design (without owls or other added motif) for the Blacker house doorknobs and plates, while they chose the *Bedford* pattern for the William R. Thorsen house in Berkeley

(1908–10). Both patterns were listed in the P. & F. Corbin catalogue in 1905, as part of the "Colonial" line of hardware, and both were cast bronze.[17] Corbin offered more than thirty different finishes or patinas from which an architect could choose. Several English furniture designers used silhouetted brass ornament as well, including C.F.A. Voysey, whose work Charles Greene would have known through magazines and might have seen in England in 1901. For the Gamble house, the Greenes designed the hardware themselves. The entry-door hardware was inspired by the shape of the *tsuba*; screws are concealed behind softly rounded square heads, similar to the square ebony plugs in the Greenes' furniture, cast in bronze to match the doorplates. The *tsuba* shape was used for the doorbell, doorplates, and the electric push-button plates (fig. 9). For the bedroom furniture on the first floor, Charles designed silver bail handles in the shape of *hikite*, or Japanese screen pulls, that are suspended from *tsuba*-shaped wooden plates.[18]

In a departure from the traditional use of metal for hardware, the Greenes occasionally substituted wood to integrate materials better. Wooden switch plates surround the electric push buttons in the Blacker house, blending with the wall surfaces. For similar effect, the Gamble dining-room sideboard has wooden keyhole surrounds.

LANTERNS

The many lanterns Greene and Greene designed for their houses flow from Arts and Crafts tradition, particularly from the Craftsman Workshops examples of Gustav Stickley, whose furnishings the Greenes purchased or specified for some of their early clients. The metal light fixtures the Greenes designed for exteriors were most often made of sheet copper with opalescent glass panels. The maker of the lanterns remains unknown, although the firm Sturdy-Lange of Los Angeles seems to have supplied and fitted most of the opalescent and iridescent glass.[19] These fixtures frequently have pagoda-like forms, resembling miniature houses with broad overhanging roofs that echoed the profiles of the structures from which they hung. The hard edges of the early lanterns gradually gave way to the softer undulating forms of the Greenes' mature style. Silhouettes of sheet lead and copper cut in a variety of patterns and designs reflect themes at the location of the fixtures. At the Blacker house, lanterns of different sizes were placed around the exterior of

the house, with the largest and most imposing at the front of the porte cochere (fig. 10). The sloping roofs of these lanterns are constructed with an inward curve on the underside, lending them a particularly graceful profile. Sheet copper silhouetted against the glass is cut in shapes of pinecones and tree branches to complement thematically the surrounding landscape. Single panes of glass are held in place by simple tabs on the interior of the fixtures, and the joints are concealed with square metal heads, again echoing the ebony plugs employed in the furniture. While some of the heads are functional, others are decorative.

For each of the great houses of the firm's classic period, Charles Greene designed a set of unique lanterns. At the Gamble house, the brass lantern over the entry doors displays the house number outlined against the interior glass (fig. 11). Fixtures of similar design and varying size hang over terraces and near doorways. The focal point of the backyard garden terrace is a tall leaded-glass lantern, mounted on a clinker-brick wall that defines the edge of

FIGURE II

Exterior lantern for front (east) terrace, brass with (oxidized) iridescent glass, David B. Gamble house

Courtesy of The Gamble House, University of Southern California. Photograph © Ognen Borissov/Interfoto

FIGURE 12

Exterior wall lantern, bronze with (oxidized) iridescent glass, David B. Gamble house

Courtesy of The Gamble House, University of Southern California. Photograph © Estate of Mark Fiennes

a Japanesque fish pond (fig. 12). The rich context of the house, terrace treatment, and adjacent garden provided inspiration for this elaborate and oft-photographed fixture, but its prototype is undoubtedly the austere and beautiful lantern for the entry terrace of the Libby house (fig. 13); its simple unleaded glass and dramatic broad roof illustrate perhaps even better the reductive design genius of the Greenes.

Metal lanterns were also featured in the Greenes' interiors, especially in some of the earlier commissions, such as the Jennie Reeve house in Long Beach (1903–04). After the Greenes had established a successful relationship with John and Peter Hall, they produced more distinctive interior lighting, including fixtures made of mahogany with leaded glass supplied by Sturdy-Lange. Other early metal examples are the Tichenor house lanterns and sconces, which combine subtle colors and textures of opalescent glass set within a cube open at the top and bottom. The central piece of glass is *tsuba*-shaped, and the outline of the bottom is a cloud lift. The sconce also has a *tsuba*-shaped back plate made of ash.

At the Gamble house, two sizes of bronzed metal lanterns illuminate the first- and second-floor halls and central staircase to harmonize with the scale of the

FIGURE 13
*Exterior wall lantern,
copper and glass,
Arthur A. Libby
house, Pasadena, 1905*
Private collection.
Photograph © Ognen
Borissov/Interfoto

respective spaces (fig. 14). These lanterns have bronze frames with a soft satiny patina and are fitted with panes of opalescent and colored glass representing the Gamble family crest: a crane with a rose in its beak. The use of the same form in different sizes according to location is another means of unifying the interior as a complete work of art.

FURNITURE

Greene and Greene rarely made furniture out of metal, preferring the mellow richness of exotic woods. An exception is a pair of brass beds that Charles Greene designed for the main guest room of the Gamble house (fig. 15). The beds were fabricated by the Pacific Ornamental Iron Works at a cost of $160.00 and were subsequently nickel-plated by contractor Peter Hall.[20] The Pacific Ornamental Iron Works were manufacturers and founders working in iron and bronze as well as hardware jobbers. The headboards and footboards of the Gamble beds are based on a traditional form, created with upright brass stiles joined at the top by rails. In contrast

to the usual treatment, however, the pieces of brass are squared, rather than tubular, and the mellow silver color of nickel-plating replaces the more common shiny yellow finish. Over time, the nickel has oxidized, imparting a softer, slightly tarnished patina. The profile of the rails is a stepped cloud lift, derived from Chinese furniture, which figures prominently in the Gamble house and in the broader design vocabulary of Greene and Greene. The plugs that cover the screw holes for the casters on the legs of the bed are analogous to the square ebony pegs of the Greenes' wood furniture. The corners of the headboards and footboards have delicately incised flowers and scrolling tendrils in a lyrical and lively design that echoes the silver and exotic wood inlay of the other furniture in this room.

Like others before him in the Arts and Crafts movement, Charles Greene adapted metal inlay as a decorative motif for furniture. These inlays, inserted into tables, chair backs, and case furniture, became increasingly delicate over time. The inlay in the Blacker house bedroom furniture is similar to that in pieces made in Stickley's

FIGURE 14
Hall lantern, bronzed
metal, David B.
Gamble house
Photograph © Ognen
Borissov/Interfoto

FIGURE 15
*Detail of
guest-bedroom bed,
brass with nickel
plate, David B.
Gamble house*
Courtesy of The Gamble
House, University of
Southern California.
Photograph © Ognen
Borissov/Interfoto

Craftsman Workshops, published in *The Craftsman* in 1903 and 1904.[21] They share the use of geometric designs and the spare, isolated application of decoration. The Greenes' metal inlays of copper and silver are combined in the Blacker pieces with abalone shell and wood to create a rich palette of materials used sparingly, with the thinnest possible vertical and horizontal lines punctuated with tiny squares of shell (figs. 16 and 17). A comparable use of inlay may be seen in the guest-bedroom furniture at the Gamble house, but pushed to a new naturalistic level of design. Sinuous scrolling vines and delicate leaves of inlaid silver are mixed with exotic woods of contrasting colors, such as vermillion and fruitwoods, to create lyrical decoration on each lighting fixture and piece of furniture.

FIREPLACES

The hearth was the focal point of a room and had social and moral overtones of family and warmth, a concept often discussed in writing of the Arts and Crafts period.

Both Greene brothers designed andirons, but Charles expanded the materials, designs, and complexity of the hearth in the houses of their classic period. These ensembles, composed of carefully selected tiles, glass mosaic, andirons, fenders, lintels, tools, hoods, grates, and other objects, were conceived as unified designs, and each was unique.

Andirons are among the first metal furnishings that the Greenes designed. Early examples were made of wrought iron in traditional but pleasing forms with simple profiles. The andirons made for Belle Barlow Bush in about 1908 incorporated an innovative feature that allowed the span of the crossbar to be adjusted to fit the interior of the fireplace (fig. 18).[22] This accommodated the fact that Mrs. Bush was a renter in the house, originally built by the Greenes for Dr. W.T. Bolton, and would take the andirons with her when she left. For the Laurabelle A. Robinson house in Pasadena (1905–06), Charles Greene designed two pairs of andirons, one of

[147]

wrought iron and the other of copper-plated cast brass, each scaled to the dimensions of a distinct fireplace.[23] Charles gave great thought to scale and proportion, and later wrote, "Most irons are made too high for the opening of [the] fireplace, so that they do not conform to the purpose for which intended, that is to hold wood without shutting in the heat of the fire."[24] Over time, his designs for andirons evolved, and the hard edges of wrought iron gave way to softer profiles in other materials that could be cast and patinated.

Copper fireplace hoods, designed to help draw smoke up the flue, also stem from the Arts and Crafts tradition. Several examples by Stickley appeared in *The Craftsman* in November 1905 and April 1907 and were typically paired with wrought-iron andirons. In the dining room

of the James Culbertson house, a hammered copper hood complemented a carved wood overmantel, showing mountain peaks and stylized clouds (see Mallek essay, fig. 1). The copper hood over the fireplace in an upstairs bedroom of the Blacker house—shown on the drawings as "bedroom #4"—is an exaggerated shape that curves outward in both width and depth, suggesting the roofline of a pagoda (fig. 19). The chased ornament evokes plumes of smoke and misty clouds.[25] This motif is further echoed in the lazy lines of applied decoration on the polished-brass andirons,[26] while the green tiles of the fire surround show meandering vines with yellow blossoms and buds in mosaic-like fragments. A harmonizing green color is picked up in the patinated copper fender that also shows leaves and blossoms. The

out-swept curve of the fender echoes the dramatic sweep of the hood, and the combination of copper, brass, and patinated copper possesses the same subtle palette as the tilework. In the andirons, the treatment of the cloud or smoke design as a close-up detail is reminiscent of Arthur Wesley Dow's interpretations of Japanese art in his highly influential book *Composition: A Series of Exercises in Art Structure for the Use of Students and Teachers* (1899).[27] Charles Greene used the same form and profile for at least three other sets of andirons: for the master bedroom of the Blacker house, for the master bedroom of the Gamble house, and for his own home. Each set has different decoration and finishes created in harmony with the patterns of the adjacent tilework.

The chased-copper fenders in the living room, dining room, and master bedroom of the Blacker house share the same profile as the fender in the guest bedroom. Like the andirons, each is designed to complement the decoration of the fireplace. The dining-room fender has a wrapped motif that resembles an obi, the wide sash used to tie a Japanese kimono. The raised parts of the decoration have a reddish patina that harmonizes with the red and green tiles of the fire surround. The same motif is repeated in the andirons, with the design wrapping around the sides.

At the Gamble house, mosaic fire surrounds and andirons share the same floral decoration. The dining-room fire surround is a combination of ceramic chip details on a field of American Encaustic Tile, with small

FIGURE 18

Andirons with adjustable bar for Mrs. Belle Barlow Bush, steel-plated cast and wrought iron, c. 1908

Courtesy of The Gamble House, University of Southern California. Photograph © Ognen Borissov/Interfoto

FIGURE 19
*Guest-bedroom
fireplace and copper
hood, andirons, and
fender, Robert R.
Blacker house*
Courtesy of Harvey and
Ellen Knell. Photograph ©
Ognen Borissov/Interfoto

FIGURE 19
*Guest-bedroom
fireplace and copper
hood, andirons, and
fender, Robert R.
Blacker house*
Courtesy of Harvey and
Ellen Knell. Photograph ©
Ognen Borissov/Interfoto

mosaic-like pieces of iridescent glass inserted as accents. A simple bronze lintel divides two areas of tilework and frames the opening of the fireplace on either side. The brightly colored iridescent glass contrasts with and complements the darker metallic surface of the bronze. Charles Greene specified that the cast-brass andirons were to be patinated to match the hardware;[28] their ornament, composed of four-petaled flowers with trailing stems, is repeated in the mosaic flowers of the tile surround.[29] Small squares scattered around the stems resemble the square plugs on the furniture and in the doorplates; even the coal grate has square-head fasteners.

The lintel over the living-room fireplace at the Thorsen house, composed of steel and inlaid with copper and brass, demonstrates the Greenes' most complex and sophisticated use of mixed metals (fig. 20). The lintel's overall shape is that of the Chinese "cloud lift,"

embellished with inlaid meandering vines and leaves. The combination of steel, copper, and brass is derived from Japanese metalwork, where sword fittings and decorative vessels often combined base and precious metals. The cast-iron andirons were made by the Pacific Ornamental Iron Works in 1911.[30] Three years later, the fire screen, also made of steel, was fabricated by the Art Metal Company of Los Angeles (fig. 1).[31] It depicts bats, flames, and birds, including a partridge and a phoenix. The bat is similar to one for an ornamental nail head illustrated in Morse's *Japanese Homes and Their Surroundings*.[32]

SUMNER GREENE, HIS TRUE MARK

Charles Sumner Greene was granted trademark #95,092 on February 3, 1914, for furniture with the motto "His True Mark, Sumner Greene." According to the patent, Greene first used the trademark in November 1910. It is

FIGURE 20
Living-room fireplace, William R. Thorsen house

Courtesy of California Sigma Phi Society. Photograph © Tim Street-Porter

[*page 153*]
FIGURE 21
Detail of living-room fire screen, William R. Thorsen house

Courtesy of The Gamble House, University of Southern California. Photograph © Ognen Borissov/Interfoto

not known what motivated him to register the trademark, but Greene's dropping of his first name coincides with changes in his aspirations. His increased artistic ambition had led him to travel once again to England for a prolonged sojourn in 1909. In 1916, he moved from Pasadena to Carmel to pursue new creative directions, including writing. His unpublished and undated novel "Thais Thayer" comes from about this period. However, between the trip to England and his move to Carmel, Greene designed some of his most important and imaginative metalwork. A remarkable number of preparatory sketches and drawings survive for the pieces that are stamped with his trademark. Charles colored many of these drawings with pencil or watercolor, showing an extra effort to express the details he wanted to achieve in three dimensions.[33] The planning of ornament and motifs was meticulous. For the Blackers and the Thorsens, Greene designed highly sophisticated fire screens to accompany the fireplace ensembles. These screens were made in 1914 by the Art Metal Company under the direction of George Burkhard and Rudolph Lensch.

It has been suggested that the complexity and high quality that Charles Greene sought in his metalwork designs was not readily attainable until he found the Art Metal Company,[34] formed by the German-born Burkhard and Lensch in 1914.[35] Burkhard was a master craftsman who also worked for the Forve-Pettebone Company making light fixtures.[36] The fire screens the Art Metal Company fabricated for the Greenes are exquisite. The three-panel design may be folded flat because vertical bars with double hinges join the panels at the top and bottom.[37] The screen portion was a "spiral woven mesh," which appears as a delicate lattice of interlacing round wire. Each fire screen has unique decoration in the reserves at the bottom of each of the three sections and on the two vertical joining pieces. Most of the screens have handles the shape of which complements the decoration.[38] The example for the Blacker house living room is bronze with finely cast lotus blossoms and cloud-shaped handles, probably inspired by cloud or mist motifs in Chinese or Japanese painting, sculpture, or furniture. Each of the bottom panels has a sunburst/flower design set within an elongated *tsuba*-shaped reserve. A knotted rope, which terminates in a lotus blossom, ornaments the vertical panel. The lotus blossom references the lotus and lily pond originally located immediately outside the house; it was also used in the leaded-glass lanterns and the gilded frieze.

The fire screen and pair of bronze andirons for the Thorsen house dining room were manufactured by the Art Metal Company in March and November 1914.[39] Charles Greene's notes specified an "old copper" patina for the screen, while the andirons were to receive a "statuary bronze" finish. A polished bronze lintel with a satiny gold finish harmonizes with the reddish-brown tiles of the fireplace surround, inset with scrolling vines and flowers made of both semi-matte ceramic and iridescent glass. Identical vines and flowers are repeated on the verticals of the fire screen. Each panel of the screen is pierced and features a bouquet of flowers and leaves suspended from ribbons.[40] This bouquet was cast as a separate piece and is attached with bronze rivets and tabs on the back. Additional pierced lines suggest highly abstracted clouds or mist. The andirons are decorated with a stylized knot. Both the screen and the andirons are raised on flat horizontal pads that lift them slightly above the surface of the hearth. The workmanship of the casting and the quality of the patination is of the highest order.

The fire screen for the Cordelia Culbertson house was probably the last of the series that Charles designed (probably in about 1914).[41] It was also the last major commission that Greene and Greene received for a house and its interior furnishings. For the first time, Charles included figures in his design; one appears to be nude, while the other wears a headdress. Each is seated in a mysterious landscape, under a tree with a silhouette of flames appearing between them. Butterflies, flowers, stars, and moons are also depicted. The central panel is pierced, much like the Thorson dining-room screen. These openings in the decoration seem intended to cast lively images of dancing flames on to the hearth as the fire burned behind the screen. In the left-hand panel, birds soar in a sky filled with billowing clouds. This fire screen was not part of an ensemble including tilework and fenders, and while it would not have been obtrusive in the interior design, neither does it fit into the more classically conceived decoration of the house. Instead, it transcends the purely decorative by pushing into the realm of narrative art.

The Greenes achieved a remarkable level of quality in the architecture, interior decoration, and landscaping of the classic bungalows for the Blackers, Gambles, Pratts, and Thorsens. Although later clients commissioned metalwork for their houses after the brothers separated, they were generally unwilling to endure the time and expense it took to create the exceptional work that characterized the Greenes' most fruitful years. Thus, the gates, straps, downspouts, hardware, furniture, inlay, andirons, and fire screens of the classic buildings stand distinct, in a period and realm of their own.

1. CSG, "Thais Thayer," unpublished typescript, GGA.
2. *The Maker's Hand: American Studio Furniture, 1940–1990*, exhib. cat. by Edward S. Cooke, Jr., *et al.*, Boston, Museum of Fine Arts, 2003, makes this argument in reference to the collaboration of the Greenes with John and Peter Hall.
3. Such specialists as E.F. Caldwell in New York provided a wide range of metalwork, including lighting, hardware, and fireplace furniture; they functioned as subcontractors for numerous architects, and their objects tended to incorporate a variety of historic styles.
4. Quoted in *The Arts and Crafts Movement in America, 1876–1916*, exhib. cat., ed. Robert Judson Clark, Princeton, NJ, Art Museum, 1972, p. 83.
5. *The Japan Idea: Art and Life in Victorian America*, exhib. cat. by William Hosley, Hartford, Conn., Wadsworth Atheneum, 1990.
6. Clay Lancaster, *The Japanese Influence in America* (New York: Abbeville, 1983), p. 109.
7. Bruce Smith, "Library of Charles Sumner Greene," typescript, GGA.
8. Edward R. Bosley, *Greene & Greene* (London: Phaidon, 2000), p. 59.
9. Randell L. Makinson, *Greene & Greene: Architecture as a Fine Art* (Salt Lake City: Peregrine Smith, 1977), p. 55.
10. Bosley, *Greene & Greene*, pp. 49, 154.
11. *Ibid.*, p. 109.
12. Charles Greene signed and dated his copy of the Glasgow International Exhibition Catalogue of 1901. List in GGA.
13. *The Arts and Crafts Movement*, exhib. cat., p. 39. The screen was published in *The Craftsman* (7, no. 5) in February 1905. The Gambles owned one of these screens.
14. Drawings dated October 16, 1905, Avery.
15. There are several full-scale drawings for the grille at Avery. The drawings are signed by L.W.C. (Leonard W. Collins), a longtime draftsman for Greene and Greene. Bosley, *Greene & Greene*, p. 103.
16. The drawing for the door escutcheon is at Avery, with a copy in the EDA. The *Albany* doorknob, plate, and related hardware pieces appear in *Hardware Manufactured by P. & F. Corbin* (New Britain, Conn., 1905).
17. *Hardware Manufactured by P. & F. Corbin*. The "Colonial" line reflects the growing popularity of the Colonial Revival after the turn of the century.
18. Similarly shaped pulls are illustrated in Edward S. Morse, *Japanese Homes and Their Surroundings* (Boston: Ticknor & Company, 1886), fig. 110.
19. A bill to Emil Lange records a cost of $142.00 for the lantern at the front entrance of the Thorsen house, $179.00 if the lantern was plated. A drawing shows the design of the lantern from all sides and has a notation of "metal $58" and "glass $179." Both record and drawing for William R. Thorsen house, Berkeley, 1908–10, EDA.
20. Bill for the Gamble house beds, April 29, 1909, GGA. Peter Hall charged $6.55 to nickel-plate the beds and add casters, April 18, 1910. The Pacific Ornamental Iron Works was run by Alfred J. Bayer, president; James F. Rothgeb, vice-president; and Harry R. Baker, secretary. In 1914, the company built a new factory and employed 160 men, according to the *Los Angeles Times*, November 22, 1914.
21. *The Craftsman*, 4, no. 4 (July 1903), p. 284; and 5, no. 4 (January 1904), p. 396. *"The Art That is Life": The Arts and Crafts Movement in America, 1875–1920*, exhib. cat., ed. Wendy Kaplan, Boston, Museum of Fine Arts, 1987, p. 245. The traditional attribution of the metal-inlaid furniture to Harvey Ellis is debated, since Ellis was more involved with architecture while working with Stickley and had never designed furniture. I thank Bruce Barnes and Joseph Cunningham for bringing this to my attention. See also Eileen Manning Michels, *Reconfiguring Harvey Ellis* (Edina, Minn.: Beaver Pond Press, 2004), esp. chap. 14, "Syracuse, 1903–04: Harvey Ellis and the Issue of Furniture Designs for Stickley." Two other men should be noted for their involvement in the furniture: LaMont Warner, who worked at Stickley, and George Harvey Jones, a supplier of marquetry in New York City. See David Cathers, *Gustav Stickley* (London: Phaidon, 2004), pp. 96–99. Catherine Zusy, a contributor to *Art That is Life*, also notes that Ellis's abstracted motifs were related to those by Mackintosh (p. 245). The same holds true here for the Greenes.
22. Identical andirons were also made for Peter Hall.
23. Drawings for the Robinson house andirons, EDA and Avery. The Avery drawings show the andirons in the fireplace opening.
24. Letter from CSG to Mrs. William Thorsen, January 7, 1911, GGA.
25. A more restrained but very similar design for the dining-room fireplace added to the James Culbertson house in 1907 prefigures the Blacker house hood.
26. Drawing for the Blacker house andirons, GGA.
27. Arthur Wesley Dow was a designer and teacher at Columbia University in New York City and in Salem, Massachusetts. His teachings had widespread influence not least among his students.
28. Charles carefully noted on the drawings that the ornament was to be raised 1/16 of an inch on the face of the casting, GGA.
29. Gamble house drawing, "Sheet #88," GGA.
30. Drawing of Thorsen house living-room cast-iron andirons, GGA. A pair of wrought-iron andirons was created for the "Jolly Room," drawing, GGA. The former pair cost $50.00, the latter cost $40.00; bill from Pacific Ornamental Iron Works, September 7, 1911, GGA. The prices are slightly higher than those for andirons made by Gustav Stickley. A metalware catalogue from 1905 lists the prices of wrought-iron andirons between $15.00 and $58.00. The most popular models cost between $20.00 and $30.00. I thank David Cathers for generously sharing this information.
31. Bill from Art Metal Company, February 2, 1914, GGA. The screen cost $223.00.
32. Morse, *Japanese Homes*, fig. 117.
33. The drawings for the Thorsen house metalwork at Avery have the decorative details highlighted in color.
34. *Last of the Ultimate Bungalows: The William R. Thorsen House of Greene and Greene*, exhib. cat., Berkeley, Calif., Thorsen/Sigma Phi House, 1996, p. 19.
35. The 1914 Los Angeles City Directory lists Burkhard & Lensch Metal Work at 806 East 9th Street. The Art Metal Company is first listed in 1915 at 1640 San Fernando. The 1930 census lists George Burkhard as aged fifty-eight. Rudolph Lensch was born August 10, 1879, in Germany and died in 1944. According to the 1920 census, he became a U.S. citizen in 1916, and his occupation is listed as a sheet-metal worker. In 1917, Charles H. Tolles joined Burkhard in the company, and Lensch is listed separately as an electric fixture maker. Tolles was also German-born and is listed in the 1920 census as a chandelier maker, born in 1867.
36. *Los Angeles Times*, December 25, 1927. Forve-Pettebone Company opened in 1901. *Who's Who in the Pacific Southwest: A Compilation of Authentic Biographical Sketches of Citizens of Southern California and Arizona* (Los Angeles: Times-Mirror Printing & Binding House, 1913), p. 293.
37. Charles Greene made careful annotations (for example, for the living-room fire screen) specifying the joints and their positions, Avery.
38. The fire screen made for the Thorsen dining room does not have handles.
39. Bills from Art Metal Company, March 1 and November 12, 1914, GGA. The screen cost $226.00; the andirons cost $94.00.
40. Drawings for the Thorsen house fire screen and andirons, EDA and Avery.
41. Sketches for the Cordelia Culbertson fire screen, EDA and GGA.

JULIE L. SLOAN

"A Glimmer of Vivid Light": The Stained Glass of Greene and Greene

To enter a Greene and Greene home, one approaches a broad, oaken doorway and is welcomed by an abstract rendering in stained glass of feathers, a branching tree, or other plantlike forms. In the bright light of the California sun, the surface decoration appears so supple and textured that at first glance it may seem to be made of wood and copper rather than stained glass. Upon entering a dim, wood-paneled hallway, the visitor is greeted by a "glimmer of vivid light"[1] as it passes through the many-colored glass to bathe the interior in a warm, honeyed glow. Sconces, wood-framed chandeliers, and smaller stained-glass windows offer additional glints throughout the house of butterscotch, amber, gold, moss, and crimson, depicting forms inspired by the surrounding landscape (fig. 1). For their distinctive interiors, Charles and Henry Greene designed stained glass with warm colors and subtle patterns that never overpower but only complement and enhance their furnished environments. Although their vision was unique, the Greenes relied on skilled craftsmen to translate that vision into glass, and it took many years before they found, in Harry Sturdy and Emil Lange, the experience, ability, and sympathy to realize it.

STAINED GLASS ON THE EAST COAST

Boston and New York were at the forefront of the American stained-glass movement from the mid-1870s until well into the twentieth century. The construction of Memorial Hall at Harvard College by architects William Ware and Henry Van Brunt in the mid-1870s was a watershed. The huge cathedral-like building served as a memorial to the Civil War dead, but its primary use was as a dining hall and theater. It included some of the finest stained glass available at the time.[2] Ware was the first director of the architecture program at the Massachusetts Institute of Technology (although he had moved on to Columbia University by the time the Greenes enrolled in 1888), and he had made decorative art, including stained glass, an important part of the curriculum.

As students, the Greenes lived in the shadow of Boston's other pivotal assemblage of stained glass, Trinity Church, which H.H. Richardson had completed in 1877. Its windows were still being installed at the time. Here again was groundbreaking work, including some of the first American windows by Edward Burne-Jones and William Morris, as well as the designs of the British Aestheticists Daniel Cottier and Henry Holiday. John La Farge's monumental *Christ in Majesty* in the west front, aglow with intense turquoise jewels, masterfully complemented the dark red and old-gold interior.[3] The Back Bay area around Copley Square boasted many other important churches with stained glass within a few blocks of the Greenes' student rooms.[4]

In Boston at this time, local architects were as much involved with craft as with design.[5] H. Langford Warren, with whom Charles apprenticed for eight months in 1891, wrote, "Architecture is essentially a Fine Art, the practice of which must be based on a thorough knowledge of construction. Great stress has therefore been laid not only on continued practice in design and drawing, but on thorough instruction in the history and principles of the Fine Arts of Architecture and *the arts allied with it.*"[6] The brothers apprenticed in the leading Arts and Crafts firms of the day, many of which employed stained glass extensively.[7] Stained glass was part of the language with which these architects worked, learning and borrowing from one another constantly. The use of stained glass filtered into the architectural vocabulary of the Greenes during their studies, and they would reinterpret it as they developed their own style.

EARLY DESIGNS

When Charles and Henry Greene began their practice in the 1890s, diamond-paned leaded glass found its way into the sidelights, transoms, upper sashes, and stair landings of their Colonial- or Federal-inspired houses. Several, including the Edward B. Hosmer (1897) and Charles W. Hollister (1898) houses in Pasadena, have sidelights and a transom or fanlight around the front door typical of those found in Federal-era houses in New England and on the eastern seaboard; a similar treatment appears in a clipping in the Greenes' scrapbook titled "Doorway at Dedham Mass" (fig. 2).[8] In the James Swan house (1898–99) in Pasadena, the stair window is a version of standard Victorian designs of the day, such as those provided by

FIGURE I
*Panel detail,
entry-hall fixture,
mahogany, ebony, and
silver, with stained
and opalescent leaded
glass, Robert R.
Blacker house,
Pasadena, 1907–09*

Courtesy of American
Decorative Art 1900
Foundation. Photograph:
Gavin Ashworth,
© American Decorative
Art 1900 Foundation

[155]

Doorway at Dedham ~ Mass ~

pattern books from lumber companies, millworks, department stores, and mail-order catalogues.[9]

Beginning in 1897, with the fanlight for the front door of the Howard Longley house in South Pasadena, Charles sketched a more lyrical floral line than he had used before. His designs a year later for the glass of the Winthrop B. Fay house in Pasadena were his most elaborate to date (fig. 3), showing a pronounced similarity to those of Louis Sullivan's Auditorium Building of 1889, designed and fabricated by Louis Millet of the Chicago decorating firm Healy & Millet.[10] Millet worked closely with Sullivan on many of his buildings, providing stained glass and other decorations, such as stencils and color schemes.[11] In 1889, he won praise for his stained glass at the Exposition Universelle in Paris.[12] The Auditorium had an abundance of stained glass in its public spaces, including the lobby bar, the dining room, and the reception room.[13] The Greenes visited Chicago and the World's Columbian Exposition in 1893 and could easily have seen the windows in Sullivan's buildings.

Charles's return from his honeymoon in Britain in 1901 marked a change in Greene and Greene's architectural style, and also in their window designs.[14] By 1902,

and until early 1906, Charles, the primary designer, employed overlays cut from sheet lead, a simple expedient that creates texture and pattern even with rudimentary stained-glass skills.[15] The overlays vary in complexity, from the naive clear-glass windows of the Samuel P. Sanborn (1903) and Jennie A. Reeve (1903–04) houses to the more detailed ornamentation of the windows for Adelaide A. Tichenor (1904–05), in which Charles's mature style began to emerge.

The Sanborn windows are deceptively simple. The line work in them is wobbly, the petals of the flowers uneven, as though drawn or cut freehand without drafting tools or straightedges. It creates the impression of an apprentice's hand, but is in fact carefully planned. The right and left halves of the windows are mirror images (with the exception of the center flower), down to the location of the warp in each vertical and horizontal line.[16] In order to glaze symmetrically crooked, the glass must be cut to this shape. The impression of inexperience is furthered by the application of simple rectilinear forms cut from sheet lead to create the small, abstracted leaves in one window and the pot and flower in the other. Soldered to the came at their edges, these elements sit proud from the surface of the window and can easily catch palms and cleaning rags on their sharp (but easily bent) corners. The carefree, playful feeling of these windows contrasts with the rigidly rectilinear designs of the Prairie School (Frank Lloyd Wright's work had been published in *Architectural Review* in 1900) and the ornate flora of Louis Comfort Tiffany's windows and lampshades (which were prominently displayed at the Columbian Exposition).[17]

An early use of a representational image in stained glass in a front door was in Charles Greene's design for the James A. Culbertson house (1902–15) in Pasadena (fig. 4). Here the glass takes a significant step forward in both design and execution. The door contains two separate images: above is a landscape with distant hills, a quiet stream, trees, and birds in the sky. Below is a rambling tree divided into three panels by two wide mullions. While the two segments bear no apparent relationship to each other, each is intimately linked to the design of the house as a whole; for, like his contemporary Wright, Charles was creating a *Gesamtkunstwerk* (a total work of art).[18] The horizontal mullion in the door aligns with the top of the wainscoting in the hall, above which are carved trees and landscapes. The glass landscape is here simply an idealized scene, with a brook meandering through willows and poplars. This might be California, but could just as easily be France or Italy. By

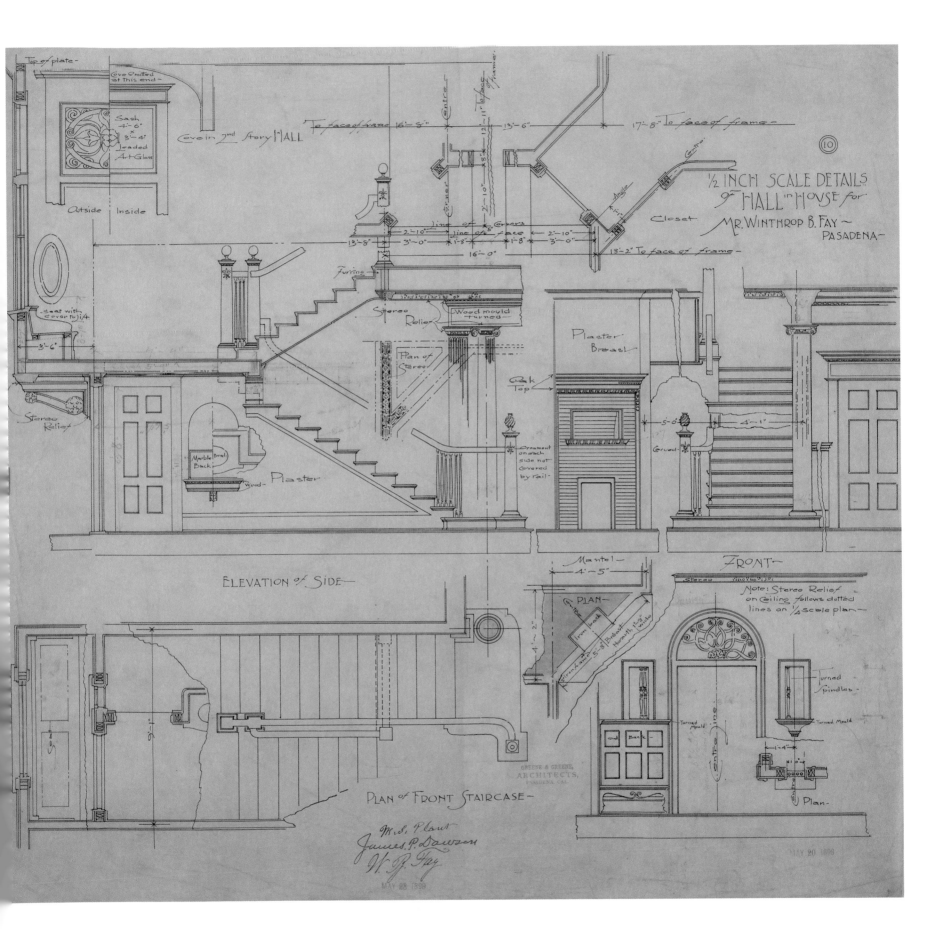

Cove omitted at this end —

Top of plate —

Sash 4'-6" x 3'-4" Leaded Art Glass

Cove in 2nd Story Hall

To face of frame 16'-5"

Centre

12'-11" To face of frame

13'-6"

17'-5" To face of frame —

⑩

½ INCH SCALE DETAILS of HALL in HOUSE for

MR. WINTHROP B. FAY —
PASADENA —

Closet

Corner

8"

2'-10"

Outside | Inside

Line of Corners

line of face

2'-10"

13'-8"

2'-10"

3'-0"

1'-8"

1'-8"

3'-0"

18'-2" To face of frame —

16'-0"

Seat with cover to 1/4

3'-6"

Furring

Stereo Relief

Wood mould turned —

Plan of Stereo

Plaster Bracket

Oak Top

Stereo Relief

Marble Bowl Back

Wood —

Plaster

Ornament on each side not covered by rail —

Carved —

5'-0"

4'-1"

ELEVATION of SIDE —

Mantel — 4'-5"

FRONT —

PLAN —

Note: Stereo Relief on Ceiling follows dotted lines on 1/4 scale plan —

Stereo

Turned Spindles —

Turned Mould

Back

Turned Mould

1'-4"

Plan —

GREENE & GREENE,
ARCHITECTS,
PASADENA, CAL.

PLAN of FRONT STAIRCASE —

W.S. Plant
James P. Dawson
W. B. Fay

MAY 28 1898

MAY 20 1898

FIGURE 4
*Front door, James A.
Culbertson house,
Pasadena, 1902–15*
Photograph © Ognen
Borissov/Interfoto

contrast, the tree in the bottom of the door is meant to appear realistic. Viewed in this context, it becomes a low bush, such as boxwood or manzanita, that might realistically be viewed through the door surrounding the porch or stoop. This detail view of the plant, without landscape or details of setting, became Charles's preferred composition for plant forms in stained-glass designs.

The door also reveals the improved quality of fabrication of the Greenes' stained-glass designs. The texture of the tree trunks below and the weepy branches of the willow tree above are created with sheet-lead cutouts like those in the Sanborn windows, but these are more detailed and sophisticated. The leaves of the willow tree are quite rectilinear and somewhat ungainly, like the tulips of the Sanborn house. Although the holes are rectangles (a shape not often associated with willows), there are many of them and they are close together. The quality of craftsmanship in the door also shows improvement, though the maker remains unknown.

The branches of the tree in the lower half of the door are more lyrical and graceful in design and execution. Curved and elongated cutouts give them texture and color. The cutouts were created with a jeweler's saw or a similarly delicate tool by someone with a practiced hand, though even this level of craftsmanship seems amateurish compared to the fine work that soon followed. Two matching overlays were cut, one for the interior of the door, the other for the exterior. Overlays

of this kind for large windows hide the lead came that holds the pieces of glass together.

Charles continued to work out his ideas for glass in the Reeve house. In the living-room china cabinet (fig. 6), two asymmetrical lines swoop from the top center to each side in the upper pane, like tied-back curtains. In this subtle but surprising detail are the seeds of the graceful, organic, Asian-inspired curves that would emerge more fully within a year. In the entry hall, the door-sized window at the foot of the stairs is divided into a horizontal panel above, center and sidelights, and seven vertical sections below (fig. 7). At the center is a landscape, rendered as though the viewer were looking through a window at the hills, sky, flowers, and birds. The image is quite abstract, however, with simple rounded shapes depicting leaves, flowers, and rocks, with no differentiation. The outline is somewhat awkward, lacking the flow and grace of the Greenes' later work. At the bottom, mullions give the effect of a slatted fence, with tall, simple flowers—perhaps hollyhocks—behind it. A watercolor for the door (fig. 8) is slightly different; the fence and flowers at the bottom are there, but instead of a landscape, the center is a view into the boughs of a tree. The palette is somber: dark brown, amber, and dark teal blue. Only the birds are sheet-lead cutouts.

The stained-glass hanging lamps for the Reeve house (fig. 9) were the first major lighting fixtures designed by the Greenes.[19] Their pierced-lead overlays look like

FIGURE 5

Dining room, showing leaded-glass cabinet doors, double sconce, and hanging fixture, Jennie A. Reeve house, Long Beach, 1903–04

Courtesy of Charles Sumner Greene Collection (1959-1), Environmental Design Archives, University of California, Berkeley

FIGURE 6

Corner of living room, showing leaded-glass cabinet and hanging fixtures, Jennie A. Reeve house

Courtesy of Charles Sumner Greene Collection (1959-1), Environmental Design Archives, University of California, Berkeley

FIGURE 7
Entry-hall leaded-glass panel, Jennie A. Reeve house
Private collection. Photograph courtesy of Sotheby's New York

FIGURE 8
Watercolor design for entry-hall panel, Jennie A. Reeve house
Courtesy of Greene and Greene Archives, The Gamble House, University of Southern California

FIGURE 9
Exterior leaded-glass fixture, Jennie A. Reeve house
Courtesy of Guardian Stewardship. Photograph courtesy of Sotheby's New York

construction-paper cutouts, made with tin snips rather than jeweler's saws. Their construction is heavy, with large, lumpy soldering holding the panels together. The hangers of bent metal rod are rather crude. On the chandeliers, the large hooks on the top look sharp and dangerous (fig. 5).[20] Yet here Charles's style has become recognizable: the meandering line that represents a floral stem, interrupted irregularly by curling leaves; the Japanese quality of composition; the asymmetrical arrangement of both floral components and panels, combined into lampshades with marked Asian influence.

The windows of the Tichenor house, completed in early 1906, were the last to feature sheet-lead overlays.[21] They embellish the dining-room buffet windows with flowering branches and the master-bedroom windows with a flock of birds (fig. 10). But there is a change in the treatment of the overlays: not only are they fine and delicately cut, but they are also coated with solder that

has been worked into textures suggesting the bark of branches and the cup of a petal or the bellies and hollows of a bird's breast and wings. Solder is naturally a bright silver color that eventually dulls to a dark gray over the course of a number of years. In most of the Greenes' overlay windows, the solder was artificially aged by brushing on an acidic compound.

The Tichenor dining-room and bedroom windows are made with brilliantly colored glass, individual opalescent sheets combining green, yellow, pink, and white in imitation of sunrise. Such glass composed of so many different colors is sometimes called "end of day" glass, because at the end of the day, when there was too little molten material left to make a complete sheet of a single hue, the glass makers poured the tag ends of their pots of melted glass together to create a sheet or two and not waste the material.

The Tichenor house is the first to which the Los Angeles stained-glass studio of Sturdy-Lange can be

FIGURE 10
*Pair of bedroom
windows, Adelaide A.
Tichenor house, Long
Beach, 1904–05*
Courtesy of Guardian
Stewardship. Photograph
© Bill Bachhuber

connected with documentation. It is not known who fabricated the Greenes' windows previously. Only one photograph of the Sturdy-Lange studio is known to survive (fig. 11).[22] At the top of the right pane in the third window from the right is a silhouette of a flock of birds in flight. This matches one of the panels in the Tichenor house bedroom windows.[23]

In other windows in the Tichenor house, Charles's formerly wobbly lines, seen in the Reeve and Sanborn windows, have evolved into Chinese-like cloud forms.[24] The absence of straight edges is now clearly intentional, representing the horizon, or a band of clouds or water, or whatever Charles or the viewer brings to it. This band in the design, with a wide came on one side and a narrow one on the other, and irregularly spaced colored squares, also bordered by cames of dissimilar width, was similarly used as the upper border of the lanterns in the Reeve house; the vertical, fork-like elements in the windows for the C.J. Willet house in Pasadena (1904); and the vertical trellis in windows in the Laurabelle A. Robinson house (1905–06), also in Pasadena. Without any Western representational imagery, the freehand quality of the lines is both organic and lyrical, enabling the viewer to bring his or her own interpretation to it in ways that would be hampered by absolutely straight and symmetrical compositions.

TECHNICAL REFINEMENTS

In 1906, the Greenes' stained-glass output changed dramatically, not in style—which, as has been shown, was developing apace—but in execution. Until this time, both lampshades and windows had been assembled with lead came in the medieval tradition. Suddenly, the copper foil that gave Tiffany lamps their distinctive elegance and their rigid strength appears in the Greenes' work, bursting out in the astonishing complexity of the dining-room chandelier for the Robinson house. Copper foil, cut into narrow strips and wrapped around the edges of the glass, forms a narrower, more uneven line than came. Solder holds the pieces together. The technique was patented in Boston in 1886 by an otherwise unknown stained-glass craftsman, Sanford Bray, "to provide a cheap, simple, convenient, and expeditious means for joining colored-glass mosaics for church-windows."[25] Tiffany Studios began using foil in the early 1890s for windows and by 1897 for lampshades; within a few years, foil had been

FIGURE 12

Dining-room chandelier, Laurabelle A. Robinson house, Pasadena, 1905–06

Courtesy of The Huntington Library, Art Collections, and Botanical Gardens, San Marino, California. Gift of Randell L. Makinson, an anonymous donor, and the Virginia Steele Scott Foundation. Photograph © Ognen Borissov/Interfoto

FIGURE 13

Watercolor design for dining-room chandelier, Laurabelle A. Robinson house

Courtesy of Charles Sumner Greene Collection (1959-1), Environmental Design Archives, University of California, Berkeley

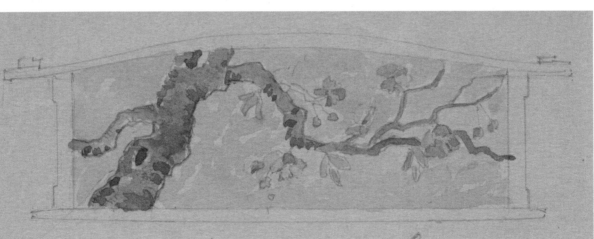

adopted by other makers.[26] Stained-glass craftspeople tended to be peripatetic, frequently moving from one studio to another, sharing new materials and methods. The copper-foil technique may have been brought to Los Angeles by the ex-Tiffany employees who operated the MacKay Company.

The design for the Robinson chandelier, depicting cherry branches in bloom, is Charles's most sophisticated yet, portraying on the side of the shade the branches in profile and from below the impression of looking up into the blooming tree (figs. 12 and 13). Further adding to the complexity of the design is the undulation of the glass panels, which flow inward at the corners and belly outward on the sides. To achieve this

serpentine form, the craftsmen had to divide the background and stems into myriad tiny pieces that could be bent around a mold and soldered to shape, the same way a Tiffany lampshade was formed. Charles's watercolor, inscribed *Glass $150*, does not indicate or even hint at such background detail, implying that this labor-intensive construction may have been the craftsmen's suggestion. At this price, the Robinson chandelier was more expensive than most Tiffany shades.[27]

Partitioning the background into hundreds of pieces, each smaller than one square inch, could have been done randomly without any attempt to depict forms or textures. Instead, the pieces are treated like tesserae in a mosaic, used to create bands and concentric

arcs. These bands, executed in iridescent amber glass, suggest woven reed basketwork, much like Tiffany's shades of about 1899 based on Native American baskets.[28] The Robinsons collected such baskets and other Native American objects, and the Greenes designed their house to reflect this interest.[29]

The chandelier demonstrates the new possibilities of the copper-foil technique. The line created by the foil is very thin, and in bright light it is practically invisible. The delicacy of the foil permits fine detail, since it does not obscure as much glass as does came. Structurally, it is very sound; because the edges of the glass practically touch, there is little room for it to bow or sag. A copper-foiled lampshade is surprisingly rigid. This factor is particularly important for windows installed in doors, where movement often causes leaded panels to bow.

The windows of 1907 for the James Culbertson house are a further exultation in the delicacy of copper foil. On the stairs is a *tour de force* window of unprecedented individuality (figs. 14 and 15). Below transoms of clear roundels laid out in an ordinary geometric pattern are clear panels of extraordinary calligraphic complexity that provide an intricate counterpoint to the rigid rectilinearity of the staircase woodwork. Floral vines twine a wall or trellis, yet from a distance, the design could be a skeleton: the rounded horizontal lines in the middle evoke a rib cage; the dense black flowers and their dangling lianas suggest the flanges of the pelvis and the shape of legs. The solder is again sculpted, mimicking and enhancing the odd anthropomorphism of the vines. The effect is both enchanting and slightly sinister, like the best fairy tales.

The final material change in the Greenes' windows that makes their work truly extraordinary is the use of iridized colored glass (fig. 16). Until 1907, the Greenes had employed clear glass or plain opalescent glass in either monochromatic hues or extravagantly multicolored

FIGURE 15

Detail of single staircase window, James A. Culbertson house

Photograph © Ognen Borissov/Interfoto

sheets, as in the Tichenor house. In the great cathedrals, the richly hued windows were primarily viewed by day; since there were few services at night, the fact that the windows go dark without any sun was not a drawback. But in homes, it was important that stained glass retain color at night, when interior lighting reflected off its surfaces. Opalescent glass does just this; its dense, non-transparent body reflects color. This was one of the factors that made a happy marriage between opalescent glass and residential stained-glass windows.

Iridescent glass was a further refinement. This colored glass has a surface finish that reflects the myriad colors of a soap bubble. Erroneously termed "Tiffany glass" by past Greene and Greene scholars, the glass used by Charles Greene is more like that employed by Frank Lloyd Wright in his windows for Susan Lawrence Dana (1902–04, Springfield, Illinois) and Darwin D. Martin (1903–05, Buffalo, New York).[30] Glass is iridized by exposure to metallic fumes in a process that has been known for centuries. Louis Comfort Tiffany, Frederick Carder of Steuben Glass, Emile Gallé in France, and the Lötz Witwe firm in Austria, to name but a few, admired ancient iridescent glass and strove successfully to duplicate it. Tiffany Studios produced iridescent glass objects, such as vases and bowls; whatever flat glass it made was solely for its own use. The glass used by the Greenes and other artists was produced by other glass houses, including Dannenhoffer Glass Works in Brooklyn and the Opalescent Glass Works in Kokomo, Indiana.[31] Most iridescent flat glass was transparent cathedral (machine-rolled) and not opalescent, because the heating process required for the finish could change the color of the opalescent glass.[32] Like Wright in the Dana and Martin houses, the Greenes preferred a palette of green and gold iridescent glass that gives the interior a warm, sunny glow.

In three of the firm's greatest commissions—the Robert R. Blacker (1907–09), David B. Gamble (1907–09), and William R. Thorsen (1908–10) houses—Charles used iridescent glass enthusiastically, designing more windows, lanterns, and cabinet inserts than ever before. These houses overflow with stained glass, but they are not gaudy or even remotely religious. Nor are they claustrophobic, as a house can be when the view through a window is blocked by busy designs. There is no discordant blue or strident red, no hot yellow or acidic green. The warm golden and olive tones of the exterior windows blend with the rich, rubbed-wood finishes of the interior and the muted, faded tones of the Oriental carpets. Charles employed iridized glass in lanterns, cabinets, interior windows, and fireplace surrounds; the rainbows of

reflected color are subtle and gentle, sparkling quietly in the ever-changing light that filters through the trees and diaphanous curtains. In the evening, when the warm light of incandescent bulbs passes through the fixtures, it becomes the color of honey. The control of light and color in glass in the Blacker, Gamble, and Thorsen houses is masterful, never overpowering or ostentatious.

The choice of subjects and imagery was important in these spaces. While obviously deeply influenced by Asian art, Charles adapted the ancient forms and compositions to their surroundings. Seagulls in white opalescent glass float through Chinese clouds in the lanterns of the Blacker house (see page 2). The twisted trunks and branches that welcome visitors to the Gamble and Thorsen houses evoke gnarled old specimens, symbols of longevity both in Japanese prints and in Chinese scrolls.[33] Vines of grape, ivy, wisteria, and bougainvillea twine through transoms and lampshades, while *tsuba* and various auspicious symbols, including lotus, peach, and pomegranates, outline lantern panels and china-cabinet doors. The effect is at once familiar and exotic, quotidian and spiritual.

Charles's largest window compositions were for the doors of the Blacker and Gamble houses (fig. 17). Both employ the technique of layering glass, called plating, borrowed from opalescent-window artists; the Blacker door has three layers of glass, the Gamble door has two.[34] Despite the high artistic quality of the windows, the method used in the Blacker and Gamble doors was quite rudimentary. Although there was no single method of assembling plated windows, typically the layers were built up as the window was made and soldered together as the panel progressed. The Gamble door, however, was made as two separate windows and then placed together, joined by a wrapping of copper foil around the perimeter and set into the woodwork. It is fortunate that the individual panels of the door are small: had they been wider or taller, the two layers could have separated, one bowing to the inside, the other outward. Many of the sconces and chandeliers of this period were also plated, but in select areas only, usually on the details of flowers or clouds.

The detail of the tree bark in the Gamble door is made with a copper overlay. The delicate profile was

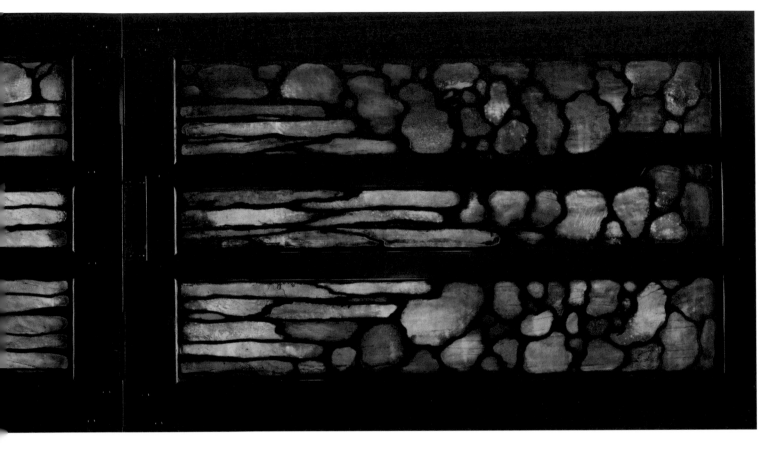

FIGURE 16

Iridized glass in breakfast-room transom window, Robert R. Blacker house

Courtesy of American Decorative Art 1900 Foundation. Photograph: Gavin Ashworth, © American Decorative Art 1900 Foundation

cut from very thin copper and soldered over the foiled joints in the glass in the same way the lead overlay was in the Culbertson door.[35] Copper is thinner, lighter, and stronger than lead, which makes it easier to cut. The overlay was cut in duplicate, as in the Tichenor windows, and applied to the interior and exterior surfaces. The copper was coated with textured solder that was patinated with copper sulfate to impart a warm brown tone with a greenish cast.

After 1915, Charles became more consumed with his own pursuits, and his involvement with the office lessened; in 1916, he left Pasadena to move to Carmel-by-the-Sea, about 300 miles (480 km) north of Los Angeles.[36] Although he continued to design houses for clients, his use of stained glass was minimal. He drifted back toward the firm's pre-bungalow days with Gothic designs for the bay windows of the James Culbertson house (1914; see Mallek essay, fig. 15) and for the addition to the Mortimer S. Fleishhacker, Sr., estate in San Francisco (1929–32; it was never built). Several of the windows of his own studio in Carmel (1923–24) are of blown-glass

roundels, a type that can be found in medieval houses in Europe.[37]

In 1929 or 1930, Charles designed a library addition to the home of Martin Flavin, called Spindrift, in Carmel. An unusual three-part window features bands of what could be egg-and-dart molding and Asian fish-scale motifs, crossed in front of a pattern resembling a wall of flat stones. When one of the panels broke during shipping by rail to the house, Charles reused the pieces for a small wall lamp above the library door.[38]

Henry Greene designed a few pieces of stained glass, but he never attained his brother's lyricism of drawing or mastery of colored light. Instead, he retreated to old-fashioned Federal-style glass for the bookcases of the Theodore A. Kramer house in South Pasadena (1918). But Henry retained an interest in birds, decorating the ceilings of these bays with cutout silhouettes similar to the windows of 1906 for Adelaide Tichenor's bedroom. In 1918, he revisited the Tichenor birds in the Carrie Whitworth house in Altadena, placing them against an almost-clear background with clouds (fig. 18). In his most

adventurous use of colored glass, Henry designed a pair of sunrise and sunset windows for the Kate A. Kelly house in Los Angeles (1921), where birds float through cumulus clouds worthy of N.C. Wyeth. By far his most interesting glass was also practically his last: china-cabinet doors (later converted to exterior windows) for the Thomas Gould, Jr., house in Ventura (1924) that featured hummingbirds feeding at fuchsias. Although they recall Charles's vine designs in the Blacker house, Henry's windows are startling in their use of glass paint to delineate the tiny faces and tail feathers of the birds. No other glass art in the careers of the brothers had resorted to this medieval expedient.

REGIONAL STAINED-GLASS STUDIOS

Los Angeles hosted only a handful of stained-glass studios in the first decade of the twentieth century, unlike the East Coast, where hundreds of makers were in operation in the major cities. Which of these studios provided services to Greene and Greene is only partly known. The Warren Glass Company, which opened in the late 1880s, provided a variety of art glasses: embossed, beveled, and silvered, as well as stained.[39] In 1894, Edward A. Bellringer founded the Los Angeles Art Glass Company, incorporating it in 1897; Frederick W. Schneider, one of the founding partners, took over the studio in 1912, and ran it until his death in 1924.[40] The MacKay Company, "one of the most important art glass works on the Pacific Coast," started up in 1904, founded by Joseph Evan MacKay, a former employee of Tiffany Studios.[41]

In the 1890s, Herman Raphael, a commercial glazier in Los Angeles, had a stained-glass department run by Walter Horace Judson. Judson opened his own studio in Los Angeles, the Colonial Art Glass Company, in 1897, changing its name to W.H. Judson Art Glass Company in 1906. In 1921, it became Judson Studios, the name under which it still operates.[42] The firm made bookcase windows at Henry Greene's direction for Charles M. Pratt in Ojai in 1937, nearly thirty years after Greene and Greene designed the house.[43] Designed and built 1908–11, the Pratt house contained light fixtures similar to those in the Blacker house, as well as interior windows in cabinets, bookcases, and between rooms. It is not clear which cabinet windows were made by Judson Studios.

For his triptych windows in the Flavin house of about 1930, Charles commissioned the Oakland-based Cobbledick-Kibbe Glass Company. Begun in 1890 as L.N. Cobbledick & Bros., a distributor of such building materials as glass, paints, oil, and wallpaper, the firm switched exclusively to glass in late 1906 or early 1907.[44] By 1914, Cobbledick-Kibbe Glass Company was "one of the leading concerns of its kind in Oakland … The company also has a department given to the exclusive manufacture of leaded art glass and trade along this line is also extensive and gratifying."[45] The firm ultimately became one of the largest distributors of window glass in America, closing around 2001.[46]

STURDY-LANGE STUDIO
The stained-glass studio that produced the majority of windows for Greene and Greene was Sturdy-Lange, located in Los Angeles. Their relationship can be documented only between 1906 and about 1910. Both the company and its principals, Harry Sturdy and Emil Lange, are today elusive, and made little mark on the local horizon at the time. The firm did not advertise and was not listed in business directories, local publications, or maps. The only billheads for Sturdy-Lange known to survive are those in the Greene and Greene Archives (GGA), and they date only to a short period between December 1909 and February 1910.[47]

Emil Lange's name is recognized today largely because of Randell Makinson's efforts to give credit to the craftspeople who made the Greenes' houses. Unfortunately, much of Makinson's information was erroneous.[48] A purported connection between Lange and Tiffany—that Lange had worked for the New York

studio or used its glass in his windows for the Greenes—cannot be substantiated. Prior to his move to Los Angeles, there is no evidence that he had any experience in stained glass or any other field in art or craft.[49]

Lange was born on December 2, 1866 in St. Louis, Missouri, to German-born parents, Rudolph and Caroline Schlapp Lange.[50] In 1870, the family moved to Iowa, where Rudolph bought the Arsenal Brewery in Davenport.[51] By the time he died in 1897, he was a pillar of the community; he was buried in Davenport's most fashionable garden cemetery, Oakdale.

Emil Lange briefly studied mining engineering in 1888 at Freiburg University in Germany, although he seems not to have completed his studies.[52] In 1893 or 1894, he married a local girl, Emma Stracke, from Burlington, Iowa; they had two daughters, Agnes and Vera, in 1896 and 1899, respectively.[53] In 1893, Lange bought an interest in a large lumber company in Burlington, run by John D. Harmer;[54] he served as secretary of J.D. Harmer & Co. between 1894 and 1898.[55] When the company failed between 1898 and 1900, Emil "suffered heavy losses."[56] He soon moved his family back to Davenport, where they lived in his father's house with Emil's mother and younger sister.[57]

By March 1900, Emil was secretary of the Iowa Mantle Manufacturing Co., and perhaps also an investor.[58] He seems to have flourished in Davenport until at least early 1904, but his apparently comfortable life came apart in 1905, when he moved to Los Angeles without his wife and daughters.[59] By mid-1906, Emma had lost touch with Emil. In a letter to her sister, she related, "Did I tell you that Ella [Emil's sister] and her mother spent the winter with Emil in Los Angeles[?] He went into a new factory & they make Art Glass and other novelties. Ella sees a great future for him, I hope she will not be disappointed."[60] In a letter otherwise filled with the minutiae of Emma's life, the detachment with which she writes about her husband is disturbing. This suggests that they were not only estranged, but that Emil may not have been providing for her and the children.

The family's story does not have a happy ending. Emma narrated a litany of health problems to her sister, including, "nervousness" and "melancholia." Despite her doctor's assurances, on October 10, 1906, Emma shot herself in her bedroom, where her seven- and ten-year-old daughters found her later in the day. She was thirty-eight years old; the newspapers gave the reason for her suicide as "ill health."[61] There is no indication that Emil returned for her funeral.[62] Lange's children were raised in Burlington by his wife's family; he seems never to have

FIGURE 17
Front door, David B. Gamble house, Pasadena, 1907–09
Photograph © Estate of Mark Fiennes

returned to Iowa.[63] There is virtually no record of Emil's life in California, other than sparse references to him in Greene and Greene's papers. Emma's obituary states that he was "trying to retrieve in the west" the losses sustained in the failure of J.D. Harmer & Co. but provides no details of where he was living or what he did for work.[64]

The first mention of Lange in Los Angeles is in a classified advertisement from November 1906 for Sturdy-Lange, Manufacturers of Art Glass and Decorators.[65] There is no record of when or how Lange met Harry Sturdy. On the company's billheads, Sturdy is listed as president and Lange is given as secretary and treasurer. Lange was a businessman, after all, not an artist. Sturdy, the president and first listed name of the firm, was the artist and craftsman.[66]

In the 1910 census, Lange described himself as an artist in art glass; by this time, he probably was designing windows. By 1920, when Sturdy-Lange no longer existed, he called himself a wholesaler in the art-glass business, suggesting that he hired others to design and maybe even manufacture windows that he then provided to other companies (such as lumberyards and department stores). Yet he appeared in the ledgers of W.H. Judson Art Glass Company in the same year, with irregular payments suggesting that he subcontracted work from them on occasion, receiving hourly wages.[67] Emil Lange died on July 28, 1934, of liver disease, survived by his mother, sisters, and daughters.[68]

Harry Sturdy is more historically obscure than Lange. Born in Canada in 1869 of English parents, he immigrated to the United States in 1885. By 1900, he lived in Chicago with his wife, Mary Leahy, at 634–36 Fifty-sixth Street, about a mile west of Midway Plaisance, the southwestern edge of the 1893 Columbian Exposition grounds. At age thirty-one, he was an interior decorator.[69]

Sturdy, the principal artist of Sturdy-Lange, probably gained experience in the craft of stained glass in Chicago. It was a popular art form in the city in the 1890s: at least four local studios exhibited at the Columbian Exposition in 1893; Tiffany Studios had an enormous display at the fair as well as an office downtown; and at least six other local firms advertised or received notice in *Inland Architect* in the decade.[70] By the mid-1890s, Chicago was noted for its production of residential art glass: "The old notion about the incapacity of Chicago artists engaged in the production of art glass is rapidly dying out, and the wealthy and refined of our city are now honoring the artistic creations of local artists by placing them in their residences, and employing glass decorations profusely to embellish their homes."[71] As an interior decorator, Sturdy probably worked for one of these firms.

Sturdy moved to California sometime after 1900. His name first appears in March 1906, in the society pages of the *Los Angeles Times*, eight months before the classified ad for Sturdy-Lange.[72] In the 1910 census, Sturdy styled himself an artist and interior decorator, living at 2807 La Salle Avenue in Los Angeles, an upper-middle-class neighborhood.[73] By February 1910, however, his name had been omitted from the company billhead with a stamp announcing "Emil Lange / Successor to" before the firm's name. Sturdy died sometime before 1920, leaving a wife and three sons aged between eight and seventeen. He clearly must have been living in 1912 to have an eight-year-old son in 1920. No obituary or death notice has been located.[74]

Harry Sturdy's disappearance from the records around 1910 coincides roughly with the end of Greene and Greene's use of elaborate leaded glass. Although they may have continued to employ Lange, the decorative windows created for the Whitworth, Kelly, and Gould houses are different in style and simpler in construction. If Sturdy-Lange was the force behind the complexity and artistry of the Greenes' windows beginning around 1906, and if Sturdy was in fact the more talented glazier of the pair, it is reasonable that this quality would have changed when he departed the firm.

Whatever the reason, the amount of leaded glass used by the brothers declined after the Thorsen house was completed in 1910. The style of their architecture was beginning to change, and stained glass was no longer part of their designs. Perhaps they were unconsciously responding to conditions of bright light (which washes out the colors of glass) and warm climate (which demands windows that open) that are thought to have influenced the medieval development of European stained glass, making such glass less popular in sunny locales, such as Italy and Spain, than in cloudier northern Europe and Great Britain.[75] Perhaps the Greenes began to think stained glass was old-fashioned, no longer cutting-edge decoration, although this attitude would come more slowly to the eastern United States, where the craft began to lessen in popularity only in the 1920s. It may have been for reasons more personal or more practical. Like other architect-designers of stained glass (notably Frank Lloyd Wright and the Prairie School), Charles and Henry Greene never articulated their thoughts about the medium, and so their motivations can be only imagined.

FIGURE 18
Three-panel leaded-glass window, 1918, designed by Henry Greene for Carrie Whitworth, Altadena
Courtesy of Guardian Stewardship. Photograph courtesy of Sotheby's New York

[pages 175 and 176]
FIGURES 19 AND 20
Panel details, living-room light fixture, Robert R. Blacker house
Courtesy of American Decorative Art 1900 Foundation. Photograph: Gavin Ashworth, © American Decorative Art 1900 Foundation

1. Samuel Howe, "The Making of the Glass," *The Craftsman*, 3, no. 6 (March 1903), p. 368.

2. Memorial Hall included the pioneering work of John La Farge with his first public opalescent window, *Battle* (1878–82), and windows by Louis Comfort Tiffany, Daniel Cottier, William J. McPherson, Sarah Wyman Whitman, and Henry Holiday. La Farge was the first to use opalescent glass in windows; Tiffany popularized the material, particularly in the 1890s with his lampshades; see Julie L. Sloan, "The Rivalry Between Louis Comfort Tiffany and John La Farge," *Nineteenth Century*, 17, no. 2 (Fall 1997), pp. 27–34. Cottier was a decorator born in Scotland and trained in London; he opened a New York office in 1873 and is credited with bringing the Aesthetic style to the United States; see Mark Girouard, *Sweetness and Light: The "Queen Anne" Movement, 1860–1900* (New Haven, Conn.: Yale University Press, 1977), p. 210. McPherson was a decorator who produced many Aesthetic-style windows in the Boston area; see Lance Kasparian, "The Stained-Glass Work of Donald MacDonald of Boston: A Preliminary Study," *Journal of Stained Glass*, 28 (2004), pp. 12–30. Whitman was a Boston socialite; see Betty S. Smith, "Sarah de St. Prix Wyman Whitman," *Old-Time New England*, LXXVII, no. 266 (Spring–Summer 1999), pp. 46–64. Holiday was a major London artist; see Henry Holiday, *Stained Glass as an Art* (London: Macmillan & Co., 1896).

3. Morris and Burne-Jones provided the baptistery window (1882) and the north-transept window (c. 1883); Holiday created three windows in the nave (all c. 1878); and Cottier designed four small windows in the south transept. La Farge had covered the church's interior with richly colored murals in 1876–77; he returned to provide windows in 1883–87 and again in 1902.

4. These included New Old South (1873–75); Brattle Square (First Baptist) by Richardson (1873); Central Congregational by Richard Upjohn (1867; now Church of the Covenant); First Church (Unitarian; 1868; burned in 1968, leaving only the front façade); South Congregational, where Edward Everett Hale preached (1883–84, later sold); First Spiritual Temple (1885; now a commercial building); Emmanuel Episcopal

Church (1861); and Notre Dame Catholic Church. Moses King, *King's How to See Boston; a trustworthy guidebook* (New York: King's Handbooks, 1895), pp. 138–50, 157.

5. Edward S. Cooke, Jr., "Talking or Working: The Conundrum of Moral Aesthetics in Boston's Arts and Crafts Movement," in *Inspiring Reform: Boston's Arts and Crafts Movement*, exhib. cat., ed. Marilee Boyd Meyer, Wellesley, Mass., Davis Museum and Cultural Center, Wellesley College, 1997, pp. 18–28.

6. Quoted in Cooke, 'Talking or Working," p. 24, emphasis mine. Warren was describing the architecture program at Harvard, which he headed from 1893 until his death.

7. Edward R. Bosley, *Greene & Greene*, (London: Phaidon, 2000), pp. 15–19.

8. CSG and HMG, Scrap Album, begun 1890, p. 40, GGA.

9. The window is illustrated in Randell L. Makinson, *Greene & Greene: The Passion and the Legacy* (Salt Lake City: Gibbs Smith, 1998), p. 16.

10. "Mosaics," *Inland Architect and News Record*, 11, no. 8 (July 1888), p. 89; Kathleen Cummings, "Sullivan and Millet: Stained Glass in Chicago's Auditorium Building," *Style 1900*, 14, no. 2 (Spring/May 2001), pp. 44–48.

11. Collaborations between Millet and Sullivan included McVicker's Theater, the Transportation Building at the World's Columbian Exposition, the Schiller Building, and the Chicago Stock Exchange; see David A. Hanks, "Louis J. Millet and the Art Institute of Chicago," *Bulletin of the Art Institute of Chicago*, 67 (March–April 1973), p. 14.

12. E. Didron, "Le Vitrail depuis cent ans et à l'exposition de 1889," *Revue des arts décoratifs*, 10 (1889–90), pp. 145–47. According to the article, the French government purchased all of Millet's windows for its own collections.

13. Cummings, "Sullivan and Millet," p. 46. Most of this glass is no longer in the building. Millet also designed a set of figural lunettes for the entrance to the Auditorium itself.

14. Bosley, *Greene & Greene*, p. 38. Charles's first English-inspired glass is the lantern at the base of the stairs for the James A. Culbertson house in Pasadena (1902). The vertical fixture is Japanese in sentiment, its broad, flat top sheltering the leaded-glass sides. Its floral design, executed in opalescent glass, is similar to textile

and inlay patterns by M.H. Baillie Scott and Will Bradley; Baillie Scott was published often in *International Studio*, while Bradley's work appeared frequently in 1901–02 in *Ladies Home Journal*: 18 (November 1901), p. 7; 19 (December 1901), p. 17; 19 (January 1902), p. 11; 19 (February 1902), p. 13; 19 (March 1902), p. 15; 19 (May 1902), p. 13; 19 (July 1902), p. 15. Charles subscribed to the former, and may have seen Baillie Scott's work on his honeymoon in Britain. He admired Bradley's work enough to paste one of his articles into his scrapbook; Scrap Album, pp. 43–47.

15. By the 1910s, other artists used this technique very expressively, including Nicola D'Ascenzo of Philadelphia and G. Owen Bonawit of Cleveland.

16. The manufacturer of the Sanborn window is unknown.

17. Robert C. Spencer, Jr., "The Work of Frank Lloyd Wright," *Architectural Review*, 7 (1900), pp. 61–72; Tiffany Glass and Decorating Company, *A Synopsis of the Exhibit of the Tiffany Glass & Decorating Company in the American Section of the Manufactures and Liberal Arts Building at the World's Fair, Jackson Park, Chicago, Illinois, 1893, with an Appendix of Memorial Windows* (New York: Tiffany Glass and Decorating Co., 1893).

18. Julie L. Sloan, *Light Screens: The Complete Leaded-Glass Windows of Frank Lloyd Wright* (New York: Rizzoli, 2001), p. 261.

19. Regarding the hanging lamps, see Bosley, *Greene & Greene*, p. 61 n. 33.

20. I am grateful to Nina Gray, Joseph Cunningham, and Bruce Barnes for drawing my attention to issues of fabrication in these lamps.

21. In a letter to Charles Greene of December 7, 1905, Adelaide Tichenor complains that the windows are not yet installed; Randell L. Makinson, "Greene and Greene," in *Toward a Simpler Way of Life: The Arts and Crafts Architects of California*, ed. Robert Winter (Berkeley: University of California Press, 1997), pp. 129–30.

22. Makinson, *Passion*, p. 79. The photograph is a gift from Emil Lange's granddaughter, Joan Kass, in the GGA.

23. I am grateful to Edward Bosley and Ted Wells for sharing their discovery of this with me.

24. Bosley and others have related the appearance of Asian forms at this time to Charles's visit with Adelaide Tichenor to the Louisiana Purchase Exposition in St. Louis, in July 1904; Bosley, *Greene & Greene*, p. 67.

25. Sanford Bray, "Joining Glass Mosaics," patent no. 349,424, granted September 21, 1886.

26. Martin Eidelberg *et al.*, *A New Light on Tiffany: Clara Driscoll and the Tiffany Girls* (New York: New-York Historical Society, 2007), pp. 30–32. Several references on the Internet state that Tiffany bought the rights to Bray's patent, preventing anyone else from using it until its expiration around 1903, but this claim cannot be substantiated.

27. In Tiffany Studios' price list for 1906, no. 342, a large Wisteria, complete with a bronze base and wired for electricity, was $400, while an oil lamp with a bronze base and large Peacock shade, no. 224, was $115; see Robert Koch, *Louis C. Tiffany's Glass, Bronzes, Lamps* (New York: Crown Publishers, 1971), p. 169.

28. *Louis Comfort Tiffany at The Metropolitan Museum of Art*, exhib. cat. by Alice Cooney Frelinghuysen, New York, The Metropolitan Museum of Art, 1998, p. 75.

29. Bosley, *Greene & Greene*, pp. 81–84.

30. Sloan, *Light Screens*, pp. 228–51, 257–63; Randell L. Makinson, *Greene & Greene: Furniture and Related Designs* (Salt Lake City: Peregrine Smith, 1979), pp. 35, 99; Randell L. Makinson, *Greene & Greene: Architecture as a Fine Art* (Salt Lake City: Peregrine Smith, 1977), p. 166; Makinson, *Passion*, p. 79.

31. Nina Gray, *Tiffany by Design: An In-Depth Look at Tiffany Lamps* (Atglen, Pa.: Schiffer Publishing, 2006), p. 10; Paul Crist, *Mosaic Shades* (Sante Fe Springs, Calif.: Paul Crist Studios, 2005), II, pp. 26–29; Sloan, *Light Screens*, pp. 321–22, 328–29.

32. Opalescent glass can "strike" if refired after manufacture. Striking usually turns the glass more opaque. Opalescence caused by striking can often be seen in iridescent glass.

33. See, for comparison, the *Great Pine* murals (1624–26) by the school of Kanō Tanyū in Nijō Castle, Kyoto; Joan Stanley-Baker, *Japanese Art* (London: Thames & Hudson, 1984), p. 140.

34. Originally developed for use in American windows by John La Farge in the late 1870s, plating was adopted by Tiffany, J. & R. Lamb, and many other artists working in opalescent glass; Sloan, "Rivalry." I am indebted to stained-glass craftsman John Hamm for his insights into the manufacture of the Gamble and Blacker windows, based on his experience with their restoration.

35. Makinson, *Furniture*, p. 99, was in error in his descriptions of the processes.

36. Bosley, *Greene & Greene*, pp. 163, 167, 170, 176, 226.

37. A panel of roundels is also visible in the photograph of the Sturdy-Lange studio, GGA.

38. Bosley, *Greene & Greene*, pp. 212–13. "Am sorry to say the largest light was broken in transit but I have put in a claim with the railroad and believe will get the cost of repair back." Letter from CSG to Martin Flavin, March 17, 1933, EDA.

39. "Warren Glass Company," *Los Angeles Times* (*LAT*), November 22, 1887, p. 5.

40. "Flotsam and Jetsam: Miscellaneous Driftwood Thrown into the Courts," *LAT*, February 2, 1897, p. 8; "Glass Maker Dies," *LAT*, October 8, 1917, p. I-8; "Schneider Funeral is Tomorrow," *LAT*, August 18, 1924, p. I-1. The studio was also listed as having failed to pay a state license tax, "Proclamation by Governor," *LAT*, September 27, 1910, p. II-10.

41. "Wouldn't Work with Any Jap," *LAT*, August 13, 1905, p. II-5. The story is about a Japanese man who had worked for Tiffany in New York coming to work for MacKay.

42. Jane Apostol, *Painting with Light: A Centennial History of the Judson Studios* (Los Angeles: Historical Society of Southern California, 1997), pp. 19–21.

43. Letter from HMG to Judson Studios, July 19, 1937, noting enclosure of check "for the leaded glass in bookcase doors for Mrs. C.M. Pratt. They look very well in the case now that it is all finished up. Thank you for your cooperation on this small job." The studio invoice notes two 24 × 27 in. (60.9 × 68.5 cm) door lights with "Lead as per Architect's detail." I am grateful to Anne Mallek for bringing this correspondence, in the Judson Studios Archives, to my attention.

44. *Past & Present of Alameda County, California* (Chicago: S.J. Clarke, 1914), II, p. 192, gives the date as 1906; as of October 30, 1906, the company's advertisement in the Oakland *Tribune* still listed wallpaper as its business (p. 5). On May 13, 1907, a *Tribune* classified advertisement lists L.N. Cobbledick Glass Co.

45. *Past & Present*, p. 192. The name changed at the time of L.N. Cobbledick's death, but the date of this was not located.

46. Dez Farnady, "Cobbledick and the PM," *U.S. Glass*, 36, no. 4 (April 2001).

47. Invoices from Sturdy-Lange Company to D.B. Gamble, all in the GGA, for "5 lanterns for bracket frames for Bedroom #0"; iridescent glass for various fixtures, doors, and windows; "5 dining room lanterns"; "2 Door Lights Mantel Bedroom #6"; and "1 Lantern Living Room / 2 Lanterns Living Room / 2 Lanterns Living Room." All invoices were signed by Lange, the company treasurer, noting receipt of payment from Greene and Greene on April 22, 1910. Curiously, these invoices are dated December 25, 1909; two dated January 20, 1910; and two dated February 15, 1910—a period spanning only seven weeks. They do not cover all of the glass in the Gamble house.

48. Makinson, *Furniture*, pp. 34–35, 99–100; Makinson, *Architecture as a Fine Art*, p. 166. Makinson did correct some of his errors in his most recent book, *Passion*, p. 79, but his information is anecdotal, coming from interviews that were confusing at best.

49. Several scholars have stated that Lange had a stained-glass studio in Burlington, Iowa; see Makinson, *Passion*, p. 79, and Bosley, *Greene & Greene*, p. 84. There is no historical evidence of that, however. In the Lange files, GGA, photographs of blue-and-yellow opalescent diamond-paned windows from the First Congregational Church of Burlington, Iowa, are accompanied by notes attributing these windows to Lange. The church has no records of any kind connecting Lange or his family with the church or the windows, which were installed in 1900; e-mail to the author from Ellen Fuller, First Congregational Church Historian, March 14, 2007.

50. "Death Notices: Lange," *Davenport Daily Times*, July 30, 1934, p. 6. Lange's father's name is alternately spelled Rudolf. He had emigrated in 1854, arriving in the bustling Mississippi River town of Burlington, Iowa, the following year, where he married and opened a grocery store. By the mid-1860s, he had moved on to St. Louis, where Emil and his two sisters, Ella and Adele, were born. Lange's name is pronounced "Lāng-ee," in two syllables, as in German, although the German pronunciation would have been "Lahng'-eh." I am grateful to Joan Kass, Lange's granddaughter, for pronunciation guidance.

51. The Arsenal Brewery's previous owners included George H. Schlapp, Rudolph's father-in-law. Rudolph renamed the firm Koehler & Lange Brewery two years later; Henry Koehler, Rudolph's partner, was Caroline Lange's brother-in-law; "Obituary: Schlapp [Marie, Mrs. George Schlapp]," *Davenport Daily Leader*, December 10, 1897, p. 1. The brewery achieved local fame by challenging a state prohibition law in 1882 and having it overturned; "Koehler & Lange vs Hill: The Old Davenport Suit up for the Last Time," *Davenport Daily Leader*, January 23, 1894, p. 2[?]. Rudolph sold the brewery in 1896 to Davenport Malting Co.

52. "Death Notices: Lange"; "Emil Lange," *Davenport Democrat and Leader*, July 30, 1934, p. 15. Emil never listed any college education in census records.

53. "Death Notices: Lange" places Emma and Emil's wedding in Davenport in September 1893. A later date of May 1894 appears in the Family Search International Genealogical Index, vol. 5, Salt Lake City. Most references give the 1893 date. Emma was born in Madison, Iowa. Her parents were Louis Stracke, b. 1832, and Victoria Heiser, b. 1841, both born in Germany. She was adopted by Ed and Catherine Hagemann (alternately spelled Hageman and Hagerman) and lived with them in Burlington; Iowa State Census Collection, 1836–1925, Burlington, Ward 6, Des Moines County, 1885, pp. 633–34, lines 19–24; the family's address was Starr and West Avenues, later given as 907 Starr Avenue. "Obituary: An Incineration," *Davenport Weekly Democrat and Leader*, October 18, 1906, p. 11; "Iowa News," *Frederickburg [Iowa] News*, October 18, 1906, n.p. In Emil's obituaries in the *Davenport Daily Times* and the *Davenport Democrat and Leader*, Emma is referred to as Emma Stracke Hagemann and Emma Hagemann, respectively.

54. "Mr. Lange, who takes charge of the business department of the concern, is an energetic and capable young man and his Davenport friends wish him every success in his new and important business enterprise"; *Davenport Daily Leader*, June 4, 1893, p. 5. Since Emil was only twenty-six, and either newly or soon to be wedded, it is probable that his father had provided the funds for this ambitious purchase. It was another

two years before the Burlington press reported that J.D. Harmer & Co. would open: "Before the year [1895] closes Burlington will have another great lumber milling industry, involving an investment of nearly $150,000, employing from two to three hundred men and covering nearly 30 acres of ground. John D. Harmer & Co. ... will erect ... a complete saw mill, planing mill, shingle mill, sash, door and blind factory"; *Davenport Daily Leader*, June 24, 1895, p. 3 The Mississippi River and its major tributaries were home to many lumberyards at this time; see Arthur A. Hart, "M.A. Disbrow & Company: Catalogue Architecture," *Palimpsest*, 56, no. 4 (July–August, 1975), pp. 98–119; and Joseph C. Bigott, *From Cottage to Bungalow: Houses and the Working Class in Metropolitan Chicago, 1869–1929* (Chicago: University of Chicago Press, 2001), pp. 28–40.

55. *Gould's Burlington [Iowa] City Directory*, 1894, p. 209; Emil is listed as working for J.D. Harmer & Co. and residing at 1018 N. Seventh Street. Four years later, *Gould's Burlington [Iowa] City Directory*, 1898, p. 232, lists him as secretary of J.D. Harmer's Manufacturing Co. and living at 934 N. Fifth Street.

56. On the failure of J.D. Harmer & Co., see "Frank Millard," *Biographical Review of Des Moines County, Iowa* (Chicago: Hobart Publishing Co., 1905), p. 994.

57. It is likely that this move was financially necessary. Emil had lost a great deal of money, and he had not inherited anything from his father. Caroline Lange was the sole beneficiary of her husband's estate; "Will of Rudolph Lange," *Davenport Daily Leader*, December 23, 1897, p. 2. Caroline outlived Emil by five years.

58. "Directory," *Davenport Times*, March 22, 1900; 1900 U.S. Census, Davenport, Scott County, Iowa, line 76. The Iowa Mantle company made mantles for gas and kerosene lamps, not fireplace surrounds. Mantle technology was somewhat new, having been invented in Germany in the late 1880s and perfected in the early 1890s.

59. Lange was a member of the local *Turnverein*, or social club, and he was on the board of his father's former company, the Davenport Malting Co.: "29 New Members Are Initiated: Turner Society Holds an Enthusiastic Meeting," *Davenport Weekly Leader*, November 17, 1903, p. 5: Lange was

one of the initiates; "Davenport Malting Company Stockholders: Meet and Re-elect Members of Old Board of Directors," *Davenport Republican*, January 9, 1903, p. 8; "Malting Company Elects Officers: Annual Meeting of the Davenport Malting Company Held Last Evening," *Davenport Daily Leader*, January 6, 1904; Harry E. Downer, *History of Davenport and Scott County* (Chicago: S.J. Clarke, 1910), II. Emma and her children are recorded with the Hagemann family in Burlington; Iowa State Census Collection, 1836–1925, Burlington, Des Moines County, 1905, cards 953–57. This listing also includes a Maud Lange, whose name does not show up elsewhere in family records; this record does not indicate her age.

60. Letter from Emma Stracke Lange, Burlington, to her sister [no name or address], July 24, 1906, GGA.

61. "A Darkened Home / Mrs Emma Lange Found Dead at Her Home on Starr Ave. / Had Been in Poor Health for Some Time and Ended Her Life in a Fit of Mental Aberration," unidentified clipping, October 11, 1906, GGA; "Obituary: An Incineration"; "Iowa News." Fairmount Cemetery Association, "Cremation Record," 1906, line 307, confirms the cremation of the body, but not the place of interment. (Emil's parents were originally interred in Oakdale; their remains were moved to Fairmount in 1949, according to records from both cemeteries.) No record of a divorce was located.

62. Lange's mother and sisters arranged for the cremation and interred Emma's remains in the Lange family vault in Davenport; "Darkened Home."

63. Agnes A. and Vera C. Lange are listed as residing at the Hagemanns' Burlington address in the census of 1915; Iowa State Census Collection, 1836–1925, Burlington, Des Moines County, 1915, cards D460 and D461, respectively. Lange's daughters grew to adulthood without knowing him, and his grandchildren knew nothing of him; related to the author by Joan Kass, daughter of Vera Lange, January 31, 2007.

64. "Darkened Home."

65. The advertisement does not mention Lange personally. It was placed by Sturdy-Lange, looking for a "good active strong boy willing to work as smudger in art glass shop" (a smudger waterproofed windows by rubbing putty beneath the lead cames); *LAT*, November 5, 1906. This advertisement is the first record of the company.

66. There is only one known sketch for a window signed by Lange, for a large rectangular, geometric window, probably a skylight, Judson Studios Archives. Lange's name and address are in the lower right corner, but the client and location are not identified. Lange's address is Ninth Street, indicating that he drew the design prior to 1920, when his address changed to Birch Street.

67. Log Books, Judson Studios Archives. On August 1, 1920, Lange received $159.35 and $50.00; on August 6, he was paid $59.35. I am grateful to David Judson for bringing this to my attention. Lange may have had similar work from other studios, but the records have not been located.

68. "Death Notices: Lange"; "Emil Lange"; "Deaths," *LAT*, July 31, 1934, p. 18. Neither the death notice in Los Angeles nor the two obituaries in Iowa described Lange's occupation, saying only that he had been in business in Burlington before moving to California.

69. 1900 U.S. Census, Schedule no. 1.- Population, Hyde Park Township, Cook County, Illinois, lines 59–60. There are no census records for Cook County from 1890, and a search for Harry Sturdy elsewhere in the country in the surviving census records of that year revealed nothing.

70. The firms at the fair were Wells Glass Company, McCully & Miles, Flanagan & Biedenweg, and George E. Androvette & Co.; "Interesting World's Fair Exhibits," *Inland Architect and News Record*, 22, no. 2 (September 1893), pp. 22–23. Tiffany Glass Company opened its office in Chicago in 1887; "Mosaics," p. 65. The firms advertising in *Inland Architect* included Linden Glass Company (part of Spierling & Linden), Healy & Millet, F.D. Kinsella & Co., George A. Misch, Chicago Art Glass, and F.X. Dahinten. See also Sharon Darling, *Chicago Ceramics and Glass* (Chicago: Chicago Historical Society, 1979).

71. *Arts for America*, 5 (March 1896), p. 67.

72. "Events in Local Society," *LAT*, March 16, 1906, p. I-16; untitled notice, *LAT*, March 17, 1906, p. I-16.

73. 1910 U.S. Census, Precinct 74, Los Angeles Township, Los Angeles County, line 76.

74. Sturdy's wife, however, continued to be mentioned in the society pages of the *Los Angeles Times*; see "At the City's Gates: The Southwest," *LAT*, February 25, 1907, p. 14, noting that the couple hosted a game of progressive whist, and "What Hostesses Have Been About Lately," *LAT*, September 5, 1925, p. D-1. Her death was noticed in the paper on July 13, 1931, p. 14; July 14, 1931, p. 22; and July 15, 1931, p. 18. The newspapers followed the Sturdys' sons as well. Announcements on Frederic H. Sturdy included "Society in Sunny Southland and What It is Doing and Planning for Diversion," *LAT*, October 9, 1927, p. C-1; "Other Engagements: Hancel-Sturdy," *New York Times*, February 20, 1932, p. 12; "Betrothed to Frederic H. Sturdy," *New York Times*, March 10, 1932, p. 18; "Eastern Girl Bride-Elect," *LAT*, March 24, 1932, p. A-6; "New York Society Girl to Wed Here Thursday," *LAT*, July 31, 1932, p. B-2; "Simplicity Marks Wedding Held in All Saints Church," *LAT*, August 7, 1932, p. B-3; "Newlyweds to Be Domiciled Here," *LAT*, August 7, 1932, p. B-4; and Juana Neal Levy, "Of Interest to Women: Society," *LAT*, August 18, 1932, p. A-5. Juana Neal Levy, "Of Interest to Women: Society," *LAT*, April 12, 1933, p. A-6, announced Paul Sturdy's marriage. "Troth Announcement Made," *LAT*, July 30, 1933, p. B-4, announced Herbert F. Sturdy's engagement.

75. This concept is something of a chestnut in medieval stained-glass history. Modern writers surmise that it was not so much the brightness of the light as it was the trapping of heat inside buildings with large window openings; see, for example, Lawrence Lee, George Seddon, and Francis Stephens, *Stained Glass* (New York: Crown Publishers, 1976), pp. 72, 94. Other historians believe that the Gothic style (characterized by the pointed arch, which permits larger window openings) was not as popular in Italy (in particular) because of its ever-present heritage of Classical architecture. Because Italy barely adopted Gothic architecture, its buildings had fewer and smaller window openings and greater expanses of wall, which led to a preference for fresco over stained glass; G. Marchini, *Italian Stained Glass Windows* (London: Thames & Hudson, 1957), p. 10.

ANN SCHEID

Independent Women, Widows, and Heiresses: Greene and Greene's Women Clients

From Greene and Greene's first client, Pasadena widow Martha Flynn, to their most celebrated one, presidential widow Lucretia Garfield, through Nellie Blacker, Mary Pratt, and Elisabeth Severance Allen Prentiss—faithful patrons in the firm's later years—women played an important role in the Greenes' architectural practice. Mary Darling, Adelaide Tichenor, and Laurabelle Robinson gave the brothers chances to experiment. Nellie Blacker and Mary Gamble offered the opportunity to build grandly. In later years, such patrons as Elisabeth Prentiss (fig. 1) and such new clients as Dr. Edna Hatcher sustained them in hard times. These women found in the Greenes congenial professionals who were comfortable working in the domestic sphere and attuned to the details of function, efficiency, and beauty desired by their well-educated, sophisticated clients. Charles Greene's considerable charm, artistic sensibility, and persuasiveness, combined with Henry's straightforward solutions, proven competence, and organizational skills, inspired confidence in clients who sought something extraordinary. The Greenes also offered what no other architect could supply: a complete designed environment—landscape, architecture, and interior—a concept especially appealing to women with the means to achieve it.

For the first time in the country's history, the 1860 census showed more women than men living in the United States. In the last two decades of the nineteenth century, the situation of these "superfluous women" began to bring about substantial social changes.[1] In the aftermath of the Civil War, more women became employed outside the home.[2] For the uneducated, there was factory work, but for women able to gain some higher education, teaching became the "natural" profession. Women were considered "better with children," and would also work for less money than men.[3] States established normal schools to train teachers; at the same time, a number of private female colleges were founded in the East and the South. In the more socially progressive Midwest, coeducation became the norm, with

Oberlin College, Ohio, and the University of Michigan among the first to admit women.[4]

As women gained increased access to higher education, their attitudes about marriage changed. They tended to marry later or not at all. Early college graduates came from middle-class backgrounds; their fathers were self-made men. These families saw education as the opportunity for "a fuller life, intellectually, socially and economically." The eastern elites, on the other hand, "preferred to educate their daughters privately at home, in boarding school, and through travel abroad."[5] Several of the Greenes' early clients were independent, educated women. The "new woman" (a term coined by Henry James)[6] was emerging from the constraints of Victorian society, financially independent and able to play a larger role in civic and business affairs.

In general, the Greenes' clients, almost all Midwesterners, were politically and socially progressive. If wealthy, they were supporters of social causes, art, and culture. In most cases, they were not self-made, but had fathers who were. Products of the Gilded Age, some were heirs to vast fortunes based in steel, oil, railroads, or allied industries, or in lumber, produced by the unceasing westward advance of clear-cutting through the seemingly endless virgin forests. The Greenes' less affluent clients, often the children of clergymen, came from the educated class. They tended to be in the professions: teaching, law, or medicine.

Most of the Greenes' clients were still only one or two generations removed from the more humble origins of their families. They did not belong to the New England aristocracy, and many were better educated than their fathers. Wives were often better educated than their husbands or brought wealth to the marriage, strengthening their hands in making decisions about the architecture and design of their new homes. The Greenes' single or widowed women clients had inherited wealth from husbands or fathers, or had been able to achieve their own financial independence. For the

FIGURE 1
Wedding portrait of Elisabeth Severance Allen Prentiss on the occasion of her marriage to Francis Fleury Prentiss, 1917
Courtesy of Western Reserve Historical Society

well-to-do at the turn of the twentieth century, coming to Pasadena represented an escape from the polluted air of the industrialized cities to a healthier environment, from cold winters and hot, humid summers to a warm, dry, equable climate. In some cases, it was also a desperate attempt to prevent or cure the scourge of the era, tuberculosis.

THE "NEW WOMEN" CLIENTS: DR. EDITH CLAYPOLE, DR. EDNA HATCHER, AND ADELAIDE TICHENOR

Outstanding among the Greenes' early clients was Dr. Edith Claypole (1850–1915). Before earning her medical degree from the University of Southern California in 1904, Edith Claypole asked the Greenes to design a bungalow for her in 1903 that included a laboratory where she could carry out her research. Her father, Edward Claypole, professor of natural science at Throop Polytechnic Institute (now the California Institute of Technology), had died in 1901, and Edith and her twin sister, Agnes, also a scientist, were appointed to the faculty to replace him. Both sisters had degrees from Buchtel College (now University of Akron) in Ohio and master's degrees from Cornell, and both had taught at Wellesley. Agnes held a PhD from the University of Chicago.[7]

Edith Claypole began her career as a physician in 1905, working as a pathologist at Pasadena Hospital and practicing with Dr. Norman Bridge, a specialist in respiratory diseases.[8] Her research on an infectious disease of the lungs, differentiating it from tuberculosis, won her an award from the American Medical Association. In 1911, she left Pasadena for Berkeley, where she carried out research on the typhoid bacillus, working on developing a typhoid vaccine. She died in 1915 of typhoid fever from an accidental infection with the bacillus.[9]

Four years after Dr. Claypole graduated from USC medical school, Dr. Edna Hatcher (1888–1975) became the first woman awarded the degree of Doctor of Dental Surgery from USC. Edna Hatcher was born in Wildomar, California, and graduated from high school in San Jacinto, where her father was the stationmaster for the Santa Fe Railroad. Dr. Hatcher opened a dental practice in Pasadena in 1910; in 1924, she hired Henry Greene to design an English Revival house on Club Road for herself, her two sisters, and her father, who had moved to Pasadena following his wife's death (fig. 2). After marrying Harry Herbert Hughes in 1927, Dr. Hatcher retired briefly from dentistry to raise her two children, John Kevin and Kingdon, but returned to practice after World

FIGURE 3
*Adelaide Alexander
Tichenor, c. 1920*
Courtesy of Long Beach
Public Library

FIGURE 4
*Wedding portrait
of Lucretia Rudolph
Garfield, 1858*
Courtesy of Western
Reserve Historical Society

War II, specializing in the treatment of children, initially in the public schools and later in private practice. The National Museum of Dentistry in Baltimore displays some of her equipment in an exhibit entitled "Edna Hughes: Pediatric Practitioner."

Although most of the Greenes' work was in Pasadena, Adelaide Tichenor (1846–1924; fig. 3) sought out the brothers in 1904 to design a house for her in Long Beach, probably on the advice of her friend Jennie Reeve. A leader in Long Beach society and civic affairs, as well as a successful businesswoman, Mrs. Tichenor had founded the local Ebell Club, a woman's civic organization, and had secured funds to establish the public library and build a public day nursery. She served on the boards of directors of a number of companies and was a member of the chamber of commerce. Lauded for her many achievements by the local press, Mrs. Tichenor was singled out for her work in "awakening women to a realization of their responsibilities and opportunities in politics."[10]

Born Mary Adelaide Alexander in Ravenna, Ohio, a small town between Youngstown and Cleveland,[11] the young Miss Alexander moved with her family to Oberlin and then to St. Louis. After graduating from St. Louis Normal College, she taught school in the city, making a

strong impression on William Torrey Harris, superintendent of schools and renowned philosopher and educator; he reportedly said that she was the best teacher he had ever known.[12]

As evidence of her adventuresome spirit, in 1884 Adelaide set out on a trip around the world. She got as far as California, where in 1885, at age thirty-nine, she married the much older Lester Schuyler Tichenor, who owned lumber businesses in San Bernardino and Hawaii. Following his death in 1891, she invested in a ranch at Redlands and taught school there, later moving to Long Beach in the mid-1890s, where she began to acquire property. She commissioned only one house from the Greenes, her own, but she built a total of twenty houses as investments for resale: sixteen in Long Beach and four in Topeka, Kansas.[13]

Mrs. Tichenor visited Europe in 1901, and in the fall of 1902, she embarked on that longed-for trip around the world with several friends, including fellow Greene and Greene client Jennie Reeve. They sailed from Los Angeles in September, arriving in Honolulu in October. The trip took many months and included extensive travel in Asia. By the summer of 1903, Mrs. Tichenor was back in Long Beach. The house commissioned after her return was the

first overtly Asian-derived design by the Greenes (see Smith essay, figs. 15–17). In the summer of 1904, she returned to St. Louis to visit the Louisiana Purchase Exposition.[14] At her behest, Charles Greene traveled back to his childhood home to see the fair, where he purchased Grueby vases and other items for the Tichenor house.[15]

Greene's visit to the exposition was undoubtedly significant in the development of his design aesthetic. In addition to the Japanese exhibits,[16] he and his client would have seen rooms by the Vienna Secessionists and German Jugendstil architects and designers, who had also impressed Frank Lloyd Wright. Their coordination of architecture, furniture, and textiles into a *Gesamtkunstwerk*, unified by a repeated design motif, may have given the impetus for the Asian-inspired furniture designs for the Tichenor house, the Greenes' first major attempt to create fully integrated architecture and furnishings.

THE WIDOWS: LUCRETIA GARFIELD, BELLE BARLOW BUSH, AND JOSEPHINE VAN ROSSEM

The most prominent client of the Greenes was Lucretia Garfield (1832–1918; fig. 4) widow of the assassinated president, for whom the Greenes began work in 1903. Following several months of design, the relationship was broken off, then taken up again in March 1904, with the house ready for Mrs. Garfield's arrival in Pasadena that October. The correspondence between the client and Charles Greene reveals a determined woman who continually questioned the architect and requested multiple design changes. Always hanging over the project was the question of funds.[17]

Born into a religious family in Garretsville, Ohio (her father, Zebulon Rudolph, was a leader of the Disciples of Christ), Lucretia Rudolph graduated from the Western Reserve Eclectic Institute (now Hiram College), which her father cofounded. Later she taught at the institute and elsewhere; in 1858, she married her former Greek teacher, James Garfield, despite reservations on both sides (he found her cold but intellectually stimulating; she resigned herself to his repeated infidelities).[18] An intelligent, independent-minded woman, "Crete" Garfield bore seven children, with five surviving to adulthood. Shortly after her husband returned from the Civil War, she supervised the building of the family house in Washington, where Garfield was serving in Congress. Later she referred to the Washington house: "I built a home once, bought all material and hired the workmen and although it was in wartime, I have never done anything so cheaply since, nor

ever had anything better done."[19] After Garfield's assassination in 1881, she altered and expanded Lawnfield, their Ohio farmhouse. These experiences no doubt gave her the confidence to question the Greenes' design.

Belle Barlow Bush (1865–1948) arrived in Pasadena around 1906 from New York, fleeing from the breakup of her marriage. By 1909, perhaps as early as 1908, she was renting the Dr. W.T. Bolton house on Elevado Drive (now West Del Mar). The Greenes had designed the house in 1906 for Bolton, who never occupied it. Mrs. Bush became an important client of the Greenes, asking Charles to make alterations to the house and to create several pieces of furniture that he had already designed for Dr. Bolton in early 1907: two hall chairs and a table, and a dining-room set (see Cooke essay, figs. 8 and 9). For Mrs. Bush he also designed an exquisite curio cabinet and a mantel clock. Charles Greene must have felt close to the family, for he designed personal bookplates for them (fig. 5).

Born Mabelle Barlow to a prosperous merchant from New York in Ridgeway, Michigan, Belle married Irving Ter Bush (1869–1948), also a Ridgeway native, in 1891. The son of Rufus Ter Bush, a founder of Standard Oil, Irving was heir to a vast fortune, an inheritance he was to multiply many times over. A *New Yorker* profile of 1927 characterized him as having the "uneven, angry energy of a man who has been confronted all his life with the opportunity to loaf."[20] At the age of nineteen, he set out to sail his father's yacht around the world.[21] Beginning in 1902, he created Bush Terminal, a port and railroad facility in Brooklyn that became one of the great transportation centers of the world. In Manhattan, he built Bush Tower, a much-admired Gothic skyscraper. He also built Bush House, one of the largest office buildings in central London at the time.[22] Bush's "uneven, angry energy" carried over into his private life. Belle Barlow was the first of his three wives. To mute the social stigma of divorce, Belle Bush styled herself a widow.

A member of the board of the Los Angeles Symphony, Belle Bush traveled to Europe in the summer of 1914 with Greene and Greene client Nellie Blacker and other board members. When World War I broke out in August, they cut short their trip, returning on ships from England.[23]

Mrs. Bush lived in the Bolton house in Pasadena with her two daughters, Beatrice and Eleanor, until about 1915. In 1920, she was living on Beacon Street in Boston, but she returned to Pasadena in 1923, when she commissioned

local architects Johnson, Kaufmann & Coate to design a house for her on Hillcrest Avenue in the Oak Knoll neighborhood. She continued to live there, near her friend Nellie Blacker, until the early 1940s.

Josephine Van Rossem (1867–1960), arrived in Pasadena in 1895 shortly after the death of her husband. Born Josephine Williams in Goderich, Ontario, where her father operated a sawmill and shipping business, she married Adriaan C. Van Rossem, scion of a prominent Dutch family with interests in Rotterdam and the Dutch East Indies. They settled in Chicago, where Van Rossem engaged in international trade. In 1894, Van Rossem's health failed, and the couple, with two young sons, traveled to The Netherlands and Switzerland, seeking a cure. In February 1895, Adriaan died in Leysin sur Aigle, Switzerland, touted as the "village of perfect health."[24] Later that year, the young widow moved with her two small sons to Pasadena, another health resort (fig. 6).

The family home, a Swiss chalet on Arroyo Terrace across the street from Charles Greene's house, was not designed by the Greenes, but Josephine Van Rossem did commission three houses from the brothers: two on Arroyo Terrace as investment properties, and one on North Orange Grove for her residence, where she lived briefly. Her brothers, John and Joseph, were professional photographers, and in 1897, Josephine began working with Pasadena photographer Eugene F. Kohler in his studio on Colorado Boulevard. She worked with Kohler for fifteen years, until 1912. Later she was the proprietor of a lending library, variously known as the Book Box or the Bookends. Her elder son, Adriaan J. Van Rossem, graduated from Throop Polytechnic and became a celebrated ornithologist at the University of California, Los Angeles; her younger son, Walter Johannes (Jack) Van Rossem, followed in the family tradition, becoming a commercial photographer in Los Angeles.[25]

THE VASSAR CONNECTION: JENNIE REEVE, MARY DARLING, NELLIE BLACKER, MARY PRATT, AND CAROLINE THORSEN

Vassar College was founded in 1861 in Poughkeepsie, New York, by brewer Matthew Vassar with the ambitious goal of providing "education to women equal to that of Yale and Harvard."[26] Five of the Greenes' clients were associated with Vassar: Jane Eliza ("Jennie") Allen Reeve, her daughter Mary Allen Reeve (later Darling), Mary Seymour Morris (later Pratt), Caroline Canfield (later Thorsen), and her older sister Nellie Canfield (later Blacker).[27] In the academic year 1879–80, four of them were in Poughkeepsie. Mary Reeve, a Poughkeepsie

native, was a special student at the college, living in town with her widowed mother, Jennie, whose late husband, Erastus Reeve (c. 1824–1874), had been a partner in the Vassar brewery.[28] Mary Morris and Caroline Canfield had been studying at Vassar since 1875 and were in their senior year. At the time, the college had only one building, where students lived and all classes were held,[29] so it is likely that the three young women knew one another and that Jennie Reeve knew the Canfield and Morris girls. Carrie Canfield's sister Nellie, though she was older, entered Vassar later, graduating in 1887.

Mary Reeve Darling (1860–1946) was the first of these women to consult the Greenes; they designed her house in Claremont in 1903. The Darling house, the first by Greene and Greene to receive international attention, marked a new step in the evolution of their California version of the Arts and Crafts style.[30] Mary had married Henry A. Darling in 1883; they had two sons, Harold and Kenneth, born in 1887 and 1890, respectively. Accompanied by Jennie Reeve, the Darlings visited Southern California in 1886 at the beginning of the great land boom, which prompted them to begin buying and selling real estate in the area.[31] The Darlings lived for a time in Los Angeles and in Long Beach. In 1903, while Mary was planning and building her house, Henry Darling and his son Harold were traveling abroad; ship's records show them arriving in San Francisco from Australia in July of that year. In September, Henry sued for divorce; he remarried shortly afterward and died in 1910. Mary Darling continued to live in the Claremont house for many years; however, by 1930, she was living in Cambridge, Massachusetts, with her son Kenneth. She died in 1946 in Westborough State Hospital in Massachusetts.

In the mid-1890s, Jennie Reeve (1838–1911) established herself in Long Beach, where she invested in real estate and was active in local society. After returning from her trip with Adelaide Tichenor to the Far East and around the world in 1902–03, she reported to the Ebell Club on her impressions of Korea.[32] Her house by Greene and Greene was scheduled to be ready by November 1904, but the design and fabrication of the light fixtures caused delays. Mrs. Reeve and Mrs. Tichenor, who had scheduled a reception at the new Reeve house for a large group of clubwomen from Los Angeles, were disappointed, or as Adelaide Tichenor put it in a letter to Charles Greene (dated less than a week before the event): "You have about broken my heart—in other words broken my health and happiness. After all the hard work, after the programs were all published—Mrs. Reeve tells me today that we cannot have the reception at her house—and that

FIGURE 6
Josephine Van Rossem tutoring her sons, Adriaan and Walter (Jack), at their home, 371 Arroyo Terrace, Pasadena, c. 1900. The framed photograph on the wall at right is probably of her deceased husband, Adriaan.

Courtesy of Greene and Greene Archives, The Gamble House, University of Southern California

it is your fault that the work is left undone—that she cannot now possibly get her house ready."[33]

The Greenes also designed a cottage for Jennie Reeve in Long Beach as an investment, and a cottage retreat in Sierra Madre nearer her daughter in Claremont. Charles Greene trusted Mrs. Reeve's business acumen and corresponded with her regarding investments; her letters to him are full of advice and tips.[34] Upon her death following a streetcar accident in 1911, Jennie Reeve was lauded as "one of the most progressive business women in the city."[35] She was also one of the wealthiest.

Nellie and Carrie Canfield, born in Racine, Wisconsin, had grown up in Manistee, Michigan, a lumber town on the shore of Lake Michigan. Their father, John Canfield (1830–1899), was the town's wealthiest citizen, owning several lumber mills, a store and office building in the town center, and a tugboat line.[36]

Nellie (1854–1946), the eldest of six children, married Robert Roe Blacker in Manistee in 1900, the year after her father's death. A widower with two adopted children, Robert Blacker (1845–1931) was fifty-four years old, Nellie was forty-five. The son of a prosperous brick manufacturer in Brantford, Ontario, Robert Blacker started in Manistee as a lumber inspector in 1870, when he was living in a boarding house with five other young men of the same profession. That same year, the census recorded that his future father-in-law, John Canfield, lived with his wife, four children, and four servants, and had $80,000 in real estate assets and $20,000 in personal property. Within a few years, young Blacker started a shingle mill, which he later expanded into a lumber mill. As he prospered, he invested in a second lumber company, a salt works, a wholesale drug company, local banks, and railroads. Blacker gained political prominence with his election to the state legislature and a term as Michigan's secretary of state. He also served as mayor of Manistee and was twice a delegate to the Democratic National Convention.

Nellie and Robert Blacker began visiting Pasadena in 1901. After purchasing 5 acres (2.02 ha) in the new Oak Knoll subdivision in 1905, they engaged Myron Hunt and Elmer Grey to design a house for them (fig. 7). The Blackers rejected their proposal, however, and turned to the Greenes in late 1906, a few months after Robert's sisters, Mary and Annie, had returned from a trip to Japan.[37] The resulting design and its execution mark a major achievement in the Greenes' work (see Streatfield essay, figs. 4 and 5).[38] The Greenes may have come recommended to the Blackers by the Hawks family, for whom the brothers built a house that year.[39] Mrs. David Linnard, wife of the owner of the Maryland Hotel, held a reception in honor of Helen Hawks and Nellie Blacker in December 1906. Helen's father owned a large paper mill in Wisconsin and may have had connections with lumber businesses in Manistee.

Carrie Canfield (1858–1942) married William Randolph Thorsen (1860–1942) in 1886 in Manistee.[40] Thorsen's father, John, a prosperous Milwaukee merchant, made his fortune in 1868 investing in the Stronach Lumber & Salt Company in Manistee, a competitor of the Canfield mills, and installed his son William as secretary-treasurer.[41] In the small town of Manistee (population 5000 in 1873), the Canfields, Thorsens, Thorsen's Canadian partner Charles Paggeot, and fellow Canadian Robert Blacker would have known one another and mixed socially, although John Thorsen continued to reside in Milwaukee, only a few hours by ferry across Lake Michigan.

The younger Thorsens moved west around 1903, when William became president of West Side Lumber Co. in Tuolumne, California. They spent summers in Tuolumne, living in Berkeley the rest of the year, where they built a house by Greene and Greene, a choice surely influenced by Nellie Blacker (see Bosley essay, fig. 4).[42] Already patrons of architecture, the Thorsens had hired William Le Baron Jenney to design their house in Manistee, and New York architects Emory & Emory to build their Tuolumne house, which is still extant, as are the sycamore trees planted along the town's streets at the behest of Carrie Thorsen.[43]

Mary Morris (1857–1947), daughter of Luzon Morris, a prominent attorney in New Haven, Connecticut,[44] married Charles Millard Pratt (1855–1935) in 1884. Pratt was the son of Charles Pratt, a founder of Standard Oil, and served as secretary of the company and president of the board of trustees of Pratt Institute, also established by his father. Both father and son were important patrons of architecture. The Pratt Institute and the campuses of Vassar and Amherst (the younger Pratt's alma mater) were enhanced by buildings funded by the Pratts and designed by eminent architects, including the Boston firms Shepley, Rutan & Coolidge (onetime employers of Henry Greene) and Allen & Collens, as well as New York architects Ebenezer Roberts, William B. Tubby, and York & Sawyer. Tubby also designed family homes for the Pratts in Brooklyn, while New York architect Charles Alonzo Rich was responsible for the design of Seamoor, Charles and Mary Seymour Pratt's estate at Glen Cove, Long Island.[45]

When the Pratts decided to build a rustic retreat in the remote Ojai Valley in California, they turned to the Greenes, probably led to them through Mary's friendship

FIGURE 7

The three Canfield sisters and their husbands in the Blacker house garden, Pasadena, c. 1920. From left to right: Ida Canfield Frost (sister of Nellie and Carrie), Edward Wheeler Frost, Nellie Blacker, Carrie Thorsen, William Thorsen, Robert Blacker.
Courtesy of Greene and Greene Archives, The Gamble House, University of Southern California

with the Canfield sisters. The elder Pratt's goal for the Pratt Institute, founded to elevate the dignity of hand labor, and his building of one of the first rustic camps in the Adirondacks, signaled an Arts and Crafts ethic that carried over into the younger generation.[46]

Particularly poignant is a note in the Greene and Greene Archives from Mrs. Pratt's secretary in March 1948, responding to an invitation to attend the American Institute of Architects ceremony in Los Angeles honoring the Greenes and their work. The secretary replied that Mrs. Pratt had died only a few months earlier, in October 1947.[47]

SCIONS OF INDUSTRY FROM WESTERN PENNSYLVANIA AND OHIO

Many of the Greenes' most prominent clients came from western Pennsylvania and Ohio, where their families had made great fortunes during and after the Civil War in steel and its allied industries, railroads, oil, lumber, and, in the case of the Gambles of Cincinnati, a new industrial consumer product, soap. Heirs to these fortunes—such as Robert Pitcairn, Jr., of Pittsburgh; James A. Culbertson and his sisters, Cordelia, Katharine, Margaret, and Belle; David B. Gamble; Freeman Ford; Laurabelle Arms Robinson; and Elisabeth Severance Allen Prentiss—were able, by the turn of the century, to indulge in winter residences in fashionable Pasadena.

An important cohort of Greene and Greene clients came from the city of Youngstown in Ohio's Western Reserve. Youngstown was the center of the coal, iron, and steel industries of the Mahoning Valley, and its leading citizens, the Wick, Tod, Ford, and Arms families, lived along Wick Avenue, the town's "Millionaires' Row." These families intermarried to an astonishing degree, forging alliances and preserving fortunes.[48] In Pasadena, they clustered together on South Grand Avenue, overlooking the Arroyo Seco.

Carrie Arms Ford, wife of Tod Ford, Sr.; their two sons, Tod Ford, Jr. (1887–1954), and Freeman Arms Ford (1881–1945); and Carrie's first cousin, Laurabelle Arms Robinson (1862–1943), were descended from Israel Arms, whose three sons, Myron, Freeman, and Charles, moved to Youngstown in the 1840s. The Arms brothers invested in the coal and steel industries; the Tods developed coal mines and achieved prominence in politics and banking.[49] By 1900, these families and others among the Youngstown elite had sold their holdings to the large steel combines, Bethlehem Steel and U.S. Steel, and founded the Youngstown Sheet & Tube Company. Members of the Tod and Ford families, as well as John Long Severance

and Francis Fleury Prentiss of Cleveland, brother and husband of Elisabeth Prentiss, served on the board of the new company, which in the 1920s was the third largest steel company in the United States. Youngstown Sheet & Tube was formed with the help of Laurabelle's husband, the ambitious lawyer, banker, and politician Henry Robinson (1866–1937).[50] Robinson's close personal and business ties to his wife's family are emphasized by the fact that he shared offices for thirty years in various downtown Pasadena buildings with her relatives: Tod Ford, Jr., an attorney, and Freeman Ford, a businessman. Also linked to the Youngstown group was Greene and Greene client Mrs. George A. Guyer of Chicago, whose daughter, Lillian, married Freeman Ford in 1905.

The Greenes' fruitful association with these families was initiated with a job for Tod Ford, Sr. (1854–1907), to design two bungalows for property at Ocean Park near Santa Monica in 1901. The following year, the firm designed alterations for Mrs. Guyer's house on the southwest corner of Mariposa and Santa Rosa in Altadena. Originally the home of Colonel G.G. Green, the sprawling three-story Shingle-style house with an expansive porch and large gardens set the tone for the Guyers' prominent social position in Los Angeles and Pasadena.[51] The Greenes' alterations included adding a panel with a carved motto over the living-room fireplace and installing dining-room cabinets and paneling, giving the rooms a strong Arts and Crafts character.

Just as the plans for Mrs. Guyer's house bear her name instead of her husband's, so the Robinson house documents are in the name of Laurabelle, not Henry. As part of the usual procedure in an architect's office, a drawing's title records the name of the person billed for the work. In the case of Laurabelle Arms Robinson, it is safe to assume that she was the person most responsible for the design and interaction with the architects; moreover, it was probably her personal fortune that was paying for the house, commissioned in 1905.[52]

One year earlier, Laurabelle's younger sister, Olive Arms, who had married a distant cousin, Wilford Arms, began building her own house, Greystone, on Youngstown's Wick Avenue. Designed by the Cleveland architects Meade & Garfield, Greystone was an English Arts and Crafts mansion, for which Olive made the decisions down to the smallest detail, noting that the architect "is inclined to build merely for himself—he builds his house, not yours."[53] Although little personal information survives about Laurabelle Arms's interest in architecture, her sister wrote an essay filled with ideas about the design of her house. Since the sisters were very close, it is

FIGURE 8
*Laurabelle Arms and
Olive Arms, c. 1880*
Courtesy of Mahoning
Valley Historical Society

probable that Laurabelle was familiar with Olive's ideas, and may have been influenced by them (fig. 8).

Olive's essay reveals preferences that also appear in Laurabelle's house. She calls for "the honest use of natural unpainted materials, which time beautifies," and for fitting the architectural style into the landscape: "The first requirement of architectural beauty is suitability to situation. A house should seem to belong where it stands. The colonial house should be placed on an elm-bordered street, on its own wide lawn, against the green of a wooded background, the thatched roof cottage should be on a wooded lane." As for the interior, the living room should have "plenty of light … and attractive views." Regarding furnishings, she writes, "If we happen to have an abundance of ornaments, we can do as the Japanese do, select a chosen few."[54]

However similar the sisters' motivations, Laurabelle's house was a bold departure from Olive's traditional English manor; instead, it reflected California traditions. Its adobe-like plastered buttress and chimney forms were derived from the early architecture of California and the Southwest, and the house's setting in an orange grove was a natural extension of California's agricultural landscape. The main living rooms are light-filled, with large

windows framing views of the arroyo (see Cooke essay, fig. 6). Japanese motifs in interior details and furnishings, as well as the use of light, natural-colored woodwork in the 1918 sunroom addition, with its Japanese-style carved frieze, hark back to Olive's essay.

Construction began on the Robinson house in August 1905 at the time Laurabelle's relative Freeman Ford and his new wife, Lillian, were beginning to consider building a home of their own. The newlyweds had lived first in a bungalow on Tod Ford, Sr.'s, estate on South Grand Avenue, where records show Craftsman-style additions designed by the Greenes.[55] The titles on the original drawings for the additions record Freeman Ford as the client; his name was later crossed out and Todd [*sic*] Ford substituted, perhaps indicating that Tod Ford, Sr., was paying for the work, while Freeman and Lillian were directing the design.

For the Fords, the Greenes produced designs for a low plaster-walled house arranged around a courtyard, similar in plan to the Arturo Bandini house of 1903. A second scheme for a larger house was put aside, and a revised version of the original design was built on property between the Tod Ford and Robinson places in 1907–08. Lillian Ford (1884–1959; fig. 9), in her early twenties at the time, was much younger than Laurabelle Robinson; her choice of a design evoking early California may have been influenced by the imposing house of her husband's cousin that was going up next door. The need to compete with the Robinson house in terms of size and presence, Lillian's desire to fit in with her new family, and of course the fact that her father-in-law was probably footing the bill may explain much about the choice of architects, revisions to the design, and the final result. The young couple also must have been aware of the house of fellow Chicagoan Arthur Jerome Eddy, built on nearby California Street a couple of years earlier. With the help of architect Frederick Roehrig, Eddy had built his own interpretation of an Arts and Crafts house appropriate for Southern California, an adobe-like courtyard *hacienda*, similar in plan to the Ford house.

Although the Fords and Robinsons of Youngstown financed two of Greene and Greene's most important early houses, the Ohio client with whom they had the longest relationship was Elisabeth Severance Allen Prentiss (1865–1944) of Cleveland. Mrs. Allen's purchase in 1917 of the house the Greenes had designed for the Culbertson sisters in 1911 was the beginning of a series of commissions that lasted for twenty years. Daughter of Louis Henry Severance, a founder of Standard Oil (like Charles Pratt, Sr.), Elisabeth and her brother

John Long Severance were major patrons of the arts, especially the Cleveland Orchestra and the Cleveland Museum of Art. Elisabeth Prentiss also left one-third of her fortune to a foundation to fund medical research and care. At Wellesley College in the 1880s, Elisabeth was close to its president, Alice Freeman Palmer, a progressive thinker and leader in education for women. Elisabeth later said that she might never have developed "the social values that have colored her life, if she had not been at Wellesley when Alice Freeman Palmer was president."[56]

Elisabeth Severance married Dr. Dudley Peter Allen in 1892. He was forty and she was twenty-seven. A well-known surgeon and pioneer in the development of surgery as a specialty, Allen became president of the Ohio State Medical Association and the American Surgical Association. In 1910–11, the Allens made a world tour, spending most of their time in Asia. Notes from her travel diary indicate that Mrs. Allen was impressed with the beautiful screens, carved panels, and lacquered wood that they saw in Kyoto.[57] Dr. Allen was known as "a connoisseur of fine arts and expert on Chinese porcelain."[58] He even brought back a structure from Korea to install in the Japanese garden of their new house in Cleveland, Glen Allen, completed after his death in 1915.

In the spring of 1917, Elisabeth Allen purchased the house on Hillcrest Avenue in Pasadena from the three Culbertson sisters, as well as two adjacent oak-studded parcels to protect the view to the north across the canyon and to extend the garden (see Streatfield essay, fig. 12). She may have been inspired to buy the house, with its dramatic landscaping, by her brother's estate in neighboring San Marino, which boasted a spectacular garden.[59] The vaguely Chinese character of the house's exterior; the beautifully proportioned, open, simple rooms; and the gallery around the courtyard, suitable for displaying art, may have also been attractions. In September 1917, Mrs. Allen (fig. 1) married Francis Fleury Prentiss, a Cleveland businessman. Christening her new house "Il Paradiso," Elisabeth Prentiss embarked on a series of commissions to enhance the estate.[60] Like other Greene and Greene clients, she had to contend with Charles Greene's tardiness in finishing projects and was sometimes unpleasantly surprised by the bills.[61] An undated letter from Laurabelle Robinson to Charles Greene in Carmel attests not only to Elisabeth Prentiss's concerns about completion of the work but also to the social connections among the clients: "Am glad to note by your letter that you plan to have Mrs. Prentiss' work all completed by the time she arrives here, because some friends of hers who have just come out from Cleveland have been telling me of some very serious threats that she has made if the work is not completed ..."[62]

Of all the houses by Greene and Greene, the Gamble house is the most renowned, not only because it has been open to the public since 1966, but also because it is preserved almost intact, with most of its accompanying furnishings. The clients, however, were naturally retiring, living quietly and eschewing society for good works.[63] Mary Huggins Gamble (1855–1929), described by her son Sidney as a "matriarch," made all the decisions about the Pasadena house, except for the den, which she left to her husband.[64] Born Mary Augusta Huggins in Kalamazoo, Michigan, Mary had three younger siblings, William, Julia, and Marie (Minnie). Her father, William Sidney Huggins, a Yale graduate and Presbyterian minister, died when Mary was seven; her mother soon remarried, to Lucius D. Chapin, a Presbyterian minister in Ann Arbor and professor of philosophy at the University of Michigan. Early in their marriage, Mr. and Mrs. Chapin made an extended trip to Europe, accompanied by Mrs. Chapin's sister Augusta, known as "Duttie." During their trip, they met Miss Mary Gamble of Cincinnati and her brother George; Duttie and Mary Gamble became good friends. This encounter set the stage for the eventual meeting and marriage of Mary Gamble's brother David and Mary Huggins.

In her third-person autobiography, Mary Huggins Gamble relates that severe headaches and eye trouble caused her to leave school at fifteen.[65] Bored at home and missing school, she credited her mother with teaching her how to draw, play instruments, and appreciate music and art. Mary had a second chance at an education when her stepfather became the president of Ingham University in LeRoy, New York, ranked at the time as one of the best institutions of higher education for women in the country.[66] Mary reveled in her classes and new friendships, but after a happy year, she began to suffer headaches again, writing: "I must smother my ambitions," one of which had been to become a doctor. Her own delicate health had made her interested in health and hygiene. After a period of recuperation at a spa and at home, Mary went to Smith College for a year as a special student, "one of the happiest years of her life."[67] By this time, her stepfather had resigned his post at Ingham University and eventually took a pastorate at a Presbyterian church in Chicago's Hyde Park.

In the fall of 1881, David Gamble traveled from Cincinnati to visit Mary and her family in Chicago, going on to visit Mary's Aunt Duttie in Milwaukee, where

FIGURE 10
*Mary Gamble
in animated
conversation with
Charles Greene (left)
and David Gamble
(center) while
standing on the site
of their future
house, n.d. [1907]*
Courtesy of Greene
and Greene Archives,
The Gamble House,
University of Southern
California

Mary's sister Julia was staying. David visited Chicago again on the way home, "and there, I suppose, the deed was done," Mary wrote laconically, describing her engagement to David Gamble.[68] Implicit in Mary's description of the episode is the notion that her suitor may have been courting Julia as well, but there is no hint as to whether Julia rejected him or he preferred Mary from the beginning. Mary's family was not happy with the engagement, her stepfather saying "she was very foolish to throw away all the opportunities which he expected to give her—a home on the Hudson, a trip to Europe and so forth."[69] Mary remained unmoved. The wedding took place in September 1882 in Hyde Park in Chicago, followed by a grand reception the next day with her mother's family in Milwaukee. Mary was twenty-seven and David was thirty-five.

David Gamble had graduated from high school in Cincinnati and soon entered the family business, Procter & Gamble, where he eventually became secretary-treasurer.[70] The Gambles built a house in the late 1880s in Avondale, a Cincinnati neighborhood, to accommodate their growing family, and a summer "cottage" in Harbor Point, Michigan, in 1893.[71] By 1894, Mary and David had three sons, Cecil, Sidney, and Clarence; a daughter, Elizabeth, had died in 1890 from diphtheria.

The Gambles purchased property overlooking the Arroyo Seco in Pasadena in 1907, and commissioned Greene and Greene to build a house (fig. 10; see also Streatfield essay, fig. 3). Charles Greene's handwritten notes document Mary's dominant role in the design. She wanted the color of the living-room rugs "to be more green," she specified the size and shape of the lantern on the west terrace and the height of the doorknobs, wanted reading lights for "Mr. G." in the living room and bedroom, no vents or windows in the closets, bright light in the kitchen, and a set of hall chairs ("not like Mrs. Bush's").[72]

Beginning in the fall of 1909, a series of letters from Mary and David to their youngest son, Clarence, documents their plans for moving into their new home.[73] Sent out to Pasadena in September to start the school year, the fifteen-year-old Clarence had the task of attending to last-minute details in preparation for his parents' arrival in the late fall. In her affectionate letters to her youngest boy, Mary expressed concerns about fresh air and health that illuminate the motivation behind the three large covered sleeping porches on the new house. She wrote that the window in Clarence's room at Harbor Point had been altered to swing "on hinges and I wish you had had the extra air all summer."[74] Fresh air was a preoccupation of the time, when tuberculosis and other respiratory ailments were believed to fester in the cities, with their putrid atmosphere and unsanitary conditions. In another letter, Mary wrote of Don Armour, her nephew, who was about Clarence's age and resting in a sanitarium "in a serious condition and will never be strong. How pitiful!" Later from Cincinnati, she complained, "The air is heavy, as usual. I am certainly glad we are to be in a place [Pasadena] where there is more to breathe."[75]

Mary bombarded Clarence with questions about the construction: "How does the house look? Are you pleased with it?" "How does the furniture look? Are the views full? Can you see where the fire has been back of the Armours'?"[76] On October 7, she thanked Clarence for sending photographs, especially a print of the stairway. On November 10, she wrote, "We are quite excited to think you are actually in our new house, and I do wish we were there ..."[77]

The Gambles' trip west was delayed, first by surgery on Mary's eyes in New York, then by her mother's unexpected illness at the Armours' home in Evanston. Mary's sister Julia, who was supposed to have arrived in Pasadena earlier to help Clarence prepare the house, had to stay behind to care for her mother. Mary and David finally arrived in Pasadena just before Thanksgiving; on the day after Thanksgiving, "Mr. Greene" had scheduled "Mr. Huff [Hough] to do the walls."[78] They moved into an incompletely furnished house; additional pieces kept arriving throughout 1910.

The notes reflecting Mary Gamble's role in the details of the design, much like the Tichenor and Garfield letters, provide a model for the typical interaction between client and architect in the Greenes' practice. Compared to their contemporaries, the Greenes attracted more women clients, perhaps because they confined their practice almost exclusively to residential work.[79] The smaller scale of residential projects allowed them greater control over the outcome and afforded them a more intimate relationship with the client and with the workmen. The Greenes probably found this satisfying, for it fulfilled the Arts and Crafts ideals of the cooperation of the artist, the craftsman, and the client in the creative process. By their intense involvement, the Greenes' women clients, well-educated and artistically inclined, challenged the firm to produce path-breaking, artistic works, and nurtured the brothers' stylistic development. Their joint efforts have given us the legacy that we enjoy today.

The author wishes to thank friend and colleague Paul Secord, whose genealogical research significantly aided this essay.

1. Thomas Woody, *A History of Women's Education in the United States* (New York and Lancaster, Pa.: Science Press, 1929), II, p. 1.

2. Barbara Miller Solomon, *In the Company of Educated Women: A History of Women and Higher Education in America* (New Haven, Conn.: Yale University Press, 1985), p. 45.

3. Woody, *Women's Education*, II, p. 460.

4. *Ibid*.

5. Solomon, *Educated Women*, pp. 64–65.

6. Henry James was referring to wealthy American women living in Europe who were directing their own lives. Later the term referred to the new American professional women, arising in the last two decades of the nineteenth century. Ruth Bordin, *Alice Freeman Palmer: The Evolution of a New Woman* (Ann Arbor: University of Michigan Press, 1993), http://www.press.umich.edu/bookhome/bordin (accessed January 13, 2008).

7. Marilyn Bailey Ogilvie and Joy Dorothy Harvey, *Biographical Dictionary of Women in Science* (London: Taylor & Francis, 2000), p. 267. See also California Institute of Technology, "The Prehistory of Biology at the Institute," http://biology.caltech.edu/about/history/Prehistory.html (accessed January 13, 2008).

8. The State Board of Medical Examiners refused Dr. Claypole a license on a technicality, but after protests from Dr. Bridge and others, the board capitulated. See "Doctors War on Woman's Status," *Pasadena Star*, March 30, 1905, p. 1; "License is Granted Dr. Claypole," *Pasadena Star*, October 26, 1905, p. 9. See also Norman Bridge, *The Marching Years* (New York: Duffield & Co., 1920), pp. 203–205.

9. Ogilvie and Harvey, *Women in Science*, p. 267. See also "Dr Claypool [*sic*] is Suddenly Summoned," *Pasadena Star*, March 29, 1915.

10. "Mrs. Adelaide Tichenor," *Long Beach Telegram*, May 18, 1924. In 1907, after a change in the city charter excluding women from public office, Mrs. Tichenor and her friend Jennie Reeve were forced to resign from the library board. See "Feminine Members Sorry," *Los Angeles Times* (*LAT*), December 31, 1907, p. II-8.

11. Ravenna was also the hometown of another Greene and Greene client, Henry M. Robinson, born 1868.

12. During Harris's tenure in St. Louis, school board president and Washington University professor Calvin Woodward opened the Manual Training School, a public high school affiliated with Washington University, where Charles and Henry Greene studied in the mid-1880s; see Edward R. Bosley, *Greene & Greene* (London: Phaidon, 2000), pp. 11–13. Citing health problems, Harris left his post in St. Louis in 1880 to join the transcendental philosophers near Boston. In 1889 he was appointed the U.S. Commissioner of Education. See "William Torrey Harris," in *National Cyclopedia of American Biography*, XV, p. 1. According to her autobiography, Adelaide Alexander also spent time in Boston, perhaps in the early 1880s, teaching and studying art. See "Adelaide Alexander Tichenor," in *History of Los Angeles County*, ed. John Steven McGroarty (Chicago: American Historical Society, 1923), p. 465.

13. "Adelaide Alexander Tichenor," p. 465.

14. Reports of some of Tichenor's travels appeared in the *Los Angeles Times*: "Women's Clubs: Long Beach Ebell," January 15, 1902, p. 10; "Redlands Brevities," September 16, 1902, p. A-4; "Long Beach Brevities," October 9, 1902, p. A-7; "Beach Briefs," July 26, 1903; "Out-of-Town Society: Long Beach," March 27, 1904. Harris also returned to St. Louis in 1904 to give a lecture at the exposition.

15. Letter from Adelaide Tichenor to CSG, June 10, 1904, EDA; letter from CSG to Grueby Faience Co., August 1, 1904, EDA.

16. See Bosley, *Greene & Greene*, pp. 67–69.

17. Bosley gives an account of the polite struggle between Lucretia Garfield and Charles Greene. *Ibid.*, pp. 57, 65–66.

18. National First Ladies' Library, "Lucretia Rudolph Garfield," http://www.firstladies.org/biographies/firstladies.aspx?biography=21 (accessed January 13, 2008).

19. *Ibid*.

20. Niven Busch, "Profiles 'Over Babel,'" *New Yorker*, April 2, 1927, p. 26.

21. "Irving T. Bush," in *Builders of Our Nation: Men of 1913* (Chicago: American Publishers' Association, 1914), p. 96.

22. "Irving T. Bush Dies; Terminal Founder," *New York Times* (*NYT*), October 22, 1948, p. 25.

23. "Out-of-Town Society: Pasadena," *LAT*, April 5, 1914, p. III-15; "On Foreign Tour," *LAT*, June 3, 1914, p. II-6; "Symphony Directors in Europe," *LAT*, September 19, 1914, p. I-12.

24. H.D. Rawnsley, "The Village of Perfect Health," *Blackwood's Edinburgh Magazine*, 158 (November 1895), pp. 680–84.

25. Alden H. Miller, "In Memoriam: Adriaan Joseph Van Rossem," *The Auk*, 74 (January 1957), pp. 20–27. See also "Van Rossem, Noted Ornithologist, Dies," *LAT*, September 8, 1949, p. A-7.

26. Benson J. Lossing, *Vassar College and Its Founder* (New York: C.A. Alvord Publishing, 1867), p. 81.

27. In another connection, client D.L. James's mother, Fannie, and sister Vassie were both Vassar graduates. See "Honored by All Who Know Them," *Kansas City World*, August 1, 1897; and John Gregory Dunne, "An American Education," in *Regards: Selected Nonfiction* (New York: Thunder's Mouth Press, 2006), pp. 129–30.

28. Lossing, *Vassar*, p. 34.

29. According to the 1879–80 catalogue, there were about 220 students enrolled for that academic year. Forty-six were in the Class of 1880.

30. Alex. Koch, "American Domestic Architecture," *Academy Architecture*, 24 (1903), pp. 54–55; Bosley, *Greene & Greene*, pp. 54–56.

31. "Iron Sulpher [*sic*] Springs," *LAT*, August 12, 1886, p. O-3.

32. "Out-of-Town Society: Long Beach," *LAT*, March 27, 1904, p. A-2.

33. Letter from Adelaide Tichenor to CSG, postmarked November 9, 1904, EDA. See also "Festal Days Slated for the Club Women," *LAT*, November 3, 1904, p. 6; the article publicized the reception at the Reeve house to be held on November 15.

34. Reeve letters are in the EDA.

35. "Mrs. Jennie A. Reeve, Prominent Club and Society Woman, Dies of Hurts Received in Accident," *Long Beach Press*, February 24, 1911, p. 1.

36. *History of Manistee County, Michigan* (Chicago: H.R. Page & Co., 1882), http://www.rootsweb.com/~mimanist/1882ManHist.html (accessed January 13, 2008).

37. Ancestry.com, "California Passenger and Crew Lists, 1893–1957," http://www.ancestry.com (accessed January 13, 2008). Mary and Annie Blacker arrived at San Francisco from Yokohama on the *Korea* on May 29, 1906.

38. For a discussion of the background and significance of the Blacker house, see Bosley, *Greene & Greene*, pp. 104–11.

39. The Hawks family lived in their Greene and Greene house at 408 Arroyo Terrace briefly, before moving to the Hansen house by Greene and Greene on San Pasqual. They left Pasadena a few years later.

40. *Vassar College Miscellany*, October 1886, p. 36.

41. "John Thorsen," in *Men of Progress: Wisconsin*, ed. Andrew Jackson Aikens and Lewis A. Proctor (Milwaukee: Evening Wisconsin Co., 1897), pp. 459–60. See also Bosley, *Greene & Greene*, p. 129.

42. See Bosley, *Greene & Greene*, pp. 129–37.

43. *Ibid.*, pp. 129, 222 n. 39. See also TCMM Historical Research Committee, "A Brief History of the West Side Lumber Co., Tuolumne, California," http://www.tuolumnemuseum.org/westside.htm. Excerpts taken from Mark V. Thornton *et al.*, "Tuolumne Community Context Statement," County of Tuolumne, September 1999.

44. Luzon Morris was a judge, a state legislator, and governor of Connecticut in 1893–95.

45. Karen Van Lengen and Lisa Reilly, *Vassar College: An Architectural Tour* (New York: Princeton Architectural Press, 2004); Scott Meacham, "The Buildings and Projects of Lamb & Rich Architects and Related Firms, 1876–1935," 2004, Dartmo.: The Buildings of Dartmouth College, http://www.dartmo.com/rich/buildings.html (accessed January 13, 2008).

46. On the camp in the Adirondacks, see Bosley, *Greene & Greene*, p. 127. In 1915, alterations to Seamoor (built in the 1880s) included the addition of Mercer tiles. See Meacham, "Lamb & Rich."

47. Letter from (Miss) Elisabeth Hiscox, Secretary to the late Mrs. C.M. Pratt, to Mr. [David C.?] Allison, March 2, 1948, GGA.

48. Patricia Gillespie, "Wick Avenue, 1940–1967: Millionaires' Row and Youngstown State University" (master's thesis, Youngstown State

University, 2006), pp. 7–23.

49. David Tod, uncle of David Tod Ford, Sr. (known as Tod Ford), served as governor of Ohio in 1862–64.

50. Rockwell Hereford, *A Whole Man and a Half Century* (Pacific Grove, Calif.: Boxwood Press, 1985), p. 21. See also *50 Years in Steel: The Story of the Youngstown Sheet and Tube Company* (Youngstown: Youngstown Sheet & Tube Company, 1950), http://www.youngstownsteel.com/ images/yst/youngstown.html (accessed January 13, 2008).

51. The original architect of the Guyer house was Frederick L. Roehrig. Eventually the Guyers donated the property as the site for the Altadena Public Library.

52. Bosley, *Greene & Greene*, p. 80.

53. Abram Garfield, partner in Meade & Garfield, was the son of Lucretia Garfield; he advised his mother on the house being built for her by the Greenes. Olive Arms, "The Story of My House," Mahoning Valley Historical Society, http:// www.mahoninghistory.org/ armmyhse.stm (accessed January 13, 2008).

54. Olive Arms, "The Story of My House."

55. "Radiant Vision, Girlish Bride," *LAT*, January 19, 1905, p. III-1. According to the *Times*, the newlyweds "would be at home in a charming little bungalow built for them upon Tod Ford's place." In 1917, Tod Ford, Jr., replaced both the bungalow and the main house on his father's estate with an elegant Italian villa designed by Reginald Johnson.

56. Quoted from notes by Diana Tittle, author of a history of the Severance family, from an article in *The Clevelander*, December 1928. Elisabeth funded construction of a dormitory at Wellesley, Severance Hall, in 1927. Mary Cross Ewing, "Severance Hall Completes the Tower Court Group," *Wellesley Alumnae Magazine*, XI, no. 4 (April 1927).

57. Diary excerpts furnished by Diana Tittle in an e-mail to the author, December 12, 2006. According to Tittle, Elisabeth Severance was a stylish, attractive woman with a deeply felt aesthetic sense.

58. "Peter Dudley Allen," in *Encyclopedia of Cleveland History* (Cleveland: Case Western Reserve University, 1997), http://ech.case.edu/ ech-cgi/article.pl?id=ADP (accessed January 13, 2008).

59. John L. Severance's garden, designed by landscape architect Paul Thiene, was widely published.

60. The Greenes' records show twenty-five different job numbers assigned to Mrs. Prentiss between 1917 and 1937. Bosley, *Greene & Greene*, p. 160.

61. *Ibid.*, p. 209.

62. Letter from Laurabelle Robinson to CSG, Carmel, December 11 [no year], EDA.

63. In contrast to most of the Greenes' other clients, whose social rounds are noted in the local newspapers, almost nothing appears about the Gambles' social life. Staunch Presbyterians, they focused on donating to the church, supporting missionary work abroad and missionaries' retirement at home, building the Pasadena YMCA headquarters, and supporting Occidental College, where David Gamble served as a trustee.

64. Notes on interview with Sidney Gamble by Randell Makinson, 1967, GGA.

65. Mary Huggins Gamble, "Autobiography," typed transcript, 26 pp., GGA. Mary's eye condition may have been inherited from her father; "the failure of his eyes obliged him … to give up … study for nearly two years." See Rev. Samuel Haskell, *In Memoriam: Three Sermons to Young Men* (Philadelphia: Presbyterian Publication Committee, 1862), p. 31.

66. Woody, *Women's Education*, II, p. 146.

67. Gamble, "Autobiography," p. 24.

68. *Ibid.*

69. *Ibid.* Lucius Chapin may have disapproved of the match because he felt the Gambles were of inferior social or educational background.

70. "David B. Gamble," in *History of Cincinnati and Hamilton County Ohio* (Cincinnati: S.B. Nelson & Co., 1894), p. 471.

71. The S. Hazard Halsted family, who built a Greene and Greene house on North Grand Avenue in Pasadena in 1905, also lived in Avondale.

72. CSG, handwritten notes on conversation with Mrs. David Gamble, n.d., EDA.

73. Ten letters to Clarence Gamble in Pasadena, dated September 17, 1909, through November 18, 1909. Sarah Bradley Gamble Papers, Schlesinger Library, Radcliffe Institute, Harvard University, Cambridge, Massachusetts.

74. Letter from Mary Gamble (MG), Harbor Point, to Clarence Gamble (CG), September 17, 1909.

75. Letters from MG, Avondale, to CG, September 23 and November 10, 1909. Don is in a sanitarium taking a water cure (letter from MG to CG, October 7, 1909).

76. Letters from MG, Avondale, to CG, September 17 and September 23, 1909. Mary's sister and brother-in-law owned a large tract in the Linda Vista hills across the arroyo from the Gambles' property.

77. Letters from MG, New York and Avondale, to CG, October 7 and November 10, 1909. Clarence had moved into the new house on November 1. Servants had already arrived.

78. Letter from MG, Chicago, to CG, November 18, 1909. "We have actually started on our westward journey …"

79. Contemporaries Myron Hunt and Sylvanus Marston took on larger institutional and commercial projects, respectively. Frederick Roehrig designed large residences in Los Angeles, where the clientele was more conventional than in Pasadena's arts-oriented environment.

73

ALAN CRAWFORD

Charles Greene and Englishness

This essay describes two kinds of Englishness in the life and work of Charles Greene.[1] One is the personal sense that Greene had of England, partly because it was his wife's country of origin. The other is the public image of England, and specifically of an English house, that operated in his work. The relationship between them was not simple.

Before the Greene brothers had finished their architectural training in Boston, they started keeping a scrapbook.[2] The first page is dated March 15, 1890, and they went on using it until at least 1906. It contains many images cut out of magazines: views of new buildings in Boston by the Anglophile architect Ralph Adams Cram and others; Swiss chalets; New England clapboard houses; drawings by the illustrator Daniel Vierge, of Spanish towns and marketplaces populated with swaggering noblemen in sixteenth-century dress and big hats; engravings of late nineteenth-century paintings with a sentimental sense of the European past, such as *The Last Moments of Mozart* or two fat monks surrounded by casks of wine. There are old houses on a street in Plymouth, England; timber-framed houses in Saxony; views of Coutances, Normandy; two pages of photographs of Native Americans; and an image of the Mission Santa Inés near Santa Barbara.[3]

There are also about seventy photographic reproductions of houses, all apparently from the same source, all about two to three inches square, and mostly of large English houses in the country (fig. 1). It seems that they come from a magazine called *Country Life in America*, which was published from 1901 in New York. This was an American version of the English magazine *Country Life*, the opening pages of which were filled with advertisements for houses to rent or buy in the English countryside. *Country Life in America* carried some of the same advertisements, which the brothers must have cut out with great regularity.

It is difficult to draw conclusions from specific images in this scrapbook. We do not know how much of it was assembled by Charles and how much by Henry; and there are no obvious similarities between individual pictures and Greene and Greene's work. But, taken as a whole, the scrapbook is invaluable as evidence of the Greenes' architectural eye on the world in the 1890s and early 1900s. It shows their interests as houses of the

middling sort; the past (there are far more old buildings than new in the scrapbook); Europe (particularly England); and the setting of houses in part-natural and part-artificial gardens and parks. They pasted in pictures that have distinct national or regional associations: clapboard houses, the *Country Life in America* images, half-timbered buildings in Saxony, Vierge's drawings with their corny Spanishness. The perception of buildings as having strong associations and meanings, and of national and regional identity being one of the strongest of those associations, is important in this essay.

In 1901, Charles Greene married Alice Gordon White, who grew up in England, in the Lake District. Her father was a wealthy English engineer and industrialist who had settled in Pasadena; he died in 1896, leaving his four daughters comfortably off. Alice was fifteen when she came to the United States with her father, and she kept a strong sense of being English. The wedding between Charles and Alice took place on February 11, 1901, and, about six weeks later, they set off on a four-month tour of Europe. The main records of this journey are two small diaries in which Charles erratically recorded their travels; a collection of about 320 photographs, presumably taken by Charles; and a similar number of postcards.[4] The postcards are of popular tourist sites and seem to have been bought indiscriminately. The photographs, on the other hand, are carefully taken. They are almost all of buildings; only a few are devoted to people or to scenery.

Charles and Alice were in Europe by early April and spent the next two months in Italy and France, visiting the obvious cities and tourist sites: Rome, Florence, Paris, Rouen. As Edward R. Bosley has written, on this stage of their journey, they were typical tourists.[5] Judging by the surviving images, Charles Greene did not use his camera much on this part of their trip. They crossed to England in late May and spent the next fortnight in rented accommodation in Pembroke Square, in London's fashionable western suburbs. In London, they went to museums and visited the usual sights. But when they left the city, they began to explore the country more individually, and Charles began to use his camera more.

The couple went westward first, through Somerset, where Charles photographed the ruins of Glastonbury Abbey, and on to the cathedral towns of Wells and Exeter. Then they turned north through Barnstaple to

FIGURE 1

A page from a scrapbook kept by Charles and Henry Greene, showing images taken from Country Life in America

Courtesy of Greene and Greene Archives, The Gamble House, University of Southern California

FIGURE 2
*The Ship Inn at
Porlock, Somerset.
Photograph by
Charles Greene, 1901*

Courtesy of Greene
and Greene Archives,
The Gamble House,
University of Southern
California

the little town of Lynton on the north Devon coast. Lynton is perched high up on tree-covered slopes above the little fishing village of Lynmouth, about which Shelley and other Romantic writers had enthused. Greene photographed the houses around the harbor and the fishing boats at low tide. From Lynton, the couple went on to Porlock, farther along the coast, where they stayed in the Ship Inn (fig. 2). There Charles took pictures of the inn in its picturesque village setting and of other similar buildings in the neighborhood: cottages of stone with thick plastered walls and equally thick thatch on the roof.

From the southwest, the Greenes traveled up to Bowdon, a wealthy Manchester suburb, where they presumably had relatives or friends, and from there they made excursions into the Peak District to see two great country estates, Haddon Hall and Chatsworth. At Chatsworth, Greene focused his camera not on the grand classicism of the big house but on the self-consciously picturesque houses at Edensor, a planned village created by the sixth Duke of Devonshire in about 1840.

The couple's destination in the north of England was the southernmost part of the Lake District, above Morecambe Bay, and in particular Newby Bridge, where Alice had grown up; she still had family there. Charles photographed the mid-seventeenth-century bridge with its massive cutwaters, which would have made a perfect subject for the early nineteenth-century watercolorist John Sell Cotman (fig. 3). After that came York and Ripon, more cathedral towns and more Gothic work, ruined and otherwise. Charles and Alice took the train north to Scotland, where they stayed for five days in Edinburgh. On the second day in Scotland, they visited the International Exhibition in Glasgow, the most ambitious British exhibition of its kind in those years.[6] Charles

FIGURE 3
*Newby Bridge,
Cumbria. Photograph
by Charles Greene,*
1901

*Courtesy of Greene
and Greene Archives,
The Gamble House,
University of Southern
California*

Greene probably recalled the larger and more monumental World's Columbian Exposition in Chicago, which he had visited in 1893, but one can only speculate, for we have no record of his reflections on either event. On July 13, the couple sailed for New York.

Not surprisingly, the photographs that are the main documentation of this trip show some of the same interests and tastes as the scrapbook: here are the houses of the middling sort, the sense of buildings in their natural setting, the camera turned away from the monumental.[7] And there is an odd note, a suggestion that Charles Greene looked at England through early nineteenth-century eyes. He had a taste for the Picturesque, dominant in England in the early nineteenth century: the rustic cottage, the village nestling in the landscape, Gothic architecture both in ruins and preserved, buildings and nature in juxtaposition. This was apt; the Picturesque as a

perception of specifically British landscape beauty, and a guide to what to admire, developed partly because warfare and revolution had made the traditional Grand Tour in continental Europe too dangerous. The Picturesque was a way of traveling around Britain instead, and finding beauty, which is just what the Greenes were doing.

Some Greene and Greene scholars have seen this English trip as an important moment of change in Charles Greene's creative life and in the brothers' work. There are two common forms of this argument, one particular, the other general.

The particular argument is put most strongly by Bosley in his classic study of Greene and Greene: on the trip of 1901, Charles Greene "came into contact with significant examples of the architecture and decorative arts of the English Arts and Crafts movement, an exposure that would have an immediate effect on his work back home."[8] Bosley argues that Charles and Alice may well have taken tea in the Green Dining Room of the South Kensington Museum (now the Victoria and Albert Museum), decorated by William Morris's firm; that they must have traveled close to and perhaps had seen major works by the architects C.F.A. Voysey and M.H. Baillie Scott in the Lake District; and that they almost certainly saw booths designed by Charles Rennie Mackintosh at the Glasgow exhibition. Bosley is too good a scholar not to note that these points of contact are conjectural.[9] The argument turns to some extent on the state of the evidence. The principal documents, as already mentioned, are the two diaries, the photographs, and the postcards. What do they show? The diaries do not have any indication that the Greenes looked closely at Arts and Crafts work or met any figures in the movement. None of the surviving photographs taken by Charles Greene is of Arts and Crafts work, although one postcard does relate to the movement, showing the Canterbury Weavers, a women's Arts and Crafts workshop set up in 1898. On this evidence, we cannot say with any certainty that Charles Greene came into personal contact with English Arts and Crafts. But equally clearly, we cannot say that he did not, for the documentation of the trip is so poor. There are no diaries with substantial entries, no letters, no reminiscences, nothing that would give a rounded sense of what the Greenes did. We know hardly anything about what they thought and said, or whom they met. If there were more documents, the evidence of contact with Arts and Crafts might be there. At present, on Charles Greene, England, 1901, and Arts and Crafts, the jury is out.

The other, larger argument turns not on documents but on the shape of the Greene brothers' creative story after 1901. It is that their work takes on a different and more impressive character after 1901, culminating in the classic bungalows of 1907–11, and that this is in some way due to Charles Greene's visit to England.[10] This argument works well as chronology: there was a new coherence and originality in their designs after 1901. But it is not always easy to connect these qualities with Charles Greene's experiences in England, to see the English trip as a cause of the new spirit in their architecture, rather than as simply marking its beginning.

Let us take the most obvious example of Englishness in Greene and Greene's work immediately after 1901, the Culbertson house at 234 North Grand Avenue, Pasadena. In 1902, the Greenes were approached by James A. Culbertson, a Pennsylvania lumberman who lived in an English-style house in an artistic suburb of Chicago. He wanted a summer home in Pasadena along the same lines. The Culbertson house stands against the backdrop of the San Gabriel Mountains, but if it stood in a leafy English suburb, it would not look much out of place (see Mallek essay, fig. 6). The roof with its long ridge and medley of gabled wings and dormers, the house and garden treated in combination, the stucco below with timber framing above, the diamond-leaded windows: all these were part of the stock-in-trade of English detached suburban houses from the 1880s onward, reflecting the popularity of the Old English style pioneered by Richard Norman Shaw. It is only some of the details that give the design away: the shakes on the upper story where English houses would have clay tiles, the boulder work in the garden walls.

But does this character, do these features derive from Charles Greene's visit to England? Is it merely pedantic to point out that none of the buildings Greene photographed in England has much bearing on the Culbertson house? Perhaps we should look not just to Greene's personal experience and development but also to the context in which he worked, and to the public language of American architecture, in order to explain the appearance of this house. Within the rich stylistic eclecticism of American suburban domestic architecture at the time, there was a reasonably distinct language of national and regional types that made it possible for a client to ask for an English house or a French house, and for the architect to know roughly what was wanted. The phenomenon is probably countrywide, but I saw it very clearly in Pasadena when I was researching this essay and walked each day to the Huntington Library along Lombardy Road, between Hill and Allen. The national types are each distinct yet equal: the houses the same, their function in the street the same, but each has its own national dress and associations. They work as stereotypes, using a handful of familiar features to convey the national type: a broken roofline and half-timbering for England, mansard roofs and tall windows for France, arcades and curving gables for Mission, clapboards and classicism for Colonial Revival.[11] And they were shaped more by the market than by professional or progressive architectural taste; it was generally the client who wanted the English house. This is the public image that I mentioned at the start, and which forms the second thread of Englishness in my story.

Charles Greene was well placed to meet the demand for such houses, as we have seen from the brothers' scrapbook. He liked the idea of a house with strong national associations. So it was with the Culbertson

house. To get the design going in his mind, he did not turn to the photographs he had taken in England; he turned to the stereotype, an American design for a house in the English style. The earliest versions of the Culbertson house were based on Ralph Adams Cram's "Country House of Moderate Cost," in the architect's usual Anglophile style, published in the *Ladies Home Journal*.[12] The "English" of the Culbertson house was only one among several styles that the Greenes could provide. On their drawing board at the same time was the George H. Barker house in Pasadena, in full-blown Colonial Revival style.[13] The language of the Culbertson house was available to a skillful architect in Pasadena in the early twentieth century, and it may be that the Greene brothers would have designed the house as they did whether or not Charles had been to England eighteen months before. The same can be said of two other Greene and Greene houses in the English style: the Mary M. Kew house in San Diego of 1912–13, where the shingles of the roof were shaped to look like thatch (a device we will meet again), and Henry Greene's reticent Henry A. Ware house in Pasadena of 1913.

The interiors of these post-1901 Greene and Greene houses, and their furniture when it was specially designed, are another matter. Here we find hints that align them more closely to England and the Arts and Crafts movement there, though still nothing that makes a clear connection with Charles Greene's trip. For instance, Charles plainly felt that the interiors he designed in 1902 for Culbertson were in the spirit of the Arts and Crafts, for when the client recommended particular furnishings, Greene replied, "The suggestions enclosed in your letter for the living room pleased me very much, as I am in through [sic] sympathy with the Wm Morris movement, in fact the whole inside of the house is influenced by it in design."[14] "The Wm Morris movement": it is difficult to know here whether Greene meant that his work breathed the spirit of English Arts and Crafts or if he was using the phrase more loosely, to refer to the Arts and Crafts movement in England *and* the United States.

The Englishness of some of the Greenes' early twentieth-century interiors is a minor and subtle theme, often stronger in the eye of the beholder than in the fabric of the building, and more obvious to an American eye than to that of an English art historian. I have visited the Robert R. Blacker house in Pasadena (1907–09), but I never caught a hint of England in it until I read what Mrs. Beswick-Purchas wrote about staying there as a guest in a letter to her brother and sister-in-law, Mr. and Mrs. William R. Thorsen, while their Greene and Greene house was being built in Berkeley in 1909:

It is the bedrooms that suffer and seem a little cold in this handling. Two heavy beams transect the large guest room and broad bands surround this frieze. The idea, taken from the old English taverns, does not seem suitable to a bedroom … there is not a deep, soft chair or sofa in the house. It is all as the style of office furniture though it is built on fine old English plain lines and beautiful work.[15]

In January 1909, the architect and designer C.R. Ashbee, one of the leading figures of the Arts and Crafts movement in England, went to Pasadena on a lecture tour. Ashbee, usually perceptive about professional colleagues, wrote an entry about Charles Greene in his journal. It was as if the English movement had paid him a visit, and was holding up a mirror to his work. Charles Greene, Ashbee wrote,

fetched us in his auto again this afternoon and drove us about, then took us to his workshops where they were making without exception the best and most characteristic furniture I have seen in this country. There were chairs of walnut and lignum vitae, exquisite dowelling and pegging, and in all a supreme feeling for the material, quite up to our best English craftsmanship, Spooner, Barnsly [sic], Lutyens, Lethaby. I have not felt so at home in any workshop on this side of the Atlantic—(but then we have forgotten the Atlantic, it is the Pacific!).[16]

Ashbee seems to have responded more strongly to the Greenes' furniture than to their architecture, as if the furniture were closer in spirit to the English movement in which he worked. He was probably shown pieces for the Gamble house. He saw in it the use of fine woods and designs that exploit the quality of the grain, a slight self-consciousness about joints and construction, and a creative handling of tradition. (Elsewhere in the same journal entry he described himself as "fingering the surface of Greene's scholarly panelling," "scholarly" being a term he used to praise the intelligent reinterpretation of past forms.) The qualities he recognized in the Greenes' work were precisely those of the leading English Arts and Crafts furniture designers whom he lists, Charles Spooner, Sidney Barnsley, Edwin Lutyens, and W.R. Lethaby, and also of Barnsley's colleague Ernest Gimson (fig. 4). Ashbee felt suddenly at home with the Greenes' fine work, though he also knew how far away from home he was; in another part of the same journal entry, he wrote of their designs: "it is California that speaks."[17]

FIGURE 5
*North Hill, Clovelly,
Devon, from
"Sixteen Permanent
Photographic Views
of Clovelly,"
purchased by Charles
Greene, 1909*

Courtesy of Greene
and Greene Archives,
The Gamble House,
University of Southern
California

NORTH HILL, CLOVELLY

Three months after Ashbee's visit, Charles and Alice Greene, now with four children, set out for England, where they stayed for the next six months. This trip is even less documented than their honeymoon, and it is not obvious why they were abroad for so long, leaving Henry Greene to run the office in Pasadena by himself. A stay of three months would have been enough for visiting Alice's family and touring the country, and that seems to have been their original plan.[18] But Charles later recalled how exhausted he was creatively at this time, and they may have extended the sojourn to allow him to regain his strength.

The Greenes were based once again in London's western suburbs, at 72 Scarsdale Villas, West Kensington, and they had outings to Paris in October and perhaps to the Lake District to see Alice's family.[19] In July, they spent more than two weeks on the north coast of Devon and Cornwall, which had so attracted them in 1901. This time they stayed for about a week at Tintagel, a dangerous-seeming place, with its ruined castle perched on a massive rock, around which strong seas and Arthurian legends swirl with equal force. Charles Greene made many drawings of buildings in and around Tintagel, and he took a photograph of the late medieval manor house known as the Old Post Office, with its massive walls and crumpled roof (fig. 9). From Tintagel, the Greenes traveled north to Clovelly, a village with houses tumbling over one another down a narrow gulley toward the sea. Clovelly had been tended to for centuries by the lords of the manor, the Hamlyn family, the cottages carefully preserved, the surrounding landscape picturesquely planted in the early nineteenth century.[20] Here Charles made many drawings, including two of North Hill. The streets of Clovelly are so narrow, steep, and uneven that the only practical form of transport was, and still is, a sledge (fig. 5).

Back in London, Charles and Alice did the usual things, visited museums, shopped. As in 1901, there is no evidence that Charles Greene made any contacts with architects or designers, or that he looked up his recent visitor, C.R. Ashbee. The documentary evidence for this trip consists mostly of tradesmen's bills and commercial catalogues. We find Greene looking for and buying new and antiquarian books, on early nineteenth-century topography, on Japan, and on metalworking techniques; buying enamels and a muffle furnace for enameling; and looking at equipment for jewelry and metalworking.[21] We can perhaps imagine Greene, exhausted by his professional responsibilities, letting his creativity flower into smaller, more personal, more speculative things: the decorative arts, literary matters, the past. But these are just scraps of evidence and should not be overinterpreted. As in 1901, documentation is so scanty that it may give a quite false impression of what happened. When Charles returned to Pasadena, the *Pasadena News* reported that he had made "an extended tour of England and Europe," during which he had "secured many ideas applicable to the practice of his profession in Southern California. He was particularly impressed with the beautiful old classic architecture found in the ancient cities of the Old World."[22] Was this journalistic hype, or did Charles Greene have important experiences in England in 1909 of which no documentary evidence survives?

A year or more after Charles returned from England, Mortimer Fleishhacker, a San Francisco businessman, asked the Greene brothers to design a summer house for his family on a large estate at Woodside, about 33 miles (53 km) south of San Francisco. Fleishhacker and his wife, Bella, specifically asked for an English-style house with "a thatched roof if possible."[23] So we are back with the language of national types that we met at the Culbertson commission.

The Fleishhacker house looks out to the south, first over a formal garden designed by Greene, and beyond that to blue horizons of pine-clad mountains (fig. 6). The size of the garden and its relationship to the house immediately strike one as more English than American. The house is long and low under a hipped roof, with single-story elements huddled around it and gables and bays breaking up the elevation. English country buildings that have grown over the centuries look a bit like this. The walls are covered with gunite, a sprayed-on patent material favored by the Greenes at this time, which looks like the rough plaster known in England as "render" or "roughcast." The roof, like that of the Mary M. Kew house, is covered with shingles that are swept up in gentle curves over changes in level and around dormer windows; rolled, most tellingly, around the eaves; and curved themselves, by a steaming process, to fit the details of the roof (fig. 7). It seems that this was an alternative to the thatch requested by the clients.

The Fleishhacker house created powerful echoes of English originals, but not necessarily the types of old houses or cottages Charles Greene photographed in 1901. It is closer to modern Arts and Crafts houses for wealthy commuters in the countryside around London and other large cities, though it is not obviously influenced by any known example.[24] There are some features that do not feel truly English. The layout of the garden is sparser and more formal than in English gardens, with their curving lawns and lush herbaceous borders; when Greene and

FIGURE 7
*Detail of roof
shingles, Mortimer
Fleishhacker, Sr.,
estate*

Photograph by
Alan Crawford

Fleishhacker added a spectacular Italianate pool at a lower level, the difference was even more marked. Also, shingles have not been common as a roof covering in England since the Middle Ages, and they do not look at all like thatch. But none of this alters the character or effectiveness of the house. Its Englishness does not depend on how closely it is modeled on originals, but on how convincingly it fits the stereotype. To American eyes, the Fleishhacker house sends out a clear message of Englishness.

The last and strangest house that Charles Greene designed was also the last and strangest example of Englishness in his work. In 1918, when he had decided that his architectural career was over, he was approached by a Kansas City businessman, D.L. James, who wanted him to build a summer house on a rocky promontory in the Carmel Highlands, looking out over the Pacific (fig. 8). The extraordinary site must have caught Greene's imagination, for he quickly produced a design, which he was then left to create, relatively free from constraints of time or money. Built of granite irregularly but carefully laid and roofed with pantiles, straightforward in plan but endlessly complex in elevation, advancing and receding in bays, porches, window recesses, and arcaded stairways, and crowned with a series of massive chimney stacks, the James house looks from the air like a giant iguana basking in the sun, all ridges and awkward, organic-looking angles.

At the start, perhaps, Greene may have been thinking of a Tuscan farmhouse, for the shallow pitch of the roofs, the pantiles, and the arcading give that suggestion. But Tuscan farmhouses are generally loosely planned, simple, and straight-lined. They have none of the furious complexity of the James house. Where does that come from?

The answer is that, remarkably, at this last moment of his career, Charles Greene drew for the first time and very directly upon his English experiences. The situation is simple. The James house stands on a cliff. In England, Greene had been drawn to the seaside villages of Lynmouth and Clovelly, where the houses tumble down into the sea; and on his second trip, he had made a special study of Tintagel, where the cliffs are sheer and the sea boils at the bottom of them, as it does around the James house. He built a very specific reminiscence of Tintagel, re-creating an archway from the ruins of the castle alongside the house, looking down in the same way over the sea (figs. 10 and 11). And as for the jumbled-together, additive quality of the house and its reptilian roofs, they echo the Old Post Office at Tintagel, which Charles had photographed and drawn in 1909: "low, dark, picturesque,

with roofs like a cluster of hills, and of a slaty hue like elephant's hide" (fig. 9).[25] It is a long way from Cornwall to Carmel Highlands, but Charles Greene's experiences of England had at last found a place in his architecture.

We end where we started, with the Greene brothers browsing the art and architecture magazines, only this time they do not cut out the images; they flag them with slips of paper. The Greene and Greene Archives of the University of Southern California include the forty-five

bound volumes of Charles Greene's run of *International Studio*, from 1897 to 1912, just the period when English influence may have been strongest on their work. *The Studio* was published in London from 1893 as a monthly magazine of fine and decorative art, English in emphasis but international in scope. It was never officially identified with Arts and Crafts, but it carried a great deal of information about the movement in England, and disseminated it in Europe and the United States more

FIGURE 8
Aerial view to the southeast, D.L. James house, Carmel Highlands, 1918–22
Photograph © Estate of Mark Fiennes

FIGURE 9
The Old Post Office, Tintagel, Cornwall. Photograph by Charles Greene, 1909
Courtesy of Greene and Greene Archives, The Gamble House, University of Southern California

[*page 210*]
FIGURE 10
Arch at D.L. James house inspired by Charles Greene's drawing of a similar arch at Tintagel Castle, Cornwall
Photograph © Estate of Mark Fiennes

[*page 211*]
FIGURE 11
Stone arch at Tintagel Castle, Cornwall. Watercolor by Charles Greene, 1909
Courtesy of Greene and Greene Archives, The Gamble House, University of Southern California

powerfully than any other magazine. *International Studio*, published monthly from 1897 in New York, was broadly the same magazine, with special American material.

Small slips of yellow paper inserted in many of the volumes of *International Studio* are thought to have been put there by Charles Greene.[26] It is difficult to say when they were inserted, except that it was probably some time after the volumes were bound. The pages Greene marked are as miscellaneous as the cuttings in the early scrapbook. He was browsing, keeping his eyes open for things that interested him, not searching for anything in particular. He noted striking visual motifs in paintings and scribbled on the slips "geese," "clouds," "sea-foam." Articles on old decorative techniques, such as gesso and enameling, and on Indian painting caught his attention. He flagged a drawing of Don Quixote by Daniel Vierge, and a good deal of German and Austrian furniture between about 1901 and 1908. Slips also appear by some English and rather more Scottish material, but, considering the amount of such work that the magazine carried, it is more remarkable how much was passed over.[27] Voysey, one of the darlings of *The Studio*, Charles ignored completely.[28]

I have jumped around a lot in this essay, from archive to archive and place to place, and it is time to bring together some conclusions. First, it is clear that Charles Greene had a quite specific sense of England, based partly on reading and partly on direct experience. He saw a rural, history-laden landscape dotted with cathedral towns, big houses and small cottages, buildings and landscape in harmony inland, but in tension at the edges, around the cliffs of Devon and Cornwall. And, curiously, his sense of the country had an early nineteenth-century feel to it.

But Greene evidently did not develop a strong sense of English Arts and Crafts, despite the fact that he was such a distinctive exponent of the movement in America. He had the opportunities to do so, through *International Studio* and other journals; on two extended visits; and with Ashbee in 1909. It seems to us in retrospect that connections should have been made, but they were not. And equally it seems to us that Greene's close study of English buildings should have had an impact on his work, but it did not until the last minute.

There were, of course, "English" buildings in Greene's work. But they were shaped not so much by his experience of England as by a public American architectural language, a stereotypical language that could be easily shared between client and architect and easily read on the street.

It is perhaps an odd and negative conclusion that there should be so little connection between Charles Greene's personal experience of England and the character of the English houses he designed. But we should not be surprised by this. There are countries of the world, and there are countries of the mind, and they work in very different ways. Charles Greene's English houses were designed in the England of his imagination. In much the same way, the Japanese elements that are such an important feature of his mature work were designed in his imagination. He never visited Japan.

1. A word on the scope of this essay: I have written about Charles Greene because England played a much larger part in his life than it did in that of his brother, Henry. But much of their work was done together, and it is not easy to separate their different contributions, so that what is said here of Charles's work may often also be true of Henry's. Scotland comes into this story a little, and, strictly speaking, I should use the words "Britain" and "Britishness." I have chosen the terms "England" and "Englishness" because they are more familiar and richer in associations.

2. CSG and HMG, Scrap Album, begun 1890, GGA.

3. A smaller and miscellaneous collection of cuttings in the EDA contains images of work by important English architects, such as John Belcher and Mervyn Macartney, taken from the English *Building News* and *American Architect and Building News* in the early 1890s.

4. The two diaries are Parkins & Gotto purse diaries for 1901, EDA. The photographs and postcards are in the GGA. It may be that a portion of the photographs and postcards date from the Greenes' later trip to England, in 1909.

5. Edward R. Bosley, *Greene & Greene* (London: Phaidon, 2000), p. 37.

6. Charles's library contained a guide for the show: *Glasgow International Exhibition: Official Guide* (Glasgow: Charles P. Watson, 1901).

7. Of course, some of the scrapbook entries may have been made *after* the English trip; those from *Country Life in America* almost certainly were.

8. Bosley, *Greene & Greene*, p. 37.

9. *Ibid.*, p. 38.

10. That the trip to England influenced the Greenes' style after 1901 is implicit in Bosley's argument, and was nicely expressed by Bruce Smith in a letter to me of April 13, 2007: "What has always amazed me is how distinctly different their work became after Charles's return from his first trip to England ... The work the brothers did before England was so mundane, so many diverse elements patched together, and after England, it became so interesting, so fun."

11. The language is lightly sketched in Lester Walker, *American Shelter: An Illustrated Encyclopedia of the American Home* (Woodstock, NY: Overlook Press, 1981).

12. Charles Greene kept a cutting

of this design; see Bosley, *Greene & Greene*, p. 47.

13. *Ibid.*

14. Letter from CSG to James Culbertson, October 7, 1902, GGA.

15. Quoted in Bosley, *Greene & Greene*, pp. 134–35. Mrs. Thorsen and Mrs. Blacker were sisters.

16. For the full quotation, see *ibid.*, p. 140. Taken from Ashbee Papers, Modern Archive Centre, King's College Library, Cambridge University, doc. nos. 72–74.

17. *Ibid.*

18. The rental agreement on 72 Scarsdale Villas, West Kensington, originally ran from May 1 to July 31. On June 30, it was extended to October 23, GGA.

19. In Charles Greene's "Datebook" for 1909 (EDA), there is an entry under July: "Mrs Boulton, Croft House, Roose, Near Barrow-in-Furness."

20. Bridget Cherry and Nikolaus Pevsner, *The Buildings of England: Devon*, 2nd edn (Harmondsworth: Penguin, 1989), pp. 553–56.

21. For early nineteenth-century works, see some of the titles listed in Greene's "Datebook" for 1909 (EDA), under December. (The EDA also has invoices for this kind of material from William Downing, an antiquarian bookseller in Birmingham, England, between 1913 and 1924.) See also the copy of *Excursions in the County of Sussex* (1822), which Charles Greene bought in July, GGA.

22. *Pasadena News*, December 24, 1909, p. 9. See also an article by Charles Greene in the *Los Angeles Builder and Contractor* for December 23, 1910, in which he says that in England he was "much impressed with the beauty of the old classic and Gothic work." I am grateful to Anne Mallek for telling me about both passages.

23. Quoted in Bosley, *Greene & Greene*, p. 149.

24. The Fleishhacker house would not look out of place in any of the volumes of *Small Country Houses of To-day* published by *Country Life* between 1910 and about 1925.

25. Nikolaus Pevsner and Enid Radcliffe, *The Buildings of England: Cornwall*, 2nd edn (Harmondsworth: Penguin, 1970), p. 221.

26. I am grateful to Ann Scheid for guidance on Charles's annotations to *International Studio*. From volume 26 on, the bindings are lettered "C. Sumner Greene."

27. Since these flagged passages are documented examples of some kind of interest in English Arts and Crafts, they are worth listing. Greene marked the following with his yellow slips: F.A. Jones, "Art in Grid Irons," 4 (1898), pp. 99–103; George Walton's work at Elm Bank, York, 13 (1901), pp. 36–42; Alexander Fisher on enameling, 13 (1901), pp. 242–54, and 14 (1901), pp. 88–95; Aymer Vallance, "The Revival of Tempera," 14 (1901), pp. 155–65; W.R. Watson, "Some Recent Scottish Domestic Fittings and Decorations," 18 (1902), pp. 104–10; Ernest Radford, "Mr G.P. Bankart's Lead-Work," 20 (1903), pp. 90–93; George Logan's furniture,

21 (1904), pp. 204–05; cabinets by M.H. Baillie Scott, 22 (1904), pp. 56–57, and 23 (1904), pp. 240–41; a fire screen by the Artificers' Guild, 23 (1904), p. 341; a four-poster bed by Ambrose Heal, 24 (1904–05), pp. 82–83; a bedcover by Frances A. Jones, 24 (1904–05), pp. 148–49; J. Taylor, "A Glasgow Artist and Designer: The Work of E.A. Taylor," 24 (1904–05), pp. 216ff; a washstand by Ambrose Heal, 24 (1904–05), p. 360; and work by Ernest Gimson, 34 (1908), p. 63.

28. Two views of houses by Voysey are included in the Scrap Album, pp. 47, 51, GGA.

DAVID C. STREATFIELD

Divergent Threads in the Garden Art of Greene and Greene

In 1905, Charles Greene wrote an article titled "California Home Making," emphasizing the importance of gardens and the difficulty of their design: "There is much being written about gardens and there are those willing to tell me readily enough what to do; but fine gardens are like fine pictures, only it may take longer to paint them with nature's brush." He continued, proposing "an arbor leading at the side to a secluded spot, sheltered but not gloomy, where one may leave one's work or book and take it up again at will, where one could look out into the bright sunlight on groups of flowers and where one may hear the tinkle of water and see the birds drink, where the shapely branches of tree or bush cast their lacey shadows fitly around a winding path."[1]

The social role of the garden as a place of leisure was clear; however, the most remarkable section of the article was Greene's hope that "California with its climate, so wonderful in possibility, is only beginning to be dreamed of, hardly thought of yet. It is not beyond probability that where the sounds of the desert now idly drift and only the call of the coyote breaks the stillness, there may rest a Villa Lante or a Fukagawa garden."[2]

The latter statement confirms that the Greene brothers considered the garden a work of art in its own right. This implicit recognition of the garden as "third nature" made no reference to the complex symbolism underlying the two visually distinct design traditions represented by the Villa Lante and the Fukagawa gardens.[3] This is not surprising, since at this time, garden history was little more than a recitation of chronology. Charles cited two old and contrasting visual representations of nature as standards of excellence that could become ideals for new garden design. In doing so, he clearly distanced himself from William Morris's simple definition of a garden: "It should be well fenced from the outside world. It should by no means imitate either the wilfulness or the wildness of Nature, but should look like a thing never to be seen except near a house."[4]

We can speculate that Charles was setting up the challenge of creating fine garden art that would be equivalent to these high ideals. Much later, Henry Greene said, "We were able to do our best design when we could control a complete landscape and then decorate it, as well as

the house. This is the only possible way to achieve integration of all three."[5] Despite the importance the Greenes placed on their garden designs, this work has attracted little scholarly attention.[6] The difficulty of disengaging the gardens from the houses is compounded by the lack of specific information on the gardens in surviving correspondence and writing. The drawings, with a few notable exceptions, display little more than the most basic information on setting out houses and piping arrangements. Since many of the gardens have been subjected to major alterations, archival photographs have become the principal record of the Greenes' intentions.

The most notable gardens Greene and Greene created between 1907 and 1929 employed the seemingly distinct naturalistic and formal design traditions, either singly or, more frequently, in a synthesized manner. This essay will explore the interweaving of these divergent threads in the Greenes' attempt to create an appropriate California Garden idiom within the American Arts and Crafts movement. This body of work differs from other American regional garden traditions. It eschews the Prairie School insistence on the use of native plants and close respect for the subtlety of existing topography. It is unlike the Hillside Gardening of the San Francisco Bay area, where house siting was determined by topography, and a palette of plants that bloomed all year long. It does not follow Kate Sessions's insistence in San Diego on drought tolerance as a determining factor, nor does it follow the abstract formalism of Irving Gill.[7]

1893–1906: DESIGN SYNTHESIS

The architectural designs undertaken during the Greenes' early period represent an evolving search for an appropriate "California House."[8] The accompanying garden designs represent a parallel search for a "California Garden" that countered the prevailing popular stylistic pluralism in Pasadena homes and gardens, devoid of a sense of regional specificity. Abundant irrigation allowed gardens to be assembled with plants from all over the world in complete disregard of the dry climate.

In creating a "California Garden," the Greenes drew from a wide range of sources, including California missions and ranch houses, English Tudor gardens, and

FIGURE I

Garden stairs and jardinière, 1927–28, Mortimer Fleishhacker, Sr., estate, Woodside, 1911–12

Photograph © Estate of Mark Fiennes

Japanese gardens. Many scholars have emphasized the centrality of Japan, citing Charles's expressed regret that he had never visited that country, his familiarity with Edward Morse's book *Japanese Homes and Their Surroundings*, the comment by C.R. Ashbee that "the spell of Japan is on him," and the obvious physical evidence in some gardens of stepping stones and stone lanterns.[9] Japanese gardens were not, however, the sole source of inspiration for the Greenes' naturalistic landscape designs. The brothers' familiarity with Japanese gardens was limited to a few examples seen at expositions and the images in Morse's book, none of which was equivalent in size to their larger gardens.

On a grander scale, English landscape gardens and American gardens informed by Picturesque theory almost certainly served the Greenes as important models. Charles visited two major English landscape gardens, Stourhead in Wiltshire and Studley Royal in Yorkshire, on his honeymoon. In Boston, Charles and Henry saw public and domestic landscape designs by Frederick Law Olmsted, derived from English precedents that employed Picturesque concepts.[10] Another potential source are photographs of larger water landscapes in Gertrude Jekyll's *Wall and Water Gardens* (1905).[11]

The physical evidence of the Greenes' gardens supports the hypothesis that Picturesque theory and techniques formed the principal ordering system for their naturalistic landscape designs, joined with Japanese flourishes. The consistent use of sequences of pictorially composed spaces focused on distant mountainous panoramas differentiates their gardens from the more introverted and constricted spaces depicted in Morse's book. This may be further supported by recognizing that the brothers' borrowings from English Tudor and Japanese design idioms resulted from client requests rather than from their own preference.

It has been assumed that Charles's leading role in design development relegated Henry to the relatively minor role of producing construction documents and specifications and supervising the office. Yet Henry clearly played an important part in disciplining his brother's artistic nature and ensuring, through careful detailing, that the designs could be carried out; his contributions should not be understated. Careful examination of the nineteen garden and landscape designs undertaken by Henry on his own makes clear that he was a distinguished designer in his own right, whose penchant for more austere form complemented his brother's artistic boldness.

During this period, the Greenes' exploration of the "California Garden" depended on the development of a distinctive vocabulary of garden features, including walls, paths, fences, entrance platforms, and pergolas, just as their "California House" integrated regionally expressive walls and paths.[12] The Greenes fashioned walls from cobbles and boulders taken from the Arroyo Seco and mixed with clinker brick, as in the boundary walls of Charles Greene's house (1902) and the James A. Culbertson house (1902), both in Pasadena. While the use of boulders was criticized in small walls, their later use in boldly fluid terrace walls, graded upward in sweeping curves, as at the James W. Neil house in Pasadena (1906), made possible sensuous transitions with the ground plane.[13] Paths using local brick and stones were equally important elements of this new design vocabulary, as shown in the extensive brick paths at the Edward Crocker garden in Pasadena (1911–12) and the service path at the Jennie Reeve house in Long Beach (1903–04). Each of these superbly crafted features was conceived as a work of art in its own right.[14]

A distinctive element of the Greenes' landscape design that has gone unnoticed is their treatment of entry platforms to enhance the presence of the front door. These platforms supported pots filled variously with yuccas, clipped boxwood cones, or cypresses.[15] An alternative design contained the stairs to the front door with low cheek walls, as at the Dr. W.T. Bolton house in Pasadena (1906), sometimes flared outward—emulating such Italian Baroque precedents as the water staircase at Palazzo Corsini, Rome[16]—or with small flanking platforms often bearing pots, as at the David B. Gamble house in Pasadena (1907–09). The perspectival effect of these designs emphasized the front door as a focal feature. Pots, filled with plants, were also used to provide rhythm and emphatic vertical contrast on entrance porches.

Detached pergolas, such as the one at the Robert R. Blacker garden in Pasadena (1910), functioned as leisurely destinations within the garden and were designed with large projecting rafters inclined at a shallow angle.[17] Longer pergolas, as in the Crocker garden, created shelters over pathways and sitting areas, and were given a distinctive delicate quality with longer, more slender, overhanging rafters with rounded ends.[18] An abundant planting of vines invariably enveloped the pergolas.

The Greenes used plants lavishly—both in the garden and inside the house, in stained glass, furniture panels, and ceiling ornaments—to create a real and imagined "perfected nature." Picturesque theory advocated visually marrying buildings with the landscape. This was achieved by the careful choice of wall colors and regional materials and by an abundant use of hanging plants in window boxes. Trellis fences were lushly enveloped with vines.

FIGURE 2
View of driveway from the front steps, Freeman A. Ford house, Pasadena, 1906–08. Photograph by Leroy Hulbert, c. 1915

Courtesy of Avery Architectural and Fine Arts Library, Columbia University

This interpretation of Picturesque theory complemented the Greenes' use of Picturesque spatial techniques.

Although both brothers were fascinated by nature, their collective knowledge of plants was not extensive.[19] Late in life, Henry told Jean Murray Bangs, who was preparing to write a book on the Greenes, that they could not find landscape designers to assist them, and consequently they used the services of the nurseryman George Chisholm.[20] It is not known how this relationship worked; it is most probable that the Greenes described the effects that they desired, and Chisholm selected appropriate plants.

1907–09: NATURALISTIC GARDENS

By 1907, the Greenes had developed a distinctive design approach and vocabulary. This coincided with commissions by enlightened clients with substantial financial means for the houses that are now recognized as the apogee of Greene and Greene's architecture. Their equally significant landscape designs, using Picturesque compositional techniques—sequential views related to irregular lines of movement through space, carefully framed views, manipulation of the ground plane, and careful siting of structures in the landscape—constitute a unique landscape idiom.

The Greenes often used oval and gently curving drives to create sequences of changing views that cumulatively created illusions of larger space. Massed planting and changes in the ground plane controlled diagonal sight lines. Plants also framed the mass of houses into visual units. The small park space between the house and road on the Freeman A. Ford property in Pasadena (1906–08) was framed by a series of gently graded mounds and masses of evergreen trees to provide multiple framed diagonal views both for the pedestrian and the visitor (fig. 2). The sophisticated planting also created textural contrast with the carefully composed masses of the house. A single orange tree to the left of the shallow entry steps not only offered contrast in texture and form but also served as a fragrant and symbolic reference to California's extraordinary fecundity.

Beyond the shallow steps, the entrance followed a diagonal sight line through the flanking planting of pine trees to a low pergola. Within the pergola, the visual axis shifted to the axis of the front door, bisecting the formal courtyard that was centered on a slightly depressed central pool. This axis was reinforced using pots of clipped orange trees at the corners of the pool and by smaller pots planted with clipped evergreens.

FIGURE 3
View northwest from Westmoreland Place, David B. Gamble house, Pasadena, 1907–09. Photograph by Leroy Hulbert, c. 1915

Courtesy of Avery Architectural and Fine Arts Library, Columbia University

FIGURE 4
View of south façade, looking toward dining room and pergola, Robert R. Blacker house, Pasadena, 1907–09. Photograph by Leroy Hulbert, c. 1915

Courtesy of Avery Architectural and Fine Arts Library, Columbia University

The pergola was the fulcrum that linked the asymmetrical balance of the outer landscape garden and the geometric courtyard. Passing through it to descend the shallow steps, the visitor was presented with two framed vistas, a technique consistent with English Picturesque practice and strikingly similar to Humphry Repton's design for Stoneleigh Abbey in Warwickshire, where this effect also created an enhanced sense of distance.[21]

The design of the David B. Gamble garden (1907–09) was controlled by the presence of three large eucalyptus trees, rolling topography, and the siting of the house parallel to the street. Placing buildings in close relationship to existing trees was another Picturesque device used to marry architecture and landscape. The tall eucalyptus trees and the flanking Italian cypresses and shrubs between the street and the house framed the building into smaller visual units. Passage through this planting along the semi-oval drive ensured a sequence of changing views as well as access to the front door and the detached garage. This perfected naturalism was further enhanced by grading the undulating topography into a sensuous surface of geometrically rolled terraces and a shallow swale-like feature leading diagonally across the rear lawn. The front lawn rises gently into a berm that hides from view the high-crowned brick drive (fig. 3).

The Greenes' extraordinary attention to seemingly prosaic details enhanced the naturalism of the design. The low points of the high-crowned brick drive serve as drainage channels and are continued across the sidewalk as grooves discharging runoff water directly into the street so that pedestrians do not have to step down from the curb. The three ridges of the curved brick planes of the drive that meet at the junction with the branch drive to the garage are crowned with carefully cut wedges of brick.

The Greenes considered the garden for the Robert R. Blacker house to be their finest design. This 5-acre (2-ha) garden (1909–28), their largest commission in Pasadena, united geometric and naturalistic modes.[22] The large U-shaped house sits on the highest part of the rolling topography near the northwest corner of the property; it overlooked an expansive landscape with a large central pond containing a small island and a bridge.

The large central section was subtly defined by two axial vistas that extended from the house. The dining-room axis ran south toward the garage, keeper's cottage, and lath house through a massive wisteria-draped pergola (1910) supported by prominently braced posts on low brick piers (fig. 4). A parallel axis through the front door extended across a terrace and over a later large marble fountain basin (1927–28; see Bosley essay, fig. 5)

Leroy Hulbert

FIGURE 5
*View of east façade,
lily pond, and
landscape, Robert
R. Blacker house.
Photograph by
Frederick Martin,
n.d. [after 1914]*
Courtesy of the California
History Room, California
State Library, Sacramento

FIGURE 6
*View of north (front)
and west façades,
Margaret B.S.
Clapham Spinks
house, Pasadena,
1907–09. Photograph
by William R.
Current, n.d.*
Courtesy of Greene
and Greene Archives,
The Gamble House,
University of Southern
California

to command a symmetrical vista of tall palm trees alternating with rectangular flower beds and terminating in a simple exedra of Italian cypresses. The spacing of the palms and their vertical profile ensured a level of spaciousness markedly different from the more confined allées of historic Italian formal gardens. The understated and subtle geometry of this design was an effective transition to the flowing naturalism below.

The Greenes extended the cross axis through the living room along a low ridge above the large pond marked by pots of orange and cypress trees; it terminated in a detached pergola (1910) with the typical shallow profile. The pond was thus enfolded between two axial walks providing shade and a variety of diagonal views down to the water. It was one of the clearest expressions of Charles's ideal garden with "an arbor leading at the side to a secluded spot, sheltered but not gloomy, where one may leave one's work or book and take it up again at will ..."[23] The naturalistic forms of the pond, planted with water lilies and lotus, and of the massive groups of

shrubs and trees, evoked on a large scale the character of Japanese and English landscape gardens (fig. 5). This was in contrast to the firm but subtly expressed geometry of the outer walks. The changing sequence of views was experienced, as in a Japanese garden, from a series of stepping stones carefully placed in the grass. These vantage points afforded views through mature stands of trees of the advancing and retreating masses of the large house. The seemingly instantaneous maturity coupled with the synthesis of three design traditions resulted in an artistic *tour de force* not seen before in the Greenes' work.[24]

The Margaret B.S. Clapham Spinks house and garden in Pasadena (1909), probably designed by Henry on his own, demonstrated an austere and restrained use of Picturesque devices on a smaller lot.[25] Henry took full advantage of the fine eastern prospect by siting the house close to the point where the eastern slope descends into the canyon. The view from the street was carefully orchestrated to provide a subtle diagonal sight line, expanding the sense of spaciousness (fig. 6). The edges of the drive appear to converge, creating a perspectival effect of distance complemented by the gentle terracing of the front lawn in three falls. The drive terminates at the garage, discreetly sited so that it is not visible from the street.

This small naturalistic park afforded privacy for its owners, who could enjoy unobstructed views of the distant landscape from an open terrace at the rear, approached through French doors from the living and dining rooms. Color was not conspicuous, since flowers were relegated to a rose garden aligned on the axis of the front porch.

The Charles M. Pratt house (1908–11) is something of an anomaly in the Greenes' work, as it sits on a high site in the dry Ojai Valley in the middle of an orchard, and thus has virtually no garden. Yet it was a splendid union of structure and landscape because of its wide V-shaped plan that follows the ridge and provides sweeping views toward the mountains (see Bosley essay, fig. 1). Swirling tiered plant boxes at the front door are an artistic flourish that helps anchor the house into the rugged setting. The house is perceived as a structure fully integrated *into* the landscape rather than an object placed *on* the landscape.[26] Regional identity is also expressed in the remarkable stone walls along the road. Charles had supervised their construction almost obsessively, prompting Pratt to complain about the size of the invoice.[27]

1901–23: FORMAL GARDENS

The Greenes used geometry to order space in a relatively small number of their garden designs. The gardens for the Mrs. Charlotte A. Whitridge (1904) and Dr. W.T. Bolton houses in Pasadena were developed on sloping sites with simple symmetrical layouts.[28] The brothers' courtyard designs were rarely geometrical. The Arturo Bandini house in Pasadena (1903), based on Mexican rancheros with all the rooms opening directly on to colonnades, had a courtyard of irregularly shaped beds with trees, a fountain, a trellis, and an axial entry pergola on the fourth side (see Smith essay, figs. 11 and 12). This differed markedly from the simple formal layout of the courtyards of such ranch houses as Rancho Camulos in Ventura County.[29] The courtyard of the Cora C. Hollister house in Hollywood (1904–05) was a subtle variant of the Mexican design, with corridors on two sides opening directly on to a paved rectangular area with an offset basin. Carefully balanced planting was enhanced by a curving path leading to a rear garden.[30]

The most ambitious and sophisticated courtyard design was for Charles's unbuilt "Dwelling Place … for W.B.T." (1903). The L-shaped house, crowning a low hill,

was envisioned as two separate wings linked together by arcades enclosing two sides of a large depressed formal garden; the other sides defined by vine-draped pergolas. The interior garden was geometrically organized with a central formal parterre leading to a lower sitting area and an exedra-like feature (see Smith essay, fig. 9). This design is a most assured and skillful essay in manipulating geometric forms.[31]

Henry consistently employed geometry to order garden space, and his largely unexamined designs reveal considerable and distinctive skill. His design for the relatively small Dr. S.S. Crow house in Pasadena (1909–10) is widely acknowledged to be one of the finest by Greene and Greene.[32] The subtlety of the street façade is an unquestioned masterpiece, revealing a superb command of form and proportion (fig. 7). Central to the success of this façade is the garden setting. The house is approached across a gently graded front lawn that rises into a rolled terrace below the porch. Bauer "Indian" flowerpots are placed on low brick pedestals at the driveway, along the entrance pathway, and on the entry platform. Filled with yuccas and boxwood cones, these created subtle vertical accents and contrasts of texture and forms.

The Crow property was expanded to occupy the entire end of a block following Edward Crocker's purchase of the house and more land in 1911. In Henry Greene's designs for Crocker, the area behind the house was fenced and planned as a series of room-like spaces, some of which were fully enclosed by fences or hedges (fig. 8). The path from the narrow court between the western wings of the house led directly to the motor court, screened by a laurel hedge. The path on the right led past a rose garden laid out in two long, formal rectangular beds. Beyond this was the large principal garden enclosed by regularly spaced brick piers supporting wooden trellis panels embowered with climbing roses. A *torii*-like gate with extended beams gave entrance to a small grove of orange trees, separated from the caretaker's cottage by a laurel hedge. The grove was protected from the main part of this garden by a trellis supporting white, pink, and lavender sweet peas.

Henry conceived the simple geometric layout of the main space with the most rigorous attention to detail using *sharawadgi*, the Japanese practice of inserting an asymmetrical element within a symmetrical space. The path continued beyond the orange grove between two flower beds to terminate at a basin of water lilies with a fountain. This was backed by small shrubs and pots filled with plants marking the path intersection. From this point, the rectangular shape of the space was reinforced

FIGURE 7
*View of east (front)
façade and lawn,
Dr. S.S. Crow house,
Pasadena, 1909–10.
Photograph by Leroy
Hulbert, c. 1915*
Courtesy of Avery
Architectural and
Fine Arts Library,
Columbia University

[pages 222–23]
FIGURE 8
*Plan of garden,
c. 1911, for Edward S.
Crocker, second owner
of the Dr. S.S. Crow
house*
Courtesy of Avery
Architectural and
Fine Arts Library,
Columbia University

by a simple layout of brick paths linking a tea pavilion on the left and a long pergola spanning the path on the right. Greene reinforced the corners of the lawn with L-shaped beds of shrubs and small trees.

The placing of the two structures in relation to the path, coupled with the inclusion of a crepe myrtle, a gazing ball, an Italian cypress, and lilacs, provided necessary visual counterpoint of form and massing to what otherwise would have been a relentlessly symmetrical scheme. The detailing of the tea pavilion, which was raised four steps above the brick paving with long cantilevered beams and a rear brick wall, was similar to that of the long pergola at the Blacker garden, designed a year before. The pergola, with 6-foot-long (1.8-m-long) cantilevered beams, supported on posts with braces on the end and central bays, was an exceptionally graceful structure.

The design for Crocker differed from others by Greene and Greene in making productive space a critical element in the garden experience. Henry's treatment of the garden as a series of discrete zones was the closest that either of the Greenes ever came to English Arts and Crafts gardens, although the main space had no visual connection to the house.[33]

The Cordelia A. Culbertson garden in Pasadena (1911–13) was the brothers' last collaboration; thereafter, Henry and Charles designed houses and gardens on their own.[34] A remarkable and sophisticated essay in geometric forms, the Culbertson garden was a conceptual conflation of the mission courtyard tradition and the Italian Mannerist hillside garden. The unusual plan was a creative response to the exigencies of the site as well as the distinctive tastes of two sets of clients,[35] with the three wings of the house embracing an irregular splayed upper court carefully graded around an octagonal tiled fountain basin (1915). A massive wisteria-draped pergola led gracefully downward from the living porch to a platform above the garage and on to a large terrace above an immense Engelmann oak tree. The stairs around the tree led to a long, narrow terrace that ran parallel to the two-story bedroom wing, from which one could descend to the lower water garden (fig. 12).

A set of outwardly splayed stairs flanked by Italian cypress trees descended the slope to a terrace from which they divided and partially defined the oval basin at the bottom. This clearly recalls the Dragon Fountain at the Villa d'Este, Tivoli, which Charles visited on his honeymoon.

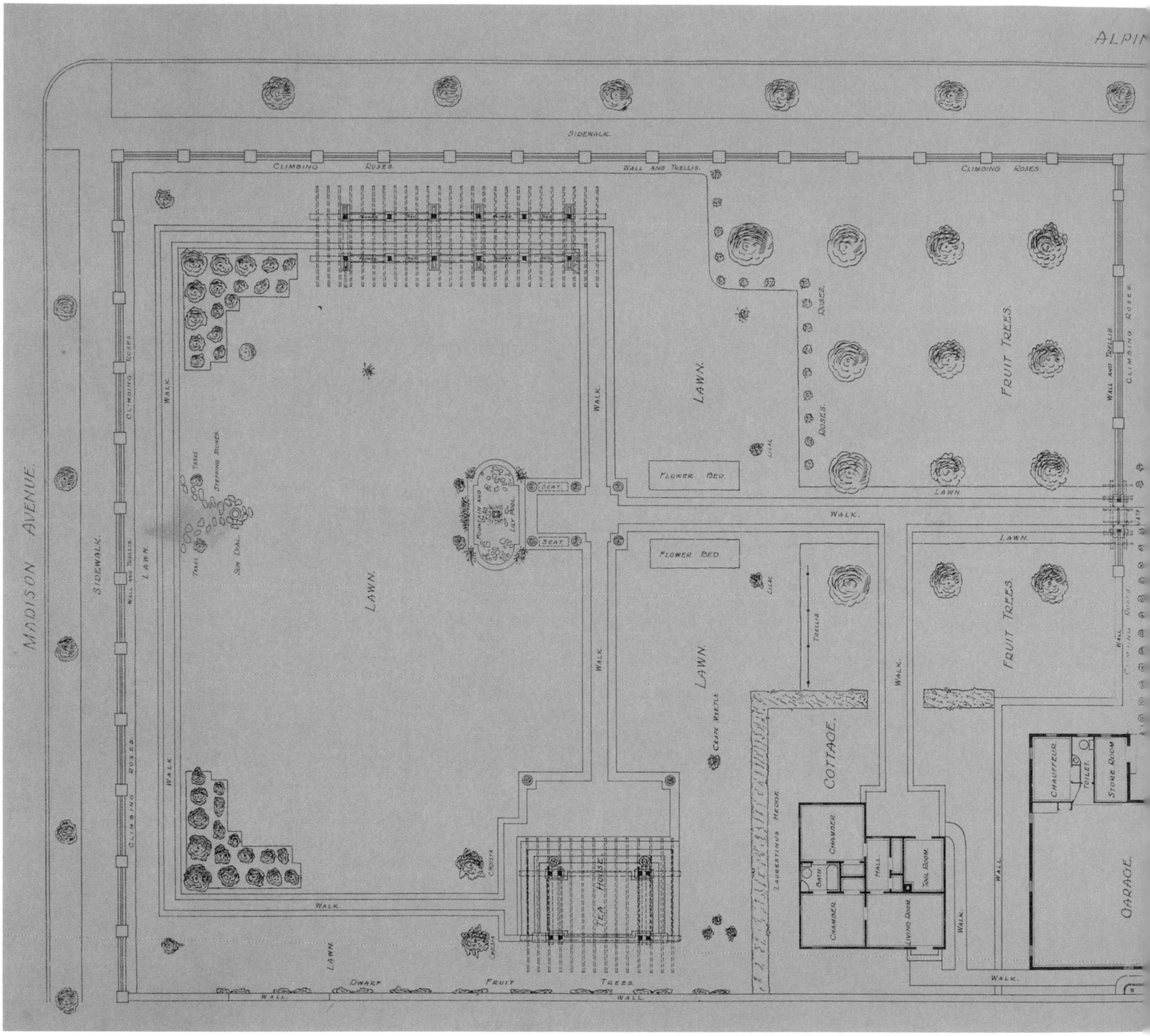

MADISON AVENUE
SIDEWALK
CLIMBING ROSES
WALL AND TRELLIS
LAWN
WALK
TREES
STEPPING STONES
SUN DIAL
LILY POOL
SEAT.
SEAT.
FLOWER BED
FLOWER BED
LILAC
ROSES
ROSES
FRUIT TREES
FRUIT TREES
TRELLIS
CREPE MYRTLE
LAURESTINUS HEDGE
COTTAGE
CHAMBER
CHAMBER
BATH
HALL
TOOL ROOM
LIVING ROOM
TEA HOUSE
CHAUFFEUR
TOILET
STORE ROOM
GARAGE
DWARF FRUIT TREES
WALL

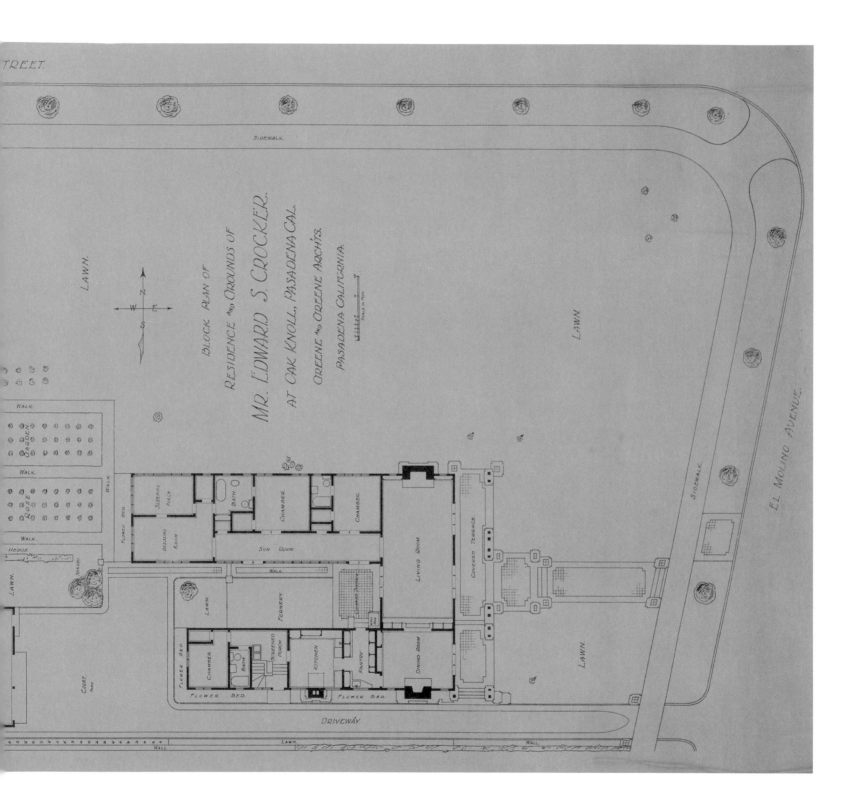

STREET.

SIDEWALK.

LAWN.

BLOCK PLAN OF
RESIDENCE AND GROUNDS OF
MR. EDWARD S. CROCKER.
AT OAK KNOLL, PASADENA CAL.
GREENE AND GREENE ARCH'TS.
PASADENA CALIFORNIA.

SCALE IN FEET.

LAWN

WALK

GARDEN

WALK

ROSE

WALK

WALK

HEDGE

LAWN

COURT

FLOWER BED

SLEEPING PORCH

BEDDING ROOM

BATH

CHAMBER

SUN ROOM

CHAMBER

WALK

LIVING ROOM

COVERED TERRACE

SIDEWALK

LAWN

EL MOLINO AVENUE.

FLOWER BED

CHAMBER

LAWN

BATH

SCREENED PORCH

FERNERY

KITCHEN

COVERED PASSAGE

PANTRY

DINING ROOM

FLOWER BED

FLOWER BED

DRIVEWAY

WALL

LAWN

WALL

LAWN

WALL

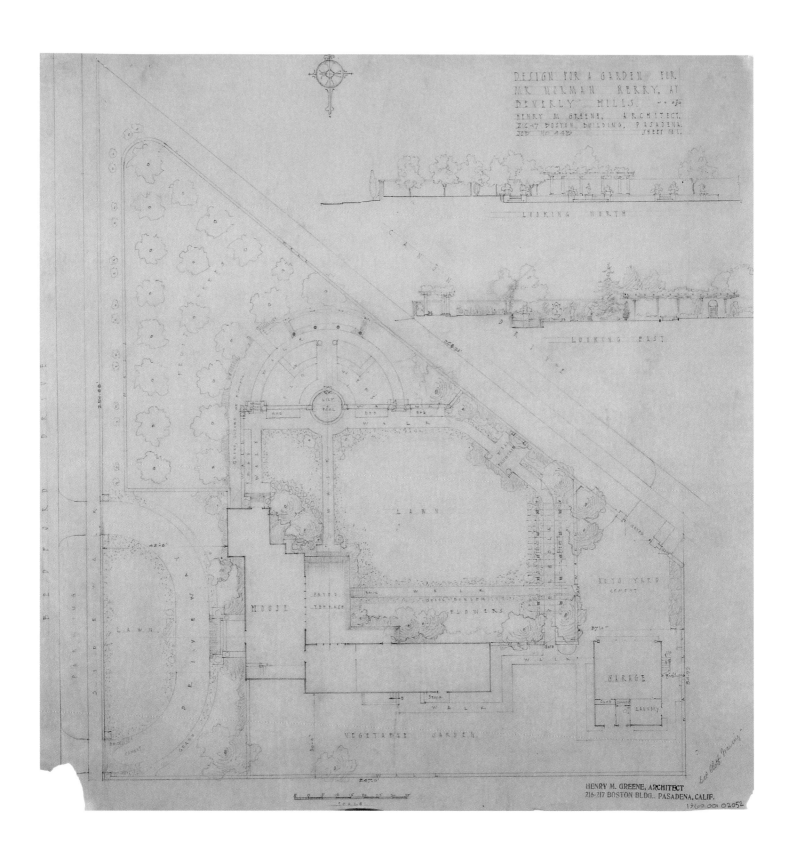

DESIGN FOR A GARDEN FOR
MR NORMAN KERRY, AT
BEVERLY HILLS.
HENRY M. GREENE, ARCHITECT.
216-17 BOSTON BUILDING, PASADENA.
JOB NO 449   SHEET NO 1.

LOOKING NORTH

LOOKING EAST

LAWN

LILY POOL

HOUSE

PAVED TERRACE

LAWN

FLOWERS

KITCHEN YARD
CEMENT

GARAGE

LAUNDRY

WALK

VEGETABLE GARDEN

SCALE

HENRY M. GREENE, ARCHITECT
216-217 BOSTON BLDG., PASADENA, CALIF.

His design was a romantic evocation of the original's time-worn forms, although it lacked any iconographic references.[36] The romantic descent was further enhanced by the sound of running water in two small fountains and in narrow tile-lined channels in the stair treads.

In 1918, Theodore A. Kramer commissioned Henry to make internal alterations to his late Victorian house in South Pasadena and to redesign the garden on the large corner lot, on which there were several big trees. One of these became the visual focus of formal flower gardens between the house and the garage, while a large oak tree became the centerpiece of the main lawn. This was characteristic of the Greenes' practice of using natural elements as framing and focal features. The large lawn was separated from the street by a long vine-draped pergola terminating with a gently curving bench oriented toward a gazing ball.[37]

The strong geometry of the areas around the house gave way to a more naturalistic treatment of the low mound surrounding the large oak, which became the dominant feature of the lawn. The simple restraint of the plan contrasts strikingly with the rich planting. The surviving drawings provide more information on planting than any other scheme by either of the brothers, indicating either Henry's greatly enhanced knowledge or heavy reliance on a nurseryman.

Henry designed two gardens for the Earle C. Anthony house (Los Angeles, 1909–10). The first, relatively small garden was embraced by the wings of the L-shaped house and an L-shaped pergola, one arm of which extended from the house, running parallel to the street. The central lawn space could be viewed from the vine-covered pergola and from a deeper pergola set in the angle of the house that opened off the large living room and dining room through French doors.[38]

In 1923, the new owner of the Anthony house, the actor Norman Kerry, relocated the building to a larger, triangular site in Beverly Hills (fig. 9). The new site allowed Henry Greene to position the house farther back from the road, with a narrow oval drive and a separate walled garage court approached from the rear street. The new walled rear garden offered complete privacy on the gently sloping site; a semicircular flower garden raised slightly above the main lawn by a low wall and centered on a small circular pool recalls the Renaissance practice of placing such features in the middle of a change of level. This feature and the loggia against the enclosing wall are axially related to the new terrace in the angle of the house, creating a much stronger relationship of garden to house.

Mortimer S. Fleishhacker, Sr., selected Charles Greene to design his large estate, Green Gables, in Woodside (1911–12). This was the largest commission undertaken by Greene and Greene, and it exemplifies the enlightened patronage of the Fleishhacker family, which extended, with several breaks, for over two decades. The clients requested a thatched English house, an unusual choice both for such a dry site and for a large house. After a lengthy study of the property, Charles placed the house on the middle slope of an isolated, tree-covered hill commanding panoramic views of the distant Santa Cruz Mountains.[39]

A magnificent California live oak, removed in the 1950s, dominated a large brick terrace and broke up the broad mass of the flat façade of the house into a series of visual units, an effect emphasized by the flanking living-room wing and open loggia. Below the paved terrace are rolled grass terraces above a simple lawn. Two paths traverse the lawn, drawing the eye toward a T-shaped reflecting pool at the top of an abrupt slope that from the terrace appears suspended in space. The spacious and simple formality of this scheme evokes the geometry of English Tudor and Jacobean gardens as they appeared at the beginning of the twentieth century; devoid of their original elaborate parterres, they became simple grass plats (see Crawford essay, fig. 6).[40]

In 1926, Fleishhacker recalled Charles "to do something" with the area lying some 60 feet (18 m) below the reflecting pool. The result is one of the most extraordinary geometric garden designs ever created in the United States and is a superb demonstration of Charles's inventive artistic genius. He extended the central axis between two Monterey pine trees to direct the eye from the end of the upper garden to a distant peak in the mountains. Twin stairs, seemingly embedded in the topography, descend in sweeping curves to a broad terrace overlooking a long pool of water, known as the "Roman pool," that terminates in a semi-oval arcade (figs. 10 and 11). The details recall such Italian Baroque gardens as the Villa Aldobrandini, Frascati, in the Alban Hills east of Rome (1600), which Charles had visited on his honeymoon. The sculpted swirling staircases are Baroque in spirit but are set apart from that precedent by the use of three different kinds of stone for the treads, walls, and copings (fig. 1). Subtle gradations of color and texture underscore the different roles of each element in the composition. Charles was almost certainly attracted by the seemingly ruined and rustic character of the water features and fountains in the upper garden at Villa Aldobrandini. The wall fountains below the semicircular terrace recall the organization of the outdoor dining area at the villa.[41]

FIGURE 9

Plan and elevations for garden, 1923, for Norman Kerry, second owner of the Earle C. Anthony house, 1909–10, relocated to Beverly Hills

Courtesy of Avery Architectural and Fine Arts Library, Columbia University

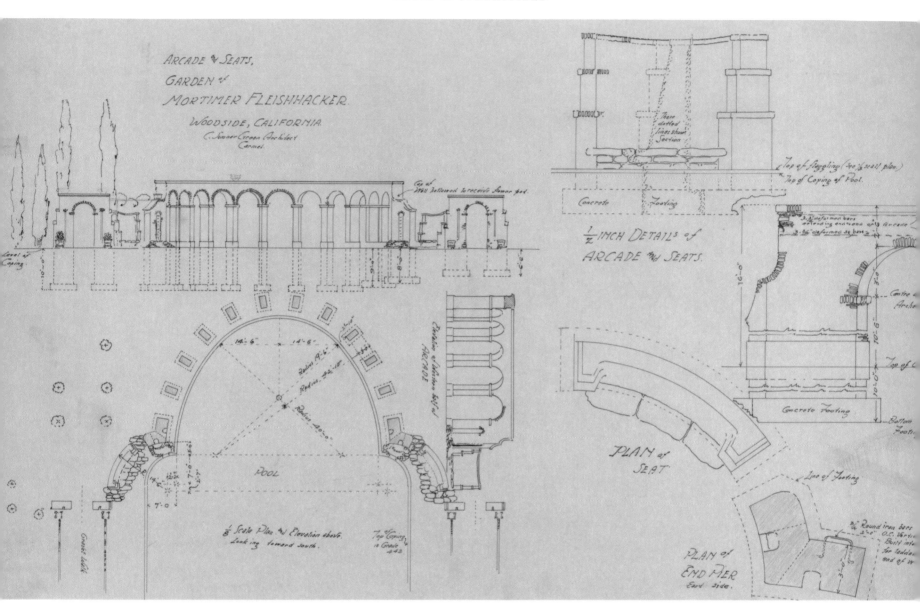

The process of selecting a suitable termination for the outer end of the long pool was protracted and involved the creation, over two years, of three alternative designs, each framing the vista of the distant mountains. In an early proposal, a continuous wall was pierced by a trio of closely grouped small arches; one scholar suggested that this use of three reflects Charles's interest in Theosophy.[42] Charles presented the final design for the arcade in 1929. Several sources have been proposed for the arcade, the most plausible being a small photograph in Charles's collection of a distant aqueduct in the Roman Campagna.[43] The protracted design process was matched by an equally lengthy construction sequence, underscoring the difficulty that patron and architect experienced in creating an appropriate conclusion for the semi-oval terminus of the long pool.

While the upper garden and the Roman pool are resolutely formal, the adjacent planting effectively blurs their edges. The arcade at the edge of the garden partially veils the outer view and draws a subtle line in space. In

FIGURE 10
Plans and elevations for arcade and seats, n.d. [c. 1928], Mortimer Fleishhacker, Sr., estate

Courtesy of Charles Sumner Greene Collection (1959-1), Environmental Design Archives, University of California, Berkeley

FIGURE 11
Arcade, 1928–29, and reflecting pool, 1927–28, Mortimer Fleishhacker, Sr., estate

Photograph © Estate of Mark Fiennes

[page 229]
FIGURE 12
View of lower garden, stairs, and pool, Cordelia A. Culbertson house, Pasadena, 1911–13. Photograph by Leroy Hulbert, c. 1915

Courtesy of Avery Architectural and Fine Arts Library, Columbia University

this way, the garden is distinct from the distant prospect but is also experienced as belonging to the landscape.

CONCLUSION

Charles and Henry Greene's "California Garden" is a complex contribution to the art of garden design in the American Arts and Crafts movement. It is clearly different both from William Morris's conception of the garden and from the regional traditions of the Midwest and other parts of California. The invocation by Charles of the aristocratic art of Villa Lante and the Fukagawa garden further emphasizes the ambiguity of the Greenes' work within the Arts and Crafts movement.

The ability of Charles and Henry Greene to weave the seemingly divergent threads of refined geometry and naturalism into a unique and creative synthesis of disparate sources, coupled with consummate craftsmanship, has never been surpassed. It was a remarkable achievement of garden art, reflective of both time and place.

1. CSG, "California Home Making," *Pasadena Daily News*, January 2, 1905, pp. 26–27.

2. *Ibid.*, p. 27. The references to the Villa Lante and the Fukagawa garden come from A.D.F. Hamlin, "The Italian Formal Garden," and K. Honda, "Japanese Landscape Gardening," in *European and Japanese Gardens*, ed. Glenn Brown (Philadelphia: Henry T. Coates & Co., 1902), pp. 35–37, 139, 144. CSG owned a copy of this title. For the iconography of Villa Lante, see Claudia Lazzaro, *The Italian Renaissance Garden* (New Haven, Conn.: Yale University Press, 1990), pp. 243–69.

3. "Third nature" is a Classical concept first advanced by Pliny the Younger to define the progressive transformation of wild, untamed nature ("first nature") to settled landscapes ("second nature") and finally to the union of art and nature ("third nature"). The last idea was developed by Jacopo Bonfadio in 1541. See Thomas E. Beck, "Gardens as a 'Third Nature': The Ancient Roots of a Renaissance Ideal," *Studies in the History of Gardens and Designed Landscapes*, 22, no. 4 (October–December 2002), pp. 327–34.

4. William Morris, *Hopes and Fears for Art* (London: Longmans, Green & Company, 1908), pp. 126–27.

5. HMG, quoted in Esther McCoy, "Who Starts a Style?" *Los Angeles Times*, Home Magazine, July 19, 1953.

6. The most comprehensive discussion of Greene and Greene gardens is provided in Janet Lynn Brown, "Charles Sumner Greene and Henry Mather Greene, Architects: The Integration of House and Garden—Southern California, 1893–1914" (master's thesis, University of California, Berkeley, 1988). See also Thaïsa Way, "Arts and Crafts Gardens in California" (master's thesis, University of Virginia, 1991). A typology of Californian Arts and Crafts gardens is provided in David C. Streatfield, "The Arts and Crafts Garden in California," in *The Arts and Crafts Movement in California: Living the Good Life*, exhib. cat., ed. Kenneth R. Trapp, Oakland, Calif., Oakland Museum, 1993, pp. 35–54. For general treatments of Arts and Crafts gardens, see Wendy Hitchmough, *Arts and Crafts Gardens* (New York: Rizzoli, 1997); and Judith B. Tankard, *Gardens of the Arts and Crafts Movement* (New York: Harry N. Abrams, 2004).

7. For a discussion of the landscape designs of the Prairie School, see O.C. Simonds, *Landscape-Gardening* (Amherst: University of Massachusetts Press, 2000), pp. ix–lvi; and Robert E. Grese, *Jens Jensen, Maker of Natural Parks and Gardens* (Baltimore: Johns Hopkins University Press, 1992). For the San Francisco Bay area, see Charles Keeler, *The Simple Home* (Santa Barbara, Calif.: P. Smith, 1979). For Kate Sessions, see Mac Griswold and Eleanor Weller, *The Golden Age of American Gardens: Proud Owners, Private Estates, 1890–1940* (New York: Harry N. Abrams, in association with the Garden Club of America, 1991), pp. 345–56; and Elizabeth MacPhail, *Kate Sessions, Pioneer Horticulturist* (San Diego: San Diego Historical Society, 1976). For Irving Gill, see Thomas S. Hines, *Irving Gill and the Architecture of Reform: A Study in Modernist Architectural Culture* (New York: Monacelli, 2000).

8. Edward R. Bosley, *Greene & Greene* (London: Phaidon, 2000), pp. 40–71.

9. Clay Lancaster called the Greenes "the West Coast foremost Japanophiles," in *The Japanese Influence in America* (New York: Abbeville, 1983), p. 186. Edward S. Morse, *Japanese Homes and Their Surroundings* (Boston: Ticknor & Company, 1886); C.R. Ashbee is quoted in Robert W. Winter, "American Sheaves from C.R.A.," *Journal of the Society of Architectural Historians*, 30 (December 1971), p. 321.

10. The word "Picturesque" means "like a picture" and was used throughout the eighteenth century to describe landscapes worthy of depiction. At the end of that century, it was classified as a style characterized by roughness, sudden variation, and irregularity. Such American landscape designers as Andrew Jackson Downing and Frederick Law Olmsted were well read in Picturesque theory and applied it in their work. For a general discussion, see David Watkin, *The English Vision: The Picturesque in Architecture, Landscape and Garden Design* (London: John Murray, 1982); and John Dixon Hunt, *The Picturesque Garden in Europe* (London: Thames & Hudson, 2002), pp. 60–89. For an excellent discussion of the Shingle style and related landscape designs in Boston, see Barbara Ann Francis, "The Boston Roots of Greene and Greene" (master's thesis, Tufts University, 1987), pp. 26, 88. For an

excellent discussion of Olmsted, see Charles E. Beveridge and Paul Rocheleau, *Frederick Law Olmsted: Designing the American Landscape* (New York: Rizzoli, 1995).

11. Charles Greene owned a copy of Gertrude Jekyll, *Wall and Water Gardens* (London: Country Life and George Newnes, 1905), plates facing pp. 125, 154, 158.

12. Bosley, *Greene & Greene*, pp. 40–71.

13. Herbert Croly [Arthur C. David, pseud.], "An Architect of Bungalows in California," *Architectural Record*, 20, no. 4 (October 1906), p. 312. Charles acknowledged the correctness of David's criticism in "Bungalows," *Western Architect*, 12, no. 1 (July 1908), pp. 3–5. Iwan Serrurier specifically instructed the Greenes not to use large boulders on his house.

14. Francis, "Boston Roots," p. 78.

15. Frank Lloyd Wright also used planted pots on terrace walls and at the entrances to some of his Prairie School houses, but these have a more insistent presence.

16. A photograph of the water staircase in the garden of Palazzo Corsini, Rome, is in Brown, *European and Japanese Gardens*, frontispiece, p. 63.

17. The shallow-angled pergola first appears at the James A. Culbertson house. This profile was used again on the roofs of the gate piers at the Oaklawn Residential Park (1904–05) and of the "tea house" of the Adelaide A. Tichenor house, Long Beach (1904–05). Randell L. Makinson, "Charles and Henry Greene," in *Toward a Simpler Way of Life: The Arts and Crafts Architects of California*, ed. Robert Winter (Berkeley: University of California Press, 1997), p. 128.

18. The first use of long, projecting horizontal rafters was on the garage of the James Culbertson house, added in 1906, which was designed to appear as an elegant pavilion in the garden. Bosley, *Greene & Greene*, p. 50.

19. Henry particularly admired the formal order of orange orchards. HMG, "The Use of Orange Trees in Formal Gardens," *California Southland*, April 1918, p. 8.

20. Jean Murray Bangs Papers, Avery.

21. Charles and Henry were not familiar with the design of Stoneleigh Abbey, but the similarity reinforces their understanding of Picturesque practices. Mavis Batey and David Lambert, *The English Garden Tour: A View into the Past* (London: John Murray, 1990), p. 251.

22. Clay Lancaster, "My Interviews

with Greene and Greene," *Journal of the American Institute of Architects*, 28 (July 1957), p. 206. A reconstructed plan of the garden is given in Randell L. Makinson and Thomas A. Heinz, *The Blacker House* (Salt Lake City: Gibbs Smith, 2000), p. 40; the detached pergola is shown on pp. 28–29. Early photographs suggest a strong Japanese quality in the pond area. However, photographs taken after the garden had matured show it was much closer to English landscape gardens.

23. CSG, "California Home Making," pp. 26–27.

24. In Southern California, the transplanting of large boxed trees was pioneered by William Hertrich at the Henry Huntington estate in San Marino. William Hertrich, *The Huntington Botanical Gardens, 1905–1949, Personal Recollections of William Hertrich* (San Marino, Calif.: The Huntington Library, 1949), pp. 34–36.

25. Bosley, *Greene & Greene*, pp. 141–42.

26. *Ibid.*, pp. 127–29.

27. *Ibid.*, pp. 166–67.

28. *Ibid.*, pp. 65, 89.

29. *Ibid.*, pp. 58–59. For Rancho Camulos, see Charles F. Saunders, "California," in *Gardens of Colony and State: Gardens and Gardeners of the American Colonies and of the Republic before 1840*, ed. Alice B. Lockwood (New York: Charles Scribner's Sons for the Garden Club of America, 1931 and 1934), II, pp. 391–402.

30. Randell L. Makinson, *Greene & Greene: Architecture as a Fine Art* (Salt Lake City: Peregrine Smith, 1977), p. 89.

31. Bosley, *Greene & Greene*, pp. 63–64. CSG's sketch for a house for "W.B.T." was exhibited at the St. Louis exposition of 1904, and published in *Architectural Club of Los Angeles, Year Book, 1911, of the Second Annual Exhibition under the auspices of the Architectural League of the Pacific Coast, Los Angeles, Ca., January 17–21, 1911.*

32. Bosley, *Greene & Greene*, pp. 142–45.

33. Hermann Muthesius, *The English House* (London: Crosby Lockwood Staples, 1979), p. 107. Translation of *Das englische Haus* (Berlin: Wasmuth, 1904–05).

34. Bosley, *Greene & Greene*, pp. 155–60; *Pacific Coast Architect*, 7, no. 3 (March 1914), pp. 10–11.

35. The three unmarried sisters of James Culbertson commissioned the

house in 1911, but were forced to sell it in 1917. In 1914, job records reflect the construction of pergolas, lath house, and trellis, and, in 1915, a fountain. The next owner, Mrs. Dudley P. Allen of Cleveland, Ohio, commissioned alterations to the grounds in 1917; gunite fences and a gate in 1918; a full planting plan in 1921; step stones in the lower garden in 1927; and potting shed and paving in 1931. See Bosley, *Greene & Greene*, pp. 231–235. All told, the Greenes worked on the house and gardens for more than twenty years.

36. Henry Hawley, "An Italianate Garden by Greene and Greene," *Journal of Decorative and Propaganda Arts*, 1, no. 3 (Fall 1986), pp. 32–45. Photographs and plans of the Villa d'Este garden appear in Brown, *European and Japanese Gardens,* pp. 17, 22, 54. The photographs emphasize the overgrown and romantic appearance of the fountain early in the twentieth century. Georges Gromort, *Jardins d'Italie* (Paris: A. Vincent, 1922–31), plate 57, confirms that this condition still obtained in the 1920s. For differing iconographic interpretations of the Villa d'Este garden, see David R. Coffin, *The Villa*

d'Este at Tivoli* (Princeton, NJ: Princeton University Press, 1960); and David Dernie, *The Villa d'Este at Tivoli* (London: Academy Editions, 1996).

37. Bosley, *Greene & Greene*, p. 179.
38. Makinson, *Architecture as a Fine Art*, p. 185.
39. David C. Streatfield, "Echoes of England and Italy: 'Green Gables' and Charles Green," *Journal of Garden History*, 2, no. 4 (October–December 1982), pp. 377–98. Anne Bloomfield, "The Evolution of a Landscape: Charles Sumner Greene's Design for Green Gables," *Journal of the Society of Architectural Historians*, 47 (September 1988), pp. 231–44, provides a comprehensive history of the garden and repeats much of Streatfield's analysis.
40. A photograph in R. Clipston Sturgis, "English Gardens," in Brown, *European and Japanese Gardens*, p. 90, is quite similar to the upper garden at Green Gables. For images of Tudor and Jacobean gardens in their original state, see Roy Strong, *The Renaissance Garden in England* (London: Thames & Hudson, 1979).

41. When Charles visited Villa Aldobrandini, the upper garden was considerably overgrown, emphasizing the rustic nature of several features. This overgrown quality persisted for decades. E. March Phillips, *The Gardens of Italy with Historical and Descriptive Notes*, ed. Arthur T. Bolton (London: Country Life and George Newnes; New York: Charles Scribner's Sons, 1919), fig. 175. The sculptural stairs at Villa Torlonia, Frascati, may have served as a model for the staircase. *Ibid.*, fig. 165.
42. Travis Lee Culwell, "The Spirituality of Charles Greene" (master's thesis, University of California, Berkeley, 1995), fig. 35 and p. 79.
43. The suggestion made in 1982 that the source for the arcade at Green Gables was the arcade at Canopus at Villa Adriana, Tivoli, can be discounted, since this feature was not revealed until excavations and a subsequent restoration between 1951 and 1954; Streatfield, "Echoes of England and Italy," p. 389. For the reconstruction, see Salvatore Aurigemma, *Villa Adriana* (Rome: Istituto Poligrafico dello Stato,

Libreria dello Stato, 1961), pp. 10–126. Photographs of Canopus after its restoration and before water was introduced are in Elena Calalandra, "Il programma figurativo del Canopi," in *Adriano: Architettura e progetto* (Milan: Electa, 2000), pp. 74, 75.

Vincenzo Cazzato proposed the terminal arcaded hedge at the water-parterre at Villa Gamberaia, Settignano, near Florence, as Charles's source. In 1898, this feature was redesigned by Princess Ghyka and her companion, Florence Blood, in an unauthentic manner. Vincenzo Cazzato, "The Rediscovery of the Villa Gamberaia in Images and Projects of the Early 1900s," *Studies in the History of Gardens and Designed Landscapes*, 22, no. 1 (Spring 2002), p. 90. Since Charles did not visit the garden at Villa Gamberaia, he could only have known it through photographs in such books as Gromort, *Jardins d'Italie*, plate 134; Luigi Dami, *The Italian Garden*, trans. L. Scopoli (New York: Brentano's, 1925, plate CCXLVIII); and Phillips, *The Gardens of Italy*, p. 322. None of these books was in his library, so this attribution is at best inconclusive.

EDWARD R. BOSLEY

Out of the Woods: Greene and Greene and the Modern American House

In 1952, the American Institute of Architects awarded Charles and Henry Greene with a Special Citation, heralding the brothers as "formulators of a new and native architecture" (see page 6).[1] One might reasonably assume that this was in just recognition of the Greenes' focused dedication some forty-five years earlier to a remarkable output of work that demonstrated a unified aesthetic, uncompromising craft, and a pursuit of domestic architecture that was supremely suited to its climate, culture, and topography. However true this may be, to assume that this was the only reason for the AIA award risks missing the intriguing context that brought the Greenes out of decades of relative obscurity and into the national limelight for their influence on Modernism.

Architectural polemics in the interwar and post–World War II eras frequently turned on establishing or discrediting, depending on the critic, a continuum of architectural pedigree in America down to the present day. Modernism in its many forms, and whether it related to the American past, was a topic of politically charged debate. Greene and Greene were portrayed by admirers during this period as progenitors of a uniquely American "style" of home design that had provided a legitimate source of modern inspiration to young American architects. Given the migration of architects with bold and influential ideas from Europe, the argument for an indigenous American Modernism could be seen as a defensive posture with an offensive edge. The ideological struggle had been forming since the 1920s, generally between those who believed that modern architecture should be adaptable to any place or popular need (the International Style had its name for a reason) and those who believed that regional considerations, individuality, and tradition should inform design. The differences between these views—and there were other views as well—generally mirrored global and domestic political forces at work before and after World War II, and so politics as much as design caused an architect's star to rise to national notice or not. This essay examines how two such reputed antimodernists as Charles and Henry Greene could be "rediscovered" by American Modernists, and why this may not be as counterintuitive as it seems.[2]

THE AMBIVALENCE OF ANTIMODERNITY

Throughout their partnership in Pasadena, the Greenes were well regarded and widely published. By the end of World War I, however, the firm had effectively closed, with Charles having moved to Carmel in 1916 and Henry remaining in Pasadena primarily to respond to the needs of existing clients and occasionally to find new ones. The Arts and Crafts movement itself, with its antimodern message and an emphasis on fine craftsmanship and natural materials, had gradually begun its own decline, and by 1930 it was an irrelevance, if not an embarrassment, in the face of political, social, and economic upheaval. Throughout, the Greenes had remained apolitical in their work: they strived to create beauty and usefulness in their architecture and decorative arts, and in doing so took advantage of modern technological resources (such as structural steel and gunite) along with more traditional building methods. But, though they operated effectively as architects and citizens in the modern world, Charles and Henry Greene also harbored a persistent antimodern sentiment.

During the busiest period of the Greene and Greene partnership, from 1903 to about 1913, their typical client was educated, discriminating, and comfortably well-off, even very wealthy in several cases. As the Greenes developed relationships with contractors, especially after about 1901, their houses were increasingly well built and not inexpensive. More modest bungalow builders could fashion an attractive and useful dwelling by consulting published examples of the Greenes' houses or flattering copies of their work. In an article that congratulated California architects for resolving the "problem" of an increasing need for a servant-less house, *International Studio* published the Greenes' work in January 1907, featuring Charles Greene's own home (1902) and the Arturo Bandini house (1903), both in Pasadena (see Smith essay, figs. 5 and 12).[3] The "servant-less house" was a problem the Greenes and their clients may not have known they had, but the writer chose this path to justify to the reader why such houses as these—simple, unpainted board-and-batten or shingle cottages with rustic boulders—appeared in an international publication. The Arturo Bandini house was designed for the scion of a prominent Spanish land-grant family, and his wife, Helen Elliott Bandini,

FIGURE I

Detail of eaves at balcony, with view to east and the Topa Topa Mountains, Charles M. Pratt house, Ojai, 1908–11. Photograph by Maynard L. Parker, 1947

Courtesy of The Huntington Library, San Marino, California

daughter of one of Pasadena's founders. For many years after its construction, it was this simple structure that architecture writers pointed to as a characteristically Californian house. It respected tradition, recognized the needs of the owners, and was yet livable in the modern sense. Its U-shaped plan was reminiscent of the Spanish *casa de campo*, and so responded to local colonial history, while its materials—redwood and stone—were the readily available currency of construction in the region. The central open courtyard acted simultaneously as the entertainment patio and circulation core of the house and was naturally suited to the warm, semi-arid climate of Southern California. Readers could imagine for themselves how such a dwelling—steeped in tradition yet mindful of contemporary life—could become the idyllic focus of domestic bliss.

Even for the Greenes' progressive clients (and despite the brothers' reliance on modern machines and new methods of building), much of the allure of the Arts and Crafts movement was historical and anti-industrial; it was romantic and nature-based. And it was personal. Greene and Greene and their like-minded colleagues sought to respond meaningfully to how and where people lived, and they were fortunate to have such clients as the Bandinis, Culbertsons, Robinsons, Fords, Gambles, Blackers, Thorsens, Pratts, and others who appreciated them for the personal approach they took to their work. Charles and Henry Greene offered up their creativity utterly in the course of divining their clients' needs and desires. Only in this way could they produce practical living spaces of artistic beauty and superior craftsmanship (fig. 2). This was not merely to please their clients, but also to honor the art of architecture and the materials that produced it. In this, they were in select company, particularly after World War I, when high-quality materials and craftsmanship became scarce. If other architects strived to remain relevant in a modernizing society, Greene and Greene clung to their art and craft and compromised for no one. Charles was fifty and Henry forty-eight when the war ended in 1918. Clients had been few since the war began, and Charles had taken his family to Carmel two years earlier, lamenting to a friend that he had been "prostituting his art" in Pasadena.[4] He vowed to quit designing houses but recanted, spectacularly, for D.L. James in 1918. Henry remained to struggle with what little work there was for an antimodernist in a rapidly modernizing world, and he occasionally found a kindred spirit. The Greenes' days at the top of their profession were behind them, and more than once they may have wondered whether they had taken the right fork in the road.

SPLENDID ISOLATION

In 1930, *The Carmelite* magazine published an essay by Hugh Ferriss (1889–1962), who had spent the winter of 1927 in the coastal California artists' colony where Charles had settled. Ferriss was internationally known for his futuristic architectural renderings and for his book *The Metropolis of Tomorrow* (1929); his soulless monochromatic cityscapes represented the antithesis of Charles Greene's vision of a picturesque built environment. By this time, Greene had become absorbed in the study of Buddhism and Theosophy and had little to do with architecture, designing only the occasional piece of furniture for increasingly rare clients. In *The Carmelite*, Ferriss tried to sound a conciliatory note toward artists, lamenting the "logical structures, the impersonal and mechanistic masterpieces, the cold triumphs of science, from which the spirit of art is excluded." Making reference to Carmel's Hawk Tower, hand-built by the poet Robinson Jeffers, Ferriss wrote, "It is true many Modernists do not realize what they lack; discrediting the heart, they affirm that the hand and the head are the only essentials of architectural accomplishment. But it is precisely here that the stone tower of Carmel might become a symbol to illuminate their darkness. [It is] undubitably [*sic*] the work of the *poet*."[5] Greene responded in the following issue, dismissing Ferriss's sympathy for artists; echoing William Morris's indictment of a gritty and unlivable London "overhung with smoke" in *The Earthly Paradise* (1868–70), he took Ferriss to task for portraying the future as an impersonal society under a "heavy vaporous pall."[6] Henry Greene wrote approvingly of his brother's reply in a letter to Charles's wife, Alice, adding his own feelings on the subject: "Most people have succumbed to the 'machine' and are trying hard to think they like it when, in truth, they do not … But it surely dominates everything just now, willy-nilly."[7]

Charles had shown his antimodern inclination toward a romantic English past in the cliff-side stone dwelling he had designed for D.L. James in the Carmel Highlands (see Crawford essay, fig. 8); and his own Carmel studio (1922–23) was no less evocative of history in referencing the California missions. However beautiful and well crafted, though, both designs feel poignantly regressive compared with the brothers' earlier teamwork in Pasadena. The adobe-and-timber ranch house that Henry Greene designed for Walter L. Richardson in 1929 in Porterville, California, was also obstinately romantic, particularly in its construction. Local boys made bricks of mud and straw from the site, then stacked them nearby to bake on the ground (fig. 3). This was quaint and

FIGURE 2
Dining room, Robert R. Blacker house, Pasadena, 1907–09. Photograph by Maynard L. Parker, 1947
Courtesy of The Huntington Library, San Marino, California

anachronistic compared to what the world was paying greater attention to at the time: the cool aloofness of the much-admired and published Lovell "Health" house in Los Angeles, designed by Richard Neutra (1892–1970) and completed the same year as the Porterville adobe. Henry Greene's late-career ode to the California Arts and Crafts movement was virtually ignored by the press, who were captivated instead by Neutra's creation, what Kenneth Frampton later called "the apotheosis of the International Style."[8]

Ironically, Neutra himself appreciated thoroughly the important connection between a house and its landscape, and even sought to reconcile European Modernism with California's regional dictates. The work of Neutra's fellow Austrian émigré and onetime associate, Rudolph Schindler (1887–1953), also showed an exuberant willingness to adapt to the climate, materials, and culture of his adopted Los Angeles. In his own house of 1921–22, Schindler used unadorned redwood and tilt-slab concrete panels pioneered by Irving Gill—the Arts and Crafts architect turned Modernist—to create an indoor–outdoor compound for flexible California living. Schindler, Gill,

and Neutra had had the opportunity to absorb directly the principles of Frank Lloyd Wright's organic architecture, but each had turned it to distinctly different aesthetic uses. The Greenes may even have appreciated a certain kinship in Schindler's attitude toward materials, despite the formalistic gulf that separated his work from theirs. They probably would have approved of Schindler's judgment, too, that "Functionalism, with its white stucco, stainless steel, glass, and poster color schemes is here more out of place than anywhere else on this continent."[9]

As early as the mid-1920s, various manifestations of modern architecture imported from Europe, including the International Style, had set roots in America. But it was not until 1932 that the Museum of Modern Art in New York (MoMA), under its young architectural curator, Philip Johnson, held the first of many exhibitions to celebrate such work and the American and European architects who emulated it. Entitled *Modern Architecture*, the exhibition was later described by the museum as "virtually the first presentation of modern architecture to the American public and to American architects."[10] The implication that rankled some was that the nation and its architects were barely aware of Modernism and probably could have produced none of their own without influence and help from Europe. The exhibition included work by the German Ludwig Mies van der Rohe, the Hungarian Marcel Breuer, Berliner Walter Gropius, and the Swiss William Lescaze, as well as Richard Neutra. Each had come to America rejecting historical styles and materials in favor of taut, spare compositions, often of steel and glass. Many young American architects followed their lead. Throughout the 1930s and 1940s, the Museum of Modern Art continued to exert an influence on American preferences in architecture toward functionalism. But with MoMA's exhibition in 1935 entitled *Modern Architecture in California*, regionalism attained some legitimacy. (By this time, Philip Johnson had left MoMA to dabble in fascist politics.)[11] While Neutra's California work was featured, Schindler was excluded. Included, however, was the work of native son William Wilson Wurster (1895–1973), whose houses purposefully expressed a regional identity, particularly in the use of wood. In Wurster's case, it was an interest honestly come by and rooted in respect for the simple wood-shingled houses of the turn of the century in Berkeley, where he had graduated from the school of architecture at the University of California in 1919. Wurster also would have known of the Greenes' nearby William R. Thorsen house (1908–10; fig. 4), adjacent to the university campus, though he may not have known who designed it. He did, however, know something about the origins of the Arts and Crafts movement in the Bay Area thanks to an epiphany as an incoming freshman. Of the unfinished redwood interior at the Charles Rieber house designed by Ernest Coxhead (1904), Wurster later recalled: "Such a place as this doesn't need permanence, or really precious materials or workmanship to make it convincing ... I know that many were inspired by this sort of thing, and you find it in much of the work of [A.C.] Schweinfurth, Coxhead, the Greenes, [Willis] Polk, [John Galen] Howard and [Bernard] Maybeck."[12] Wurster was included in MoMA's exhibition of California architecture probably because his manipulation of space and reductive expression of surfaces were recognizably "modern" to curator Ernestine Fantl. Wurster's generous use of wood—a hopelessly *retardataire* material in the eyes of Johnson and such Modernists as Gropius and Breuer—was probably tolerated because of its spare and airy presentation. It may have helped, too, that he sometimes painted the surfaces white. Five years after the MoMA exhibition, Charles Greene wrote to his brother: "There is lots of building going on here but mostly cheap

and ill-adapted to the location. However, when the ground is finally covered it will be one grand accumulation of commonplace."[13] In this deceptively simple statement, Greene revealed his continued personal concern for the suitability of a house to its location, the quality of its workmanship, and the value of designing to the uniqueness of the clients. From today's perspective, it is difficult to appreciate to what degree this point of view had gone out of fashion by 1940. Relative to the new generation of Modernists, the Greenes may have felt that the relevance of their work was firmly situated in the past, despite a few kindred spirits, such as Wurster.

EMERGING FROM THE SHADOWS

Beginning in the late 1930s and early 1940s, through the rare but favorable opinions published by educators Howard Moise and Talbot Hamlin and by the eminent architectural historian Henry Russell Hitchcock, the meaning of Greene and Greene within American architecture slowly began to be discerned, and finally publicized and promoted.[14] Soon, appreciation of Greene and Greene would become consonant with trends that had been emerging in California architecture since the late 1920s, and the brothers would be cultivated as one of the missing links in the continuum of American architectural history. In January 1941, a young architect named Whitney R. Smith (1911–2002) visited Henry Greene to ask if he might be permitted to produce a book on the brothers' work, with new drawings and photographs. Smith, then thirty years of age, had grown up in the Pasadena area and had visited clients of the Greenes socially in their homes.[15] He had graduated from the University of Southern California School of Architecture in 1934 and worked briefly for architect Harwell Hamilton Harris in Los Angeles before going into independent practice. After the visit from Smith, Henry Greene wrote with enthusiasm to his brother in Carmel:

What would you think about going into an arrangement to publish some of our work in book form with illustrations (photographs) and drawings of plans and some of our details? ... He [Smith] means a book without advertisements—somewhat on the order of Guy Lowell's book and like the book of Frank Lloyd Wright's work, etc. Not in any way to be propaganda, but to become a record of our work ... This young man believes in original work and has, with a small group of the younger architects (with good educations and training), been great admirers [sic] of our work and has visited and seen some of our work inside as well as outside. They seem in earnest and show considerable interest.[16]

[pages 236–37]
FIGURE 4
View of west (front) façade, William R. Thorsen house, Berkeley, 1908–10
Photograph © Alexander Vertikoff

FIGURE 5

Garden and bird
fountain, Robert R.
Blacker house.
Photograph by
Maynard L. Parker,
1947

Courtesy of
The Huntington Library,
San Marino, California

FIGURE 6

Living room, Robert
R. Blacker house.
Photograph by
Maynard L. Parker,
1947

Courtesy of
The Huntington Library,
San Marino, California

Smith also wrote to Charles Greene directly to ask his cooperation: "I believe that your work here is the only true development of a California house." Unmoved, Charles scribbled "unanswered" at the bottom of the letter. The persistent Smith wrote again several months later: "I am still very desirous of making a study of your work … The Gamble house especially should be done soon as I believe there may be some changes there soon."[17] Finally, in January 1942, Charles gave his "consent to go ahead."[18] A week later, Henry wrote to Charles confirming that he had obtained permission for Smith to visit and photograph the David B. Gamble and Robert R. Blacker houses in Pasadena. Then, in a poignant passage that expressed sensitivity to the potentially ephemeral nature of their work, Henry shared this about his visit to the elderly Mrs. Blacker:

The place looks lovely now with the green lawns and trees and shrubbery, vistas, bird bath and pool (fig. 5). The inside of the

house is perfect yet; apparently not a scar or shrinkage or blemish … Mrs. B. said she had great joy living there. I asked her what she would do with the furniture when she passed on. She replied, she did not know. I suggested she place some of the finer pieces in some good museum where students and art lovers could see it (figs. 6 and 7).[19]

Two days later, Charles wrote to his brother, objecting to magazine publication of their work. Henry responded, saying he had gotten Smith on the phone to tell him, adding: "He promised to make a statement as you requested and would mail it direct to you."[20] Apparently feeling the need to reassure further the skeptical Charles, he continued:

Mr. Smith is known to some of the good architects here, and has worked for some whom I know. So, except for lack of knowledge of his own work, I believe he may be able to work it out. He wants to make the re-drawings necessary, and wants to

FIGURE 7
*Living-room music
cabinet, mahogany
and ebony, with inlay
of silver, ebony, and
other contrasting
woods, 1909, Robert
R. Blacker house*

*Private collection, Courtesy
of Tim Gleason, New York.
Photograph © Ognen
Borrisov/Interfoto*

study our work critically as most younger men do the work of older men; and put it in shape for about a hundred of the younger architects here to study it, because they admire it. He is especially interested to know our philosophy behind it.

Again Smith wrote to Charles: "Without a doubt the most important thing to me is the inspiration that I am receiving personally from the contact with your work. The personal contact, too, with your brother has been of great value in learning of your philosophy and trying to form one of my own."[21] He went on to say what he would require in the way of photographs (noting that photography of the Blacker house was starting that day), drawings, a philosophy, and a "story of the problem." He asked for information on how the Greenes developed their furniture designs. With all of this, he wrote, he felt he could "submit ... to publishers to see if anyone would be interested ..." Then he added, probably thinking about the delay in getting to this stage of discussions, "I naturally need your cooperation or the work will be of little value to me or anyone else." By this time, however, the country was fully engaged in World War II, and Smith was soon needed for war work. The book project was dropped, and the rediscovery of the Greenes would have to wait, but not, as it happened, for long.

In the late 1930s and early 1940s, Smith's former employer, Harwell Hamilton Harris (1903–1990), and his wife, Jean Murray Bangs (1894–1985), were commuting between their home in Los Angeles and a leased house in Berkeley while Harris completed three commissions in the Bay Area. Among them was the Weston Havens house (1940–41), situated on a steep Berkeley hillside overlooking San Francisco Bay to the west. Harris was born and raised in Southern California, and as a young man had been aware of the Greenes' houses without knowing who designed them. He was familiar, too, with others in the Craftsman idiom.[22] Bangs had also seen the Greenes' work in her youth. Born in Calgary, Alberta, Bangs went to California with her family in 1904. She lived in Pasadena not far from the Greenes' house for David and Mary Gamble, which was built when she was a teenager. One of Jean's childhood friends was the daughter of architect Louis B. Easton, whose work had been illustrated in the same *International Studio* article that had published the Greenes' Bandini house in 1907.[23] In a letter to a publishing colleague in 1955, Bangs, in recalling buildings that were meaningful to her, wrote, "Just like Greene & Greene, I remember them from my childhood."[24] As a student at Berkeley, where she graduated with a degree in economics in 1919, Bangs had

probably been aware of Bernard Maybeck's shingled houses on the hillsides. By the time she and Harwell Harris were returning regularly to Berkeley to work on the Bay Area projects, Jean's interest in the reasons for her husband's innate love of wooden architecture must have been piqued. Through Walter Steilberg, supervisor on the Havens house (and assisting engineer for Julia Morgan on several of her projects), Jean met and interviewed Maybeck,[25] who was known then mainly as a colorful local character who had designed the Palace of Fine Arts in San Francisco (1913–15) and some idiosyncratic but charming wooden structures around Berkeley. Walter Webber, a retired architect whom Harris hired to assist him on his projects in the San Francisco area, knew the local architecture, including Greene and Greene's Thorsen house, not far from the Havens house job site. As Lisa Germany recounts in her book *Harwell Hamilton Harris*, Webber ominously warned Bangs: "They got Greene and Greene and they'll get your husband, too."[26] Webber believed that the Greenes had been doomed to disregard because their work was so widely copied by less talented architects and builders. Bangs was intrigued, and, fearing Webber might be right about her husband facing a similar fate, she resolved to learn as much as she could about the Greene brothers while simultaneously pursuing her interest in Maybeck.

Jean and Harwell spent the remaining war years in New York, where he taught and she researched topics of interest to her. Both made important contacts, including Elizabeth Gordon (1906–2000), the dynamic editor of *House Beautiful* magazine, with whom they shared an interest in the American origins of modern architecture. Harwell Harris was not unfamiliar with *House Beautiful*. His first house, the Pauline Lowe residence in Altadena, California (1933), and the groundbreaking Fellowship Park house that he had designed for himself and Jean in Los Angeles (1935) had both been published in the magazine previous to Gordon's editorship. During Gordon's tenure—from January 1942 through December 1964—the magazine featured, illustrated, or mentioned Harwell Harris and his work dozens of times, often in articles written by Jean Murray Bangs. An editorial of 1945, "People Who Influence Your Life—Meet Harwell Hamilton Harris," was accompanied by a portrait of the architect taken at the Museum of Modern Art by the photographer Yousuf Karsh. Gordon revealed to readers that Harris felt "American culture ... is based on a belief in the supreme importance of the individual man."[27] She repudiated the European Modernists in the pages of her magazine, so this particular comment seems calculated to position Harris in opposition to such architects and designers as the former Bauhaus leaders who had emigrated to America. In an era of desperate scarcity and political hardships in their native Europe, Marcel Breuer and Walter Gropius had rejected the supremacy of the individual in favor of collective, democratic architecture. Gordon was using Harris to make a political point, but it was presumably one Harris was comfortable helping her to make. Bangs may have also recognized the opportunity to further her husband's career, and her own, by cooperating with Gordon. For nearly two decades, starting in 1945, Bangs contributed numerous articles to *House Beautiful* about food, home design, and architecture.

Returning to Los Angeles from New York by November 1944,[28] Bangs began her investigations of the Greenes. Although she made it known that she was preparing books on the Greenes and on Maybeck, neither book was ever published. Material she collected would instead become the basis for several magazine articles dedicated to promoting the importance of the architects' work, and especially its influence on modern American architecture.

Meanwhile, California architecture had another spotlight directed on it by Lewis Mumford in one of his "Skyline" essays for the *New Yorker* in October 1947, in which he coined the phrase "Bay Region Style." Mumford noted the emerging architecture of the region as a "native and humane form of modernism," which he saw as linked to the work of Bernard Maybeck and Greene and Greene. He singled out William Wurster and Harwell Harris as modern architects of particular note who worked in this idiom. Mumford had been interested in historical antecedents in Berkeley since 1941, when he had stood in front of Maybeck's First Church of Christ, Scientist (1910), and "learned from William Wurster's lips ... the direct effect of Maybeck's poetic architectural imagination on his own work ..."[29] Mumford's article was followed by a firestorm of criticism from the local Modernist elite, and on February 11, 1948, he moderated a public symposium at the Museum of Modern Art that included the museum's director, Alfred Barr, Jr.; Henry Russell Hitchcock; Philip Johnson; Walter Gropius; and Marcel Breuer. A panel less sympathetic to his notion of a legitimate regional modernism would have been difficult for Mumford to assemble.

From a public-relations standpoint, it seems that Jean Murray Bangs, a believer in Mumford's point of view, had begun researching Greene and Greene at the right moment. She had visited the Greenes in 1945, interviewed them, and borrowed the drawings that had come from the firm's office, many of which had been left in a rodent-infested cabinet in the back of the garage in Henry Greene's former residence on Bellefontaine Street in Pasadena. Thanks to her persistent efforts, and with help from Henry Eggers and the Southern California chapter of the American Institute of Architects, the Greenes' drawings were rescued, and their work was documented with new photography by Maynard Parker in 1947, when the interiors of their greatest commissions were still largely intact.

On March 9, 1948, only four weeks after the MoMA symposium, the Southern California AIA honored Greene and Greene at its annual banquet with a special award and an exhibition of the Maynard Parker photographs.[30] Henry Greene and Charles's son Patrickson together received the citation from Henry Eggers on behalf of the Greene and Greene firm. Telegrams from across the country congratulated the brothers.[31] Merle Armitage, art director at *Look* magazine, wrote, "Glad to add my congratulations to the brothers Greene who originated an indigenous, sturdy and particularly happy architectural concept that has brought such great credit to themselves and their profession." Henry Wright, managing editor of *Architectural Forum*, wrote on behalf of Howard Meyers, the magazine's editor, calling the Greenes' work "a Western tap root of best contemporary design trend today," adding that the magazine planned to publish a "comprehensive article" on Greene and Greene later that year. Not to be outdone, *Architectural Record* weighed in with a message from Kenneth K. Stowell (editor at *House Beautiful* prior to Elizabeth Gordon) and Elisabeth Kendall Thompson, "honoring Greene and Greene for their outstanding contributions to the art and science of architecture." Particularly meaningful may have been the telegram from William Wurster, then dean of architecture at the Greenes' alma mater: "With pride and warmth of heart the Architectural School of Massachusetts Institute of Technology sends greetings to Greene and Greene, pioneers who helped to give freedom and new vitality to American architecture. As a fellow Californian I add my personal feeling of debt and appreciation." Talbot Hamlin, author, architect, editor of *Pencil Points*, and professor of architectural history at Columbia University, called the Greenes "forward looking imaginative architects whose work was important in [the] birth of modern architecture." A tribute from Bernard Maybeck, referring to the D.L. James house, was poetic if not strictly accurate: "Beyond Carmel Greene and Greene have built on the rocks by the sea one of the most beautiful pictures of our time. By such work we know them."[32]

OUT OF THE WOODS

Greene and Greene emerged quickly from obscurity in 1948. No longer ignored, they were brought to the attention of the broader public through several national publications, including professional and general-readership periodicals. The earliest of the magazine articles that showed the fruits of Jean Murray Bangs's research was, ironically, one she did not write. In May 1948, the *Architectural Record* contained an editorial entitled "A New Appreciation of 'Greene and Greene,'" which quoted Henry Eggers speaking at the AIA recognition banquet, where he in turn quoted text provided by Jean Murray Bangs in anticipation of a major article; her article would ultimately appear in *House Beautiful* in 1950, illustrated with Parker's photographs. The *Architectural Record* editorial was probably composed by Elisabeth Kendall Thompson, western editor of the magazine at the time.[33] This borrowing of her words would not have pleased Bangs, who was scrupulously protective of the physical material she possessed on the Greenes lest it escape her control before her book could be published.[34] By 1947, Bangs had some five thousand drawings by the Greenes and hundreds of photographs she had borrowed from the architects.[35] The *Architectural Record* editorial quoted Bangs's "forthcoming book of 1948 on the work of Greene and Greene."

"The development of the Greene and Greene style began with a small house they designed for Arturo Bandini in 1903," the *Record* recounted, going on to describe the Spanish origins of the plan and how it was emblematic of California and the West: "The Greene brothers went on to execute it in wooden construction which raised logic and common sense into a supremely unified language and expression, of a vivid and solidly reassuring virtue." These were words perhaps chosen to incite the New York Modernists, particularly since such terms as "logic" and "common sense" could have come from their own lexicon. The article extols the virtues of the Greenes' work, often in the context of its modern conveniences or technological developments: "modern fenestration and facilities for outdoor living equaled in few houses of today … In the Thorsen house and the Crowe [*sic*] house (designed by Henry M. Greene) are large flush panel ceiling lights … The Crowe house has a long gallery on the south, one side of which is almost entirely of glass" (fig. 8). Quotes from Bangs conclude by stating, "Greene and Greene helped pioneer the modern house, and built it so conveniently, so graciously, and so without talk that people accepted it hardly knowing what it was." This may have felt true in 1948, but it is also true

that the Gambles and the Blackers probably knew what it was, as did *The Craftsman*, *International Studio*, and the other publications that featured the work of Greene and Greene at the time it was constructed. It was important, however, for Bangs to make the point that enlightened California architects of the 1940s (including Harris and Wurster) may not have known the Greenes by name until recently but were nonetheless influenced by the way their houses looked and worked. Nearly single-handedly, it seems, Jean Murray Bangs had launched the Greenes into the national architectural consciousness.

Another proponent of the Greenes appeared in the mid-1940s who helped to fortify Jean Murray Bangs's arsenal of material. L. Morgan Yost (1908–1992), a young architect and instructor at the Art Institute of Chicago, had become interested in the Greenes through early issues of *Architectural Record*. As Yost recalled for an oral history taken in 1986, "I would take a moment or two and go into the Burnham Library [Art Institute of Chicago] and look through the old periodicals. I was interested in Frank Lloyd Wright … [and] came across some houses, which I greatly admired, by Greene and Greene … I had to see those houses. My parents lived in San Gabriel, California, so when we had the first opportunity after the war we went … to find out about Greene and Greene."[36] Yost first visited Charles and Henry Greene, and the Blacker house, in February 1946; in an article that appeared in September 1948 in *American Lumberman*, Yost, like Bangs, referred to the Greenes as innovators and noted such contemporary amenities as "flush panel lighting" and "modern 36-inch high kitchen cabinets" (fig. 9).[37] He remarked in a later article in the same vein, "clerestory windows brought in high light where needed and the larger window areas were protected from the south sun by overhangs."[38] Yost betrayed a far more dispassionate scholar's appreciation for the Greenes' use of materials than Bangs had, and he was comparatively specific and authoritative about quality of construction, integration of furnishings, and the relation of house to garden. In recounting his visits in 1946 to Charles Greene in Carmel, and to Henry Greene and Mrs. Blacker in Pasadena, Yost later conceded that the Blacker house was for him the most influential pre–World War II residence.[39] "This was to be an experience never to be repeated," he lamented, "as Mrs. Blacker died the next year, the property was sold, divided and disfigured, and the furniture dispersed." Yost pointed out that the "workmanship in [the Greenes'] houses will never be approached" and that "it was the last beautiful bloom of handcraft."[40] "These are the most perfect houses, I

believe, that have ever been built." He added, "I now had facts to build on and I transmitted them to Jean Murray Bangs who, with Los Angeles as a base of operations, decided to do a book on the work of Greene & Greene."[41] "It was the perfect expression of that decade in California. Out of it came lessons in truth of construction, in the use of native and inexpensive materials, of considerate design that today after a period of neglect serve as inspiration for thoughtful architects."[42] In a congratulatory letter to Henry Greene at the time of the AIA award in 1948, Yost wrote, "Others, like me, of a later generation, have rediscovered your work and it has had a sudden, though belated, impact on the thoughts and the work of the architects of today."[43] Yost felt his own architecture (fig. 12) related to the Greenes' in that he was "looking for something that would make the house more human."[44]

MODERN INTERPRETATIONS

No postwar architect showed a greater devotion to the Greenes' aesthetic than Harwell Hamilton Harris (fig. 11). While his interest was doubtlessly linked closely to his wife's passion for the Greenes, Harris had grown up surrounded by Craftsman houses being built, and had demonstrated an affinity as well as a gift for wooden architecture since his early career. Harris admired Frank Lloyd Wright's work above all—he counted Hollyhock House in Los Angeles as the building that set his career in motion—but as his design philosophy matured, he was also able to see how the architecture of Maybeck and Greene and Greene could hold valuable lessons in developing the designs of the future. As his wife gathered information on the Greenes, Harris allowed their influence to penetrate his work in recognizable ways.

Harris's Clarence H. Wyle house in Ojai (1946–48; fig. 10) is surprising for its elegant yet bold recapitulation of the Greenes' wooden architecture, in deep overhanging eaves, rolled roofing, and exposed beams and rafters, here used on long purlins two bays past the termination of the roof itself. These rafters were deeper than those actually supporting the roof to remove any suspicion that roofing had flown off. The form of the house nonetheless conveys the postwar originality and optimism that could be expected of such a talented and influential architect as Harris. Like the Greenes' Charles M. Pratt house (1908–11; figs. 1 and 13), also in Ojai, the Wyle house opens itself completely to the stunning vistas of its site, using sectional glass walls and French doors to draw one visually and physically to the outdoors. Sheltered exterior walkways, defined by deep overhangs and simple wooden posts, recall the Greenes' courtyard for the Bandini house. Harris's Ralph Johnson house in Los Angeles (1947–48; fig. 14) also took the Greenes' structural vocabulary to an inventive degree of deconstruction and reassembly exacted from familiar materials.

While Harris was designing these commissions, he was also teaching design at the University of Southern California School of Architecture, where students and other faculty would have been aware of the Greenes and their influence on Harris's work. In 1951, this influence migrated with Harris to the University of Texas at Austin,

FIGURE 13
*Charles M. Pratt
house. Photograph by
Maynard L. Parker,
1947*
Courtesy of
The Huntington Library,
San Marino, California

FIGURE 14
*Harwell Hamilton
Harris, Ralph
Johnson house,
Los Angeles, 1947–48.
Photograph by
Maynard L. Parker*
Courtesy of
The Huntington Library,
San Marino, California

FIGURE 15
*Harwell Hamilton
Harris, "Pace Setter"
house, Dallas Fair
Park, Dallas, Texas,
1954–55. Photograph
by Maynard L. Parker*
Courtesy of
The Huntington Library,
San Marino, California

where he was the director of the School of Architecture until 1955. Here, the interests of Harris and his wife neatly merged again, this time with the "Pace Setter" house of 1955 for *House Beautiful*, designed by Harris and his students and constructed in Fair Park in Dallas (fig. 15). Harris is credited with the words describing the project, but Bangs's self-assured tone can be felt behind them: "The 1955 Pace Setter house has many elements of the California Bungalow as developed in its purest and finest form by Greene and Greene."[45]

Although Harwell Harris left USC in 1951, his influence carried on under Calvin C. Straub (1920–1998), a former apprentice to Richard Neutra who had been a student at USC under Harris and went on to lecture in architecture there from 1946 to 1961. Straub attributed much of his design inspiration to the work of Greene and Greene (fig. 16). As was noted in the text accompanying an exhibition of his work at Arizona State University in 1995, "his engagement in post-war rhetoric did not alter the course of his lifelong exploration of timber construction."[46] Among the many influenced by Straub were Donald Hensman and Conrad Buff, who partnered with Straub, even as students, under the firm name of Buff, Straub & Hensman. While the firm's modern designs could rarely be confused with the Greenes' aesthetic, the materials and workmanship honored the spirit of Greene and Greene. Frank O. Gehry, a student and apprentice of Straub's, credited his teacher with "a profound influence on my architectural life … [and for] the discipline of designing everything from the plan itself to the wood members framing a building not only to look right but to be functionally logical."[47]

The decision by the American Institute of Architects to award the Greenes a Special Citation in 1952 was due primarily to the efforts of L. Morgan Yost, who felt compelled to garner formal, if long-overdue, praise from their peers across the country.[48] More than fifty-five years later, the influence of the Greenes can be sensed in many forms today, from new houses in Shell Beach, Durango, Healdsburg, Jackson Hole, San Francisco, Jacksonville, Oregon, and Pasadena to hotels in La Jolla and Anaheim. More subtly, USC architects Whitney R. Smith, H. Douglas Byles, Gilbert L. Hershberger, and even Frank O. Gehry each owe a separate debt to Greene and Greene (fig. 17). From the recent outright copies of the Greenes' design vocabulary to the more academic homage expressed in the intelligent use of natural materials, the sympathetic placement of a house in the landscape, and the careful response to a client's needs in daily life, the values to which Greene and Greene held fast, regardless of fashion, are the values that continue to inspire others a century later.

1. "A Special Citation to Henry Mather Greene and Charles Sumner Greene," *Journal of the American Institute of Architects*, 18 (July 1952), p. 5.

2. I am particularly grateful to Bruce Smith for sharing so generously and collegially his valuable and well-informed views on this subject.

3. Florence Williams, "The Southern California Bungalow: A Local Problem in Housing," *International Studio*, xxx (January 1907), pp. lxxvi–lxxxi.

4. Janette Howard Wallace, interview of June 13, 1988. I am grateful to Robert Judson Clark for sharing with me the notes of the interview he conducted with the daughter of John Galen Howard, then dean of the School of Architecture ("The Ark"), University of California, Berkeley, and a close friend of Charles Greene. The Howards had a vacation home in Carmel near the Greenes.

5. Hugh Ferriss, "The Architecture of New York—and Carmel," *The Carmelite*, 3, no. 37 (October 23, 1930), pp. 1, 6–7.

6. CSG, "Architecture and the Machine Age: A Reply," *The Carmelite*, 3, no. 38 (October 30, 1930), p. 3.

7. Letter from HMG to Alice Greene, November 12, 1930, EDA.

8. Kenneth Frampton, *Modern Architecture: A Critical History*, 3rd edn (London and New York: Thames & Hudson, 1992), p. 248.

9. Quoted in Wayne Andrews, *Architecture, Ambition and Americans: A History of American Architecture* (New York: Harper, 1955), p. 276.

10. Elizabeth Mock (ed.), *Built in USA, 1932–1944* (New York: Plantin Press for The Museum of Modern Art, 1944), p. 124.

11. Franz Schulze, *Philip Johnson: Life and Work* (Chicago: University of Chicago Press, 1996). This excellent biography (written during Johnson's lifetime) unflinchingly reports on the many facets of this complex figure in American art and architecture.

12. Quoted in Daniel Gregory, "William W. Wurster," in *Toward a Simpler Way of Life: The Arts and Crafts Architects of California*, ed. Robert Winter (Berkeley: University of California Press, 1997), pp. 246–47.

13. Letter from CSG to HMG, June 17, 1940, EDA.

14. Howard Moise, "California Architecture," *Architect and Engineer*, 126 (November 1936), pp. 52–54; Talbot Hamlin, *Architecture through the Ages* (New York: G.P. Putnam's Sons, 1940), p. 647; and [Henry] Russell Hitchcock, "An Easterner Looks at Western Architecture," *California Arts and Architecture* (December 1940), pp. 20–25, 40–41, Greenes mentioned on p. 23. I am grateful to Ann Scheid at the GGA for locating and providing copies of these early writings on Greene and Greene.

15. My thanks to Bruce Smith for sharing this information from his own interview with Whitney R. Smith.

16. Letter from HMG to CSG, January 17, 1941, EDA.

17. Letters from Whitney R. Smith (WRS) to CSG, March 8 and November 27, 1941, EDA.

18. Letter from CSG to WRS, January 26, 1942, EDA.

19. Letter from HMG to CSG, February 4, 1942, EDA.

20. Letter from HMG to CSG, February 17, 1942, EDA.

21. Letter from WRS to CSG, February 14, 1942, EDA.

22. Lisa Germany, *Harwell Hamilton Harris* (Austin: University of Texas Press, 1991), p. 94. This superb text provides rich background and insightful perspective on the opposing agendas among Modernists in the mid-twentieth century.

23. Thanks are due Bruce Smith for telling me about Jean Murray Bangs's childhood in Pasadena and about her friendship with the daughter of Louis B. Easton.

24. Letter from Jean Murray Bangs to "Doug," September 24, 1955, Alexander Architectural Archives, University of Texas Libraries, Austin. "Doug" was apparently a publishing contact; among other clues the letter contains the sentence: "Please don't ask for text till I have seen the illustrations."

25. Germany, *Harris*, p. 97.

26. *Ibid.*, p. 94.

27. Elizabeth Gordon, "People Who Influence Your Life—Meet Harwell Hamilton Harris," *House Beautiful*, July 1945, pp. 54–55.

28. Germany, *Harris*, p. 107.

29. Lewis Mumford, "The Architecture of the Bay Region," reprinted in *Domestic Architecture of the San Francisco Bay Region*, exhib. cat., San Francisco Museum of Art, 1949, n.p.

30. The Huntington Library, San Marino, California, holds the Maynard Parker archives of original negatives, including envelopes marked "Mrs. HHH," which contain ninety images of Greene and Greene houses taken in 1947, most likely in anticipation of the AIA recognition and exhibition championed by Bangs (Mrs. Harwell Hamilton Harris).

31. All of the telegram messages to the Greenes on the occasion of the 1948 award are in the EDA.

32. The James house was the exclusive design of Charles Greene, not the Greene and Greene firm.

33. [Elisabeth Kendall Thompson], "A New Appreciation of 'Greene and Greene,'" *Architectural Record*, 103 (May 1948), pp. 138–40.

34. Bangs complains of requests for Greene and Greene illustrations coming from Elisabeth Thompson at the *Architectural Record*: "I certainly don't want to provide the illustrations for other people's articles. And I am counting on you to strong arm the *Record*. I am sick of well-meaning people with no brains. The boys are certainly out to get me, but so far they have only succeeded in working up interest in my book." Letter from Bangs to William Helburn at *Architectural Review*, March 12, 1949, Alexander Architectural Archives, University of Texas Libraries, Austin.

35. In 1960, after years of the Greene families trying to secure their return or their deposit at the AIA's Octagon, Bangs "donated" the items to Avery, where they remain well cared for today. See relevant correspondence at the GGA.

36. "Oral History of L. Morgan Yost," interviewed by Betty J. Blum, 1986. Compiled under the auspices of the Chicago Architects Oral History Project, Department of Architecture, The Art Institute of Chicago, p. 91.

37. L. Morgan Yost, "American Houses from Victorian to Modern," *American Lumberman* (September 11, 1948), p. 222.

38. L. Morgan Yost, "Greene & Greene of Pasadena," *Journal of the Society of Architectural Historians*, 9, nos. 1–2 (March–May 1950), p. 13. This article was republished with the same title and with nearly identical text in the *Journal of the American Institute of Architects*, 14 (September 1950), pp. 115–25.

39. "Oral History of L. Morgan Yost," p. 114.

40. Yost, "American Houses," p. 222.

41. Yost, "Greene & Greene," pp. 13, 11. Yost may have heard that Bangs was working on a book on the Greenes through Henry Greene, or perhaps even through Harwell Harris. In 1945 or 1946, Yost was asked to join with seven other architects, including Harris, to design houses around the Ingersoll Utility Unit that Harris had designed with Donald Deskey in New York in 1945. See Germany, *Harris*, pp. 99–100. Yost may have met Bangs through Harris in Los Angeles in 1946 when he was visiting his parents, the Greenes, and their houses.

42. Yost, "American Houses," p. 222.

43. Letter from L. Morgan Yost to HMG, March 1, 1948, EDA.

44. "Oral History of L. Morgan Yost," p. 94.

45. [Jean Murray Bangs], typescript of draft text describing the "Pace Setter" house of 1955 for *House Beautiful*, February 1955. Text as published resembles the draft, but mention of Greene and Greene is not included. Harwell Hamilton Harris Papers, Alexander Architectural Archives, University of Texas Libraries, Austin. My thanks to Nancy Sparrow and Monica Penick.

46. Robert Alexander Gonzales, "The Work of Calvin C. Straub," booklet (Gallery of Design, School of Architecture, Arizona State University, November 3, 1995), n.p. I am grateful to Sian Winship for her help in locating this information on Straub.

47. Quoted in *ibid*.

48. "Oral History of L. Morgan Yost," p. 93: "The Greenes were most pleased, almost overcome, by the certificates of honor which the AIA did bestow, which I regard as one of my signal accomplishments, reinforced by the California AIA group."

Bibliography

PRIMARY SOURCES

BANGS, Jean Murray, "Greene and Greene,"
Architectural Forum, 89, no. 4 (October 1948)

BROWN, Glenn (ed.), *European and Japanese Gardens*,
Philadelphia: Henry T. Coates & Co., 1902

CRAM, Ralph Adams, *American Country Houses of Today*,
New York: Architectural Book Publishing Co., 1913

CROLY, Herbert [Arthur C. David, pseud.], "An
Architect of Bungalows in California," *Architectural
Record*, 20, no. 4 (October 1906)

"Domestic Architecture in the West: California's
Contribution to a National Architecture: Its Significance
in the Work of Greene and Greene, Architects,"
The Craftsman, 22, no. 5 (August 1912)

GREENE, Charles Sumner, "Architecture and the
Machine Age: A Reply," *The Carmelite*, 3, no. 38
(October 30, 1930)
———, "Bungalows," *Western Architect*, 12, no. 1 (July 1908)
———, "California Home Making," *Pasadena Daily
News*, January 2, 1905, pp. 26–27
———, "Impressions of Some Bungalows and
Gardens," *The Architect*, 10 (December 1915)

HOPKINS, Una Nixson, "A Study for Home-Builders,"
Good Housekeeping, March 1906

KOCH, Alex., "American Domestic Architecture,"
Academy Architecture, 24 (1903)

LANCASTER, Clay, "My Interviews with Greene and
Greene," *Journal of the American Institute of Architects*,
28 (July 1957)

MORRIS, May (ed.), *The Collected Works of William
Morris*, 24 vols., London: Longmans, Green & Company,
1915

MORSE, Edward S., *Japanese Homes and Their
Surroundings*, Boston: Ticknor & Company, 1886

"A Special Citation to Henry Mather Greene and Charles
Sumner Greene," *Journal of the American Institute of
Architects*, 18 (July 1952)

YOST, L. Morgan, "Greene & Greene of Pasadena,"
Journal of the Society of Architectural Historians, 9, nos. 1–2
(March–May 1950)

SECONDARY SOURCES

ANDREWS, Wayne, *Architecture, Ambition and
Americans: A History of American Architecture*, New York:
Harper, 1955

*"The Art That is Life": The Arts and Crafts Movement in
America, 1875–1920*, exhib. cat., ed. Wendy Kaplan,
Boston, Museum of Fine Arts, 1987

The Arts and Crafts Movement in America, 1876–1916,
exhib. cat., ed. Robert Judson Clark, Princeton, NJ,
Art Museum, 1972

*The Arts and Crafts Movement in California: Living the Good
Life*, exhib. cat., ed. Kenneth R. Trapp, Oakland, Calif.,
Oakland Museum, 1993

BECKERDITE, Luke (ed.), *American Furniture 1993*,
Hanover, NH: University Press of New England, 1993

BIGOTT, Joseph C., *From Cottage to Bungalow: Houses
and the Working Class in Metropolitan Chicago, 1869–1929*,
Chicago: University of Chicago Press, 2001

BLAKESLEY, Rosalind P., *The Arts and Crafts Movement*,
London: Phaidon, 2006

BOSLEY, Edward R., *Greene & Greene*, London:
Phaidon, 2000

BROWN, Janet Lynn, "Charles Sumner Greene and
Henry Mather Greene, Architects: The Integration of
House and Garden—Southern California, 1893–1914,"
master's thesis, University of California, Berkeley, 1988

BROWN, S. Azby, *The Genius of Japanese Carpentry:
The Secrets of a Craft*, Tokyo, New York, London:
Kodansha, 1995

California Design 1910, exhib. cat., ed. Timothy J.
Andersen *et al.*, Pasadena, Calif., Pasadena Center, 1974

CHERRY, Bridget, and Nikolaus Pevsner, *The Buildings of
England: Devon*, 2nd edn, Harmondsworth: Penguin, 1989

CRANZ, Galen, *The Chair: Rethinking Culture, Body, and
Design*, New York: Norton, 1998

*Culture and Comfort: People, Parlors, and Upholstery,
1850–1930*, exhib. cat. by Katherine C. Grier, Rochester,
NY, Strong Museum, 1988

DAVEY, Peter, *Arts and Crafts Architecture: The Search for Earthly Paradise*, London: Architectural Press, 1980

The Distinction of Being Different: Joseph P. McHugh and the American Arts and Crafts Movement, exhib. cat., Utica, NY, Museum of Art, Munson-Williams-Proctor Institute, 1993

DUDDEN, Faye E., *Serving Women: Household Service in Nineteenth-Century America*, Middletown, Conn.: Wesleyan University Press, 1983

EIDELBERG, Martin, *et al.*, *A New Light on Tiffany: Clara Driscoll and the Tiffany Girls*, New York: New-York Historical Society, 2007

Fine Homebuilding, Great Houses: Craftsman-Style Houses, Newtown, Conn.: Taunton Press, 1991

FOY, Jessica H., and Thomas J. Schlereth (eds.), *American Home Life, 1880–1930: A Social History of Spaces and Services*, Knoxville: University of Tennessee Press, 1992

FRAMPTON, Kenneth, *Modern Architecture: A Critical History*, 3rd edn, London and New York: Thames & Hudson, 1992

FRANCIS, Barbara Ann, "The Boston Roots of Greene and Greene," master's thesis, Tufts University, 1987

FRELINGHUYSEN, Alice Cooney, *Louis Comfort Tiffany at The Metropolitan Museum of Art*, New York: The Metropolitan Museum of Art, 1998

GERMANY, Lisa, *Harwell Hamilton Harris*, Austin: University of Texas Press, 1991

GIROUARD, Mark, *Sweetness and Light: The "Queen Anne" Movement, 1860–1900*, New Haven, Conn.: Yale University Press, 1977

GRAY, Nina, *Tiffany by Design: An In-Depth Look at Tiffany Lamps*, Atglen, Pa.: Schiffer Publishing, 2006

GRISWOLD, Mac, and Eleanor Weller, *The Golden Age of American Gardens: Proud Owners, Private Estates, 1890–1940*, New York: Harry N. Abrams, in association with the Garden Club of America, 1991

HAFERTEPE, Kenneth, and James F. O'Gorman (eds.), *American Architects and Their Books, 1840–1915*, Amherst: University of Massachusetts Press, 2007

HALES, Virginia Dart Greene (ed.), *The Memoirs of Henry Dart Greene and Ruth Elizabeth Haight Greene*, 2 vols., La Jolla, Calif.: Virginia Dart Greene Hales, 1996–2001

HUNT, John Dixon, *The Picturesque Garden in Europe*, London: Thames & Hudson, 2002

Inspired by China: Contemporary Furnituremakers Explore Chinese Traditions, exhib. cat. by Nancy Berliner and Edward S. Cooke, Jr., Salem, Mass., Peabody Essex Museum, 2006

Inspiring Reform: Boston's Arts and Crafts Movement, exhib. cat., ed. Marilee Boyd Meyer, Wellesley, Mass., Davis Museum and Cultural Center, Wellesley College, 1997

International Arts and Crafts, exhib. cat., ed. Karen Livingstone and Linda Parry, London, Victoria and Albert Museum, 2005

The Japan Idea: Art and Life in Victorian America, exhib. cat. by William Hosley, Hartford, Conn., Wadsworth Atheneum, 1990

KAPLAN, Wendy, *The Arts and Crafts Movement in Europe and America: Design for the Modern World*, New York: Thames & Hudson, 2004

KRENOV, James, *A Cabinetmaker's Notebook*, New York: Van Nostrand Reinhold, 1976

LAMBOURNE, Lionel, *Japonisme: Cultural Crossings between Japan and the West*, London and New York: Phaidon, 2005

LANCASTER, Clay, *The Japanese Influence in America*, New York: Walton H. Rawls, 1963

LANG, Robert W., *Shop Drawings for Greene & Greene Furniture*, East Petersburg, Pa.: Fox Chapel Publishing, 2006

LAZZARO, Claudia, *The Italian Renaissance Garden*, New Haven, Conn.: Yale University Press, 1990

LEE, Lawrence, George Seddon, and Francis Stephens, *Stained Glass*, New York: Crown Publishers, 1976

MaCCARTHY, Fiona, *William Morris: A Life for Our Time*, London: Faber & Faber, 1994

The Maker's Hand: American Studio Furniture, 1940–1990, exhib. cat. by Edward S. Cooke, Jr., *et al.*, Boston, Museum of Fine Arts, 2003

MAKINSON, Randell L., *Greene & Greene: Architecture as a Fine Art*, Salt Lake City: Peregrine Smith, 1977
———, *Greene & Greene: Furniture and Related Designs*, Salt Lake City: Peregrine Smith, 1979
———, *Greene & Greene: The Passion and the Legacy*, Salt Lake City: Gibbs Smith, 1998
———, and Thomas A. Heinz, *The Blacker House*, Salt Lake City: Gibbs Smith, 2000

MARCHINI, G., *Italian Stained Glass Windows*, London: Thames & Hudson, 1957

McWILLIAMS, Carey, *Southern California Country: An Island on the Land*, New York: Duell, Sloan & Pearce, 1946

MOCK, Elizabeth (ed.), *Built in USA, 1932–1944*, New York: Plantin Press for The Museum of Modern Art, 1944

PARRY, Linda, *William Morris Textiles*, London: Weidenfeld & Nicolson, 1983

PEART, Darrell, *Greene & Greene: Design Elements for the Workshop*, Fresno, Calif.: Linden Publishing, 2005

PEVSNER, Nikolaus, and Enid Radcliffe, *The Buildings of England: Cornwall*, 2nd edn, Harmondsworth: Penguin, 1970

RAND, Marvin, *Greene & Greene*, Layton, Ut.: Gibbs Smith, 2005

SATO, Hideo, and Yasua Nakahara, *The Complete Japanese Joinery*, Vancouver, BC: Hartley & Marks, 1995

SCHARF, Frederic A. (ed.), *"A Pleasing Novelty": Bunkio Matsuki and the Japan Craze in Victorian Salem*, Salem, Mass.: Essex Institute, 1993

SCHEID, Ann, *Pasadena: Crown of the Valley*, Northridge, Calif.: Windsor Publications, 1986

SCHULZE, Franz, *Philip Johnson: Life and Work*, Chicago: University of Chicago Press, 1996

SHI, David, *In Search of the Simple Life: American Voices, Past and Present*, Layton, Ut.: Gibbs M. Smith, 1986

SIMONDS, O.C., *Landscape-Gardening*, Amherst: University of Massachusetts Press, 2000

SLOAN, Julie L., *Light Screens: The Complete Leaded-Glass Windows of Frank Lloyd Wright*, New York: Rizzoli, 2001

SMITH, Bruce, *Greene & Greene and the Duncan-Irwin House: Developing a California Style*, Salt Lake City: Gibbs Smith, forthcoming
———, and Alexander Vertikoff, *Greene & Greene: Masterworks*, San Francisco: Chronicle Books, 1998

SOLOMON, Barbara Miller, *In the Company of Educated Women: A History of Women and Higher Education in America*, New Haven, Conn.: Yale University Press, 1985

STANLEY-BAKER, Joan, *Japanese Art*, London: Thames & Hudson, 1984

STARR, Kevin, *Inventing the Dream: California through the Progressive Era*, New York: Oxford University Press, 1985

STEWART, Suzanne, and Mary Praetzell (eds.), *Sights and Sounds: Essays in Celebration of West Oakland*, Rohnert Park, Calif.: Anthropological Studies Center of Sonoma State University, 1997

THOMPSON, Eleanor McD. (ed.), *The American Home: Material Culture, Domestic Space, and Family Life*, Winterthur, Del.: Henry Francis du Pont Winterthur Museum, 1998

TOMITA, Kojiro, *A History of the Asiatic Department: A Series of Illustrated Lectures Given in 1957 by Kojiro Tomita (1890–1976)*, Boston: Museum of Fine Arts, 1990

WALKER, Lester, *American Shelter: An Illustrated Encyclopedia of the American Home*, Woodstock, NY: Overlook Press, 1981

WATKIN, David, *The English Vision: The Picturesque in Architecture, Landscape and Garden Design*, London: John Murray, 1982

WAY, Thaïsa, "Arts and Crafts Gardens in California," master's thesis, University of Virginia, 1991

WINTER, Robert (ed.), *Toward a Simpler Way of Life: The Arts and Crafts Architects of California*, Berkeley: University of California Press, 1997

WOODS, Mary N., *From Craft to Profession: The Practice of Architecture in Nineteenth-Century America*, Berkeley: University of California Press, 1999

ZWERGER, Klaus, *Wood and Wood Joints: Building Traditions of Europe and Japan*, Basel, Berlin, Boston: Birkhauser, 2000

VIX EA NOSTRA VOCO

Acknowledgments

The editors would like to thank the Ahmanson Foundation, without the very generous financial support of which this publication would not have been possible. We also appreciate the generous assistance of the American Decorative Art 1900 Foundation and of Thomas K. Figge.

This book not only interprets the work of Charles and Henry Greene and their associated craftsmen, but also features a talented group of photographers, without whom many of the objects would not appear to such stunning advantage. We would especially like to thank Ognen Borissov for his time and talent, sometimes at a moment's notice. Photographs by the late Mark Fiennes and the late Linda Svendsen serve as testimonial to their great artistic abilities and to their sensitive appreciation of the Greenes' work. We are also grateful to be able to include the fine work of Gavin Ashworth. Additionally, without the time and assistance of Bryce Bannatyne, Bruce Barnes, John Caldwell, Joseph Cunningham, Caroline Fiennes, Thomas K. Figge, Tim Gleason, Nancy McClelland, Jack Moore, Jodi Pollack, and Ted Wells, we would not have had access to some of the fine objects and photographs represented in these pages.

For their invaluable time, assistance, and expertise in retrieving objects and information, we would like to thank the following individuals and archives: Gerald Beasley, Janet Parks, and Inna Guzenfeld at Avery Architectural and Fine Arts Library, Columbia University, New York; Waverly Lowell and Miranda Hambro at the Environmental Design Archives, University of California, Berkeley; Jennifer Watts and Erin Chase at the Huntington Library in San Marino, California; Melinda Kwedar at the Kenilworth Historical Society, and Kenilworth historian Kathy Cummings; Kurt Helfrich at the University of California, Santa Barbara; Beth Dodd and Nancy Sparrow at the Alexander Architectural Archive, University of Texas Libraries, Austin; Mary Woolever, Art and Architecture Archivist, Ryerson and Burnham Libraries, The Art Institute of Chicago; and Sian Winship for her help with material on architect Calvin Straub. We are also very grateful to our colleague Ann Scheid, Archivist of the Greene and Greene Archives at the Huntington Library, for her many kindnesses and thoughtful suggestions.

Many others contributed to this publication—as colleagues, editors, and experts—and we would particularly like to acknowledge Lee Hershberger, David Jameson, Wendy Kaplan, Susan Mallek, and Monica Penick.

The editors are grateful beyond measure to the essay contributors, who in many cases were willing to investigate and interpret unfamiliar territory. Indeed, they embraced the challenge, and this publication has benefited enormously from the new perspectives and scholarship that they have offered. Our thanks also go to Frank O. Gehry, FAIA, for offering his perspective in the foreword. We would also like to acknowledge the staff at Merrell Publishers in New York and London, who were great supporters from the beginning and true collaborators at every turn.

Although this publication is not strictly an exhibition catalogue, it shares the title of a coincidental exhibition of the work of Greene and Greene. The editors, who are also the co-curators of the exhibition, would like to take this opportunity to record their gratitude to the following individuals, lenders, and donors for collectively making available works of Greene and Greene, some of which have never before been seen by the public, others not for decades, and most not at all at venues outside California. For their generosity as major financial supporters, we thank the following: The Ahmanson Foundation; Ayrshire Foundation; The Henry Luce Foundation; Steven and Kelly McLeod Family Foundation; Joseph D. Messler, Jr.; Peter Norton Family Foundation; The Ralph M. Parsons Foundation; Ann Peppers Foundation; Resnick Foundation; Laura and Carlton Seaver; Andy Warhol Foundation for the Visual Arts; Wells Fargo; Windgate Charitable Trust; Margaret Winslow; and Elsie de Wolfe Foundation. We also wish to extend gratitude to those contributors whose gifts were received after publication. For their participation, enthusiastic cooperation, and support in so many ways, we also thank: Mary Ellen Porter Anderson; Bryce Bannatyne; Bruce Barnes and Joseph Cunningham; John and Susan Caldwell; California Sigma Phi Society; Detroit Institute of Arts; Kenneth J. Dukoff; Delia Ehrlich; David and Vicki Fleishhacker; Mortimer and Franny Fleishhacker; Louise K. Franke; Joan Frederick; Olivier Gabet; Tim Gleason; the Goldstein family; François-Joseph Graf; John Griswold; Guardian Stewardship; Jan Hurff; Betty and Robert Hut; James Ipekjian; Wendy Kaplan; Robert Ewing Kelly and Maria John Nicholas Kelly; Harvey and

Ellen Knell; Los Angeles County Museum of Art; Nancy McClelland; Jack Moore Antiques; Dottie O'Carroll; Robert and Arlene Oltman; Lorraine Petersen; Greg Porter; Richard Porter; Norman Selby and Melissa Vail; Ray W. Springer and Susanna Springer in memory of Frank N. Springer; Ted Wells; Steve Yamaguchi; and private collectors who wished to remain anonymous. We would also like to extend particular gratitude to Brenda Levin, Robert Stone, and Alice Gates of Levin & Associates for contributing the beautiful design of the exhibition space at the Huntington, and to Kelly Sutherlin McLeod of Kelly Sutherlin McLeod Architecture for her design of the Bandini house component. Bryce Bannatyne deserves thanks for suggesting the idea several years ago that such an exhibition could happen.

A final and essential note of thanks goes to our colleagues and staff at the Huntington Library, Art Collections, and Botanical Gardens; Smithsonian American Art Museum's Renwick Gallery, Washington, D.C.; Museum of Fine Arts, Boston; and last but not at all least, to the staff, docents, and friends of The Gamble House and University of Southern California School of Architecture.

Edward R. Bosley and Anne E. Mallek

Contributors

EDWARD R. BOSLEY is James N. Gamble Director of The Gamble House, a program of the University of Southern California School of Architecture. His publications include *Greene & Greene* (2000) and other books and articles related to the Greenes and the Arts and Crafts movement. He lectures widely on these subjects and on historic preservation.

EDWARD S. COOKE, JR., the Charles F. Montgomery Professor of American Decorative Arts in the Department of the History of Art at Yale University, New Haven, Connecticut, specializes in American material culture and decorative arts. He has published extensively on both historical and contemporary furniture.

ALAN CRAWFORD is an independent scholar based in London. He has written about the history of British architecture and decorative arts in the years around 1900, and is currently working on a book about the Arts and Crafts movement in England.

NINA GRAY is an independent curator and scholar specializing in decorative arts and architecture of the nineteenth and early twentieth centuries. Her publications include "Tiffany's Contemporaries: The Evolution of the American Interior Decorator," in *Louis Comfort Tiffany: Artist for the Ages* (2005), *Tiffany by Design: An In-Depth Look at Tiffany Lamps* (2006), and *A New Light on Tiffany: Clara Driscoll and the Tiffany Girls* (2007).

VIRGINIA GREENE HALES is one of eight grandchildren of Henry Mather Greene. She has edited two volumes of *The Memoirs of Henry Dart Greene and Ruth Elizabeth Haight Greene*, published in 1996 and 2001. She is currently writing volume three, *Greene & Greene: Their Family Ancestry, 1550–1900*.

MARGARETTA M. LOVELL, the Jay D. McEvoy Professor of History of Art at the University of California, Berkeley, has curated exhibitions on William Morris and Morris & Company at Berkeley and at the Huntington Library, San Marino. She teaches British and American art, and writes about eighteenth-century portraiture and decorative arts, nineteenth-century landscape painting, the Arts and Crafts movement, and vernacular aesthetic theory of the present.

ANNE E. MALLEK is Curator at The Gamble House. She curated the exhibition *William Morris: Creating the Useful and the Beautiful* (2002) at the Huntington Library, San Marino, and helped prepare the exhibition *The Beauty of Life: William Morris and the Art of Design* (2004) and its accompanying publication. She contributed an essay to *American Architects and Their Books, 1840–1915* (2007).

ANN SCHEID is the author of several books on Pasadena history, most recently *Early Pasadena's Downtown Architecture* (2006), as well as articles on the history of architecture and city planning. She is currently Archivist of the Greene and Greene Archives, located at the Huntington Library, San Marino.

JULIE L. SLOAN is a stained-glass consultant based in North Adams, Massachusetts. She has worked in stained glass since 1982. The author of *Conservation of Stained Glass in America* (1995) and *Light Screens: The Complete Leaded-Glass Windows of Frank Lloyd Wright* (2001), as well as many articles, she is currently writing on John La Farge and the history of American stained glass.

BRUCE SMITH is an independent researcher and writer who has been examining the life and work of Charles and Henry Greene for more than fifteen years. He is the co-author of *Greene & Greene: Masterworks* (1998) and author of the forthcoming *Greene & Greene and the Duncan-Irwin House: Developing a California Style*.

DAVID C. STREATFIELD, Professor Emeritus of Landscape Architecture at the University of Washington, is a historian with a specialization in nineteenth- and twentieth-century landscape architecture and the landscapes of the American West. He is the author of *California Gardens: Creating a New Eden* (1994) and numerous articles and essays.

Index